THE STORY OF INSTRUCTION

THE CHURCH, THE RENAISSANCES AND THE REFORMATIONS

THE MACMILLAN COMPANY
NEW YORK · BOSTON · CHICAGO · DALLAS
ATLANTA · SAN FRANCISCO

MACMILLAN & CO., Limited
LONDON · BOMBAY · CALCUTTA
MELBOURNE

THE MACMILLAN COMPANY
OF CANADA, Limited
TORONTO

THE
STORY OF INSTRUCTION

THE CHURCH, THE RENAISSANCES, AND THE REFORMATIONS

BY

ERNEST CARROLL MOORE

NEW YORK
THE MACMILLAN COMPANY
1938

To

DOROTHEA MOORE

91372

PREFACE

"HISTORY," said Coleridge, "is the essence of innumerable biographies." There are other notions of it. Preformitarian philosophies, religious and secular, attribute it to Fate, The Absolute or the Forces of Nature. We prefer Coleridge's account to theirs. Viewed as a human enterprise, the Christian church stands between Greece and Rome and our own time. The ages of the church are the bridge over which antiquity passes to reach our day. But the church is more than a bridge and a highroad, it is the conservator of the past; and more than the conservator of the past, it is the tiller of the fields of the human spirit.

I like particularly the words in which Windelband [1] estimates the function of the church in the history of mankind:

"When the migration of the peoples broke in devastation over the Roman Empire, and the latter lacked the political strength to defend itself against the northern barbarians, scientific civilization, also, was in danger of becoming completely crushed out; for the tribes to whom the sceptre now passed brought less mind and understanding for the finely elaborated structures of philosophy than the light forms of Grecian art. And withal ancient civilization was in itself so disintegrated, its vital force was so broken, that it seemed incapable of taking the rude victors into its school.

"Thus the conquests of the Greek spirit would have been given over to destruction beyond hope of rescue,

[1] *A History of Philosophy*, transl. James H. Tufts, 263 (New York: Macmillan, 1923).

if in the midst of the breaking down of the old world, a
new spiritual power had not grown strong, to which the
sons of the North bowed, and which, with firm hand, knew
how to rescue for the future the goods of civilization, and
to preserve them during the centuries of subversion. This
power was the *Christian Church*. What the state could not
do, what art and science could not achieve, religion accomplished. . . . Only from this point of religious excita-
tion, therefore, could the process of the appropriation of
ancient science by the peoples of Europe of today begin;
only at the hand of the Church could the new world enter
the school of the old. . . . The Church had grown to its
great task of becoming the educator of the European Nations, first of all, because from the invisible beginnings of
a religious society it had developed with steadily growing
power to a unified organization, which amid the dissolu-
tion of political life presented itself as the only power that
was firm and sure of itself. And since this organization
was supported by the thought that the Church was called
to become the means of bringing the salvation of redemption to all humanity, the religious education of the barbarians was a task prescribed by its own nature. . . . The
education of the European peoples, which the history of
the philosophy of the Middle Ages sets forth, has then for
its starting point the Church doctrine, and for its goal the
development of the scientific spirit. The intellectual civilization of antiquity is brought to modern peoples in the
religious form which it assumed at its close, and develops
in them gradually the maturity for properly scientific
work."   ERNEST CARROLL MOORE

*The University of California
at Los Angeles.
December 29, 1937.*

CONTENTS

CONTENTS

THE STORY OF INSTRUCTION

THE CHURCH, THE RENAISSANCES
AND THE REFORMATIONS

I

THE OLD WORLD AND THE NEW FAITH

GREEK philosophy began in Ionia in an effort to understand the material world. In Socrates it became an effort to control human conduct. When Platonism at length evolved into Neo-Platonism its concern was with the Absolute, the substantial as opposed to the phenomenal. Its last stage is otherworldly, through and through. Its eye is upon the Eternal. For the things of time the thinker has only contempt. The course which Greek philosophy ran then was from materialism through humanism to the intensest spiritualism. Its last stage was a denial of interest in and concern for this world, a bankruptcy and abandonment of science, ethics, and politics, which brought on barbarism for it abandoned the people to superstition.[1]

The Neo-Platonists claimed to derive from Plato. In fact they put under tribute every philosophy which capitalized the dualistic separation of soul from body. Plato had done that in certain passages, though in other great ones, as for example his definition of the true musician,[2] the business of the soul is the harmonizing of life. Mr. Guthrie[3] quotes from the *Cratylus* (400 *c.*): "Now some

[1] Harnack, *History of Dogma* (transl. Buchanan), Vol. I, Appendix III, "Neoplatonism" (London: Williams and Norgate, 1905).

[2] *Republic,* 412.

[3] *Orpheus and Greek Religion*, p. 157. By permission of the author and of Methuen & Co., Ltd.

say that the body (*soma*) is the *sema* of the soul, as if it
were buried in its present existence; and also because
through it the soul makes signs of whatever it has to express, for in this way they claim that it is rightly named
from *sema*. In my opinion it is the followers of Orpheus
who are chiefly responsible for giving it the name, holding that the soul is undergoing punishment for some
reason or other, and has this husk around it, like a prison,
to keep it from running away." Mr. Guthrie's comment
deserves to be quoted also: "This central doctrine of the
Orphics had a tremendous and one is sometimes tempted
to say unfortunate fascination for Plato. Some of the
finest parts of the dialogues give the impression not that
he despised the body, but that, although the soul was the
higher principle and must maintain the lead, soul and
body could work in harmony together. Yet this un-
natural dualism of the Orphics, which divides the two so
sharply and makes the body nothing but an encumbrance,
the source of evil, from which the body must be purified,
permeates the *Phaedo*, together with a great deal of language borrowed from 'the initiators.' I would go so far as
to name the Orphics as at least one of the influences
which went to form the most characteristic part of Platonism, the sharp separation of the lower world of *sensa* from
the heavenly world of ideas. It is often puzzling to see
how this doctrine, which in itself leads naturally to a
lack of interest in the sensible world and a concentration
on the higher, seems to be at war with Plato's inborn
longing to interfere effectively in practical matters. I
believe in fact that it was the teaching of the *hieroi logoi*
that set the feet of the philosopher on the upward path
from the Cave into the Sunlight, whereas it was the voice
of Plato's own heart that sternly bade him return and
help his fellow-prisoners still fettered in the darkness of

the cave. The same Orphic ideal appealed to Aristotle in his Platonic youth."

Pythagoreanism, another influence which played upon Plato, had much in common with the Orphic religion. Both were "ways of life" which forbade the eating of meat, for all life is one and the considerate man would not be a cannibal. Each of these religions had the purification of the soul for its object, and to that end preached the transmigration of souls and their need to break the bondage to the body. But Dionysos was Orpheus' God, and Apollo was Pythagoras' deity. Pythagoras taught a cosmology and explained the universe; the Orphics, a religion. If the Pythagoreans were Orphics in their teaching of religion—which they may have been—they taught their own mathematical philosophy in addition to that doctrine. Mr. Guthrie points out that both Orpheus and Pythagoras were musicians and protagonists of a heavenly order and harmony which they urged men to adopt. Plato's interest in mathematics was a sufficient warrant for his giving great attention to the followers of Pythagoras. And if one will recall the conditions of Athens' life in Plato's day and will remember that Athens was the chief seat of the Orphic religion, Plato's readiness to acknowledge the claims of the doctrines of the Pythagorean and even of the Orphic religion may be psychologically understandable. From the Stoics the Neo-Pythagoreans took the imperiousness of the soul, but not their physics of matter. In the Epicureans alone of all the Greek schools they could find nothing to further their separation of the soul from the body. Epicureanism was to them the deadly enemy, for it preached the material identity of soul and body. Porphyry, the Neo-Platonic philosopher, writes to his wife Marcella:

"The divine law cries aloud in the pure region of the

mind: 'Unless thou consider that thy body is joined to thee as the outer covering to the child in the womb and the stalk to the sprouting corn, thou canst not know thyself.' Nor can any one know himself who does not hold this opinion. As the outer covering grows with the child, and the stalk with the corn, yet, when they come to maturity, both are cast away, thus too the body that is fastened to the soul at birth is not a part of the man. But as the outer covering was formed along with the child that it may come to being in the womb, so likewise the body was yoked to the man that he may come to being on earth. In as far as a man turns to the mortal part of himself, in so far he makes his mind incommensurate with immortality. And in as far as he refrains from sharing the feelings of the body, in such a measure does he approach the divine. The wise man who is beloved of God strives and toils as much for the good of his soul as others do for the good of their body." [4]

"For no two things can be more entirely opposed to one another than a life of pleasure and ease, and the ascent to the gods. . . . The divine Plato too made this his starting-point, summoning us away from the sensible to the intelligible. . . . Now God is not in need of any one, and the wise man is in need of God alone. . . . Next to God there is nothing great but virtue, yet God is greater than virtue. . . . God . . . delights only in the purification of the mind . . . Wherefore philosophers say that nothing is so necessary as to know thoroughly what is unnecessary, and moreover that to be self-sufficing is the greatest of all wealth, and that it is honourable not to ask anything of any man." [5] Neo-Platonism claimed to

[4] *Porphyry the Philosopher to His Wife Marcella,* transl. Alice Zimmern (London: George Redway, 1896), Sec. 32.
[5] *Porphyry the Philosopher, etc.,* Sec. 6, 10, 11, 16, 23, 28.

be the all-inclusive philosophy and at the same time the all-including religion. Its home was Alexandria, the city which Alexander had founded to be the inclusive capital of the whole world. The universalism which he had contributed to Stoicism became in turn the catholic aim of Neo-Platonism. All religions of every people were to be gathered into this one philosophy-religion of religions. The spirit of God had brooded over all hearts. There is a groping after Him in all creeds. Let but the accidental be separated from the substantial, and all can range themselves in the Neo-Platonist fold. Christianity would not perform the necessary excisions. It insisted that the world had been created in time and would be destroyed in time. Its doctrines of the Incarnation of the Lord, and of the resurrection of the body, seemed to the Platonists to make God something less than all and in all.

It is customary to say that the old pagan religions of classical antiquity were dead and their gods without worshippers when Christianity came. There is a good deal of evidence that that was not the case. Paganism's official end did not come until Justinian closed the Platonic Academy at Athens in 529. In that same year Benedict found peasants sacrificing to Apollo on Mount Casinum, which is not many miles from Rome. Pope Gregory the Great, c. 540–604, complains in a letter that there are many in Sardinia who still sacrifice to idols. There were such worshippers of the old gods in Peloponnesus in the ninth century. The altar of Victory was removed and paganism was suppressed by the Emperor Gratian in A.D. 381. There followed thirteen years of wild destruction of the ancient temples and shrines. Yet when one hundred and fifty years after that Justinian's Code was issued it pronounced heavy penalties against pagan sacrifices and the wreathing of garlands upon the temples.

Even when Christianity triumphed the old gods did not cease to exist, they were only demoted to the rank of demons.

Polytheism is hard to understand—if one has been habituated since infancy to finding reasonableness nowhere save in monotheism. But may it not be that paganism too had its reasons, its explanations which were not altogether flat and empty? The little girl who cries when her doll is being repaired, the man who kicks the chair he has stumbled against in the dark, the sensitive soul who cannot bear to use an axe with a criminal record, the student who is horrified at Descartes's teaching that animals are automata, these have the basis of understanding in them. For it is easier far to believe that all things are alive than that only some of them are alive and the rest are not. The psychological fallacy is a fateful part of our equipment. Religion is the natural feeling of awe in the presence of the mysterious forces about us. The early Roman was a practical man, practical enough to recognize such mysterious invisible forces in his world everywhere. There was a spirit, or numen, in every physical thing, a spirit of every place and process; a spirit of the earth, another of the sky, of the tree, the fountain, the river, of every person, act, and thought. The number of such spirits was limitless. Each of them was a force, for the Latin word *numen* means "will." Sixty or more of them regulated the growth of the human body, like Ossipago who knit the bones of the young child, Vagitanus who opened the infant's mouth for its first cry, Educa who caused him to eat, and Potina who taught him to drink. Cuba watched over him in his bed, Abeona taught him to walk away and Fabulinus to speak. The numen is a particular force and numina are not gods. The early Romans did not form images or make a mythology about them, but one's safety or success depends upon them. If the proper rites are carefully celebrated the numina will be constrained to respond favorably. The liturgy of the ancient festivals and household religious ceremonials, scrupulously performed, bound the spirits to accept and return in kind. There was a bargain and sale relation between the worshipper and the god in both the Greek and the Roman scheme of things. One may not speak with certainty about such disputed matters but it would seem that the chief difference between the Greek and the Roman religion is that the Greek had evolved farther. Their first stages were most likely the same; i.e., the primitive animism we have sketched as being the beginning among the Romans was the beginning stage with both of them. But the Greeks passed on to a second stage much more rapidly than the Romans did. That second stage was the anthropomorphizing or personifying of these forces of nature, the eager creative act of making gods in their own image and then telling tales, writing poems, constructing worship, shaping sculptured representations and building temples about them. The Romans were very slow in doing these things, the Greeks very fast. This is their chief difference: the one had eager-mindedness to the extreme of instability; the other, stability to the point of dullness. These differences find as striking an expression in what each people did with its religion as in anything. And the life and achievement of each people is in a very strict sense a function of its business with its religion, that is, with the awe-making forces around it.

No ancient city-state ever for a moment conceived the possibility of government without religion. In the strictest sense it was God-founded, God-directed, God-protected, and God-approved or God-abandoned. Its people were in partnership with their gods, the gods were the senior and major partners. "But as to the origin of each particular god, whether they all existed from the beginning, what were their individual forms, the knowledge of these things is so to speak, but of today and yesterday. For Hesiod and Homer are my seniors, I think by some four hundred years and not more. And it is they who have composed for the Greeks the generation of the gods, and have given to the gods their titles and distinguished their several provinces and special powers and marked their forms." [6] Rome had no Homer or Hesiod. Her backwardness was great on that account. She had to be helped by Greece, through Etruria. There was no temple at Rome until Tarquin I built the *Capitolium* for Jupiter, Juno, and Minerva. Jupiter, greatest and best, god of heaven, the thunderbolt, and of supreme power, was the protector of Rome. There were in all twelve greater gods, named in two verses of Ennius as:

> Juno, Vesta, Minerva, Ceres, Diana, Venus, Mars,
> Mercurius, Jovis, Neptunus, Volcanus, Apollo.

In addition scores of other gods were distinguished, named and worshipped together with hundreds of local deities, half distinct, and deities far more numerous than men, who were not named but only felt to exist and be like the atmosphere everywhere about one.

The Roman Commonwealth, *Senatus Populusque Romanus*, was to every Roman a corporation with six shareholders:

1. Jupiter Maximus Optimus.
2. The other major gods and goddesses.
3. The minor gods and goddesses.

[6] Herodotus, II, 53.

4. The Roman Senators.
5. The Roman *Equites*, or knights.
6. The mass of Roman citizens.[7]

The gods were gods of the state, which like the other city-states of the Mediterranean world was "a religious and military confraternity—encamped round a church." Nothing was so important for such a civic community as the continued favor of its sharing and protecting deities. They made their will known to their worshippers, (1) through changes which the priests were able to read in the internal organs of the animals sacrificed to them, (2) through birds, some of which are messengers of the gods, (3) through oracles, (4) by omens and portents. To ascertain the will of the gods and properly conciliate them the state maintained flamens and colleges of priests with a Pontifex Maximus over them. Divination was so important that even the wise Cicero was moved to write a book about it. Romulus, he says, was not only guided by augurs in founding the city of Rome, he was himself an augur. No public business either at home or in war, was ever transacted without reference to the auspices. It is the ancient and unanimous practice of nations to be guided by the omens derived from the entrails of victims sacrificed, by predictions of those who interpret prodigies or strange lights, of augurs, or astrologers, by those who interpret lots, dreams, marvels, etc. The art of divination was the supreme art at Rome, and in that branch of it which the *augurs* performed, the reading of the will of the gods from the behavior of birds, the Romans claimed to surpass all other people. The Etruscans were their superiors in interpreting the *exta* of sacrificed animals, and the Etruscans were acknowledged to be better

[7] Edward Lucas White, *Why Rome Fell*, 205. Copyright, 1927, by Edward Lucas White.

readers of portents too and were called in as experts in both these difficulties.

The twelve major deities were thought to form a Council of the Gods, and in times of great public stress they were conciliated by a *lectisternium*, or banquet of the gods. The Greeks and the Romans both made their gods, as needs they must, in their own image; they thought of them as delighting in the things which they themselves delighted in. "It is very difficult for moderns to realize that every chariot race ever run in any Roman circus, in Rome or throughout the Empire, every official governmental procession, every tragedy, comedy, farce, mime or pantomime performed at the expense of the government, just as truly as every banquet of the gods and every sacrifice to the gods, was an act of homage to Rome's gods and an act of worship to Rome's gods, whether performed for invocation, conciliation, or thanksgiving, and that every participant, every spectator, so regarded every one of these public pleasures from first to last for centuries, and all pagans felt so about them even after paganism had been forcibly suppressed." [8]

The relations of men to their gods were frankly different under paganism from what they became under the Asiatic religions of sin, mortification of the flesh, and world fleeing. "What we esteem the most agreeable things in human life," says Plutarch,[9] "are festal days, temple feasts, initiations, orgiac processions, public worship of the gods, and solemn devotions." Strabo's declaration is of like tenor: "It has been justly said that men resemble the gods chiefly in doing good, but it may be more properly said, when they are happy, and this happiness consists in rejoicing in festivals, in philosophy and in

[8] White, *op. cit.*, 210.
[9] *On Superstition*, 9.

music." [10] The great festivals are civic feasts with a definite place in the calendar and governed by the *jus divinum* which is a part of the civil law. The great state ceremonies, too, such as the triumph of a conquering general, ended in a religious consecration of his spoils to Jupiter "who inhabits the Capitol." No assemblies could be called for voting for officers or laws without the consent of the auguries, and no army could set out or begin battle unless the auspices were favorable. These prayers were and had to be public prayers formally conducted by adepts who were civic officers.

The Roman religion was a state religion, but at one point it was a terribly personal religion also. Every Roman soldier upon joining the army took an oath to obey his commander. That particular combination of words, if I could come upon it, I should regard as more important than any other statement which could come down to us from Rome, for in a very immediate sense it was the foundation of all the rest. Here is an indication of what a Roman military oath could contain. The time is 415 A.U.C. The Romans are warring upon the Latins. The two consuls are in command. This is Livy's account of what happened:

"The Roman Consuls, before they marched out their armies to the field, offered sacrifices. The aruspex is said to have shown to Decius the head of the liver wounded on the side relating to himself, in other respects the victim was acceptable to the gods; while Manlius obtained highly favorable omens from his sacrifice. 'But all is well,' says Decius, 'if my colleague has offered an acceptable sacrifice.' The ranks being drawn up in the order already described, they marched forth to battle. Manlius commanded the right, Decius the left wing. At first the

[10] Strabo, X, iii, 9.

action was conducted with equal strength on both sides,
and with the same ardent courage. Afterwards the Roman
spearmen on the left wing, not sustaining the violent assault of the Latin's, betook themselves to the principes.
In this state of trepidation the consul Decius cries out
with a loud voice to Marcus Valerius, 'Valerius, we have
need of the aid of the gods. Come, as public pontiff of
the Roman people, dictate to me the words in which I
may devote myself for the legions.' The pontiff directed
him to take the gown called praetexta, and with his head
covered and his hand thrust out under the gown to the
chin, standing upon a spear placed under his feet, to say
these words: 'Janus, Jupiter, Father Mars, Quirinus, Bel-
lona, ye Lares, ye Gods Novensiles, ye Gods Indigetes,
ye divinities, under whose power we and our enemies are,
and ye dii Manes, I pray you, I adore you, I ask your
favor, that you would prosperously grant strength and
victory to the Roman people, the Quirites; and that ye
may affect the enemies of the Roman people, the Quirites,
with terror, dismay and death. In such manner as I
have expressed in words, so do I devote the legions and
auxiliaries of the enemy together with myself, to the dii
Manes and to Earth for the republic of the Quirites, for
the army, legions, auxiliaries of the Roman people, the
Quirites.' Having uttered this prayer, he orders the lic-
tors to go to Titus Manlius, and without delay to announce to his colleague that he had devoted himself for
the army. He, girding himself in a Gabine cincture, and
fully armed, mounted his horse, and rushed into the midst
of the enemy." [11] It was lawful for a consul, a dictator,
or a praetor, when he devoted the army of the enemy,
to devote any Roman soldier he might choose out of the
legion. Cicero, in the *De Officiis* (I, xi, 36), recounts

[11] Bk. VIII, 9 (Spillan's translation).

that Cato's son served under Popilius in a legion which
was disbanded. The young Cato continued with his general, in arms. But his father wrote to Popilius requesting
that he give the young man "the military oath over
again, because his former sacrament being dissolved he
could not otherwise justify his putting himself into the
quarrel." Livy (XXII, 38) speaks of an oath dictated
by the military tribunes binding the soldiers to assemble
at the command of the consuls and not to depart without orders. Up to that time (536 A.U.C.) "the military
oath only had been employed." In addition to both these
oaths—i.e., the military oath and the one taken to the
military tribune—the soldiers on their own initiative
swore together among themselves that "they would not
depart or quit their ranks for flight or fear, except for
the purpose of taking up or fetching a weapon, and either
striking an enemy or saving a countryman. This from
being a voluntary compact among the soldiers themselves
was converted into the legal compulsion of an oath by the
tribunes." But we are still without the text of "the military oath." It is harder to find its wording than to realize that the consequences of breaking it were terrible.
Polybius tells (I, 1–7) of a Roman garrison of 4,000 invited into the friendly city of Rhegium to protect it
against Pyrrhus, which got out of hand and looted the
place, massacring its people. The 300 soldiers of that
garrison who were taken alive were sent to Rome and
marched by the Praetors into the Forum where they
were publicly scourged and then beheaded.

A Roman's relations to the gods were not all of them
state relations, and his worship was not all performed
for him in the religious ceremonies of the state. As head
of a family he conducted the rites belonging to the Lares
and Penates of his household. And while he never per-

haps in his life fell on his knees to pray or crossed himself before an image or an altar, it is certain that in the ordeals of life he no less than other men inwardly and informally called on the gods to aid him.

"For the sins of your sires, albeit you had no hand in them, you must suffer, O Roman, till you have set up again the Temples, the falling shrines of the gods and their images foul with sooty smoke. It is because you bow before the gods that you have Empire. From them entirely is the beginning of it: to them look for its end. It is the gods, because they have been forgotten, that have showered so many woes on Italy, the home of mourning." So wrote Horace in the sixth ode of his Third Book.[12]

In Augustus' own account of his reign, the *Monumentum Ancyranum*, which he wrote in his seventy-sixth year (A.D. 13–14) he declares: "I am Pontifex Maximus, Augur, one of the fifteen commissioners for religion, one of the seven for sacred feasts, an Arval brother, a *sodalis Titius*, a fetial. . . . I built . . . the temples of Apollo on the Palatine with its colonnades, the temple of the divine Iulius, the Lupercal . . . the temples of Jupiter Feretrius and of Jupiter Tonans on the Capitol, the temple of Quirinus, the temples of Minerva and of Juno the Queen, and of Jupiter Liberalis on the Aventine, the temple of the Lares at the head of the *via Sacra*, the temple of the divine Penates in the Velia, the temple of Youth, the temple of the Mater Magna on the Palatine. . . . In my sixth consulship [B.C. 28] I repaired eighty-two temples of the gods in the city in accordance with a decree of the Senate, none being omitted which at that time stood in need of repair. . . . On ground belonging to myself I built a temple to Mars Ultor . . .

---

[12] Wickham's translation.

In the temples of all the states of the province of Asia, I replaced the ornaments after my victory, which he with whom I had fought had taken into his private possession from the spoliation of the temples. . . . In my sixth and seventh consulships [B.C. 28, 27], when I had extinguished the flames of civil war, having by universal consent become possessed of the sole direction of affairs, I transferred the republic from my power to the will of the Senate and people of Rome. For which good service on my part I was by decree of the Senate called by the name of Augustus, and the door-posts of my house were covered with laurels in the name of the state, and a civic crown was fixed up over my door, and a golden shield was placed in the Curia Iulia, which it was declared by its inscription the Senate and people of Rome gave me in recognition of valour, clemency, justice, piety. After that time I took precedence of all in rank, but of power I had nothing more than those who were my colleagues in the several magistracies." [13] The same document says: "About 500,000 Roman citizens took the military oath to me.[13a] . . . By decree of the Senate my name was included in the ritual of the Salii; and it was ordained that my person should be sacred and that I should have the tribunician power for the term of my natural life."

Suetonius gives an account of the passengers and crew of an Alexandrian ship which had just docked at Puteoli, coming before Augustus who chanced to be sailing there, "dressed in white robes, with garlands on their heads and burning censers in their hands, loudly blessing and prais-

[13] In Shuckburgh, *Augustus,* 293, *et seq.*
[13a] This oath ran: "In the name of the Emperor I swear unconditionally to obey him, never to leave the ensign, nor spare my life for Emperor and State." T. A. Dodge, *Great Captains: Caesar* (1892), p. 769.

ing him and saying that they owed it to him that they were alive, that they sailed the sea, that they were enjoying their liberty and property." [14] From such heartfelt thankfulness to emperor worship was not a far cry. There were plenty of precedents for it. The Egyptians had defied their rulers. Even the Greeks had been directed in Draco's code to honor the heroes along with the gods.[15] Alexander the Great had been saluted as the Son of Zeus by the priests at Ammon. The Ptolemies and the Seleucids were deified, too. The thing was common in Asia. Oriental despots were gods. Romans when they conquered and ruled there were sometimes accorded divine honors. "Pompey, it seems, had received several temples; Cicero records with pride that he refused similar honours." [16] Julius Caesar was hailed as a god, Julian Jupiter, and given a temple and a priesthood at Rome within his lifetime.[17] It is said that an altar and a column twenty feet high were set up on the spot where his body was burned. Later Augustus erected the temple to Divus Julius there, of which he speaks in the Ancyra tablet.[18]

Caesar celebrated four triumphs on as many days, the first over the Gauls, the others for Egypt, Pharnaces, and Juba. In each of these he rode in the Chariot of the Sun, was dressed in the *toga picta* of victory, carried the ivory sceptre and the thunderbolt, and was Jupiter. Perhaps even his face was painted blood-red as the triumphator's face was in early times to denote that fact. At any rate

[14] Suetonius, *Augustus*, 98 (Forester's transl.).

[15] Erwin Rohde, *Psyche*, chap. iv, On Heroes.

[16] Strong, *Apotheosis and After Life*, 63 (E. P. Dutton, 1915). Mrs. Strong's authority for Pompey is *Anthologia Palatina*, ix, 402; for Cicero, *Letter to Atticus*, v, 21.

[17] Dio's *Roman History*, 44–46.

[18] Mrs. Strong writes that the core of that temple is still standing. *Apotheosis and After Life*, 61.

a Roman triumph must have been a heady business both for the conqueror and for the people who beheld him. It was not impossible to think of his glory as continuing. The services of Augustus were far more genuine. It is not surprising that he had worshippers. "Although he knew that it had been customary to decree temples in honour of the proconsuls, yet he would not permit them to be erected in any of the provinces, unless in the joint names of himself and Rome. Within the limits of the city, he positively refused any honour of that kind." [19] Yet a dozen places in Italy adopted the cult of his worship in his lifetime, among them Pompeii, Puteoli, Asisium, Beneventum, Pisa, Tibur, Verona.[20] Temples to Rome and Augustus or altars were set up in his lifetime at Cyme, Ancyra, Pergamus, Nicomedia, Alexandria, Sparta, and elsewhere in the east and in Spain, Moesia, Pannonia, Narbonne, Lugdunum. After his death he was declared divine by the Senate, a temple was erected to him on the Palatine and a college of Augustales was created to direct his worship throughout the Empire. So Augustus became one of the greater Roman divinities, and apotheosis was usual for emperors who succeeded him.

But Dr. Strong, basing her deduction upon an exhaustive comparative study of Roman monuments, sculptures, cameos, coins, and other surviving art objects, reaches the striking conclusion that the old gods paled and eventually disappeared before the rising *numen Augusti*. "Not Vergil, nor any Augustan poet, but the Emperor himself, or, more correctly, the Imperial idea, is responsible for 'taking the life out of Jupiter, Mars and Apollo.' The gods had perforce to efface themselves before the Imperial power emanating from the Emperor, though the

[19] Suetonius, *Augustus*, 52 (Forester's translation).
[20] Shuckburgh, *Augustus*, 196.

Emperor might for a time encourage their worship and
reinstate their cults with a new splendour. . . . On the
Syrian monument, erected about 40 B.C., the gods consent to admit the monarch to equality with themselves;
on the Roman monument [the Benevento arch erected
to glorify Trajan's home and foreign policy], some hundred and fifty years later, they yield their place to him
as their successor before they vanish for ever from the
scene." [21] In polytheistic art Jupiter is the central figure.
In the art objects which glorify the Imperial idea the
figure of the Emperor takes Jupiter's place in the centre
of the field. To make such familiar art objects take a
Christian form was easy: the figure of the Christ had
only to be substituted for the figure of the Emperor. The
same order obtained in the displacing of religions: Emperor worship drove out Jupiter worship and prepared
the way for Christianity.

But Christianity was only one of many Asiatic religions
which sought to convert Rome. The conquered East did
exactly what conquered Greece had done—it took its rude
conqueror captive. "The Syrian Orontes poured into
the Tiber." Rome experienced an invasion of oriental
religions. The worshippers of the Olympians and Caesar
were drawn off to rites of rival deities from Asia Minor,
Syria, and Egypt. Of the capturing of the city by the
advance guard of these oriental religions Franz Cumont
writes that it was as though "in modern Europe the faithful had deserted the Christian churches to worship Allah
or Brahma, to follow the precepts of Confucius or
Buddha, or to adopt the maxims of the Shinto; let us
imagine a great confusion of all the races of the world
in which Arabian mullahs, Chinese scholars, Japanese

[21] Strong, *Apotheosis and After Life*, 74, 87. Constable and Company,
Ltd.

bonzes, Tibetan lamas, and Hindu pundits would be preaching fatalism and predestination, ancestor-worship and devotion to a deified sovereign, pessimism and deliverance through annihilation—a confusion in which all those priests would erect temples of exotic architecture in our cities and celebrate their disparate rites therein. Such a dream, which the future may perhaps realize, would offer a pretty accurate picture of the religious chaos in which the ancient world was struggling before the reign of Constantine." [22]

Do not overlook the fact that the period here indicated is a long one, as long nearly as from the landing of the Pilgrims (1620) to the present day (1935). In it many religions were struggling for survival. They were all on their trial, the worship of the old Roman gods which was a civic duty, as well as the acceptance and worship of foreign gods whose appeal was purely personal, as at first they made their converts one by one. From Asia Minor the black stone supposed to be the abode of the Great Mother of Ida was brought to Rome in 205 B.C. by order of the Sibylline books which declared that its presence was necessary to drive Hannibal from Italy. Hannibal went to defend Carthage against Scipio, was defeated at Zama, and the Magna Mater was given a temple on the Palatine. This Phrygian religion included the worship of the earth goddess Cybele and her husband Attis, the god of vegetation. As Attis in the spring delighted in rushing and leaping along the mountains his worshippers must imitate him in wild delirious rites and processions which were frenzied routs. This was not in keeping with *Roman gravitas,* and so Romans were for-

[22] Cumont, *The Oriental Religions in Roman Paganism,* 196–197 (Chicago: The Open Court Publishing Co., 1911). By permission of the publishers.

bidden to join that priesthood. It was maintained by
Phrygians alone, who were allowed to march in motley
procession beating tambourines through the streets of
Rome on certain holidays and to collect money for the
support of their cult. The austerity of the Republic kept
the cult down to this attenuated expression of its zeal;
but under the Emperor Claudius the lid was lifted, Romans were permitted to join it, and its great days were celebrated with more extravagance and abandon in Italy than
in Phrygia even. A whole company of Phrygian deities
was placed on the list of Roman gods. To gain that protection other oriental religions joined the cult of the
Magna Mater. Attis and Cybele became the "Almighty
Gods." Their mysteries conferred immortality upon the
mystics through the "bloody dew" of the taurobolium.

From Egypt came Isis and Serapis. Caligula authorized
the worship of Isis at Rome. Isis and Osiris worship
spread from Alexandria to most of the Greek cities, including Athens and the Greek towns of Italy. There was
a Serapeum at Puteoli in 105 B.C. and an Iseum at Pompeii
about the same time. Republican Rome would not have
it, and five different times the Senate tore down its altars
between 59 and 48 B.C. It was an appealingly popular
religion which conservative Romans feared because of its
immoral effects and because of its being the state religion
of Rome's great rival Alexandria. To conciliate the
Roman populace it was tolerated under restrictions, then
persecuted by Tiberius, but nevertheless made its way
everywhere. At last in A.D. 38 Caligula erected a great
temple to Isis in the Campus Martius, and succeeding
Emperors advanced its cause even more powerfully. There
were Isis processions in the streets of Rome as late as
A.D. 394. But the Christian patriarch of Alexandria had
really made an end of that form of idolatry when in 391

he burned the Serapeum. Isis worship was a vague, creedless, dogmaless, and unmoral faith whose gorgeously arrayed deity was more like Venus than like Pallas Athena or the Virgin Mary. Its ritual made much of ablutions, fumigations, anointing. It was a kind of sacred hydrotherapy which was said to cleanse from moral impurity. It appealed, and mightily too, through a ceremonial purification which led to immortality.

From Syria came the Baals. The slaves who were imported into the West by tens of thousands brought with them the worship of the Dea Syria, Astargatis, and her husband Hadad. Wandering priests and queer processions of flagellants, who danced themselves to dizziness to the music of Syrian flutes and then struck themselves with swords and finally took up a collection from the bystanders, escorted Astargatis' image from village to village. Syrian peddlers penetrated into every part of the Empire and in groups lived in even its remotest towns. Phoenician trading ships brought their gods to the ports, and Syrian soldiers in the armies in the West and Roman soldiers in Syria spread the knowledge of the Syrian gods. Jupiter of Doliche, Professor Cumont says, is not mentioned in any book, but the inscriptions show that he found worshippers in every province of the Empire, even in Britain, Germany, and Africa. Heliogabalus, who ascended the throne in 218, tried to make his favorite Baal of Emesa the supreme deity of the Roman world. Fifty years after that, Aurelian set up the worship of the Sovereign Sun, transferring the gods of Palmyra, Bel and Helios, to a temple which he prepared for them at Rome. It was the worship of the Sovereign Sun which Julian tried to reinstate in A.D. 361. The Syrian religions were notorious for immorality and practiced human sacrifices. In their later development, because of Chaldean influences these faiths became astronomical religions, conceiving their god, Baal, as Lord of the Heavens and promising an endless life to devout worshippers among the never-dying stars.

"But it was, above all, the Mithraic worship which in the second and third centuries attained an extraordinary prevalence. I sometimes permit myself to say that, if Christianity had not carried the day, Mithraism would have become the religion of the world." [23] Mithra was a Persian god, the ancient spirit of light and god of truth and justice in Zoroastrianism. A moral god, protector of obligations and inspirer of fraternity, his mysteries are pure, for he himself is chaste and holy. Continence is a watchword, but not asceticism, for Mithra is a god of action. The Persian religion holds that the world is a battlefield where the good forces of Ahura Mazda fight against the legions of Ahriman. The goal to be reached is the conquest of evil and the eternal reign of the good. Mithra the invincible god assists the valiant faithful in their warfare against all evil and judges souls at death, sending the good into eternal light and releasing the evil to Ahriman and the abyss, there to await the last day when Ahriman and all whose work is evil will be utterly destroyed by fire, but the bodies of the good will be restored to their spirits that the whole of each good person may enjoy endless felicity among the stars.

Mithraism was a soldiers' religion. It was introduced into Italy by oriental soldiers from Pompey's army in 67 B.C. Its monuments are found in all parts of the Empire, particularly along the frontiers where the garrisons were, in Britain, Germany, along the Danube, the borders

[23] Renan, *Lectures on the Influence of the Institutions, Thought, and Culture of Rome on Christianity and the Development of the Catholic Church* (Hibbert Lectures, 1880), 35.

of the Sahara, and in Spain. Its conception of life as a fight and its emphasis on steadfastness and fraternity made it an appealing military cult. But it spread in time to all ranks of society. Commodus was initiated into its mysteries, and Diocletian, Galerius, and Licinius dedicated a shrine to "The Protector of Empire," at Carnuntum as late as 307. "Mithra infused a new vigor into the paganism of the occident by introducing the imperative ethics of Persia," says Professor Cumont by way of summing up its power. It had its chapels like little churches, its mysteries, its brotherhoods with their sacred suppers. The Mithraic reliefs are mostly altarpieces which decorated the ends of the chapels; in the centre is the Mithraic sacrifice of the Sacred Bull of Ormuzd, with panels that picture Mithra's miraculous birth, his encounter with the Sun, his capture of the Bull and his ascension into heaven in the Sun's chariot of fire.

A Song to Mithras

Mithras, God of the Morning, our trumpets waken the Wall!
"Rome is above the Nations, but Thou art over all!"
Now as the names are answered, and the guards are marched
    away,
Mithras, also a soldier, give us strength for the day!

Mithras, God of the Noontide, the heather swims in the heat.
Our helmets scorch our foreheads; our sandals burn our feet.
Now in the ungirt hour—now ere we blink and drowse,
Mithras, also a soldier, keep us true to our vows!

Mithras, God of the Sunset, low on the Western main—
Thou descending immortal, immortal to rise again!
Now when the watch is ended, now when the wine is drawn,
Mithras, also a soldier, keep us pure till the dawn!

Mithras, God of the Midnight, here where the great Bull dies,
Look on thy children in darkness. Oh take our sacrifice!
Many roads Thou hast fashioned—all of them lead to the Light!
Mithras, also a soldier, teach us to die aright! [24]

The climax of Mithraic holiness came through the taurobolium. The machinery needed to carry out this rite was cumbersome. There was a deep pit near the Mithraic church. It was covered over with grating. Into that pit the candidate descended naked, a bull was sacrificed above him and the blood ran down over him, he on his part bringing every part of his body under this red shower bath.

This employment of a blood sacrifice must have made an appeal to all pagans, habituated as they were to worshipping the Olympian gods with bloody offerings. But there is more than a middle term of transition in this rite. It is participation, blood transfusion, the means of identifying oneself with the god. As such it is the basis of the worship both of the Olympians and of the new gods of springtime nature fertility. The dead earth comes to life again. So shall the duly consecrated mystics who have participated in the life of the god rise with his rising and mount with his tide. The mystic who could say, "I have eaten of that which was in the dulcimer, I have drunk of that which was in the cymbal," thenceforth shared the life of Attis, his deaths and his resurrections.

Professor Guignebert points out [25] that the Attis worship of Phrygia, the Adonis worship of Syria, the Melkart worship of Phoenicia, the Tammuz and Marduk worship of Mesopotamia, the Osiris worship of Egypt, and the

[24] From *Puck of Pook's Hill* by Rudyard Kipling, c. 1905, 1906, 1934, reprinted with permission from Mrs. Kipling, Doubleday, Doran and Company, Inc., and Macmillan and Company, Ltd.
[25] *Christianity, Past and Present,* 66.

Dionysos worship of Greece are all so much alike that they may all have derived from one parenthood and be variants of one endeavor to provide humanity with immortality. Mithraism belongs to that endeavor, so does Christianity.

Why were the oriental religions welcomed in the West? They came from immemorially old lands and civilizations to a country which was new. Traders, soldiers, and teachers brought them. Franz Cumont says these foreign religions gave greater satisfaction (1) to the senses, (2) to the intelligence, and (3) to the conscience.

The Roman state religion was a pretty objective and impersonal series of relations and performances, with its priests, augurs, and diviners. It went on above the people and remotely from them. At best they were distant spectators to a pretty arbitrary series of procedures. Worship was a bargain and sale transaction which officers of state must perform to the ceremonial letter. To the people the old gods said "bow down." The new religions addressed themselves to the people. They sought to appeal to them, to make converts of them. They dressed themselves up gorgeously and employed incense, song, and spectacle to capture and delight the attention. The new gods struggled, suffered, died, and rose triumphantly from the dead. Their liturgy was the acting out of that absorbing divine tragedy.

The Greeks had made an almost inhumanly abstract thing of intelligence. They had taken it out of the matrix of human interests and concerns and treated it as though it could forever be a thing apart. But science cannot live without religion, for science is only religion become articulate, and religion is the eternal borderland of as yet inarticulate science. The peoples that did not divide too far, whose priests were wise men and whose wise men priests, made a more natural appeal than the peddlers of wisdom who left out the gods. A learned priesthood, or a wonder-working priesthood was well worth attention and got it, though of course it did not always deserve it.

It was a formal age, pretty juiceless and scientifically unenergetic. It was easier to believe what was told than put it to the test. The new religions put heart into people even though it was false heart; they taught them that they were objects of concern to the gods, and made them objects of concern to themselves.

Renan thinks that certain Syrian Jews brought the first accounts of Christianity to Rome about the year 50. We even know their names, he thinks; they were Aquila and Priscilla, tentmakers like Paul of Tarsus who lived and worked with them at Corinth. In their person Christianity, when it was introduced, did not look like a ruling religion destined to supplant the Caesars in the management of mankind. Jews had lived in Rome for more than a hundred years. They herded together in the ghetto of the Porta Portese, which was certainly as malodorous, as indescribably dirty, as want-afflicted and poverty-blighted as Jewish quarters have been in great capitals since that time. "The Jews, who by the instigation of one Chrestus were evermore tumultuous, he banished from Rome" is a sentence in Suetonius' Life of Claudius Caesar (25). The Christian church of Rome was not planted by Paul or Peter, it was a shoot from the church at Jerusalem.[26] The Christianity which Aquila and Priscilla brought was different from that which Peter and Paul introduced subsequently.

Nothing is or can be more amazing than the ordeal by which Christianity proved its survival value. What was

[26] Renan, *op cit.*, 57.

the message that was given? Jesus could not possibly have been more emphatic than in daring to add to the law of Moses a new commandment. But the kingdom which all were bidden to seek is a here and now and a future kingdom to be ushered in by obedience to the commandments—the ten with the added one.

If we ask what was the relation of Christianity to Judaism, its Founder's answer is that it is the fulfilling of the Law. The rites and ceremonies are not abrogated but "the weightier matters of the law, judgment, mercy, and faith" (Matthew 23:23), are to regulate all and themselves to be regulated by the love of God and fellow man which is the essence of the whole relation. This love is sonship. The Kingdom of God is the abounding awareness of Fatherhood and brotherhood in the divine family to which men in reality belong. A Messiah was awaited, a man of resplendent gifts to lead God's people to victory and rule in wisdom and holiness. Jesus admitted to his disciples that he was the Messiah (Mark 8:30).

The second founding of the fellowship which is the church was in that upper room in Jerusalem—about one hundred and twenty were there. Matthias was added to the eleven by lot to take the place vacated by Judas. Then came the great day of Pentecost. There were Jews present from "every nation under heaven." Peter "standing up with the eleven" preached the first public sermon, declaring that the specific promises of the Old Testament are fulfilled in this same Jesus whom ye have crucified. He has been raised up again. Therefore let all the house of Israel know that God has made him both Lord and Christ.

This was a group of Hebrews brought together by a new development of the Hebrew religion. They were a new synagogue or at most a new sect. They met to discuss their all-absorbing new interests in private houses, but they worshipped with all the rest of Jerusalem in the Temple.

The Sadducees objected to what they were saying about the resurrection, and brought them before the Sanhedrin, which enjoined them to be silent. They were not silent and were brought up a second time. Gamaliel, the Pharisee, saved them by insisting that if their cause was of God it would prevail, if it was not of God it would come to nothing; so they were scourged and sent away. Among the believers in the new doctrines there had been some murmurings by the Graecized Jews that their people were not being given a fair share of the common support funds. A committee of seven, all of them Jews with Greek names, had thereupon been appointed to oversee that distribution. One of that committee, Stephen, championed the new belief pretty vigorously in the Synagogue of Cilician Jews, where he was, it seems, pitted in argument against contenders led by a young man named Saul. The discussion went beyond bounds and Stephen was accused of blasphemy to the Sanhedrin and was sentenced to death. The trial was disorderly and the execution immediate. "And Saul was consenting unto his death."

The new belief had made enemies now among the Sadducees, the Pharisees, and the Grecians. These Grecians were Jews who lived in Greek-speaking cities like Alexandria, Antioch, and Tarsus. They came up to Jerusalem to celebrate the Hebrew religious feasts. The first disciples were Hebrews of the Hebrews, but the message had now gone to Grecian Jews who organized themselves into a group apart from that of the Twelve. The tumult about Stephen resulted in a great persecution of the infant church, "and they were all scattered abroad through the regions of Judaea and Samaria, except the apostles."

That means that both Palestinian and Grecian Jewish Christians were scattered, and the new beliefs by them spread. The Grecian Jew from Tarsus, Saul, seems to have been a leader of persecutors of the new believers after the execution of Stephen. Saul "made havock of the church, entering into every house, and haling men and women committed them to prison" (Acts 8:3). The scattered folk went preaching everywhere, and Saul sued out a commission from the high priest to hunt them down in the synagogues, particularly those of Damascus. It was on his way there that he had that Damascus road experience which changed the world. It a few days the transformed persecutor is in the synagogues of Damascus preaching Christ, "that he is the Son of God." This aroused such enmity that Saul left Damascus and went into Arabia. After a time he returned to Damascus and began his synagogue teaching about Jesus again. This brought on an effort to assassinate him and he escaped from Damascus over the wall in a basket. The time from his Damascus road experience to his departure from the city is given as three years:

"Then after three years I went up to Jerusalem to see Peter, and abode with him fifteen days. But other of the apostles saw I none, save James the Lord's brother. . . . Afterwards I came into the regions of Syria and Cilicia . . . Then fourteen years after I went up again to Jerusalem with Barnabas, and took Titus with me also. And I went up by revelation, and communicated unto them that gospel which I preach among the Gentiles, but privately to them which were of reputation, lest by any means I should run, or had run, in vain . . . They who seemed to be somewhat in conference added nothing to me: but contrariwise, when they saw that the gospel of the uncircumcision was committed unto me, as the gospel of the circum-

cision was unto Peter . . . and when James, Cephas, and
John, who seemed to be pillars, perceived the grace that
was given unto me, they gave to me, and Barnabas the
right hands of fellowship; that we should go unto the
heathen, and they unto the circumcision. Only they would
that we should remember the poor; the same which I also
was forward to do. But when Peter was come to Antioch, I
withstood him to the face, because he was to be blamed.
For before that certain came from James, he did eat with
the Gentiles: but when they were come, he withdrew and
separated himself, fearing them which were of the circumcision. And the other Jews dissembled likewise with
him; insomuch that Barnabas also was carried away with
their dissimulation. But when I saw that they walked not
uprightly according to the truth of the gospel, I said unto
Peter before them all, If thou, being a Jew, livest after
the manner of Gentiles, and not as do the Jews, why com-
pellest thou the Gentiles to live as do the Jews? We who
are Jews by nature, and not sinners of the Gentiles, knowing that a man is not justified by the works of the law, but
by the faith of Jesus Christ, even we have believed in Jesus
Christ, that we might be justified by the faith of Christ,
and not by the works of the law; for by the works of the
law shall no flesh be justified. . . . For I through the law
am dead to the law . . . I am crucified with Christ:
nevertheless I live; yet not I, but Christ liveth in me:
and the life which I now live in the flesh I live by the
faith of the Son of God, who loved me, and gave himself
for me. I do not frustrate the grace of God: for if
righteousness come by the law, then Christ is dead in
vain." [27]

Then Christianity is not a reformed Judaism. This
Greek-speaking Roman citizen, Jew of Tarsus, has given

[27] Galatians, 1:18–2:21.

it characteristics more like those of the immortality participation cults of Syria, Phrygia, and Egypt. To Paul "Christ died for our sins." To the Twelve He is the revealer of the Fatherhood of God, the Announcer of the law of love, the Usherer in of the Kingdom of God. To Paul He is the Son of God; to the Twelve, the Son of Man. To Paul, Jesus Christ is Lord at Whose name every knee should bow. In the Old Testament, Jahveh declares (Isaiah 45:23): "Unto me every knee shall bow." The relation of Jesus Christ to God thus becomes the essential problem of the Church. The question of consubstantiality is not far off, but Paul is not a metaphysician, only a raiser of metaphysical problems which will call a host of Greek gnostic theologians into being in a few days. The best Paul can do with this tremendous problem is that God's righteousness is manifested in Jesus Christ (Romans 1:17 et seq.). All have sinned. By Adam sin entered the world, and with it death. By Christ are all made alive. "Giving thanks unto the Father, which hath made us meet to be partakers of the inheritance of the saints in light: who hath delivered us from the power of darkness, and hath translated us into the Kingdom of his dear Son: in whom we have redemption through his blood, even the forgiveness of sins: who is the image of the invisible God, the firstborn of every creature: for by him were all things created, that are in heaven, and that are in earth, visible and invisible, whether they be thrones, or dominions, or principalities, or powers: all things were created by him, and for him: and he is before all things, and by him all things consist. And he is the head of the body, the church: who is the beginning, the firstborn from the dead; that in all things he might have the preëminence. For it pleased the Father that in him should all fulness dwell; and, having made peace through the blood of his cross, by him to reconcile all things unto himself; by him, I say, whether they be things in earth, or things in heaven. And you, that were sometime alienated and enemies in your mind by wicked works, yet now hath he reconciled in the body of his flesh through death, to present you holy and unblameable and unreprovable in his sight: if ye continue in the faith grounded and settled, and be not moved away from the hope of the gospel, which ye have heard, and which was preached to every creature which is under heaven; . . . even the mystery which hath been hid from ages and from generations, but now is made manifest to his saints . . . Beware lest any man spoil you through philosophy and vain deceit, after the tradition of men, after the rudiments of the world, and not after Christ." [28]

What is Paul's authority? He had not followed Jesus day by day as eleven of the Twelve had. He had had a vision on the Damascus road. It is the fulfilment-of-the-law conception of Christianity which is found in the non-Pauline writings of the first two centuries, not the Pauline conception. "In fact, the principle enunciated by James resembles closely the principle of Christ, who came not to destroy the law, but to fulfil it by revealing and emphasizing its inner meaning. And yet it is not the principle of Paul; for to him the Christian life is not obedience to any objective law, even the law of love, but the working out in the man of the life of Christ within him." [29]

Here are enough problems to keep active minds busy for all time to come. In the matrix of Christianity which the New Testament is, lie embedded all the creeds, all the orthodoxies, and all the heresies as well. The new belief was offered to the Jews. They rejected it. It was forced

[28] Colossians 1:12–26, 2:8.
[29] McGiffert, *A History of Christianity in the Apostolic Age*, 447.

to go to the Gentiles. Those "devout men of every nation" who were at Jerusalem on the day of Pentecost had a part in spreading it, particularly the Hellenists among them, for Christianity is next a Graecized, then a Greek interest. Gnosticism is Hellenism, and the Gnostics were the theologians of the first century.[30] It was the Gnostics that made Christianity a religion, declares Renan.[31] It lacked arrangement, classifications, formulations, symbolism, ceremonies, festivals, liturgies, services, creeds, sacraments; the Gnostics supplied the beginnings of them. They wrote the apocryphal books. Judaism could have no graven images. Christian art began with the Greeks, for Gnostic Christians made the first portraits of the Christ.

But inventiveness which produced so much that was fit to be incorporated in time into the organized church also ran riot in forms of shocking extravagance. Gnosticism was a centrifugal force. It multiplied interpretations and the little churches that sprang up about them, as though to be fantastically unique were its principle. It was the activity of a kind of theosophical madness that played about the slow and solid integration of the organization of the Faith. "Gnosticism" is a kind of waste-basket word. It is a name given to a lot of odds and ends which are otherwise nearly but not quite unrelated. Yet each of them claims to be Christian by being some sort of recognition of the work of Christ. It is speculative or philosophical, not historical or revealed, knowledge that Gnosticism claims to be. Simon Magus (Acts 8:9) was characterized by Eusebius as "the author of all heresy." He taught that he himself was the Supreme Power, and Christ, his forerunner. His successor, Menander, taught

---

[30] Harnack, *History of Dogma*, I, 228.
[31] *Marcus Aurelius*, "Eastern Syncretism."

that the Supreme Power is unknown to all men, but that "he himself was the Savior who had been sent down from invisible aeons for the salvation of men, and he taught that no one could gain the mastery over the world-creating angels themselves unless he had first gone through the magical discipline imparted by him and had received baptism from him." Those who received this baptism would at once become immortal and would neither grow old nor die.[32] Both these were Samaritans. The Ebionites got that name because they held "poor and mean opinions concerning Christ," denying his preëxistence and essential divinity. They rejected all the epistles of the Apostle, as they called him an apostate from the law. In one of the Ophite sects the serpent was given his ancient dignity. The Creator of the World is an evil power acting in hostility to the Supreme God, and man's fall is not an act of disobedience to the Supreme God but an emancipation from an evil being. The serpent therefore is man's emancipator. Another group of Ophites identified the serpent with the Logos or Divine Son. To one group Cain is a hero and true martyr for resisting the God of the Old Testament who was an evil being, and Judas, for he alone had the insight to assist Christ's mission of completing by his death the overthrow of the God of the Jews.[33]

Cerinthus taught that the world was not made by the Supreme God. He denied the supernatural birth of Jesus, but insisted that upon that Son of Mary and Joseph the Christ descended at baptism, leaving him at the crucifixion. The Creative God does not know the Supreme God who is over all things. The mission of Christ to the world is not

[32] Eusebius, *Church History*, III, 26, in *Nicene and Post-Nicene Fathers of the Christian Church*, 2nd Ser., Vol. I.

[33] Mansel, *The Gnostic Heresies*, Lecture VII. Legge, *Forerunners and Rivals of Christianity*, II, 25–82.

to save men from their sins but to proclaim to them the
Supreme God. Of Syrian Gnostics, Saturninus, Tatian,
and Bardesanes are foremost. Saturninus taught that the
Supreme God—the Father Unknown—made the arch-
angels, angels, principalities, and powers, but seven angels
made the world and man. The God of the Jews was one of
those seven angels. Christ, who never was born and had
but the appearance of man, being in fact without body or
form, came to depose this God of the Jews and to save
the good. Tatian also distinguished the Creator of the
world from the Supreme God. He regarded the Old and
the New Testaments as the works of different Gods. He
was a fierce ascetic, condemning marriage and the eating
of animal food. So extreme was he that in administering
the Eucharist he used pure water instead of wine.
Bardesanes held that matter, which is coeternal with God,
is opposed to Him, but that in addition Satan, an active
principle of evil, was produced from matter. The Lord,
though born of the Virgin Mary, is not flesh and blood,
but only in appearance man. He was crucified in appearance only, and there is accordingly no resurrection.

Basilides, the Egyptian Gnostic, is of abounding vitality.
"Under the pretext of unspeakable mysteries, [he] invented monstrous fables," says Eusebius (IV. 7). He
taught that the eating of burnt offerings to idols and
abjuration itself were indifferent, and required his followers like Pythagoras to observe five years of silence.
"Since therefore there was nothing, neither matter, nor
substance, nor unsubstantial, nor simple, nor compound,
nor inconceivable, nor imperceptible, nor man, nor angel,
nor God, nor in short any of the things that are named or
perceived by the senses or conceived by the intellect, but
all things being thus, and more minutely than thus, simply
obliterated, the non-existent God . . . without thought,

without sense, without counsel, without choice, without
passion, without desire, willed to make a world. When
I say *willed*, I mean to signify without will and without
thought and without sense; and by *the world* I mean not
that which was afterwards made and separated by size
and division, but the seed of the world. For the seed of
the world had everything in itself, as a grain of mustard
seed in the smallest compass comprehends all things together, the roots, the stem, the branches, the leaves, and
the innumerable seeds of other and yet other plants
mingled with the grains of the plant. Thus the non-existent
God made a non-existent world from things non-existent,
having cast down and deposited a single seed, having in
itself the universal seed of the world." [84] Valentinus, who
came after Basilides, was the best known and most influential of the Gnostics. He was born in Egypt, studied
Greek literature at Alexandria, and for thirteen years lived
in Rome in Antoninus Pius' reign. His system, which is
too vast to be outlined here, makes a pleasant appeal by
personifying the metaphysical abstractions with which it
deals. In it Basilides' non-existent God is the *Depth*.
From the *Depth* and *Silence* sprang *Mind* and *Truth;* from
these, *Logos* and *Life;* and from them, *Man* and the
Church. Logos and Life gave birth to ten Aeons. And
Man and the Church produced twelve Aeons. The first
group is the Ogdoad, the second the Decad, and the third
the Dodecad. These are personified divine attributes and
together form the *Pleroma*. They are the archetypes of
which all created things are but reflections or reminders.
Each aeon contributed that which was most excellent, and
from these contributions came "the most perfect beauty
and constellation of the Pleroma," Jesus, Savior, Christ,

[84] In Hippolytus, vii. 21, as quoted in Mansel, *The Gnostic Heresies*,
147–148.

and Logos, the *All,* because produced from all.[35] This Christ like all things else is two Christs, the one a Divine Idea, the other the created expression of that Idea or Aeon. There is a Redeemer for the Celestial World and a Redeemer for the terrestrial. The system of Valentinus is a theosophy with a kind of combined Platonic and Miltonic grandeur.

There is one other second century spirit who is not strictly speaking a Gnostic, for he does not claim to be led by knowledge but by faith; but, inasmuch as he reaches the same positions as they, he is grouped with them. That is Marcion. He was a rich shipowner of Pontus who came to Rome about 139, already a Christian, and powerfully convinced that all the churches, even then in existence, must be remade. He battled to accomplish that, and when he failed he organized a system of churches of his own. He was an extreme adherent of Paul. Maintaining that that Apostle was the only one who represented Christ worthily, he made a Bible of his own by rejecting the entire Old Testament and all of the New except ten Epistles of Paul and a pretended original Gospel, a mutilated Luke.[36] Marcion is a downright kind of man who will not compromise with revelation or palliating interpretation. He is an anti-Judaizer out and out. He will have none of them or their Old Testament. The God which those writings reveal cannot have been wise, good, and powerful, he insists, for when he had created man in his own image, he permitted him to fall, either not knowing that he would fall, or unwilling or unable to help him not

[35] Mansel, *The Gnostic Heresies,* 181. See Legge, *Forerunners and Rivals of Christianity,* II, 101.

[36] The Ten Epistles of Paul were: Galatians, I and II Corinthians, Romans, I and II Thessalonians, Ephesians, Colossians, Philemon, Philippians. From the Gospel of Luke all that relates to the genealogy, birth, and infancy of Jesus was omitted.

to fall. The Old Testament describes an imperfect God because it described the Creator of the World, not the Supreme God. And there are two Christs, too: that of the prophets, and the true Christ. The true Christ is sent by God to save all men, the Christ of the Jewish writings to restore Israel alone. The Creating God, or Demiurge, who made the world had to use matter, but the Supreme God who sent the Christ of the Ten Pauline Epistles is pure spirit and could have had nothing to do with matter. The Christ He sent then could have had nothing to do with a material body. He was not born. He did not grow up. He appeared suddenly in the world with the aspect but not the reality of a human being. He revealed his true nature when he asked "Who is my mother?" [37] He did not die on the cross, he only seemed to. Thus Marcion upheld Paul's scheme, but, may we not say, too powerfully, for does he not reduce the whole blood sacrifice atonement theory to an unnecessary appearance too?

The Church and its survival, it has been said, were determined by three great contentions: (1) its struggle with outright paganism, (2) its struggle with Gnosticism, and (3) its struggle with heresy in its own ranks.[38] Gnosticism was the effort of Hellenism to appropriate Christianity. Its Supreme God is Plato's idea of The Good, which works through the intermediary of Ideas or Aeons. It will have nothing to do with Judaism and its Old Testament writings. To maintain a complete separation between spirit and matter, it has no place for fleshly body; and, rejecting the Man Christ and all that befell him, it insists that he was ever pure spirit. In doing that

[37] Matthew 12:48. Legge, *Forerunners and Rivals of Christianity*, II, 211.
[38] Paul Elmer More, *Christ the Word*, 30.

it laid up a treasure of difficulties for Christian theologians to untangle. But while it was doing that "the splendor of the catholic and only true Church, which is always the same, grew in magnitude and power, and reflected its piety and simplicity and freedom, and the modesty and purity of its inspired life and philosophy to every nation both of Greeks and of Barbarians." [39]

[39] Eusebius, *Church History*, IV, 7.

II

THE EARLY CHURCH

The "Apostolic Age" is the period in which any or all of the Twelve and Paul were alive. The next ages are patristic ages, the ages of the Fathers of the Church. Theirs is a long period which is divided into two parts by the Council of Nicaea, A.D. 325, the period of the Ante-Nicene Fathers and the Post-Nicene period. To the Ante-Nicene period belong the work and the writings of such great leaders as Justin, Irenaeus, Clement of Alexandria, Origen, Tertullian, Cyprian, Minucius Felix, Novatian, and others; to the Post-Nicene period belong Athanasius, John Chrysostom, Basil, Gregory Nazianzen, Hilary of Poictiers, Ambrose of Milan, Augustine of Hippo, Jerome, Leo of Rome, Rufinus, John Cassian, Vincent of Lerins, Cassiodorus, Gregory the Great, and a number more. The literature which these two periods contributed is vast; in Migne's Patrologia ninety-six volumes are taken up by the Greek and seventy-six by the Latin Fathers.

He who would see a picture of how Christianity spread must read Paul's letters. They are the most vivid account of missionary labors in existence. There were little clusters of Jews in every coastal city—Jews of the Dispersion or Diaspora, scattered to the towns of the whole Roman Empire. They led their community life about their little synagogue, which perhaps was most often not a separate building but a large room in a family dwelling. These little groups were things apart—de facto ghettos. Neither the Romans nor the Greeks fellowed with the Jews, but the Jews fellowed intensively with one another. Each little ghetto was like a large patriarchal family, vigorously, almost desperately concerned in its sectarian affairs and eagerly welcoming and entertaining any journeying stranger of its own race that could talk about the national interest and the people's hopes. Such a stranger when he went to the synagogue on the Sabbath day, was asked to say a word to the congregation. That was an invitation which Paul waited for and eagerly embraced. He never failed to tell them about the redeeming work of Jesus. Sometimes they listened eagerly, and the whole group became converted; sometimes only some few of them followed Paul out and arranged to meet again with him that he might tell them more about it. Sometimes the whole congregation rose against him, put him out, and pursued him. "Of the Jews five times received I forty stripes save one. Thrice was I beaten with rods, once was I stoned." [1] The Church was not only founded on the synagogue model, it was founded in the synagogue. It was in fact a new synagogue. It was a place of holy teaching, reading of the law, counselling to piety, and the carrying on of good works. Jesus had four brothers: James, Joseph, Simon, and Judas. They were not disciples, for they did not believe in his mission (John 7:5); but they were all in that upper room in Jerusalem after the crucifixion (Acts 1:14). James, the eldest brother of Jesus, though he is not at first an apostle, seems after years of service to have been coöpted into their company and is a leader, though without any specified office, in the mother church at Jerusalem. His work and character gain for him the new name James the Just. The church in which

[1] II Corinthians 11:24-25.

he was a leading spirit was engaged in converting men to Judaism rather than away from it. Nevertheless, this good man perished by order of the Sanhedrin in A.D. 62. With the destruction of Jerusalem by Titus in A.D. 70, the remnant of that Jerusalem church fled to Pella. There could no longer be any doubt that it was not to the Jews of troubled Palestine but to the people of the outer world that Christianity must go. With the fall of Jerusalem Christianity became an independent religion. It did not choose to follow the lead of the Ebionites who continued their observance of the Jewish law, for they insisted that Christ was a mere man and rejected the whole New Testament as now known. They were dismissed as heretics and soon ran out. It went to the Gentiles, Paul took it to the Gentiles; and yet a strange thing about the Christianity that grew up in Europe is that it was not distinctively Pauline until Luther revived Pauline Christianity in the Protestant churches of the Reformation. As to the way it grew out of the synagogue, Dr. Edwin Hatch, who must be our chief guide in this chapter, points out that "when the majority of the members of a Jewish community [one of those to which Paul went in his missionary journeying outside of Palestine] were convinced that Jesus was the Christ, there was nothing to interrupt the current of their former common life. There was no need for secession, for schism, for a change in the organization. The old form of worship and the old modes of government could still go on. The weekly commemoration of the Resurrection supplemented, but did not supersede, the ancient sabbath. The reading of the life of Christ and of the letters of Apostles supplemented, but did not supersede, the ancient lessons from the prophets, and the ancient singing of the psalms. The community as a whole was known by the same name which had designated the

purely Jewish community. It was still a παροικία—a
colony living as strangers and pilgrims in the midst of an
alien society: and even when the sense of alienation lessened, the word was retained, though it was used in a new
relation to signify that upon earth none of us has an abid-
ing city." [2] Of the inner life of these earliest churches
there are intimations if not descriptions in Paul's letters.
"By one spirit are we all baptized into one body, whether
we be Jews or Gentiles, whether we be bond or free; and
have been all made to drink into one Spirit . . . there
should be no schism in the body; but . . . the members
should have the same care one for another. . . . And
God hath set some in the Church, first apostles, second-
arily prophets, thirdly teachers, after that miracles,
then gifts of healings, helps, governments, diversities of
tongues." [3] The Church, the universal Church, did not
come into being by the fusion of congregations: the congregations grew out of the church, the original conception
of Jesus of the Kingdom of God. The Apostles were
commissioned to spread that conception. The congregations were a result of their preaching. It is commonly
thought that the Apostles were limited to the Twelve and
Paul, but other Apostles were in fact added to that
number. To have had personal association with Jesus
was not the mark of an Apostle; but a divine call was.
The Prophets also functioned through a divine call, but
the Apostles were pioneer workers in new territory, shock
troops or the spearhead of the advancing Church. The
Teachers had similar qualifications, but their work of
instruction perhaps was most commonly assigned to them
by the others. All three groups possessed the charisma and

[2] Hatch, The Organization of the Early Christian Churches (Bamp-
ton Lectures, 1880), p. 60. By permission of Longmans, Green & Co.
[3] I Corinthians 12:13, 25, 28.

belonged to the general church rather than to a local church.[4] One other officer, the bishop, was appointed perhaps as head or president of the congregation to distribute the alms which were a religious due to the needy brethren. There was need too of an official always at hand to direct the services of the church. The bishop came to be that resident director of each congregation, inheriting from the Apostles, Prophets, and Teachers of the earlier day their unformulated responsibility to guide, administer, instruct, discipline, and inspire the congregation of the faithful. Each bishop had the care of his own church; when by subdividing the congregation it grew into a system of churches he had charge of the parent church and its offshoots.

"The natural result of any investigation," says Sextus Empiricus, "is that the investigators either discover the object of search or deny that it is discoverable." Just how did Christianity pass to the Greeks and the Romans and get a foothold among them? Paul preached to synagogues and made, it has been estimated, as many as a thousand converts in them. Beside him and the Twelve worked many other Apostles.[5] But the Roman Empire was a vast territory, and though it took it 300 years to do that, Christianity did become its official religion. How, we frankly do not know. The steps in that process are lost. Though rhetorical appeal is constantly made to the practices of the primitive church, it is not historical appeal. There is no recorded history of it; most likely there never was any. The days of its infancy are set down in the New Testament, but the days of its youth were too enthusiastic, too occupied, perhaps even too terrible to be written about.

[4] McGiffert, *A History of Christianity in the Apostolic Age*, 646 et seq.

[5] Romans, 16, Revelation 2.

Besides, no one knew for certain that great events were
going forward then, or merely futile failures. Even if
Eusebius had been historian enough to look for growth instead of eternal preformation, he could not have found
accurate information about the church of the first two
hundred years. There must have been a good deal of
confusion, perhaps much turbulence, a great variety of
opinions, practices, beliefs, doctrines. It is certain that
heavy hardships were the lot of some if not all the groups
of believers. In 64 when Rome burned, Nero diverted
condemnation from himself by pointing to the Christians
as possible authors of the conflagration. Their notorious
unwillingness to worship the genius of Rome or serve as
soldiers, their going apart, and their alleged practice of
secret and even horrible rites were brought forward; and
those in Rome were sent to agonizing death on the charge
that they were enemies of society. The persecution of
Christians, not because they were Christians but because
they were held to be public enemies, was in this instance
localized at Rome, but other places caught the spirit of an
imperial precedent. Upon the charge of atheism "many
who drifted into Jewish ways" were condemned by the
Emperor Domitian.[6] The Emperor Trajan's reply to the
inquiry of his legate propraetor, Pliny the Younger, who
was governor of the province of Pontus and Bithynia,
definitely makes Christianity an unlawful religion and all
Christians as such criminals. Pliny had written:

"It is my custom, my Lord, to refer to thee all questions
concerning which I am in doubt; for who can better direct
my hesitation or instruct my ignorance? I have never
been present at judicial examinations of the Christians;
therefore I am ignorant how and to what extent it is customary to punish or to search for them. And I have

[6] Dio's *Roman History*, 67–14.

hesitated greatly as to whether any distinction should be made on the ground of age, or whether the weak should be treated in the same way as the strong; whether pardon should be granted to the penitent, or he who has ever been a Christian gain nothing by renouncing it; whether the mere name, if unaccompanied with crimes, or crimes associated with the name, should be punished. Meanwhile, with those who have been brought before me as Christians I have pursued the following course. I have asked them if they were Christians, and if they have confessed, I have asked them a second and third time, threatening them with punishment; if they have persisted, I have commanded them to be led away to punishment. For I did not doubt that whatever that might be which they confessed, at any rate pertinacious and inflexible obstinacy ought to be punished. There have been others afflicted with like insanity who as Roman citizens I have decided should be sent to Rome. In the course of the proceedings, as commonly happens, the crime was extended, and many varieties of cases appeared. An anonymous document was published, containing the names of many persons. Those who denied that they were or had been Christians I thought ought to be released, when they had followed my example in invoking the gods and offering incense and wine to thine image,—which I had for that purpose ordered brought with the images of the gods,—and when they had besides cursed Christ—things which they say that those who are truly Christians cannot be compelled to do. Others, accused by an informer, first said that they were Christians and afterwards denied it, saying that they had indeed been Christians, but had ceased to be, some three years, some several years, and one even twenty years before. All adored thine image and the statues of the gods, and cursed Christ. Moreover, they affirmed that

this was the sum of their guilt or error; that they had been
accustomed to come together on a fixed day before day-
light and to sing responsively a song unto Christ as God;
and to bind themselves with an oath, not with a view to the
commission of some crime, but, on the contrary, that they
would not commit theft, nor robbery, nor adultery, that
they would not break faith, nor refuse to restore a deposit
when asked for it. When they had done these things, their
custom was to separate and to assemble again to partake
of a meal, common yet harmless (which is not the characteristic of a nefarious superstition); but this they had
ceased to do after my edict, in which according to thy
demands I had prohibited fraternities. I therefore considered it the more necessary to examine, even with the
use of torture, two female slaves who were called deacon-
esses (*ministrae*), in order to ascertain the truth. But I
found nothing except a superstition depraved and immoderate; and therefore, postponing further inquiry, I
have turned to thee for advice. For the matter seems to
me worth consulting about, especially on account of the
number of persons involved. For many of every age and
of every rank and of both sexes have been already and
will be brought to trial. For the contagion of this superstition has permeated not only the cities, but also the
villages and even the country districts. Yet it can ap-
parently be arrested and corrected. At any rate, it is certainly a fact that the temples, which were almost deserted,
are now beginning to be frequented, and the sacred rites,
which were for a long time interrupted, to be resumed,
and fodder for the victims to be sold, for which previously
hardly a purchaser was to be found. From which it is
easy to gather how great a multitude of men may be reformed if there is given a chance for repentance."

The reply of Trajan — commonly called "Trajan's

Rescript"—reads as follows: "Thou hast followed the right course, my Secundus, in treating the cases of those who have been brought before thee as Christians. For no fixed rule can be laid down which shall be applicable to all cases. They are not to be searched for; if they are accused and convicted, they are to be punished; nevertheless, with the proviso that he who denies that he is a Christian, and proves it by his act (*re ipsa*),—i.e. by making supplication to our gods,—although suspected in regard to the past, may by repentance obtain pardon. Anonymous accusations ought not to be admitted in any proceedings; for they are of most evil precedent, and are not in accord with our age." [7]

The date is 110 or 111. There was no general or empire-wide persecution until that of the Emperor Decius in 250. But the Christians refusing as they did to swear by the genius of the Emperor were definitely anti-Roman and suffered the treatment of barely tolerated dwellers in the Empire.

These are bits of evidence from Roman historians. Of Christian writers who supply details about the growth of the Faith we have next to none until near the third century. Then come Irenaeus, bishop of Lyons from 177 and author of the book *Contra Hereticos;* Justin Martyr beheaded at Rome probably in 163, who was a converted student of the Platonic philosophy and wrote an *Apology* and a work defending Christianity, *Against the Greeks;* Hippolytus Romanus, a pupil of Irenaeus, who died a martyr in Sardinia in 235 (his book *Philosophumena,* written in Greek, is a philosophical examination of Christianity). Tertullian (*c.* 150–*c.* 230) the great north African church father, was born at Carthage and did his

[7] From translator's footnote to Eusebius, *Church History,* in *Nicene and Post-Nicene Fathers of the Christian Church,* 2nd Series, Vol. I, 165.

work in that city and in Rome. He was a most vigorous defender of the Faith in a number of books. Clement of Alexandria, born at Athens about 150, died 213, was head of the Catechetical School at Alexandria and a vigorous writer against the Gnostics. He was the teacher of Origen, (185–254), who was by race an Egyptian, a fiercely energetic teacher, preacher, and author, and one of the great spirits of all time.

When these men come on the scene, Christianity is already a pretty vigorous undertaking, its momentum has been attained, it is about to become a world dominating faith. From the first it was a religion with a fierce missionary spirit. In that respect it was the very antithesis of Judaism, which was God's consideration of his peculiar people, a narrowly nationalistic message; but this an international, a universal gospel, so all-inclusive as to indicate that its propulsive motivation could not have been Jewish but must have derived from the world's first and supreme universalist—Alexander the Great. "To every creature" was the command when it was first formulated in writing, and there could be no rest for the soul of any thoroughly devout Christian until the new belief had been preached to all mankind. In the eyes of the people those who preached it were teachers, not priests, who in the pagan world celebrated rites and did not teach anything. So Christianity was from the first a teaching religion—"our divine philosophy," they called it, to distinguish it from other philosophies which were being taught all about them, some of which neither came from heaven or led there. "To every creature," God himself had come down to earth to teach the untaught and bring wisdom to the simple-minded. If you ask, "Where do we get the idea that every man should be taught?" the reply must be that the principle of the universality of teaching comes from the

new faith and was involved in the universality of individual worth which it proclaimed. Tatian, the converted
philosopher, charges the grammarians with professionaliz-
ing truth, and so preventing its spread. To him the civilization of the ancient world appeared as one great wrong,
for its principle was the neglect of the education of the
people, who because they were untaught became the un-
witting dupes of all forms of ignorance and cruelty. For
him instruction must be absolutely universal and the same
in kind for all. "Not only do the rich among us pursue
our philosophy, but the poor enjoy instruction gratuitously, for the things that come from God surpass the
requital of worldly gifts. We admit all who desire to hear,
even old women and striplings. Persons of every age are
treated by us with respect and every kind of licentiousness
is kept at a distance. . . . As for those who wish to learn
our philosophy, we do not test them by their looks, nor
do we judge of those who come to us by their outward
appearance; for we argue that there may be strength of
mind in all, though they may be weak in body. But your
proceedings are full of envy and abundant stupidity." [8]

The Apostolical Constitutions (2. 57) which prescribe
the order of service "direct the reading of two lessons
from the historical books of the Old Testament and from
the Prophets, the antiphonal singing of the Psalms of
David, and the reading of the Acts, the Epistles of Paul,
and the Gospels." [9] "We come together," says Tertullian,
"to call the sacred writings to remembrance, if so be that
the character of the present times compel us either to use
admonition or recollection in anything. In any case, by
these holy words we feed our faith, raise our hopes, es-

[8] Tatian, *Address to the Greeks*, xxxii.
[9] Hatch, *The Organization of the Early Christian Churches*, 61 n.
Longmans, Green & Co.

tablish our confidence; nor do we the less strengthen our discipline by inculcating precepts." [10]

The Old Testament was taken over by the Church. It did not follow the Gnostics in rejecting it but accepted it as a fundamental part of Christian literature. It was written in Hebrew with the exception of a few passages of Ezra, Daniel, and Jeremiah which were in Aramaic. Its text was fixed and guarded by the Sopherim. One effect of Alexander's conquest was that it necessitated a Greek translation of the religious books of the Jews. That translation, the Septuagint Bible, was made at Alexandria. This Greek version of the Old Testament was in general circulation in the time of Jesus, and the quotations in the New Testament are made from it. The oldest manuscripts of the Old Testament in existence are the Codex Vaticanus, brought to Rome in 1448 and believed to have been copied in Egypt in the fourth century; the Codex Sinaiticus found in the Convent of St. Catherine on Mt. Sinai, 1844–1859, and placed in the Imperial Library of St. Petersburg (it too is believed to date from the fourth century); and the Codex Alexandrinus now in the British Museum, which belongs to the fifth century and was sent by the Patriarch of Constantinople to Charles I of England as a gift.[11]

With the spread of the New Faith in the Roman Empire a Latin Bible became necessary; accordingly a Latin translation of the Septuagint seems to have been made in the second century. There was also an African version and perhaps others—so many in fact that their disagreement led the Bishop of Rome to commission Jerome to make a Latin translation of the Psalms and the New Testament from the Greek, which he did. Afterward,

---

[10] Quoted by Hatch, *op. cit.*, 71, from Tertullian, *Apologia*, 39.
[11] Penniman, *A Book About the English Bible*, 12.

when he lived as abbot at Bethlehem (390–405), Jerome studied Hebrew, and translated the Old Testament from Hebrew into Latin. This translation, the Vulgate Bible, is the authentic Bible of the Roman Catholic Church— though a revision was ordered some years ago by Pope Pius X, and is in progress.

The making of the New Testament has been a subject of almost endless study. There is much uncertainty about it still. It is quite clear that the story of Jesus was related orally for a number of years. Anyone who will take the trouble to read the gospels aloud will pretty certainly come to the conclusion that they are oral accounts written down. The making of the New Testament was the supreme service of the young Church in the latter part of the first and the beginning of the second century, for the Church was formed before the Testament. The Testament grew out of the Church, not the Church out of the Testament. A very interesting volume of the Everyman's Library presents an arrangement of the New Testament "in the order in which its parts came to those in the first century who believed in Our Lord." Principal Thomas M. Lindsay, who edits this arrangement, claims for it that it represents what a consensus of conservative scholarship inclines to accept; but necessarily it contains an element of conjecture. The letters of Paul come first—the two letters to the Thessalonians, and next the letter to the Galatians, then the letter of James. But before these, an effort to reconstruct the sayings of Jesus somewhat as the early Christians of the first generation must have heard them. It is believed that the *Logia* was the first effort which was made to reduce Christ's words to writing. Papias, in the beginning of the second century, makes the statement that "Matthew composed the Logia in the Hebrew language, and every one interpreted them as best he could." [12] In 1897 Hunt and Grenfell found at Oxyrhynchus in Egypt a sheet of papyrus which contains sayings of Jesus, and in 1904 a second sheet.[13]

The earliest of the Gospels is that of Mark. It is an account of Jesus' ministry by one who had not himself heard the Lord or followed him, but who followed Peter in his preaching and took down what he heard Peter report. Unlike the *Logia* of Matthew, this Gospel was written in Greek, which shows it was not meant to be read by Palestinian Jews. It seems to have been composed at Rome between 64 and 70. This Gospel was used in preparing the first and third Gospels. The first stresses the Messiahship of Jesus, and is thought not to have been written by an eyewitness but perhaps by a believer of the second or third generation. The Gospel that goes by the name of Luke is an historical account that is earlier than that which bears the name of Matthew but was written after the fall of Jerusalem in A.D. 70; the writer of this Gospel was the author of the Acts of the Apostles. Who he was, we do not know for certain, though Luke is heavily supported.[14] A Gospel, three letters, and the Apocalypse are ascribed to John. The Gospel differs from the other Gospels in that it is an interior Gospel, a study of the character of Jesus. Its author is not concerned primarily with the Teacher of Galilee but with the metaphysical Christ, the creative Logos, the mystical Saviour. This Gospel belongs to the beginning of the second century. Its author was not an Apostle, and the Book of the Apocalypse was not written by him. It is said that there are 129 uncial manuscripts of the New Testament in existence, of

[12] McGiffert, *A History of Christianity in the Apostolic Age*, 569, quoting from Eusebius' *History*, III, 39.

[13] Both of these are translated in Penniman's *A Book About the English Bible*, 68-69.

[14] See McGiffert, *op. cit.*, 433, 572-577.

which the three codices of the Bible already referred to
are the earliest. The Apocrypha of the New Testament
is extensive and highly interesting. One of the formidable
tasks of the early Church was to separate it from the
canon of authentic writings and so fix the text of the
historic New Testament. That was a work of years; the
present arrangement of the Books was fixed by the Council
of Laodicea in 363. But a more important work was the
interpretation of the inspired writings and the formulation
of the Faith from them and the preaching and teaching
of this Gospel, that is, the building of the Church.

For five hundred years the Greeks had been making
themselves expert in the interpreting of writings, the
tangling and untangling of arguments, and the making of
speeches, in that Mediterranean area to which Christianity
was now extending itself. Once more Greece took her
conqueror captive by putting the stamp of her mental
practices upon nearly all things Christian. Ever since
Protagoras had defined grammar as occupation with the
writings, and Prodicus had announced his fifty-drachma
course upon it, the whole Greek world with one accord
and much of the Roman also had sent its boys to grammar
masters to be apprenticed in that art. It had three parts:
(1) the separating of correct from incorrect speech,
(2) the reading, memorizing, and interpretation of the
poet, and (3) a study of his references and allusions.
Plato makes Socrates say: "I often envy the profession
of a rhapsode, Ion; for you have always to wear fine
clothes, and to look as beautiful as you can is part of your
art. Then, again, you are obliged to be continually in the
company of many good poets; and especially of Homer,
who is the best and most divine of them; and to understand him, and not merely learn his words by rote, is a
thing greatly to be envied. And no man can be a rhapsode

who does not understand the meaning of the poet. For the rhapsode ought to interpret the mind of the poet to his hearers, but how can he interpret him well unless he knows what he means?" [15] "We old men would have the greatest pleasure in hearing a rhapsode recite well the Iliad and Odyssey or one of the poems of Hesiod . . ." [16] The second discourse of Dio Chrysostom is a discussion between Philip and Alexander as to the power of poetry. "Why, my son," asks Philip, "have you become so infatuated with Homer that you devote yourself to him alone of all the poets? You really ought not to neglect the others, for the men are wise." Alexander's answer is that the poetry of Homer alone is truly noble and lofty and worthy of the attention of a real man such as would be a shepherd of the people. "I not only cannot endure to hear any other poet recited but Homer, but even object to any other meter than Homer's heroic hexameter" (3, 10). "Now Alexander prided himself very greatly on knowing by heart the whole of one poem, the Iliad, and much of the Odyssey likewise." [17] When, perhaps between A.D. 85 and 90, Dio, banished from Rome, wandered into the country of the remote Borysthenes north of the Black Sea, he found that they too knew Homer by heart and all their conversation was of him. Through all the Roman world Homer was studied and the grammarians shaped the young upon his poems. I know of nothing in history more heroic than a tribute one Christian teacher was constrained to pay him when in A.D. 361 Julian, the apostate emperor, interdicted all who would not sacrifice, from teaching the ancient literature. This is the account that Sozomen, the Church historian, gives of what was done

[15] Plato, *Ion,* 530.
[16] Plato, *Laws,* 658.
[17] Dio Chrysostom, *4th Discourse,* 39.

to meet that emergency: "Apollinaris [the Syrian], therefore, employed his great learning and ingenuity in the
production of a heroic poem on the antiquities of the
Hebrews to the reign of Saul, as a substitute for the poem
of Homer. He divided this work into twenty-four parts,
to each of which he appended the name of one of the
letters of the Greek alphabet, according to their number
and order. He also wrote comedies in imitation of
Menander, tragedies resembling those of Euripides, and
odes on the model of Pindar. In short, taking themes of
the entire circle of knowledge from the Scriptures, he
produced within a very brief space of time, a set of works
which in manner, expression, character, and arrangement
are approved as similar to the Greek literatures, and which
were equal in number and in force. Were it not for the
extreme partiality with which the productions of antiquity
are regarded, I doubt not but that the writings of
Apollinaris would be held in as much esteem as those of
the ancients." [18] "It is well known," says Socrates, the
Church historian, "that in ancient times the doctors of
the church by unhindered usage were accustomed to
exercise themselves in the learning of the Greeks, until
they had reached an advanced age: this they did with
a view to improve themselves in eloquence and to
strengthen and polish their mind, and at the same time to
enable them to refute the errors of the heathen." [19] The
Church had to apply Greek methods in the interpretation
of the Christian writings, in the formulation and presentation of her arguments, and in the organizing of Christian
theology. There were none other she could use, and these

[18] Sozomen, *Ecclesiastical History*, V, xviii (*Nicene and Post-Nicene
Fathers of the Christian Church*, 2nd Series, II, 340).
[19] Socrates, *Ecclesiastical History*, III, xvi (*Nicene and Post-Nicene
Fathers of the Christian Church*, 2nd Series, II, 88).

Greek methods of mental procedure were as omnipresent in the Mediterranean world as was the atmosphere men breathed. Yet there was a difficulty: if one read the old books or went to a pagan school, he was taught polytheism. The Eastern Church fathers were quite unable to give up Greek learning, the fathers of the Western Church told themselves and each other that they were not unwilling to do that. They tried and failed, though as compared with the Church of the East the Church which the Western fathers brought into existence is described as non-theological. Human learning was not a thing which could be set aside even though polytheism was woven in its texture. Acknowledgment of that fact was asserted by Rufinus at Rome about 400 in a preface to his translation of a book of Origen: "It is an absurd thing to get grammarians to explain to us the fictions of the poets' writings and the laughable stories of the comedians, and yet to think that books which speak of God and the celestial powers, and the whole universe, and which discuss all the errors of pagan philosophy and of heretical pravity are things which any one can understand without a teacher to explain them. In this way it comes to pass that men prefer to remain in ignorance and to pronounce rash judgments on things which are difficult and obscure rather than to gain an understanding of them by diligent study." [20]

After grammar comes rhetoric. Alexander tells his father Philip that a king has need of it too. Almost every Greek and Roman agreed with him about that, for in the great days of both peoples it was the supreme art of public counselling and in the days of the Empire it was the school art par excellence in all the Roman world. "Through the whole world the schools of the rhetoricians

[20] Rufinus, Preface to Book II of the περὶ 'Αρχῶν, in *Nicene and Post-Nicene Fathers of the Christian Church*, 2nd Series, III, 429.

are alive with the din of crowds of students," is Augustine's testimony.[21] The preacher's art was too much like the orator's not to borrow heavily from it. Many of the great leaders of the Church had been professional teachers of oratory before they became converted to Christianity; Tatian, Cyprian, Lactantius, Augustine, and others. The rhetorician's training, as well as the grammarian's, set problems for the Christian catechist. "There are . . . some who come from the commonest schools of the grammarians and professional speakers, whom you may not venture to reckon either among the uneducated or among those very learned classes whose minds have been exercised in questions of real magnitude. When such persons, therefore, who appear to be superior to the rest of mankind, so far as the art of speaking is concerned, approach you with the view of becoming Christians, it will be your duty in your communications with them, in a higher degree than in your dealings with those other illiterate hearers, to make it plain that they are to be diligently admonished to clothe themselves with Christian humility, and not to despise individuals whom they may discover keeping themselves free from vices of conduct more carefully than from faults of language; and also that they ought not to presume so much as to compare with a pure heart the practiced tongue which they were accustomed even to put in preference." [22]

The world was full too of the din of philosophers. The four great sects—the Peripatetics, the Stoics, the Epicureans, and the Academics—seem to have been everywhere

[21] Quoted in Hatch, *The Influence of Greek Ideas and Usages upon the Christian Church* (Hibbert Lectures, 1888), p. 36 n. (London: William & Norgate, 1890.)

[22] Augustine, *On Catechising*, IX–13, in *The Works of Aurelius Augustine* (Edinburgh, 1873), Vol. IX.

and to have had hardly less missionary zeal than the advance guard of the invading religions. Because of that zeal a significant change took place: philosophy, which for a thousand years had found its place in the pagan scheme of things, now makes its home with Christianity.[23] Greater love for Plato, perhaps, could hardly be shown than had Apollinaris of Laodicea, the son of the man who made the Bible-Homer, for being "well trained in eloquence [he] expounded the gospels and apostolic doctrines in the way of dialogue, as Plato among the Greeks had done."[24] Justin Martyr continued to wear the philosopher's dress after he became a defender of Christianity. The habitat of the first and perhaps most influential of the schools of learning of the early Church was the city of Alexandria, that great crossroads of the ancient world where Philo had fused Jewish and Greek learning and wrought out a syncretic religion which was even more Greek than Jewish. There in the home of Neo-Platonism and of Gnosticism where the very air was electrical with religious speculation, Pantaenus, a converted Stoic philosopher, some time between 150 and 180 transformed the common practice of the early Church of instructing catechumens in the elements of Christianity before admitting them to baptism, into a famous theological school for the preparation of teachers and preachers. We know little of Pantaenus save his pupil Clement's enthusiastic references to him. The school which his instruction made great continued to flourish under his successors, Clement, Origen, Heraclas, Dionysius, Didymus, etc., until the end of the fourth century, when the conflicts of the Alexandrian Church

---

[23] Hegel, *History of Philosophy* (London, 1895), III, 1.
[24] Socrates, *op. cit.*, III, xvi (*Nicene and Post-Nicene Fathers, etc.*, II, 87).

swallowed it up.[25] Dr. Charles Bigg [26] draws this picture
of it: "A large and rich community, existing in the bosom
of a great University town, could not long submit to ex-
clusion from the paramount interests of the place. Their
most promising young men attended the lectures of the
heathen professors. Some like Ammonius relapsed into
Hellenism, some drifted into Gnosticism like Ambrosius,
some like Heraclas passed safely through the ordeal, and
as Christian priests still wore the pallium, or philosopher's
cloak, the doctor's gown we may call it, of the pagan
Academy. Learned professors like Celsus, like Porphyry,
began to study the Christian Scriptures with a cool interest
in this latest development of religious thought, and pointed
out with the acumen of trained critics the scientific difficulties of the Older Testament and the contradictions of
the New. It was necessary to recognise, and if possible
to profit by, the growing connection between the church
and the lecture-room. Hence the catechetical instruction,
which in most other communities continued to be given
in an unsystematic way by Bishop or Priest, had in
Alexandria developed about the middle of the century into
a regular institution. This was the famous Catechetical
School. It still continued to provide instruction for those
desirous of admission into the Church, but with this
humble routine it combined a higher and more ambitious
function. It was partly a propaganda, partly we may
regard it as a denominational college by the side of a
secular university. There were no buildings appropriated
to the purpose. The master received his pupils in his own
house, and Origen was often engaged till late at night in

[25] *Nicene and Post-Nicene Fathers of the Christian Church,* 2nd Series,
I, 224, notes 1 and 2.
[26] *The Christian Platonists of Alexandria* (Oxford University Press,
1886), 41.

teaching his classes or giving private advice or instruction
to those who needed it. The students were of both sexes,
of very different ages. Some were converts preparing
for baptism, some idolaters seeking for light, some Christians reading as we should say for orders or for the cultivation of their understandings. There was as yet no rigid
system, no definite classification of Catechumens, such as
that which grew up a century later. The teacher was left
free to deal with his task, as the circumstances of his
pupils or his own genius led him."

Here is Eusebius' account of Origen's occupation:
"Many . . . drawn by the fame of Origen's learning,
which resounded everywhere, came to him to make trial
of his skill in sacred literature. And a great many heretics,
and not a few of the most distinguished philosophers,
studied under him diligently, receiving instruction from
him not only in divine things, but also in secular philosophy. For when he perceived that any persons had
superior intelligence he instructed them also in philosophic
branches—in geometry, arithmetic, and other preparatory
studies—and then advanced to the systems of the philosophers and explained their writings. And he made observations and comments upon each of them, so that he
became celebrated as a great philosopher even among the
Greeks themselves. And he instructed many of the less
learned in the common school branches, saying that these
would be no small help to them in the study and understanding of the Divine Scriptures. On this account he
considered it especially necessary for himself to be skilled
in secular and philosophic learning." [27]

It was in this school that Clement and Origen spent
their days, and about it they built up that Christian

[27] Eusebius, *Church History*, VI, xviii (*Nicene and Post-Nicene
Fathers, etc.*, 2nd Series, I, 264).

Platonic philosophy which is the contribution of the
Alexandrian theology. Clement, it is thought, was born
about 150, most likely at Athens. He so closely identified his life with Alexandria that he made the name of that
city a part of his own name. He studied under Pantaenus
in the Catechetical School. He became a Presbyter of the
Church, he taught in and directed the Catechetical School
for more than twenty years. Under the persecution of
Septimus Severus, Clement left Alexandria in 202 never
to return. There is one more reference to him. In 212
he carries a letter from Alexander, a former pupil, to the
church at Antioch; "My honored brethren, I have sent
this letter to you by Clement, the blessed presbyter, a
man virtuous and approved, whom ye yourselves also know
and will recognize. Being here, in the providence and
oversight of the Master, he has strengthened and built
up the Church of the Lord." [28] Professor McGiffert
holds Clement as the man who tied Christianity to Hellenism, establishing Christianity as a philosophy, and the real
father of Greek theology.[28a] His books are an "Exhortation
to the Greeks," "The Pedagogue," and "The Stromata."
The "Exhortation to the Greeks" invites them to make a
comparative study of their religion and Christianity. The
old gods are wicked; Clement condemns them even more
vigorously than does Plato. He is in reality only carrying
out Plato's outline. From the gods he passes to the philosophers. The early ones who make matter the cause of
all things are Atheists. The Stoics who say the divine
nature permeates all matter, cover philosophy with shame.
The Aristotelians speak uncertainly about God, saying in
one place that he is heaven, in another that he is spirit.

[28] Eusebius, *op. cit.*, VI, xi (*Nicene . . . Fathers, etc.*, 2nd Series,
I, 257).
[28a] *Op. cit.*, V, 11. n. 1.

"Epicurus alone I banish from memory for he pre-eminent in impiety thinks that God has no care for the world." [29] Antisthenes as a result of his intimacy with Socrates has perceived that "God is like none else, wherefore none can know him thoroughly from a likeness"; and Xenophon, when he writes of Socrates in the *Memorabilia,* says, "He who moves all things and brings them to rest again is plainly some great and mighty one, but what His form is we cannot see."

"Whom am I to take from you as fellow worker in the search? For we do not altogether despair of you. 'Plato,' if you like. How, then, Plato, must we trace out God? 'It is a hard task to find the Father and Maker of this universe, and when you have found Him, it is impossible to declare Him to all.' (*Timaeus,* 28.) Why, pray in God's name, why? 'Because he can in no way be described.' (*Letters,* VII.) Well done, Plato, you have hit the truth. But do not give up. Join me in the search for the good. For there is a certain divine effluence instilled into all men without exception, but especially into those who spend their lives in thought; wherefore they admit, even though against their will, that God is One, that He is unbegotten and indestructible, and that somewhere on high in the outermost spaces of the heavens, in His own private watch-tower, He truly exists forever." [30] "Let us then, ever listen to the voice of the divine Word." [31] "Oh, amazing mystery! The Lord has sunk down, but man rose up; and he who was driven from Paradise gains a greater prize, heaven, on becoming obedient. Wherefore it seems to me, that since the Word Himself came to us from Heaven, we ought no longer to go to human teaching to

[29] Clement of Alexandria, *Exhortation to the Greek,* Chap. V (Loeb translation).

[30] Clement of Alexandria, *op. cit.,* Chap. VI–59 p.

[31] *Op. cit.,* Chap. IX–70 p.

Athens, and the rest of Greece, or to Ionia, in our curiosity.
If our teacher is He who has filled the universe with holy
powers, creation, salvation, beneficence, lawgiving, proph-
ecy, teaching, this teacher now instructs us in all things,
and the whole world has by this time become an Athens
and a Greece through the Word." [32] "But it is the truth,
I say, which cries, 'Light shall shine out of darkness.' Let
the light then shine in the hidden part of man, in his heart;
and let the rays of knowledge rise, revealing and illuminating the hidden man within, the disciple of the light, friend
of Christ and joint-heir with Him; more especially since
there has come to our knowledge the name, worthy of all
honor and reverence, of one who is a good Father to a
good and dutiful child, Whose precepts are kindly, and
Whose commands are for His child's salvation." [33]

Of Origen, Dr. Bigg says that he was "the first great
scholar, the first great preacher, the first great devotional
writer, the first great commentator, the first great dog-
matist." [34] His dates are 185–254. He was "by race
an Egyptian." His parents were Christians, his father
dying a martyr in the persecution of Severus. At the age
of eighteen he was drafted into the mastership of the
Catechetical School left vacant by Clement's withdrawal
from Alexandria. His greatest book is the *Hexapla*, in
which he attempted to produce an accurate Greek text
of the Old Testament. It was ruled in six columns. In
the first was the Hebrew text—to prepare it Origen learned
Hebrew; in the second, the Hebrew text written in Greek
letters; in the third, fourth, and fifth, versions of Aquila,
Symmachus, and Theodotion; and in the sixth, the LXX.
The work was ponderous, requiring some 50 rolls. "Ortho-

---

[32] Clement of Alexandria, *op. cit.*, Chap. XI–87 p.
[33] Clement of Alexandria, *op. cit.*, Chap. XI–89 p.
[34] Bigg, *The Christian Platonists of Alexandria*, 115.

dox theology of all creeds has never yet advanced beyond the circle first mapped out by his [Origen's] mind," is Harnack's estimate of his power.[85] "The holy Apostles," Origen says, "in preaching the faith of Christ declared with the utmost clearness whatever they thought necessary to salvation, even to those who are slothful in the investigation of divine science, leaving the reason of their assertions to be sought out by those who should deserve the excellent gifts of the Spirit, and especially the graces of utterance, wisdom and knowledge." [86] "Origen, having been educated as a Greek in Greek literature," said the pagan philosopher Porphyry, "went over to the barbarian recklessness. And carrying over the learning which he had obtained, he hawked it about, in his life conducting himself as a Christian and contrary to the laws, but in his opinions of material things and of the Deity being like a Greek, and mingling Grecian teachings with foreign fables. For he was continually studying Plato . . ." [87] But Origen was a philosopher who took the texts of the Old and New Testaments as basic and built up a Christian philosophy by interpreting these Jewish-Christian writings according to Greek methods and standards. He did that so valiantly and finally that he made an end to the attacks of polytheism and Gnosticism and fitted Christianity with the arguments which made it a conquering religion. The whole creation moves forward with one objective, "that God may be all and in all." It is therefore a monistic or strictly monotheistic system. All things and creatures, including the entire material world, have been created by God out of nothing; but the material world is only a place

[85] *History of Dogma* (transl. from the 3rd German ed. by Neil Buchanan), II, 334.

[86] Quoted by Bigg, *op. cit.*, 141, from Origen, *De Principiis*, i, 3.

[87] Eusebius, *op. cit.*, VI, xix (*Nicene . . . Fathers, etc.*, 2nd Series, I, 265–266).

of punishment and purification for souls. The difficulty of the system is that God is the Creator of all things, and the whole creation moves forward to join its life in Him, but how came the separation and why the need for any winning back of a creation to God, which creation He himself made? How can created spirits sin unless their Creator created them to sin? And how can they be responsible for their own salvation unless they have free wills?

To Origen as to every theologian who has come after him, the doctrine of God is central. The world of things that endure for a little while and vanish away must have behind it an ultimate cause all powerful and enduring. "We have not made ourselves." The self-existent and the created then make up the universe. The theologian who was all the time reading Plato had the advantage over his master when he came to describe God. He took the Old and New Testament adjectives as revealed accounts of Him. Of His omnipotence and omniscience Origen reasons that God cannot do what He does not will; God cannot contradict Himself; God in creating cannot produce the unlimited or perfect; God being omniscient has foreknowledge, but he knows happenings before they happen because they happen, they do not happen because he knows them. All created spirits must develop and make way for new dispensations and new worlds. In exercising their God-given freedom, laxity, disobedience, and failure occur. The world was created as a place of purification of created spirits. "God wishes us to be saved by means of ourselves." To that end God created man a free rational being, but no spirit can be saved without fellowing with the Logos and receiving His instruction. Christ is the Redeemer, the God-man who buys by His sacrifice the Devil's claim to all spirits, for all have submitted to his temptation; but the supreme significance of Christ is as divine teacher. He is the manifestation of Deity, one with the Father, the Wisdom of God, the same substance, very God, a function of the Deity, yet a second person, caused by God and subordinated to Him. It cannot be denied that all the problems of Christian theology are announced here. But in the end, Origen held, all spirits, even the fallen angels and the whole brood of demons, are brought back to God by the Logos-Christ Who will deliver the Kingdom to the Father that God may be all and in all.[38] "The Alexandrian school of catechists was of inestimable importance for the transformation of the heathen empire into a Christian one, and of Greek philosophy into ecclesiastical philosophy. In the third century this school overthrew polytheism by scientific means whilst at the same time preserving everything of any value in Greek science and culture. These Alexandrians wrote for the educated people of the whole earth; they made Christianity a part of the civilisation of the world. The saying that the Christian missionary to the Greeks must be a Greek was first completely verified within the Catholic Church in the person of Origen, who at the same time produced the only system of Christian dogma possessed by the Greek Church before John Damascenus." [39]

Almost contemporary with Origen was the Latin leader Tertullian, who was born at Carthage about 160 and died about 230. He has been called "the first great Puritan of the West." [40] "He was the first man of genius of

[38] See Whitehead, *Adventures of Ideas,* 166.
[39] Harnack, *History of Dogma,* II, 319. By permission of Williams S. Norgate.
[40] Morgan, *The Importance of Tertullian in the Development of Christian Dogma* (London: Kegan Paul), 227.

the Latin race to follow Jesus Christ and to reset his
ideas in the language native to that race," says Dr. Glover
of him.[41] The language of the Latin race was the language
of law. Tertullian puts Christianity into a frame of legal
concepts and makes of it a Corpus Divinum in the likeness of the Corpus Legum which was the supreme contribution of the Roman race. The doctrines of the
Church are fixed in the title deeds of the Faith.[42]
Whether or not Tertullian was by profession a Roman
lawyer is not certain, but he poured the new Christianity
into the molds of the Roman law almost as effectively as
the first formulators of that law had fitted it to human
actions. He put its relations into terms of the law courts,
making God a great trial judge; mankind, offenders
against the divine ordinances; the world, a prison house;
death, an assize conducted by the Omnipotent. Christianity does not wear the philosopher's cloak when it
appears before Tertullian. It has nothing to do with
philosophy. Jerusalem is impassable leagues distant from
Athens. What communion can there be between the
synagogue and the porch (*Against Heretics,* vii), between
the disciple of Greece and of heaven (*Apology,* xlvi), between the talker and the doer, between the friend and the
foe of error? Pagan philosophy is the parent of heresies
(*Against Heretics,* vii). Revelation is not only higher
than human knowledge, it is contrary to it. *Credibile est
quia ineptum est; certum est quia impossibile est—credo
quia absurdum.* How is it possible for men who have inherited a divine doctrine to become seekers and enquirers?
In vain was he reminded that the words, "Seek and ye
shall find, knock and it shall be opened unto you," had

[41] *The Conflict of Religions in the Early Roman Empire,* quoted in
Morgan, *op. cit.*
[42] *Prescription Against Heretics,* XXXVII.

come from the Founder of Christianity Himself; they
are intended for those who have not yet "found" Christianity, he answers (*Against Heretics,* ix). "Away with
all attempts to produce a mottled Christianity of Stoic,
Platonic and dialectic composition! We want no curious
disputation after possessing Christ Jesus, no inquisition
after enjoying the Gospel." (*Against Heretics,* vii.) But
the man who wrote that had himself studied philosophy
quite carefully and made much use of it. The Greek
thinkers he knows most about are the Stoics and Plato.
In his *De Anima* he employs Stoic interpretations; the
Roman Stoic Seneca is, he writes, *"saepe noster."* His
references to what nature allows and demands might
have come bodily from Stoic teaching. "Everything
which is against nature deserves to be branded as
monstrous among all men, but with us it is to be condemned also as sacrilege against God the Lord of Nature"
(*De Consuetudo,* quoted by Morgan). Mr. Morgan also
cites the striking passage in the treatise "Against Marcion"
(I, 13, 14): "One flower of the hedgerow itself, I think
—I do not say a flower of the meadows; one shell of any
sea—I do not say the Red Sea; one feather of a moor-
fowl—to say nothing of a peacock,—will they speak
to you of a mean Creator?" In one respect Tertullian is
out and out a Stoic: God is both body and spirit. "All
which is is body after its kind, nothing is incorporeal, except that which is not" (*De Carne Christi*).

"We know that jurisprudence and legal thought held
the chief place in mediaeval philosophy, theology and
ethics. . . . Through the agency of Tertullian, by his
earlier profession a lawyer, all Christian forms received
a legal impress. He not only transferred the technical
terms of the jurists into the ecclesiastical language of
the West, but he also contemplated from a legal stand-

point, all relations of the individual and the Church to
the Deity, and *vice versâ,* all duties and rights, the moral
imperative as well as the actions of God and Christ, nay,
their mutual relationship. He who was so passionate and
fanciful seemed never to be thoroughly satisfied until
he had found the scheme of a legal relationship which
he could proclaim as an inviolable authority; he never
felt secure until he had demonstrated inner compulsions
to be external demands, exuberant promises to be stipu-
lated rewards. But with this the scheme of personal
rights was applied almost universally. God appears as
the mighty partner who watches jealously over his rights.
Through Tertullian this tendency passed into the Western Church, which, being Roman, was disposed to favour
it; there it operated in the most prejudicial way. If we
grant that by it much that was valuable was preserved,
and juristic thought did contribute to the understanding
of some, not indeed the most precious, Pauline conceptions, yet, on the whole, religious reflection was led into
a false channel, the ideas of satisfaction and merit becoming of the highest importance, and the separation of
Western from primitive and Eastern Christianity was
promoted." [43]

Tertullian is the author of the declaration: *Sanguis
martyrum semen Christianorum,* "The blood of the martyrs
is the seed of the Church." Much blood had been shed
in the persecutions of Decius, Valerian, Galerius, and
Diocletian. About the year 300 the Christians were felt
to be too numerous and perhaps by that time even to be
too well behaved to be put down by force. The first break
came in the Emperor Galerius' edict of 311. It read:
"Among the other things which we have ordained for the
public advantage and profit, we formerly wished to re-

[43] Harnack, *op. cit.,* V, 16–17. By permission of Williams S. Norgate.

store everything to conformity with the ancient laws and public discipline of the Romans, and to provide that the Christians also, who have forsaken the religion of their ancestors, should return to a good disposition. For in some way such arrogance had seized them and such stupidity had overtaken them, that they did not follow the ancient institutions which possibly their own ancestors had formerly established, but made for themselves laws according to their own purpose, as each one desired, and observed them, and thus assembled as separate congregations in various places. When we had issued this decree that they should return to the institutions established by the ancients, a great many submitted under danger, but a great many being harassed endured all kinds of death. And since many continue in the same folly, and we perceive that they neither offer to the heavenly gods the worship which is due, nor pay regard to the God of the Christians, in consideration of our philanthropy and our invariable custom, by which we are wont to extend pardon to all, we have determined that we ought most cheerfully to extend our indulgence in this matter also; that they may again be Christians, and may rebuild the conventicles in which they were accustomed to assemble, on condition that nothing be done by them contrary to discipline. In another letter we shall indicate to the magistrates what they have to observe. Wherefore, on account of this indulgence of ours, they ought to supplicate their God for our safety, and that of the people, and their own, that the public welfare may be preserved in every place, and that they may live securely in their several homes." [44]

Galerius died soon after this. In 312 Constantine in

[44] Eusebius, *op. cit.*, VIII, xvii (*Nicene . . . Fathers, etc.*, 2nd Series, I, 339–340).

a death grapple with the armies of Maxentius fighting
under the banner of the Sovereign Sun, at the Mulvian
bridge, opposed to them an army under a new banner—
the Cross, and in that battle Christianity conquered Sun
Worship, Mithraism, and all the congregated pagan religions.[45] In 313 the Edict of Milan was issued, which
reads in part: "When I, Constantine Augustus, and I,
Licinius Augustus, came under favorable auspices to
Milan and took under consideration everything which
pertained to the common weal and prosperity, we resolved
among other things, or rather first of all, to make such
decrees as seemed in many respects for the benefit of
every one; namely, such as should preserve reverence and
piety toward the Deity. We resolved, that is, to grant
both to the Christians and to all men freedom to follow
the religion which they choose, that whatever heavenly
divinity exists may be propitious to us and to all that
live under our government. We have, therefore, determined, with sound and upright purpose, that liberty is
to be denied to no one, to choose and to follow the religious
observances of the Christians, but that to each one freedom is to be given to devote his mind to that religion
which he may think adapted to himself, in order that
the Deity may exhibit to us in all things his accustomed
care and favor. . . ."[46] The question is sometimes asked,
At what time in his career did the Emperor Constantine
become a Christian, and in what year did Christianity
become the official religion of the Roman Empire? Professor McGiffert has an interesting discussion of Constantine's Christianity. To question it seems to him
vain. Not to remember the great variety of ways in
which being a Christian may be evidenced is perhaps to

[45] Ernest Barker, in *The Legacy of Rome* (ed. Cyril Bailey), 80.
[46] Eusebius, *op. cit.*, X, v.

be inhuman. He was a Christian as soon as his acts told forth a belief in Christ.[47] But though Constantine was a Christian, Christianity was not the official religion of the Roman Empire until Ambrose publicly restored the Church-forgiven Theodosius in the Cathedral at Milan in 390. Constantine summoned the Council of Nicaea and addressed it, but at the same time he was *Pontifex Maximus* and the old pagan rites were officially performed at Rome until the Altar of Victory was finally removed after Theodosius' defeat of Eugenius in 394. The words of Ambrose to Theodosius, who in 390 had caused, as punishment for an offence, the massacre of 7,000 persons, all the spectators in the circus at Thessalonica, are the assertion of the right and duty of the Church to direct the state in its official conduct: "Listen, august Emperor," the bishop says to the ruler of the Empire. "I cannot deny that you have a zeal for the faith; I do confess that you have the fear of God. But you have a natural vehemence, which, if any one endeavours to soothe, you quickly turn to mercy; if any one stirs it up, you rouse it so much more that you can scarcely restrain it. Would that if no one soothe it, at least no one may inflame it! To yourself I willingly entrust it, you restrain yourself, and overcome your natural vehemence by the love of piety. . . . There was that done in the city of the Thessalonians of which no similar record exists, which I was not able to prevent happening; which, indeed, I had before said would be most atrocious when I so often petitioned against it, and that which you yourself show by revoking it too late you consider to be grave, this I could not extenuate when done. . . . Are you ashamed, O Emperor, to do that which the royal prophet David,

[47] Ernest C. Richardson, in *Nicene . . . Fathers, etc.,* 2nd Series, I, 430.

the forefather of Christ, according to the flesh, did? To
him it was told how the rich man who had many flocks
seized and killed the poor man's one lamb, because of
the arrival of his guest, and recognizing that he himself
was being condemned in the tale, for that he himself had
done it, he said: 'I have sinned against the Lord.' Bear
it, then, without impatience, O Emperor, if it be said to
you: 'You have done that which was spoken of to King
David by the prophet.' For if you listen obediently to
this, and say: 'I have sinned against the Lord,' if you
repeat those words of the royal prophet: O come let us
worship and fall down before Him, and mourn before
the Lord our God, Who made us, it shall be said to you
also: 'Since thou repentest, the Lord putteth away thy
sin, and thou shalt not die.' " [48]

So the work begun by Constantine was finally perfected.
Meantime there was but one decided relapse. He who
gave the power to the Christian Constantine gave it to
the apostate Julian also.[49] Julian's restoration of the old
religion is the last brief glow of a setting sun. He is a
pathetically attractive young man who died at thirty-
two, his dates being 331–363. Constantius II killed all
his relatives save Julian and his half-brother Gallus; seem-
ing to postpone the determination of their fate to a later
day, he sent them to an imperial palace in Cappadocia
to be brought up. Here from the age of eight until he
reached young manhood Julian was under the charge of
eunuchs "who were assigned to keep watch so that he
might not waver from the Christian faith." [50] He was always a most eager student. ". . . While I was still a

---

[48] St. Ambrose, *Select Works and Letters,* Letter LI (*Nicene and Post-Nicene Fathers of the Christian Church,* 2nd Series, X, 451).

[49] Augustine, *The City of God,* V, xxi.

[50] Eunapius, *Lives of the Philosophers,* 474.

mere boy my tutor would often say to me: 'Never let
the crowd of your playmates who flock to the theatres
lead you into the mistake of craving for such spectacles
as these. Have you a passion for horse races? There is
one in Homer very cleverly described. Do you hear
them talking about dancers in pantomime? Leave them
alone! Among the Phaeacians the youths danced in
a more manly fashion. For citharode (lyre-player) you
have Phemius; for singer Demodocus. Moreover, there
are in Homer many plants more delightful to hear of
than those that we can see. "Even so did I once see the
young shoot of a date palm springing up near the altar
of Apollo on Delos." And consider the wooded islands
of Calypso and the caves of Circe and the garden of
Alcinous; be assured you will never see anything more
delightful than these.' [51] Do you want to know my tutor?
He was a Scythian, a eunuch, my grandfather brought
him up in order that he might instruct my mother in
the poems of Homer and Hesiod. . . . I was handed
over to him in my seventh year. From that time he won
me over to these views of his, and led me to school by
one straight path . . . he is of all men most responsible
for my way of life; though he too, you must know, had in
his turn been misled by others. Theirs are names that
you have often met when they are ridiculed in Comedy
—I mean Plato and Socrates, Aristotle and Theophrastus.
This old man in his folly was first convinced by them,
and then he got hold of me, since I was young and loved
literature, and convinced me that if I would emulate those
famous men in all things I should become better, not
perhaps than other men—for it was not with them that
I had to compete—but certainly better than my former
self. Accordingly, since I had no choice in the matter, I

[51] Julian, *Misopogon* (Loeb Classical Library), 351.

obeyed him, and now I am no longer able to change my character, though indeed I often wish I could, and I blame myself for not granting to all men impunity for all wrong-doing. But then the words of the Athenian stranger in Plato occur to my mind: 'Though he who does no wrong himself is worthy of honour, he who does not allow the wicked to do wrong is worthy of twice as much honour. For whereas the former is responsible for one man only, the latter is responsible for many others besides himself, when he reports to the magistrates the wrong-doing of the rest. And he who as far as he can helps the magistrates to punish wrong-doers, himself being the great and powerful man in the city, let him I say be proclaimed as winner of the prize for virtue.' " [52]

Julian, Theodoret says, while a lad had "imbibed pure and pious teaching" and was enrolled in the order of Readers and used to read the sacred books to the people in the assemblies of the Church. "Lust of Empire stripped the wretch of all true religion." He became Emperor in 361. "When Julian had made his impiety openly known the cities were filled with dissensions. Men enthralled with the deceits of idolatry took heart, opened the idols' shrines, and began to perform those foul rites. Once more they kindled the fire on the altars, befouled the ground with victims' gore, and defiled the air with their burnt sacrifices. Maddened by the demons they served they ran in corybantic frenzy round about the streets, attacked the saints with low stage jests, and with all the outrage and ribaldry of their impure processions. . . . All the honours . . . conferred on the sacred ministry by the great Constantine Julian took away." [53] "He

<hr />

[52] Julian, *op. cit.*, 353–354.
[53] Theodoret, *Ecclesiastical History*, III, i and iii (*Nicene and Post-Nicene Fathers, etc.*, III, 94, 95, 96).

enacted a law by which Christians were excluded from the cultivation of literature; 'lest,' said he, 'when they have sharpened their tongue, they should the more readily meet the arguments of the heathen.' " [54] Just what that law was and what it forbade is not definitely clear. Gregory Nazianzen in his oration against Julian quotes this statement: "Ours are the words and the speaking of Greek whose right it is to worship the gods, yours are the want of words and clownishness and nothing beyond the faith in your doctrine" (1–102). To that Gregory replies: Does the Greek language belong to a religion or a nation? "Let everyone share in my indignation who takes pleasure in words and is addicted to this pursuit—of which number I will not deny that I am one. All other things I have left to those who like them, riches, nobility, glory, power, which are of the lower world and give delights fleeting like a dream. Words alone I cleave to, and I do not begrudge the toils by land and sea that have supplied me with them. May mine be the possession of words, and his, too, whoever loves me, which possession I embraced and still embrace, first of all, after the things that be first of all—I mean Religion and Hope beyond the visible world . . ." (*Idem,* 100.) Augustine in enumerating the persecutions speaks of this act of Julian's as one of them: "Did not he persecute the Church who forbade the Christians to teach or learn liberal letters?" [55] But Julian was killed in battle with the Persians in 363, and his imperial successors all supported the Christians.

There is no better way to write of the man who was by far the greatest of the Church Fathers than that which Professor Harnack uses; namely, to let him speak for

---

[54] Socrates, *Church History,* III–12.
[55] *The City of God,* XVIII–52.

himself. This is the sum of his doctrine: "Virtues will
so increase and be perfected as to conduct thee without
any hesitation to the truly blessed life which only is
eternal: where evils, which will not exist, are not dis-
criminated from blessings by *prudence,* nor adversity is
borne *bravely,* because there we shall find only what we
love, not also what we tolerate, nor lust is bridled by
temperance, where we shall not feel its incitements, nor
the needy are aided *justly,* where we will have no need
and nothing unworthy. *There virtue will be one, and
virtue and the reward of virtue will be* that spoken of in
sacred phrase by the man who loves it: '*But to me to
cling to God is a good thing.*' This virtue will be there
the full and eternal wisdom, and it will also truly be the
life that is blessed. *Surely this is to attain to the eternal
and supreme blessing, to which to cling for ever is the
end of our goodness.* Let this [virtue] be called *prudence,*
because it will cling to the good too eagerly for it to be
lost, and *fortitude,* because it will cling to the good too
firmly for it to be torn away, and *temperance,* because
it will cling to the good too chastely to be corrupted, and
justice, because it will cling to the good too justly to be
inferior in any merit. *Although even in this life the only
virtue is to love what ought to be loved.* But what should
we choose chiefly to love except that than which we find
nothing better? This is God, and if we prefer anything
or esteem anything equal to love to him we fail to love
ourselves. For it is the better for us, *the more we enter
into him,* than whom there is nothing better. But we
move not by walking, but by loving. We may not go [to
him] afoot, but with our character. But our character is
wont to be judged, not from what anyone knows, but
from what he loves. *Nothing makes character good or bad
but good or bad affections.* Therefore, by our corruption,

we have been far from the righteousness of God. Whence
we are corrected by loving the right, that being just we
may be able to cling to the right." [56]

Augustine's dates are 354–430. He is two hundred years
after Tertullian. The Christians have withstood all the
persecutions. The great Councils have shaped the out-
lines of the faith. What is called the Theodosian imperial Church, and would more properly be called the
Ambrosian imperial Church, had command of the Empire. There are troubles ahead, the awful horrors of the
barbarian invasions. But for the moment there is almost
peace within the Church. A kind of reassessment of the
faith, a reaffirmation of belief is in order. That is Augustine's function. After the centuries of persecution and
doctrinal confusion, Christianity purified by suffering, reduced to essentials by conflict, passes through the
crucible of his mind and is formulated once more and
lo! even as it was in the beginning its name is love. Yet
its commandment is one now, not two, as in their original
formulation, but one, for to love God means to love all
that is lovable. To be rightly attituded toward God is the
essence of wisdom. The older way of saying this is, "The
fear of the Lord is the beginning of wisdom": Augustine's
way of saying it is, "Piety is the wisdom of man." The
Bishop of Hippo is an African Father no less than Tertullian was. Their conceptions of Christianity are diametri-
cally opposed. Tertullian is an exteriorist, Augustine is
an interiorist. It is the man within, the life of the man
within, the life of the soul, that concerns him. Here
Augustine is in the purest sense a Socratic, no less certainly a disciple of that great master than Plato was.
"Among the disciples of Socrates, Plato was the one

[56] Augustine, *Epistle* 155, as quoted by Harnack, *History of Dogma*,
V, 61–63.

who shone with a glory which far excelled that of the others, and who not unjustly eclipsed them all . . . For those who are praised as having most closely followed Plato, who is justly preferred to all the other philosophers of the gentiles, and who are said to have manifested the greatest acuteness in understanding him, do perhaps entertain such an idea of God as to admit that in Him are to be found the cause of existence, the ultimate reason for the understanding, and the end in reference to which the whole of life is to be regulated . . . If, then, Plato defined the wise man as one who imitates, knows, loves this God, and who is rendered blessed through fellowship with Him in His own blessedness, why discuss with the other philosophers? It is evident that none come nearer to us than the Platonists." [57] It is worth noting that Augustine is making these statements about Plato, not about the Neo-Platonists nor because of them.

Good intellects do not love words but the truth in words. It is one thing to read and another to teach reading. He who teaches reading does it that others may read for themselves. Augustine believed that everything in Scripture was of value for faith. Two things, he held, are necessary for interpreting it, the one the ascertaining of the proper meaning, the other the mode of making that meaning known. When He says, "With all thy heart, and with all thy soul, and with all thy mind," He means that there is to be no room for anything antagonistic, but whatever else is loved must be in that one current. "Whoever, then, thinks that he understands the Holy Scriptures, or any part of them, but puts such an interpretation on them as does not tend to build up this twofold love of God and our neighbor, does not yet understand them as he

[57] *The City of God,* VIII, 4-5.

ought." [58] "Instruction came by Him, because those truths which had been for men's advantage, spoken before that time on earth, not only by the holy prophets, all of whose words were true, but also by philosophers and even poets and authors in every department of literature (for beyond question they mixed much truth with what was false) might by the actual presentation of His authority in human nature be confirmed as true for the sake of those who could not perceive and distinguish them in the Light of essential Truth, which Truth was, even before He assumed human nature, present to all who were capable of receiving truth." (Letter CXXXVII.) Three languages are needed for interpreting the signs in which the Scriptures are written, Hebrew, Greek, and Latin. Let every Christian understand that, wherever truth may be found, it belongs to his Master (*Christian Doctrine* II–XV–23). All that pertains to idol worship, to augury, divination, astrology, etc., is to be repudiated. There are convenient and necessary human arrangements which are to be used. History which narrates what has been done is valuable. Those arts which, so to speak, assist God in his operations—medicine, agriculture, navigation —are valuable. Valid logical sequence is observed but not invented by man; it has its origin in God. Studious and able young men who fear God are to discriminate among the branches of learning in vogue beyond the pale of the Church. "If those who are called philosophers, especially the Platonists, have said aught that is true and in harmony with our faith," we are to claim it for our own use. It is lawful for a Christian to use the art of rhetoric since he must defend what is right and refute what is wrong. Every orator should aim at perspicuity, beauty, and persuasiveness; but eloquence without wis-

[58] *Christian Doctrine*, I, 36.

dom is vain. Now a man speaks with wisdom in proportion to his progress in the knowledge of Scripture. Some
read to remember the words, but it is plain that those
who "see with the eyes of the heart into the heart of the
Scriptures" are far above them. "The mode of existence
which is properly ascribed to the Son has to do with
training, and with a certain art, . . . and with the
exercise of intellect, by which the mind itself is moulded
in its thoughts upon things. Therefore, since by that
assumption of human nature the work accomplished was
the effective presentation to us of a certain training
in the right way of living and exemplification of that
which is commanded . . . it is not without reason that
all this is ascribed to the Son. . . . Now there is a
certain training necessary for men by which they might
be instructed and formed after some model. . . . Therefore the first thing necessary was that a certain rule and
pattern of training be plainly exhibited; and this was
done by the divinely appointed method of the Incarnation . . ." (Letter XI.) Now the Churches which are
multiplying through the world are, as it were, sacred
seminaries of public instruction in which this sound
morality is inculcated and learned, and in which above all,
men are taught the worship due to the true and faithful
God, who not only commands men to attempt but also
gives grace to perform all those things by which the soul
of man is furnished and fitted for fellowship with God
and for dwelling in the eternal heavenly kingdom. (Letter
XCI.)

Literally a vast activity of education was involved in
the new faith. Its books had to be first formulated, then
studied and read. Eusebius says that the Scriptures "were
translated into every civilized and barbarous language,
were read and pondered by all nations and the doctrines

contained in them accredited as the oracles of God." [59]
That work of translating the Scriptures which began in
the first days of the Church—the Itala version was made
perhaps in the early part of the second century—has
gone on ever since. One of the most remarkable things
that men have done was John Eliot's translation of the
entire Bible into the language of the Massachusetts
Algonquins. Eliot came to America in 1631 and spent
fourteen years in mastering that Indian tongue. The
Catechism was printed in 1653; the New Testament, in
1661; and the Old Testament, in 1663. The Scriptures
have thus far been published in 972 languages and dialects. That is the information the American Bible Society
gives us for 1935. In all, in 120 years of its existence,
268,588,636. The total issue of the three English language
Bible societies is as follows: the American Bible Society,
268,588,636; the British and Foreign Bible Society,
476,061,010; the National Bible Society of Scotland,
124,256,202; making a total of 868,905,848 volumes.
Of this number, 117,983,452 were entire Bibles. The
other were Testaments and parts.

An immense work of erudition went into the making of
those translations and into the preparation of published
arguments in defence, interpretation, exegesis, etc. Take
Ulfilas' translation of the Bible into the Gothic language.
"The barbarians dwelling beyond the Danube, called the
Goths, having engaged in a civil war among themselves
were divided into two parties"; one of these appealed to
the Roman Emperor Valens for help and got it. In
gratitude the victorious leader Fritigernes and some of
his people embraced the religion of their benefactor.
"Ulfilas, their bishop at that time, invented the Gothic
letters and translating the Sacred Scriptures into their

[59] *The Oration on Constantine*, XVII.

own language undertook to instruct these barbarians in the Divine oracles." Ulfilas did not restrict his labors to Fritigernes' people but went to other Goths as well.[60] That is a statement of fact, but what does it mean? It means that that good man made an alphabet for a people that had none. He did that by selecting from the Greek and Latin alphabets such letters as seemed to him to express the Gothic sounds which he knew. By means of that alphabet he wrote down a spoken language which had never been written before. To do that he had to invent a grammar of word and sentence forms as he went along. He had to fix the spelling of words also and idioms and to add great numbers of words to the language. Having done all these things he crowned his services to his people by giving them the whole literature of the Jewish nation. By doing so he made a book which is still reprinted and studied.[61] A Teutonic tongue three hundred years older than any other witness of it is thus preserved. "He is the Moses of the Goths," said Constantine of Ulfilas.

The intellectual labors of the early champions of the new faith were literally stupendous. Of Augustine alone the volumes are so many that one is unable to comprehend how he found time enough in one lifetime to write or even to dictate them all. Their quality is not less striking than their immensity; yet this was the output of a hardworking bishop who was constantly teaching, advising, encouraging, admonishing, directing, and protecting not only a large diocese but the whole Church as well.

These translations and explanations of the Bible were

[60] Socrates, *Ecclesiastical History*, IV, xxxiii.

[61] See *The First Germanic Bible translated from the Greek by the Gothic Bishop Wulfila in the Fourth Century*, edited and published by G. H. Balg, Ph.D., Milwaukee, 1891.

made to be read and were read, else they would not have
been made and preserved as they have been. "Who has
persuaded multitudes of either sex to devote themselves
to the study of sacred things and prefer to bodily nutri-
ment that intellectual food which is suited to the wants
of a rational soul?" [62] The thought of an ill informed
and unread laity was repugnant to the Church leaders.
The Scriptures are for the use of all men, they said. It
is neglect of them that is the cause of all ignorance,
heresies, errors, and irreligion. John Chrysostom (c. 347–
407), preaching to his congregation at Constantinople,
takes them to task in this fashion: "For this reason we
often acquaint you many days beforehand with the subject
of our discourse that taking the Bible in your hands in
the meantime, and running over the whole passage you
may have your minds better prepared to hear what is to
be spoken. And this is the thing I have always advised
and shall still continue to exhort you to: that you should
not only hear what is said in this place, but spend your
time at home in reading the Holy Scriptures . . . For
the grace of the Spirit so ordered it that they should be
originally composed and written by publicans and fishers,
and tentmakers and shepherds and private and illiterate
men that none of the most ignorant and unlearned might
have this excuse of difficulty to fly to . . . Take the
book into thy hands, read the whole history, and remember those things that are intelligible and easy and those
things that are more obscure read over and over again:
and if thou canst not by frequent readings dive into the
meaning of what is said, go to a wiser person, betake
thyself to a teacher, and confer with him about any passage, show thy diligence and desire to be informed." [63]

[62] Eusebius, *Oration on Constantine*, XVII, 6.
[63] *Homily 3,* On Lazarus.

Christianity was a teaching religion. In this respect it differed entirely from the pagan sacrifice-performing religions which it displaced. The higher officers of the Christian Church were teachers. Ambrose describes the office of bishops as chiefly an office of teaching. Cyril of Alexandria refers to the bishop's office as the dignity of teaching. Chrysostom calls the bishop's chair a teaching throne. Jerome describes Gregory Nazianzen as an eloquent teacher and the master under whom he learned the Scriptures as he explained them. A bishop who neglects his clergy or his people and teaches them not the rules of piety shall be suspended, said the Apostolical Canons.

The Scriptures were the chief studies of the teacher of the faith. They contained everything necessary for souls, and if properly administered they were diet, air and drink, medicine, fire and knife. Out of them the pagan was to be confounded and the heretic set right.

As long as a simple statement of belief or a willingness to be baptized in the name of Jesus Christ was all that was required for admission to the company there was but a single class of believers. But very early—as early as the beginning of the second century—a larger knowledge of the faith began to be required, and a certain course of training which was perhaps brief and simple at first but, in the latter part of the second and the whole of the third century, became a widely organized and highly developed activity of the Church. This was the catechetical class or school; those who received instruction in it were catechumens. This is the training school for admission into the Church. It is in operation in Tertullian's day as it was in Pantaenus', Clement's, and Origen's. The second canon of the great Council of Nicaea (325) read: "Forasmuch as either from necessity, or through the urgency of individuals, many things have been done contrary to the ecclesiastical canon, so that men just converted from heathenism to the faith, and who have been instructed but a little while, are straightway brought to the spiritual laver, and as soon as they have been baptized, are straightway advanced to the episcopate or the presbyterate, it has seemed right to us that for the time to come no such thing shall be done. For to the catechumen himself there is need of time and of a longer trial after baptism. For the Apostolical saying is clear: 'Not a novice; lest being lifted up with pride he fall into condemnation and the snare of the devil . . .' " [64] In the church services, when the different groups were assigned their places in the church building—a practice which seems to have been universal, for it receives consideration in one of the Nicene Canons—the catechumens stood along with the Jews and Gentiles, the heretics and schismatics and the energumens (or those afflicted with evil spirits) in the narthex just inside the main door.[65] There were two classes or kinds of catechumens: *audientes,* or hearers—those who heard the word of God, wished to become Christians, but were not yet looking forward to baptism; and *competentes*—those whose training was so nearly completed that they had given in their names for baptism and were being taught the great articles of the creed, the sacraments, and the penitential discipline of the Church.[66] "If a catechumen coming into the Church have taken his place in the order of catechumens and fall into sin, let him, if a kneeler, become a hearer, and sin no more. But should he again sin while a hearer, let him be cast out." This is the fifth canon of the

[64] The Seven Ecumenical Councils, 10, in *Nicene . . . Fathers, etc.,* Vol. XIV.
[65] *Idem,* 26.
[66] *Idem,* 31, 32.

Council of Neo-Caesarea, A.D. 315. "After the sermons of the Bishops, the prayers for the catechumens is to be made first by itself; and after the catechumens have gone out, the prayer for those who are under penance; and after these have passed under the hand (of the Bishop) and departed, there should then be offered the three prayers of the faithful, the first to be said entirely in silence, the second and third aloud, and then the (kiss of) peace is to be given, and after the Presbyters have given the (kiss of) peace to the Bishop, then the laity are to give it (to one another) and so the Holy Oblation is to be completed. And it is lawful to the priesthood alone to go to the altar and (there) communicate." [67] Nowhere was there a distinct order set apart to instruct catechumens; instead men were chosen from the several orders to perform this work. Classes of catechumens were trained wherever a church existed. At first this school met in the church or the regular place of assembly of the congregation. That it came to have a separate meeting place of its own is evidenced by a novel of the Emperor Leo, who calls them κατηχούμενα and says that such buildings belonged to the church.[68] The children of the Christians were thus early put to reading the sacred Scriptures and learning the principles of religion.

The Apostolic Constitutions prescribed the following course of study for those who sought initiation into the faith: "Let the catechumen be taught, before baptism, the knowledge of the Father unbegotten, the knowledge of the only begotten Son, and the Holy Spirit; let him learn the order of the world's creation, and series of divine providence, and the different sorts of legislation; let him be taught why the world and man, the citizen of the

[67] *Canon XIX of the Synod of Laodicea,* 343–381, *idem,* 136.
[68] Bingham, *Antiquities,* III–X–4.

world, were made; let him be instructed in his own
nature, to understand for what end he himself was made;
let him be informed how God punished the wicked with
water and with fire, and crowned his saints with glory
in every generation, namely, Seth, Enoch, Noah, Abraham
and his posterity, Melchisedeck, Job, Moses, Joshua,
Caleb, and Phineas the priest, and the saints of every age;
let him also be taught how the providence of God never
forsook mankind, but called them at sundry times from
error and vanity to the knowledge of truth, reducing
them from slavery and impiety to liberty and Godliness,
from iniquity to righteousness, and from everlasting
death to eternal life. After these, he must learn the
doctrine of Christ's incarnation, his passion, his resurrection, and assumption; and what it is to renounce the
devil and enter into covenant with Christ." [69] The Catechetical lectures of Cyril of Alexandria are published in
Volume VII of the *Nicene and Post-Nicene Fathers*. The
form of the catechetical instruction given by Augustine,
too, is still in existence. See his letter to Deogratias.[70]
That secular instruction was sometimes given in these
schools is shown by what was taught by Origen at Alexandria. As long as the Church had no schools of its own
for that purpose that was a difficult problem. It came
to have such schools at least in the fourth century. Before that its children did what Basil and Gregory Nazianzen did: they attended the pagan schools and ran the
risks of pagan contamination. Even the strict Tertullian
permits that, enjoining the scholar to reject all error. But
Christians he will not allow to teach in pagan schools for

[69] *The Apostolic Constitutions*, VII, xxxix (reproduced in Backhouse
and Tyler's *Early Church History*, 482).
[70] Letter CII, in *Works of Aurelius Augustine*, Rev. Marcus Dods,
Vol. XIII (Edinburgh: T. &. T. Clark).

that involves the constant worship of the old gods of the heathen. (*On Idolatry*, X.) Yet Julian's edict must have displaced many such teachers.

The school of Alexandria was not the only one which sprang up inside the Church to define the faith and teach it as a philosophical religion. About the beginning of the third century Christian seminaries similar to that of Alexandria were in existence in Rome, Antioch, Caesarea, Edessa, and several other towns. "In Rome, at the beginning of the third century, there was a scientific school where textual criticism of the Bible was pursued and where the works of Aristotle, Theophrastus, Euclid, and Galen were zealously read and utilised." [71] When war broke out in Alexandria, Origen withdrew to Caesarea and there carried out the work of explaining the Scriptures as he had formerly done at Alexandria.[72] The school of Edessa dates from the activity of Bardesanes. "A most able man and a most skillful disputant in the Syriac tongue," Eusebius calls him (IV. xxx.). He wrote scholarly works in the Syriac language which were regarded as so valuable that they were translated into the Greek tongue, which was a reversal of the intellectual practice of the time. Bardesanes' pupils, we are told, were numerous. This Christian school was active for several centuries and was one of the bridges over which Greek learning passed to the Arabs.

When Gregory the Illuminator (born about 257) converted the Armenian people to Christianity, it is said that the King Tiridates ordered schools to be set up according to the missionary's direction in every city, and masters over them to teach the Armenian children both Christian and pagan to read. Chief schools were established in

[71] Harnack, *History of Dogma*, II, 322.
[72] Socrates, *Ecclesiastical History*, IV, xxvii.

every province and smaller ones in the several communities.[73] When banished to the frontiers of Egypt by the Arian Emperor Valens, finding the inhabitants of Antinone (the place of his exile) pagans, the Catholic Protogenes, "who had received a good education and was practised in rapid writing, pitched on a suitable spot which he made into a boys' school and, setting up for a schoolmaster, he instructed his pupils not only in the art of swift penmanship, but also in the divine oracles." [74]

These accounts are preserved because of the historian's interest in the persons of whom he tells, not because he is attempting to keep a record of the instructional activity of his age. One may perhaps take it for granted that their founders were the only exceptional feature of these schools, and that schools without such striking founders were rather too common to be mentioned. In addition to the catechetical instruction, a second great historical institution of learning dates from this early period; it is the cathedral school. In the earlier days of the organized Church the boys and young men of the lesser clergy who assisted the bishop in the service frequently dwelt in the same house with him, and to that community of life and interest the episcopal school is due. John Chrysostom studied for three years as reader (lector) in the household of the bishop of Antioch. In the same way Athanasius studied with the bishop of Alexandria. In a similar case Augustine directed the work of his assistants at Hippo.

[73] Malan, *Life and Times of St. Gregory*, 298.
[74] Theodoret, *Ecclesiastical History*, IV, xv.

III

THE BEGINNINGS OF THE MONASTERIES

THE rescript of Trajan which made it a crime to be a Christian was not enforced until near the end of the second century. The Christians were odious but were tolerated until in 166 under Marcus Aurelius a raid was made upon the school of Justin at Rome and he and six of his associates were tried before the prefect of the city and executed. In that same year at Smyrna the aged Polycarp was burned at the stake. In 177 there was mob violence at Lyons and arrests, and the Emperor enforced the rescript of Trajan by beheading all who declared that they were Christians and setting at liberty all who denied that they were. The first century and a half, then, was a period of calm in which for the most part the Christians were let alone. Not so the third century. At last the government regards Christianity as a menace, an active anarchy which resists and undermines everything and must accordingly be put down by extermination. But the efforts of the state to stamp it out were intermittent and spasmodic. The fourth century was Christianity's day of coming to power. Does it make any difference that the Church which was for long persecuted is now triumphing? Crowds flock to it. After three hundred years it is at last a popular religion. The rise of monasticism synchronizes with Christianity becoming the official religion of the Empire. Instead of little struggling churches, it began to assemble great congregations.

The whole world crowded in; but some took it all much more seriously than most. Instead of being called to persecution and martyrdom as formerly, the zealot and the devotee had to find a new channel for their zeal. Christianity had ceased to be a religion in opposition and had become, or at least was becoming, a religion in conformity. As soon as they were not conscripted to bear arms against their fellows, Christians joined the army without protesting. When sacrifice to idols was no longer required, they willingly took public office and shared in the government. They ceased to withdraw from trade and the ordinary occupations. Government smiled upon them: they were no longer hunted men. The world had become theirs, and they lived in the world and expanded in the world.

The aristocracy of birth which claimed descent from Aeneas, and the aristocracy of intellect whose being was fostered by the Homeric and Virgilian traditions, were reluctant to give up the old gods. Old Christians, too, whose life object was purity, who had always believed that the new way of life was not and could not be a secular way and that the society of the faithful was never intended to be and could not be a secular society, had to find a way of going apart and living in uncontaminated holiness. Many sayings of Christ demanded a complete separation from the world, a stern asceticism, and a close following after the Master. The invitation to imitate Him was powerful. Monasticism was the left-wing movement in the Church which organized an ecclesiastical institution that made possible separation from the world and membership in the Church at one and the same time. It was a church within the Church, an undertaking of purists, of all-or-nothing Christians. So in the fourth century, while the Church in the world is being thoroughly

organized, or rather while the Roman world is being organized as a Church with specified functions assigned
to the Emperor, the Pope, the Patriarch, the Metropolitans, the bishops, the Councils, the parish priests, and the
synods, the Church outside the world is being recruited
and organized also. That Church which from the first
claimed to be more faithful than the other, embodied two
distinctive principles, asceticism and isolation. Christ had
said, "Sell that thou hast and give to the poor." The
Apostle to the Gentiles said, "Mortify your members
which are upon the earth." Now suppose one is so made
or situated that he takes these words seriously, finding in
them the substance of doctrine, the sum of the whole matter. Many did then, and do now, and have done so in
every age between. If one puts purity far above possessions or power or family or functioning in the world of
social give and take, and if one couples with purity dis-
cipleship, what appeal can be more understandable? So
"the religious life" came to mean the monastic life; and
"the secular life," the life outside a monastery. A "religious" was a man or woman who had taken monastic
vows, while a "secular" was one who had not.

Christianity did not invent the ascetic life. It was very
old when Christianity came. The Buddha organized the
Sangha, or monastic order in which the monk through
meditation cultivates control of self and learns to suppress all wants and "has his heart in his own power."
To him the one great thing is self-development. "Without covetousness, without deceit, without craving, without detraction, having got rid of passion and folly, being
free from desire in all the world, let one wander alone like
a rhinoceros." [1] Among the Jews the Essenes claimed a
dateless antiquity. They were a thoroughly organized

[1] Quoted from Fausböll's *Sutta Nipata* in Pratt, *The Pilgrimage
of Buddhism,* 46.

ascetic society, with a complete community of goods and great benevolence to one another and their fellow men. They are said to have been the first society in the world to condemn slavery. Agriculture was their occupation. Their rules were secret. They were thought to have cherished a kind of speculation. Their number seems to have been about four thousand. They did not live together in one place but were scattered in villages and towns and perhaps, later, even in the cities. They seem to have preferred the isolation of the shores of the Dead Sea. Even the Greeks, unyielding individualists though they were, maintained the military brotherhood of Sparta and the moral brotherhood of Pythagoras at Crotona. The Cynics cultivated asceticism, utterly departing from the principle of the golden mean in both their theory and their practice.[2]

Christian monasticism first appeared in Egypt, where from remote times there had been a vast monastery at Memphis for the housing of the monks of the god Serapis. This was a great communal building in which the monks lived, and which they never left. Frequent references are made to it in the papyri.[3]

The first monastery or brotherhood of monks in the Christian Church was formed about the time of the Council of Nicaea (325). Its date is sometimes given as 330, sometimes as early as 315. Its seat was an island in the Nile in the neighborhood of Thebes. Pachomius was its founder.[4] John Cassian, the first organizer of monasticism in the West, some time between 419 and 426 wrote the Institutes of the Coenobia [5] in which he reproduced some

[2] See Dio Chrysostom, *The Eighth Discourse, Diogenes or On Virtue.*
[3] See Hatch, *The Organization of the Early Christian Churches,* 157.
[4] Jerome, Letter CXXVII.
[5] *Nicene and Post-Nicene Fathers of the Christian Church,* 2nd Series, Vol. XI.

parts of the rule which Pachomius gave the original monastery of Tabenna—"whose monastery in the Thebaid," says Cassian, "is better filled as regards numbers, as it is stricter in the rigor of its system, than all the others, for there are in it more than five thousand brethren under the rule of one abbot; and the obedience with which the whole number of monks is at all times subject to one Elder is what no one among us would render to another even for a short time, or would demand from him" (IV. i.). He dwells upon "their untiring perseverance and humility and subjection, through which they remain in the monasteries till they are bent double with old age." One who seeks to be admitted to the discipline of the monastery must give an evidence of his perseverance and desire by lying outside the doors, before he is admitted, for ten days, or longer, of set purpose repelled and scorned by all the brethren who pass by. On his admission he is stripped of all his possessions, even of his clothes. When his perseverance warrants, he is clad in the garments of the monastery and given into the charge of an Elder and sent to lodge apart at the entrance and entrusted with the care of strangers and guests. Here he serves for one year without complaint. If he is sufficiently schooled in humility and patience he is then admitted to the congregation, and along with nine other juniors is put under the charge of another Elder whose chief concern is to see that each junior conquers his own wishes. By obedience a monk mortifies his wishes. The junior must not keep back any of his thoughts from the senior. He is not to do anything whatever without first asking the permission of the senior set over him. He must never say "my pen," "my book," "my sandals," "my coat," for he has nothing of his own. For every infraction of the rules, there is censure, which is adminis-

tered to the culprit lying prostrate in full congregation,
or stripes or expulsion.

At meals at Tabenna, there was strict silence. Among
the Egyptians the chief care was that every man should
work, and there was little rotation of tasks. Throughout
Egypt the number of psalms was fixed at twelve, both at
vespers and at nocturns. Two lessons, one from the Old
Testament, one from the New, uniformly followed them.
The canonical prayers followed the psalms, and each
monk was so worn "with fasting and working all day and
night" that while all stood for the prayers they were
allowed to sit for the psalms. Thus they renounced the
world, and each learned that "he was not his own maker
and had no authority over his own actions" (II. iii.). Before his death in 346, Pachomius had established nine
monasteries of men and one of women. About 410 there
were seven thousand monks under his rule. All were under
the supervision of an abbot of abbots.

This for the Thebaid, or the region near Thebes. There
was another region in Egypt which was full of monks
and monasteries, the Nitrian valley to the northwest of
Cairo, three days' journey in the Libyan desert. With
the difference that monastic life was a little less strict
there, it went on as in the Thebaid. Rufinus, who visited
this region in 372, mentions fifty monasteries as existing
there. That figure is confirmed by Sozomen.[6] Jerome
calls Nitria "the town of the Lord where day by day the
filth of multitudes is washed away with the pure nitre
of virtue" (Letter CVIII). There are, he says, in Egypt
three classes or kinds of monks. First, the cenobites live
in a community under superiors whom they must obey,
and are divided into bodies of ten and of a hundred so

[6] Gibson, Prolegomena to the Works of John Cassian, in *Nicene and
Post-Nicene Fathers, etc.,* XI, 186.

that each tenth man has authority over nine others and each hundredth has ten officers under him. Thus are the soldiers of the Lord under commanders. These monks live each in his separate cell. After the ninth hour they come together to sing psalms, read the Scriptures, and pray. Secondly, there are the anchorites, solitaries or hermits who go off by themselves and live alone. Thirdly, there is the class called Remoboth who live together in twos and threes, not under a rule, an inferior and disappointing kind of monk. "If you desire to be a monk be more careful of your soul than of your property." As between life in solitude and life in a community the preference, says Jerome, is usually given to life in solitude (Letter CXXX).

The hermits were earlier than the monasteries. The first monasteries were only solitaries brought together into an ordered common life. Henceforth most of the "religious" are to be found in monasteries; but the hermits do not cease to exist, their race has not died out. The pattern of the eremitical life is Anthony the Egyptian. Athanasius wrote a Life of Anthony which became a powerful tract in advancing the claims of the monastic devotion. Anthony's dates, incredible as they seem, are supposed to have been *c.* 251 to *c.* 356. He was reared in a pious Christian household. Shortly after the death of his parents, when he was but a youth of twenty or so, he heard the Gospel account of the Lord's command to the rich young man: "If thou wilt be perfect, go and sell that thou hast, and give to the poor, and thou shalt have treasure in heaven: and come and follow me." He obeyed the command. The promise of eternal life is bought, he said, for a trifle. Whenever we live the term of our life in the discipline, we shall reign forever and ever. For twenty years he trained himself in solitude in a ruined fort. His example called others to gather about him. He persuaded many to enroll themselves "for citizenship in heaven," and the desert was colonized by monks. The crowds of people that came to him would not let him be still, and he withdrew from that place and went into "the inner desert." There he spent the remaining forty-five years of his long life. His superiority, Athanasius maintains, was in "the serenity of his manner and the purity of his soul." He was wonderful in faith and in religion. There was about him always a fine courtesy, and his answers were not without Attic salt.

Ammon, a friend of Anthony, was the moving spirit in the Nitrian valley, filling the same place in Lower Egypt that Anthony did in the Thebaid. Their work flourished. It is said that there were 100,000 monks in Egypt in the fifth century. At the end of the fifth century Egyptian monasticism began to decline, but even to this day there are a handful of monasteries. The institution spread from Egypt to the entire Roman world. Hilarion took it to Syria. He was a Palestinian born near Gaza. While he was growing up, his whole pleasure was in the assemblies of the Church. At that time he heard of the famous name of Anthony, which was in the mouth of all the races of Egypt. He was fired with a desire to see him, and set out for the desert. He no sooner saw him than he changed his former mode of life and abode with him about two months, "studying the method of his life and the gravity of his conduct: his assiduity in prayer, his humility in his dealings with the brethren, his severity in rebuke, his eagerness in exhortation. He noted too that the saint would never on account of bodily weakness break his rule of abstinence or deviate from the plainness of his food." Hilarion, moved by the sight of Anthony's victory, entered upon "the soldier's career." It was he

who originated that mode of life in Syria. "The Lord
Jesus had in Egypt the aged Anthony; in Palestine he
had the youthful Hilarion." [7] As a sample of the conversation of such ascetics when they came together perhaps once in a lifetime for a few moments, Jerome puts
these questions into the mouth of Paul, the first hermit,
when in old age he visits Anthony. "Tell me, I pray you,
how fares the human race? Are new homes springing up
in the ancient cities? What government directs the
world." [8]

Eustathius of Sebasteia introduced the eremitical life
into Armenia.[9] Basil of Cappadocia transformed its austerities into the milder regulations of a cenobitic system.
When he left the University of Athens he travelled in
Egypt, and what he saw there affected him. His own
account is informing. "First of all was I minded to
make some mending of my ways, long perverted as they
were by my intimacy with wicked men. Then I read the
Gospel, and I saw there that a great means of reaching
perfection was the selling of one's goods, the sharing
them with the poor, the giving up of all care for this life,
and the refusal to allow the soul to be turned by any
sympathy to things of earth. And I prayed that I might
find some one of the brethren who had chosen this way
of life, that with him I might cross life's short and
troubled strait. And many did I find in Alexandria and
many in the rest of Egypt, and others in Palestine, and
in Coele Syria and in Mesopotamia. I admired their continence in living, and their endurance in toil; I was
amazed at their persistency in prayer, and at their triumphing over sleep; subdued by no natural necessity,

---

[7] Jerome, *Life of St. Hilarion*, iii, xiv.
[8] Jerome, *Life of Paulus, the First Hermit*, x.
[9] Sozomen, *Ecclesiastical History*, III, xiv.

ever keeping their soul's purpose high and free, in hunger, in thirst, in cold, in nakedness, they never yielded to the body; they were never willing to waste attention on it; always, as though living in a flesh that was not theirs, they shewed in very deed what it is to sojourn for a while in this life, and what to have one's citizenship and home in heaven. All this moved my admiration. I called these men's lives blessed, in that they did in deed shew that they 'bear about in their body the dying of Jesus.' And I prayed that I, too, as far as in me lay, might imitate them." [10]

The results were the monastery Basil organized in Neo-Caesarea in Pontus, and the Basilian Rule which put fasting and austerities below work and prayer. Seven times a day did his monks assemble for prayers; the rest of their day was given to Scripture reading and work in the fields. A novitiate had to be passed before admission. Membership in the monastery was for life. The monastery kept a school where boys were taught—boys from the world, who were not expected to join the brotherhood. The Basilian rule was the foundation of the monastic life in the Greek and Russian churches. For four centuries it was followed without change. Then it was revised by Theodore of Constantinople; but that revision was undertaken chiefly to restore the original vigor of the practice of Basil.

In the great battles about doctrine which raged in the fourth century Athanasius, the friend and later the biographer of Anthony, was banished from Alexandria to Treves on the Moselle in Gaul in 336. He had some of his priests with him, for it was "from some priests of Alexandria," from Athanasius, and subsequently from Peter,

[10] Basil, Letter CCXXIII in *Nicene and Post-Nicene Fathers, etc.*, Vol. VIII.

Jerome says, that the high-born lady Marcella at Rome
"heard of the life of the blessed Anthony." [11] Athanasius
was three times at Treves: in 336, 346, and 349. So monasticism within a generation after its beginning in Egypt
was taken to the West, and a whole crop of monasteries
shortly came into existence there. At the gates of Poitiers,
Hilary founded Ligugé in 360; St. Martin founded Tours
in 371. Sulpicius Severus' monastery was founded about
392. John Cassian, who had spent seven years in Egypt,
founded the monastery of St. Victor and the monastery
of St. Salvator at Marseilles after 410 and before 432.
In 410 Honoratus, a Gaul of consular family, founded the
great monastery of Lérins on an island a few miles from
the coast of France. About 420 St. Germain of Auxerre
was founded by the bishop of Auxerre.

St. Martin (c. 316–397) is the patron saint of France,
the warrior saint, for in his youth he was a Roman soldier.
Born in Pannonia, he determined while but a boy to live
like the hermits of Egypt. Being the son of a veteran
he had to serve in the army; but his mind was so intent
upon the monastic life that even when he was a soldier he
made himself more of a monk than a soldier. His soldier-
ing completed, he took up his work in the Church under
Hilary, bishop of Poitiers. Together they founded the
first monastery in Gaul, Ligugé at the gates of Poitiers.
From it he was forced to the see of Tours. There he spent
his life in battling against paganism and building up the
Church. This is Sulpicius Severus' account of the monastery which he founded: When he became bishop "he
made use, for some time, of the cell connected with the
Church; but afterwards, when he felt it impossible to tolerate the disturbance caused by the numbers of those
visiting it, he established a monastery for himself about
two miles outside the city. This spot was so secret and

[11] Jerome, Letter CXXVII.

retired that he enjoyed in it the solitude of a hermit. For on one side it was surrounded by a precipitous rock of a lofty mountain, while the river Loire had shut in the rest of the plain by a bay extending back for a little distance and the place could be approached only by one, and that a very narrow passage. Here then, he possessed a cell constructed of wood. Many also of the brethren had in the same manner fashioned retreats for themselves, but most of them had formed these out of the rock of the overhanging mountain, hollowed into caves. There were altogether eighty disciples who were being disciplined after the example of the saintly master. No one there had anything which was called his own; all things were possessed in common. It was not allowed either to buy or sell anything, as is the custom among most monks. No art was practiced there, except that of transcribers, and even this was assigned to the brethren of younger years, while the elders spent their time in prayer. Rarely did any of them go beyond the cell, unless when they assembled at the place of prayer. They all took their food together, after the hour of fasting was past. No one used wine except when illness compelled him to do so. Most of them were clothed in garments of camel's hair. Any dress approaching to softness was there deemed criminal, and this must be thought the more remarkable, because many among them were such as are deemed of noble rank. These, though far differently brought up, had forced themselves down to this degree of humility and patient endurance, and we have seen numbers of these afterwards made bishops. For what city or church did not desire to have its priests from among those in the monastery of Martin?" [12] Lérins on its island, protected from the invasions which disturbed the mainland, became a

[12] Sulpicius Severus, Life of St. Martin, X, in *Nicene and Post-Nicene Fathers, etc.*, Vol. XI.

great school of theology. There in 434 Vincent wrote his "Commonitory" in which is for the first time formulated that famous definition of orthodoxy: *Quod semper, quod ubique, quod ab omnibus creditum est.* There Eucher wrote his "Panegyric on Solitude." There Patrick, the patron saint of Ireland, went for his training.

The fourth century was one of vigorous life in Gaul. The province had been Romanized. Latin was at last nearly everywhere spoken. The land was prosperous. There were flourishing schools in many places. Greek was taught in them as well as Latin. They were patronized by the Christians freely, which fact accounts for the late coming of Christian schools to Gaul. At Bordeaux, Ausonius, the literary leader of a great company, finds the labor of his fellow professors worth immortalizing in his poems. The work of the teacher is to him greatly worthy. Through it indeed Ausonius attained the consulship, the greatest of civic dignities. Marseilles, though not so outstanding as in earlier time, was still celebrated. Treves, Autun, Arles were famed for the instruction of their Roman schools. That period was, as Dill has graphically described it, the Indian summer of the ancient order. The Church profited greatly that it was a century of peace. Since Christianity had imperial sanction it gathered to itself a great number of the educated better-class men of the land. So many of them became bishops that Christianity began clearly to surpass paganism in educated leadership. One result was that religious intolerance in a measure died down in Gaul; another was that the Church developed schools in which the old learning was given a place beside the new learning. Bishop Hilary had the leading episcopal school in his church at Arles. It was not so famous, however, as the young monastic school at Lérins, which was enormously

enterprising and turned out famous church leaders. The
glow of enthusiasm which radiated from Gaul in this
fourth century is both heartening and pathetic—heartening because it was so real, and pathetic in that the invasions soon smashed everything. But the Church was
planted and the bishop and the monk were there to carry
on in spite of all.

Augustine was teaching rhetoric at Milan (*c.* 386)
when a certain North African countryman of his, a high
officer of the Emperor's court, Pontitianus, came to his
house to visit him. Pontitianus noticed a book on a table
and picked it up. It was a letter by the Apostle Paul
which Augustine admitted that he was eagerly reading.
"When then I had told him that I bestowed much pains
upon these writings, a conversation ensued on his speaking of Anthony, the Egyptian monk, whose name was in
high repute among Thy servants, though up to that time
not familiar to us. When he came to know this, he lingered
on that topic, imparting to us a knowledge of this man so
eminent, and marvelling at our ignorance. . . . From
this his conversation turned to the companies in the monasteries and their manners so fragrant unto Thee and of
the fruitful deserts of the wilderness, of which we knew
nothing. And there was a monastery at Milan full of
good brethren, without the walls of the city, under the
fostering care of Ambrose, and we were ignorant of
it." [13]

Augustine, when he became bishop of Hippo, organized
the clergy of his diocese into a monastery in the bishop's
palace.[14] A monastery for women was formed at Hippo,
of which Augustine's sister was prioress. Augustine's
Letter CCXI contains the rules which he formulated in

[13] Augustine, *Confessions,* VIII, vi, 14–15.
[14] Montalembert, *The Monks of the West* I, 441. London, 1861.

423 to govern the nuns of that monastery: First of all, dwell in the house with oneness of spirit. Let all property be in common. Every other form of sin finds scope in evil works, but pride even in good works. Be regular in prayers at the appointed hours. Keep the flesh under by fastings and by abstinence from meat and drink, so far as health allows. Aspire to please by your behavior rather than your attire. Let there be no frowardness of the eye. Keep the clothes of all in one place. Those who work in making any article are to make it for others, not for themselves. Let your clothes be washed at such intervals at the prioress'orders. Let the washing of the body be at the usual interval assigned to it, i.e. once in a month. Let a physician be consulted in matters of health. The patients must do at the orders of the prioress what health demands. Let one of your number look after the care of the sick. Let manuscripts be applied for at a fixed hour every day. Quarrels should be unknown among you. If they arise they should be quickly ended. Let not her who refuses to forgive her sister expect answers to prayer. The love which you bear to each other must not be carnal, but spiritual. Obey the prioress as a mother. The Lord grant that you may yield loving submission to these rules "as persons enamored of spiritual beauty." These rules were made the basis of the monastic order of Augustinians under Charles the Great.

Milan was an imperial capital and a famous center of Roman learning in the fourth century. The education of the world, like the government of the world, was now carried on in many places. Rome had rivals, and their rivalry subtracted from her importance; but that city continued to be a great center of training and the headquarters of expiring paganism. Schools are almost the last of social institutions to yield to change. Education is traditional because it purveys the stuff of tradition: its teachers know nothing else to teach than that which they have been trained in, and even the greatest of the pupils of their training idealize their own youthful instruction and strive to keep the past upon the throne. That was true of the greatest of the leaders of the Church. Jerome and Augustine could not utterly break away from their own past; though they had moments of trying to do so, still the net effect of their practice and advice was that Christians should be trained in both the old and the new learning.

When Jerome went to live in a monastery at Bethlehem in 386 he aroused the interest of men everywhere. That great man was born at Stridon in Pannonia about 345 and died at Bethlehem in 420. He was trained in grammar at Stridon, but went to Rome in 363, where he studied under Aelius Donatus and frequented the law courts. There his record for austerity was not good; but he fell in with some young Christians, and with them visited the tombs of the martyrs in the catacombs. It is believed that he was baptized in 366. He was at Treves in Gaul from 366 to 370, studying, copying manuscripts, and writing a commentary on Obadiah. He returned to Italy in 370 and for three years lived an ascetic life at Aquileia with a little group of twelve congenial Christian young men who had a common purpose but were not under a vow or monastic rules. Here he entered definitely upon his twofold life work, the study of the Scriptures and the championing of asceticism. From here with five of his companions he travelled to the East, stopping in several places but finally reaching Antioch, where he nearly died of fever. It was in this illness that he had the life-changing dream which he afterwards described in these words: "Many years ago, when for the kingdom of heaven's sake I had cut myself off from home, parents, sister, relations and, harder still, from the dainty food to which I had been accustomed; and when I was on my way to Jerusalem to wage my warfare, I still could not bring myself to forego the library which I had formed for myself at Rome with great care and toil. And so, miserable man that I was, I would fast only that I might afterwards read Cicero. After many nights spent in vigil, after floods of tears called from my inmost heart, after the recollection of my past sins, I would once more take up Plautus. And when at times I returned to my right mind, and began to read the prophets, their style seemed rude and repellent. I failed to see the light with my blinded eyes; but I attributed the fault not to them, but to the sun. While the old serpent was thus making me his plaything, about the middle of Lent a deep-seated fever fell upon my weakened body, and while it destroyed my rest completely—the story seems hardly credible—it so wasted my unhappy frame that scarcely anything was left of me but skin and bone. Meantime preparations for my funeral went on; my body grew gradually colder, and the warmth of life lingered only in my throbbing breast. Suddenly I was caught up in the spirit and dragged before the judgment seat of the Judge; and here the light was so bright, and those who stood around were so radiant that I cast myself on the ground and did not dare to look up. Asked who and what I was I replied: 'I am a Christian.' But He who presided said: 'Thou liest, thou art a follower of Cicero and not of Christ. For "where thy treasure is, there will thy heart be also." ' Instantly I became dumb, and amid the strokes of the lash—for He had ordered me to be scourged—I was tortured more severely still by the fire of conscience, considering with myself that verse, 'In the grave who shall give thee thanks?' Yet for all that I began to cry and bewail myself saying: 'Have mercy upon me, O Lord; have mercy upon me.' Amid the sound of the scourges this cry still made itself heard. At last the bystanders, falling down before the knees of Him who presided, prayed that He would have pity on my youth, and that He would give me space to repent of my error. He might still, they urged, inflict torture on me, should I ever again read the works of the Gentiles. Under the stress of that awful moment I should have been ready to make even still larger promises than these. Accordingly I made oath and called upon His name, saying: 'Lord, if ever again I possess worldly books, or if ever again I read such, I have denied Thee.' Dismissed, then, on taking this oath, I returned to the upper world, and to the surprise of all, I opened upon them eyes so drenched with tears that my distress served to convince even the incredulous. And that this was no sleep or idle dream, such as those by which we are often mocked, I call to witness the tribunal before which I lay, and the terrible judgment which I feared. May it never hereafter be my lot to fall under such an inquisition! I profess that my shoulders were black and blue, that I felt the bruises long after I awoke from my sleep, and that thenceforth I read the books of God with a zeal greater than I had previously given to the books of men." [15]

The next five years (374–379) Jerome spent as an anchorite, living in a cell in the desert of Chalcis. Penance was his constant business, but he learned Hebrew from a converted Jew. Next he is in Antioch, is ordained a presbyter, but declines and continues to decline to take part in the active ministry; instead, he studies with Apollinaris. The next year he was in Constanti-

[15] Letter XXII *in Nicene and Post-Nicene Fathers, etc.*

nople and studied with Gregory Nazianzen. In 382 he
went to Rome and served as a kind of expert biblical and
theological adviser to Pope Damasus. It was for the
Pope that he undertook his revised versions of the Psalms
and the New Testament and began to collect the manuscript versions of the Old Testament. What occupied
him no less eagerly was a great opportunity to help to
plant devotion to the ascetic life in the minds of some
of the noblest born of Roman women. Epiphanius, a
disciple of Hilarion, was staying in Rome as a guest of
the lady Paula. Epiphanius introduced Jerome to the
lady Paula, who became his disciple in the life of self-
denial. Paula's son Toxotius and her daughters Blesilla
and Julia Eustochium were no less interested. These
with nine of their associates, all high-born Roman women,
formed a group of renunciants which met in the house on
the Aventine of Marcella, one of their number, to sing the
psalms in Hebrew, to pray together and read the Scriptures
under the direction of the pious scholar Jerome. For them
he wrote out detailed directions for leading the religious
life of self-denial which they learned by heart and practiced. When Pope Damasus died, his successor was not
sympathetic to Jerome, and a popular cry against the ascetic scholar shortly convinced him that he was trying to
"sing the Lord's song in a strange land." He resolved to
leave Rome forever and to become a monk at Bethlehem.
He sailed with two brother monks to Antioch. There Paula
and Eustochium joined them, and that little company of
renunciants journeyed through Palestine and Jerusalem
to the monks of the Nitrian valley in Egypt. In 386 they
returned to Bethlehem, to make it their home as long as
they should live. A monastery was built of which Jerome
was the head, and a convent for nuns over which Paula
presided and after her death her daughter Eustochium.

They built a hospice for pilgrims, also. Paula's wealth, as long as it lasted, provided support for these institutions. After it was gone Jerome and his brother sold their family property and used that. Here Jerome lived on bread and vegetables for thirty-four years, passing his days in a cell surrounded by his library and performing an endless work of textual study, translation, exegesis, defence of doctrine and composition and correspondence, as well as the direction of his monastery and the meeting of crowds of monks who came to Bethlehem. He taught the Latin classics, explaining "his own Maro and the comedians and lyrical and historical writers to young boys who had been entrusted to him that he might teach them the fear of the Lord," [16] and each day he explained the Scriptures to the monks of his monastery.

"I for my part am building in this province a monastery and a hospice close by; so that if Joseph and Mary chance to come to Bethlehem, they may not fail to find shelter and welcome. Indeed, the number of monks who flock here from all quarters of the world is so overwhelming that I can neither desist from my enterprise nor bear so great a burthen." [17] Writing to Laeta in Rome in 403, Jerome paints a contrast: "Even in Rome itself paganism is left in solitude. They who once were the gods of the nations remain under their lonely roofs with horned-owls and birds of night. The military standards are emblazoned with the cross. The emperor's robes of purple and his jewelled diadem are ornamented with the shameful yet saving gibbet. Already the Egyptian Serapis has been made a Christian; while at Gaza, Marnas mourns in confinement and every moment expects his temple overthrown. From India, from Persia, from Ethiopia we daily welcome

[16] Rufinus, *Apology,* II, 8 (2).
[17] Letter LXVI.

monks in crowds. The Armenian bowman has laid aside his quiver, the Huns learn the psalter, the chilly Scythians are warmed with the glow of the faith. The Getae, ruddy and yellow-haired, carry tent-churches about with their armies; and perhaps their success in fighting against us may be due to the fact that they believe in the same religion." [18]

Laeta, the wife of Toxotius, was the daughter-in-law of Paula, the supporter of the monasteries and abbess of the nuns of Bethlehem. Laeta's little daughter, who also is Paula for she bears her grandmother's name, must be educated, and the mother writes to Jerome for advice as to this. In answer she receives from him a long letter, the most important one in existence on early Christian plans for education. The directions given are for the education of a Christian woman of position, but it may be taken for granted that the attitude expressed applies to education in general, especially since the privileges which were then demanded for members of the male sex were commonly greater than those enjoyed by women. The little Paula was vowed before her birth to Christian service. She must therefore hear nothing and say nothing but what belongs to the fear of God. She must never share the company of "boys, with their wanton thoughts." Even her female attendants must be separated from worldly associates. "For if they have learned some mischief they may teach more. Get for her a set of letters made of boxwood or of ivory and called each by its proper name. Let her play with these, so that even her play may teach her something. And not only make her grasp the right order of the letters and see that she forms their names into a rhyme but constantly disarrange their order and put the last letters in the middle and the middle ones at the be-

[18] Letter CVII.

ginning that she may know them all by sight as well as by sound. Moreover, as soon as she begins to use the stylus upon the wax, and her hand is still faltering, either guide her soft fingers by laying your hand upon hers, or else have copies cut upon a tablet; so that her efforts confined within these limits may keep to the lines traced out for her and not stray outside of these. Offer prizes for good spelling and draw her onward with little gifts such as children of her age delight in. And let her have companions in her lessons to excite emulation in her, that she may be stimulated when she sees them praised. You must not scold her if she is slow to learn, but must employ praise to excite her mind, so that she may be glad when she excels others and sorry when she is excelled by them. Above all you must take care not to make her lessons distasteful to her lest a dislike for them conceived in childhood may continue into her maturer years. The very words which she tries bit by bit to put together and to pronounce ought not to be chance ones, but names specially fixed upon and heaped together for the purpose, those for example of the prophets or the apostles or the list of patriarchs from Adam downward, as it is given by Matthew and Luke. In this way while her tongue will be well trained her memory will be likewise developed. Again, you must choose for her a master of approved years, life and learning. A man of culture will not, I think, blush to do for a kinswoman or a high born virgin what Aristotle did for Philip's son when, descending to the level of an usher, he consented to teach him his letters. Things must not be despised as of small account in the absence of which great results cannot be achieved. The very rudiments and first beginnings of knowledge sound differently in the mouth of an educated man and of an uneducated. She must not learn the elided and deformed words of baby speech from silly women, for the Gracchi learned eloquence from the way in which their mother spoke to them in their earliest years. She must not acquire tricks of manner and bearing. She must be told in what army she is a recruit. Her dress and garb must be simple as is befitting a Christian. Do not pierce her ears or paint the face consecrated to Christ with white lead or rouge. Do not hang gold or pearls about her neck or load her head with jewels, or by reddening her hair make it suggest the fires of Gehenna." Directions as to religious rites and exercises, food, drink, etc. are then given. "And let it be her task daily to bring to you the flowers which she has culled from scripture. Let her learn by heart so many verses in the Greek, but let her be instructed in the Latin also. You must yourself be her mistress, a model on which she may form her childish conduct. Reading and prayer must be her chief occupations. Let her learn too how to spin wool. . . . Let her treasures be not silks or gems but manuscripts of the Holy Scriptures. . . . Let her life begin by learning the psalter, and then let her gather rules of life out of the proverbs of Solomon. From the Preacher let her gain the habit of despising the world and its vanities. Let her follow the example set in Job of virtue and patience. Then let her pass on to the Gospels never to be laid aside when once they have been taken in hand. Let her also drink in with a willing heart the Acts of the Apostles and the Epistles. As soon as she has enriched the storehouse of her mind with these treasures, let her commit to memory the prophets, the heptateuch, the books of Kings and of Chronicles, the rolls of Ezra and Esther. The Song of Songs may next be read. All apocryphal writings must be carefully avoided. Cyprian's writings let her have always in her hands. The letters of Athanasius and the treatises of Hilary she may go through without fear of stumbling.

Let her take pleasure in the works and wits of all in whose books a due regard for the faith is not neglected. But if she read the works of others let it be rather to judge than to follow them. You will ask how is this careful training to be accomplished, if one lives at Rome. Do not undertake a burden to which you are not equal. Give up this most precious of gems, to be placed in Mary's chamber and to rest in the cradle where the infant Jesus cried. Let her be brought up in a monastery, let her be one amid companies of virgins, let her learn to avoid swearing, let her regard lying as sacrilege, let her be ignorant of the world, her live the angelic life, while in the flesh let her be without the flesh, and let her suppose that all human beings are like herself." [19]

Alas! All that flourishing world of the fourth century was rapidly to be destroyed. The fear of the Goths had, like the fear of the Persians by the Greeks, never been absent from the Romans since the fatal year 390 B.C. when they captured and occupied Rome. There was much fighting in Gaul and Germany subsequent to that. In most of it the Romans were victorious, but not in all. Now the frontiers are broken and the armies driven in, the Empire is overrun, the invasions are on. Alaric is at the gates of Rome, and in 410 masters the city. In his Preface to Ezekiel, Jerome cries out against what is happening: "Who would believe that Rome, built up by the conquest of the whole world, had collapsed, that the mother of nations had become also their tomb; that the shores of the whole East, of Egypt, of Africa, which once belonged to the imperial city, were filled with the hosts of her men-servants and maid-servants, that we should every day be receiving in this holy Bethlehem men and women who once were noble and abounding in every kind

[19] Jerome, Letter CVII in *Nicene and Post-Nicene Fathers*, etc.

of wealth, but are now reduced to poverty? We cannot relieve these sufferers; all we can do is to sympathise with them, and unite our tears with theirs. The burden of this holy work was as much as we could carry; the sight of the wanderers coming in crowds, caused us deep pain; and we therefore abandoned the exposition of Ezekiel, and almost all study, and were filled with a longing to turn the words of Scripture into action, and not to say holy things but to do them." [20]

The experience of northern Italy was not different, it was only earlier than that of Rome. Bishop Ambrose, in preaching the funeral sermon over his brother Satyrus in 379, takes occasion to say: "For with the pity of thy holy mind for those near to thee, if thou knewest that Italy was now oppressed by the nearness of the enemy, how wouldst thou groan, how wouldst thou grieve that our safety wholly depended on the barrier of the Alps, and that the protection of purity consisted in barricades of trees! With what sorrow wouldst thou mourn that thy friends were separated from the enemy by so slight a division, from an enemy, too, both impure and cruel, who spares neither chastity nor life. How, I say, couldst thou bear these things which we are compelled to endure, and perchance (which is more grievous) to behold virgins ravished, little children torn from the embrace of their parents and tossed on javelins, the bodies consecrated to God defiled, and even aged widows polluted?" [21]

Not only Italy but nearly every part of the Empire was invaded. On New Year's Eve, 406, a vast army of Vandals, Alans, and Suevians crossed the Rhine and entered

[20] Jerome, Preface to Ezekiel, in *Nicene and Post-Nicene Fathers*, etc., VI, 500.
[21] Ambrose, On the Decease of His Brother Satyrus, I, xxxi–xxxii, in *Nicene and Post-Nicene Fathers, etc.*, X, 166.

Gaul. The invaders were barbarian destroyers. "The once noble city of Moguntiacum [now Mainz] has been captured and destroyed. In its church many thousands have been massacred. The people of Vangium [now Worms] have been extirpated. The powerful city of Rheims, the Ambiani [the tribe whose city was Amiens], the Altrebatae [whose city was Arras], the Belgians on the skirts of the world, Tournay, Spires, and Strasburg all have fallen, while the provinces of Aquitaine and of the Nine Nations, of Lyons and Narbonne are with the exception of a few cities one universal scene of desolation. And those which the sword spares famine destroys. I cannot speak without tears of Toulouse which has been kept from falling hitherto by the merits of its reverend bishop Exuperius. Even the Spains are on the brink of ruin and tremble daily as they recall the invasion of the Cymry; and while others suffer misfortune once in actual fact, they suffer them continually in anticipation. I say nothing of other places that I may not seem to despair of God's mercy. All that is ours now from the Pontic Sea to the Julian Alps in days gone by once ceased to be ours. For thirty years the barbarians burst the barrier of the Danube and fought in the heart of the Roman Empire. Long use dried our tears. For all but a few old people had been born either in captivity or during a blockade, and consequently they did not miss a liberty they had never known. Yet who will hereafter credit the fact or what histories will seriously discuss it that Rome has to fight within her own borders not for glory, but for bare life; and that she does not even fight but buys the right to exist by giving gold and sacrificing all her substance?" [22]

In the year 407 the horrors of civil war were added.

[22] Jerome, the letter to Ageruchia, CXXIII, xvi–xvii, in *Nicene and Post-Nicene Fathers, etc.*, VI, 237.

The Roman soldiers of Britain, having murdered two rival emperors, elected Constantine as Emperor, and Constantine at once brought his legions from Britain to Gaul and for a time fought the Vandals and Alans and then the imperial troops of Honorius intermittently for three years, during which he severed Gaul, Britain, and Spain from the Western Empire. He was conquered and beheaded. During most of that time—for two and one-half years, in fact—the Vandals and the Alans went on with their work of plundering and devastating Gaul. In the fall of 409 they passed on into Spain. "All Gaul smoked like a funeral pyre," is the way the Bishop of Auch, Orientus, described it.[23] In 412 the Visigothic conquerors of Rome moved into southern Gaul. They were forced to move on into Spain in 415; but in 418 they returned, and in Aquitaine they founded a kingdom, with Toulouse for its capital, which lasted until 507. In 451 Attila, the Hun, crossed the Rhine and fell upon and burned the city of Metz, massacring all its inhabitants. He then marched his army to Paris but did not attack it, "because of the prayers of the nun of Nanterre," but moved on to Orleans which he did attack. Aetius met him on the Mauriac plains and after a battle which lasted three days Attila withdrew across the Rhine.

In 496 Chlodovig (Clovis), King of the Franks, a heathen, but married to Hrothilde, a Christian convert, was heavily engaged in battle with the Alemanni. The day was going against him and having called upon his own gods in vain, he at last called upon the God of Hrothilde and won the battle. On Christmas Day, 496, he was baptized by Remigius, Bishop of Rheims, who received him with the command: "Bow thy neck in humility, O Sicambrian; accept as an object of worship that which thou wast wont to destroy, and burn that which thou

[23] Holmes, *The Christian Church in Gaul*, 309.

worshipped." [24] The Burgundians were in the East and North of France, the Franks were in the center, the Goths were settled in Aquitaine and Spain. The Vandals after twenty years in Spain were invited by Count Boniface to move into North Africa. Eighty thousand of them under their great leader Genseric crossed at Gibraltar in the spring of 429. They moved up and down the land and besieged its three walled cities, Cirta, Carthage, and Hippo. The aged Augustine advised his bishops to stay with their people. "What," said one of them, "is the use of our remaining, simply to see the men slain, the women ravished, the churches burned, and then to be put to the rack ourselves to make us disclose the hiding places of treasures which we have not?" [25] So Augustine gathered them about him within the walls of Hippo, and together they sat and prayed around him as his life ebbed away and death came to the foremost of Christians in August, 430. In 455 Rome was taken by the Vandals. The Empire of the West was now only a form which lasted on to 476.

What could education and the forces making for culture have done in that terrible fifth century? Now everything depends on the monk and the bishop. There is only one Church now, the Church outside the world, for all has turned to desert. Yet there are pathetic reminders of Rome's great past. One of them is the poet Prudentius who died in 410, another the poet Claudian whose last poem belongs to 405.

She alone to friendship drew the tribes that vanquished came,
She as mother, not as lord, gave all a common name,
Linking far-off lands with love a son would feel for home,
Greeting newly conquered foes as citizens of Rome.[26]

[24] Gregory of Tours, II, xxxi.
[25] Hodgkin, *Italy and Her Invaders*, II, 248.
[26] Harold Cox's translation.

The barbarian triumphed and only the Christian was left to stamp the marks of Rome upon him. The heart had gone out of the old things and valued ways of doing. Books were written and grammar and rhetoric were taught; but the style in which books were written was florid and affected, and the speeches that students learned to make were empty, verbal, and pompous. The heart had gone out of human operations, and while habitual manipulations went on where they could, they were the shadowy forms of activities that once had had energy and meaning. Here and there the Roman schools went on, at Milan, at Constantinople, at Rome, at Bordeaux, Arles, Lyons, and Autun, and of course in many other places. In 425 the Emperors Theodosius and Valentinian by edict made the government solely responsible for the conduct of education and pronounced penalties upon private persons who without authorization should open schools. But if pagan culture was expiring, Christian culture was more active than ever. The bishops had more work to do, and they did it with all the energy they possessed, for their day had come, the world depended upon them. There were five who kept the church of Gaul alive, Hilary and Caesarius of Arles, Germanus of Auxerre, Lupus of Troyes and Mamertus of Vienne. Three of them had been trained at Lérins. At Arles, Bishop Hilary, who had oversight of the whole of Gaul, founded a school for the training of the clergy. Germanus and Lupus were missionaries to Britain in 429.

The conquests of the Heruli and the Goths, and the disappearance of the Emperors from the West did not entirely change conditions in Roman society in Italy. The Teutonic rulers regarded themselves as carrying on for the Emperor at Constantinople. The public schools of Rome, Milan, Padua, Ravenna, and Naples continued to exist and the work of private teachers went on in some of the towns.[27] After the lawless years of the fifth century the schools enjoyed something like prosperity. Sicilian fathers sent their sons to be educated at Rome, which King Theodoric described as "everyone's country, the fruitful mother of eloquence, the wide temple of all the virtues. It is a striking mark of our favour to assign such a City as a residence to any of our subjects." [28] Land surveyors were still to be had there; instruction was given in the gymnasium, and Theodoric praised his officers for their zeal in the study of literature in promoting them.[29] But school education was for the Romans, not for the Goths. "Now Amalasuntha wished to make her son resemble the Roman princes in his manner of life, and was already compelling him to attend the school of a teacher of letters. . . But the Goths were by no means pleased with this . . . and all the notable men among them gathered together and coming before Amalasuntha made the charge that their king was not being educated correctly from their point of view nor to his own advantage. For letters, they said, are far removed from manliness, and the teaching of old men results for the most part in a cowardly and submissive spirit. Therefore the man who is to show daring in any work and be great in renown ought to be freed from the timidity which teachers inspire and take his training in arms. They added that even Theodoric would never allow any of the Goths to send their children to school; for he used to say to them all, that, if the fear of the strap once came over them, they would never have the resolution to despise

[27] Salvioli, *L'Instruzione pubblica in Italia nei secoli* VIII, IX and X, 6.

[28] *Cassiodori Variae*, I, xxxix, IV, vi (Hodgkin).

[29] *Ibid.*, III, lii, V, xxiii, II, xv.

sword or spear." [30] Athalaric, however, exhibited a great
interest in the work of the schools and urged the Romans
to a greater regard for them. In a letter of 533 addressed
to the Roman Senate he says: "You who are called Fathers
should be interested in all that concerns the education of
your sons. We hear by certain whisperings that the
teachers of eloquence at Rome are not receiving their
proper reward, and that the sums appointed to be paid
to the masters of schools are lessened by the haggling of
some persons. Grammar is the noble foundation of all
literature, the glorious mother of eloquence . . . The
grammatical art is not used by barbarous beings; it abides
peculiarly with legitimate sovereigns. Other nations have
arms; the lords of the Romans alone have eloquence.
Hence sounds the trumpet for the legal fray in the Forum.
Hence comes the eloquence of so many chiefs of the State,
hence, to say nothing more, even this discourse which is
now addressed to you. Wherefore, let the teacher of grammar and of rhetoric, if he be found suitable for his work
and obey the decrees of the Praefect of the City, be supported by your authority, and suffer no diminution of his
salary." [31] King Theodahad also reminds the Senate that
"the peculiar product of Rome is eloquence." [32]

In a world so troubled there was need for peace and the
organization of the means of peace. The confusion and
terror of the invasions brought despair and hopelessness
to most who were alive then. To Catholic Christians they
seemed to spell the downfall of all things: the world was
literally too bad to mend. They turned to the ancient
prophets for words bitter enough to describe their desolation and found them in the pyramided woe of Joel (1:4):

[30] Procopius, V–II.
[31] *Cassiodori Variae*, IX, xxi (Hodgkin).
[32] *Ibid.*, X, vii.

"That which the palmer-worm hath left hath the locust eaten; and that which the locust hath left hath the canker-worm eaten; and that which the cankerworm hath left hath the caterpillar eaten." Yet when despair was very heavy upon them "God raised up" a great organizer whose labors brought new and greater strength than the Church had had before. That man was Benedict (c. 480–543), and the agency which accomplished the restoring of civilization was the Benedictine brotherhood which he founded. When one views in the perspective of their accomplishment the organizations which have resulted in good and the organizations which have resulted in evil, he may indeed very properly pause and ask himself if any more fruitful banding together of human beings has taken place on the earth than Benedict of Nursia (Benedict of Monte Cassino) brought about.

He was a Roman of a noble line and was brought up at Rome, St. Gregory says, "in the study of humanity, but as he saw many by reason of such learning fall into dissolute and lewd life, he drew back his foot." He fled from the wickedness of Rome and took refuge in a cave at Subiaco. We are dealing with great stretches of time in this study. From Pachomius' first monastery to Benedict's founding of the Benedictines is two hundred years, 330 to 529.

Benedict was a solitary in that cave at Subiaco for three years, it is said, when the monks of a neighboring monastery, Vicovaro, prevailed upon him to become their abbot. They found his insistence upon a strict adhesion to their undertaking more than they had bargained for and tried to poison him; and he, despairing of their genuineness, withdrew (528) with a small band of disciples to a rocky height which surmounted the ruins of the ancient Roman town Casinum (on the river Liris, eighty-five miles south-

east of Rome and seventy-five miles northwest of Naples).
Here he preached to the peasants whom he found sacrificing to Apollo on the altar which still stood to that deity
in a grove upon the mountain top. Benedict "beat in
pieces the idol, overthrew the altar, set fire on the woods,
and in the Temple of Apollo, he built the oratory of
St. Martin, and where the altar of the same Apollo was
he made an oratory of St. John: and by his continual
preaching he brought the people dwelling in those parts to
embrace the faith of Christ." [33] On this spot he erected
the great capital city of monasticism, Monte Cassino; a
house of nuns under Benedict's sister Scholastica was
formed also. Here was formulated that constitution and
by-laws of monasticism, the famous Rule of Benedict,
which borrowed from and supplanted the earlier rules of
Basil, Cassian, and Pachomius, and has ever since been
the basic directive law of monastic life in the West. With
significant and seemingly providential appropriateness, the
year of the founding of this great organization for religious and educational culture is usually written as
A.D. 529, the very year in which Justinian by imperial
edict closed the Academy of Plato at Athens and brought
to an end the teaching of pagan philosophy. The opening
of the one interlocked with the closing of the other.

The purpose of the monastic life, as the rule declares, is
to "form a school of divine service." It has been repeatedly pointed out by those who have written of the
Rule which Benedict formulated that it was of vast
advantage to him when he came to rule-making that he
was a Roman. His rule, unlike Basil's, is not a conversation about piety, and, unlike Pachomius' or Cassian's,
is not a body of admonitions to austerity: it is a code
sharply defining what is to be done and not done by every

[33] *The Dialogues of St. Gregory,* 68 (London: Philip Lee Warner).

member of a society whose only reason for being is the common cultivation of the good life as they know it. It is not a body of ascetic orders. Though it is definite, strict, and stern, it is not inhuman, but reasonable and even kindly in its demands. Roman practicality made it workable and was the essence of its acceptability through the years, and the explanation of its great usefulness.

The opening paragraphs of the Prologue state its purpose and its appeal. They are an invitation to holy living as Christians are called to it without any admixture of Cynic or Egyptian maceration of the flesh: "Listen, my son, and turn the ear of thine heart to the precepts of thy Master. Receive readily, and faithfully carry out the advice of a loving Father, so that by the work of obedience you may return to Him, whom you have left by the sloth of disobedience. For thee, therefore, whosoever thou be, my words are intended, who giving up thy own will, dost take the all-powerful and excellent arms of obedience to fight under the Lord Christ, the true King . . . If we would live in the shelter of this Kingdom we can reach it only by speeding on the way of good works. Let us, with the prophet, ask our Lord, and say to Him, Lord, who shall dwell in Thy tabernacle? or who shall rest on Thy holy hill? And when we have so asked, let us hear our Lord's answer, pointing out to us the way to His dwelling and saying: He that walketh without spot and worketh justice: he that speaketh truth in his heart: that hath not forged guile with his tongue: he that hath not done evil to his neighbor, and hath not taken up reproach against him . . . So questioning the Lord, brethren, we have heard on what conditions we may dwell in His temple; and if we fulfil these we shall be heirs of the Kingdom of heaven. Therefore must our hearts and bodies be prepared to fight under the holy obedience of His commands, and we must beg our Lord to supply by the help of His grace what by nature is not possible to us. And if fleeing from the pains of hell, we will to attain to life everlasting, we must, whilst time yet serves and whilst we live in the flesh and the light is still on our path, hasten to do now what will profit us for all eternity. We are therefore now about to institute a school for the service of God, in which we hope nothing harsh or burdensome will be ordained . . . In living our life, however, and by the growth of faith, when the heart has been enlarged, the path of God's commandments is run with unspeakable loving sweetness; so that never leaving His school, but persevering in the monastery until death in His teaching, we share by our patience in the sufferings of Christ, and so merit to be partakers of His kingdom." [34]

The monastic laws follow in seventy-three chapters. The abbot, to be fit to rule a monastery, should ever remember that he is called, and that the dread judgment of God will inquire as to his teaching and the obedience of his disciples. Let him make no distinction of persons in the monastery. He should always observe the apostolic rule which says, reprove, entreat, rebuke. Whenever any weighty matters have to be transacted, let him call together all the community and himself propose the matter for discussion. After hearing the advice of the brethren, let him consider it in his own mind and then do what he shall judge most expedient. Seventy-two instruments of good works are listed: first of all, to love the Lord God with all our heart, with all our soul, and with all our strength. Then to love our neighbor as ourself, to respect all men, to love fasting, not to depart from charity, not to be proud, not to be slothful, not to be a murmurer, to

[34] *The Rule of St. Benedict*, transl, and ed. by Cardinal Gasquet (Medieval Library).

watch over the actions of one's life every hour of the
day, to love the young, never to despair of God's mercy,
etc. The first degree of humility is prompt obedience. Because of the importance of silence, let leave to speak be
seldom given. The first step of humility is ever to be
mindful of all God's commandments. In the winter time
the brethren shall get up at the eighth hour of the night,
"so that having rested till a little after midnight, they
may rise refreshed; let the time that remains after Matins
be used by those brethren who need it, for the study of
the Psalter or lessons." Seven psalms are to be sung, and
three lessons read, at Matins. Seven times a day were
the Lord's praises to be sung: at Lauds, Prime, Tierce,
Sext, Nones, Evensong, and Compline. All shall sleep
in separate beds in a common dormitory. If any brother
does not amend after being often corrected for a fault
and even excommunicated, let him be corrected by stripes.
Let the prayers of the brethren be used; but, if he per-
sist, let the abbot use "the severing knife." No one, without leave of the abbot, shall presume to give, or receive,
or keep as his own anything whatever: neither book, nor
tablets, nor pen; nothing at all. Let the brethren so serve
one another that no one may be excused from the work
of the kitchen. Let special care be taken of the sick. Let
baths be given them as often as expedient, but to those
in health let them "be seldom permitted." The use of meat
is allowed to the sick, but not the well. There ought
always to be reading to the brethren as they eat, by one
appointed each week to do that. To satisfy just requirements at the daily meals, at the sixth and ninth hours, let
there be two cooked dishes; and if there be any fruit or
young vegetables these may be added as a third dish. The
allowance of bread shall be one pound a day. When the
work of the community is hard the food may be increased,

but always remember that nothing is more contrary to the Christian spirit than gluttony. "Although we read that 'wine is not the drink of monks at all,' yet, since in our days they cannot be persuaded of this, let us at least agree not to drink to satiety, but sparingly, 'because wine maketh even the wise to fall away.'"

After supper let them sit together while one reads to them the Collations or Lives of the Fathers or some other book to edify the hearers, but not the Heptateuch or Books of Kings, for these will not profit at that hour; but at other times they may be read. After this let them say Compline, after which no one shall be permitted to speak at all; anyone who does shall be severely punished.

Idleness is the enemy of the soul. Because this is so, the brethren ought to be occupied at specified times in manual labor, and at other fixed hours in holy reading. They are truly monks when they live by the labor of their hands as our Fathers and the Apostles did. Six hours a day seem to have been set apart for labor, most of which was work in the fields. On the days of Lent, let each one have some book from the library "which he shall read through carefully." Two seniors are to go about the monastery to see that no one is slothful in his reading. On Sundays all not assigned to special work shall have time for reading. Let all guests be received by the prior or the brethren as Christ would receive them, with all marks of charity; but monks shall not converse with them or receive letters from the outside world. Let such craftsmen as be in the monastery ply their trade in all lowliness of mind.

Anyone on coming to the religious life should not find the entrance easy. Let him knock for four or five days; and, if his patience overcome the harshness of his reception, let him then be taken to the guest house for a few

days. Let a senior explain to him the rigor and austerity
of our journey to God. If he promises to continue, at the
end of two months the Rule shall be read to him. If he
still persevere, the Rule shall be read to him again at the
end of six months, and again after four months more. If
then he promise to keep all the law, let him be taken into
the community, knowing that now he cannot leave the
community or withdraw his neck from the yoke of the
Rule. When he is admitted into the community, he shall
"in the Oratory, in the presence of all, promise before God
and His saints stability, amendment of manners, and
obedience, in order that if at any time he shall act otherwise he may know that he shall be condemned by Him
whom he mocketh." This vow he writes out; then he
begins the verse, "Uphold me, O Lord, according to thy
word, and I shall live, and let me not be confounded in my
expectation." This verse the community repeats three
times. Then the novice casts himself at the feet of all,
asking their prayers. He must first give all he possesses
to the poor or to the monastery.

If any noble or any poor man offer his son to God, the
parent shall make oblation for the child, wrapping the
promise and the hand of the boy in the altar cloth and
"thus dedicate him to God." They shall promise that they
will never give him any property whatever. Let children
be kept by all under discipline in every way. The abbot
is held to take the place of Christ. He is chosen by the
whole community because of his virtuous life and wisdom.
If anyone in the community perceive that another is moved
against him, he shall hasten to prostrate himself before
that other until he receive a blessing. If any is too proud
to do that, let him be expelled from the monastery. Do
thou who art hastening to the heavenly country accomplish
first "this little Rule written for beginners." For the per-

fection of holy life there are the New Testament and the Lives of the Fathers.

There are no elaborate provisions for learning here, only reference to a library and the provisions that the monks shall read, that inspectors shall go about to see that they do, and that little oblati shall be disciplined until they are fifteen years of age, by all. But the Rule obligated the monks to labor, and there was one form of labor which was greatly necessary to the world of that time and well suited to the possibilities, that was being developed in another much talked-of monastery in Italy just then, and which soon found its way into the Benedictine scheme of occupations. That monastery was Cassiodorus', and its preferred form of occupation for monks was the copying of manuscripts. Cassiodorus was a great figure in the life of that day. He was born of ancestors who had for three generations held important offices of state. His father was *Comes Privatarum Rerum* and *Comes Sacrarum Largitionum* or Count in charge of the domains and of the private charities of King Odoacer; that is, he held the two great financial offices under the throne. Magnus Aurelius Cassiodorus was born at Scylacium on the east coast of Italy about 480 and died in the monastery which he had established in the home of his birth, ninety-six years later. No other man of that century saw such changes as he did or took such a great part in them. He was trained in rhetoric and philosophy. His father held the great office of Praetorian Praefect under King Theodoric and made his son his Consiliarius. It fell to that young lawyer's lot to deliver an oration in praise of Theodoric which the king of the Goths and of the Romans listened to with such delight that he at once appointed the young man to the illustrious office of Quaestor, which made him a minister of State of the highest class. Cassiodorus once

wrote a letter for King Theodoric to sign in which he tells
the duties of that office which he held for many years.
"No minister has more reason to glory in his office than
the Quaestor, since it brings him into constant and intimate communication with ourselves. The Quaestor has
to learn our inmost thoughts, that he may utter them
to our subjects. Whenever we are in doubt as to any matter, we ask our Quaestor, who is the treasure-house of
public fame, the cupboard of laws; who has to be always
ready for a sudden call, and must exercise the wonderful
powers which, as Cicero has pointed out, are inherent in
the art of an orator. He should so paint the delights of
virtue and the terrors of vice, that his eloquence should
almost make the sword of the magistrate needless." [35]   In
514 Cassiodorus was elevated to the Consulship. In 515
he received the title of Patrician, and in 526, when
Theodoric died, Cassiodorus was Master of the Offices.
Then Cassiodorus is Praetorian Praefect for the Queen
Mother, Amalasuntha, and also for Theodahad after her.
In 538 he retired from office, arranged his letters, wrote a
little treatise on the Soul, and entered a monastery which
he himself founded on his ancestral estate at Scylacium.
Indeed, he founded two of them: one for cenobites, or
monks living in a community; the other for austere re-
cluses who wanted to live apart from their fellows. Cassiodorus made a Rule of his own, largely out of the
writings of John Cassian. Cassiodorus was a learned man
whose business had been to write state papers and make
public pleas for the measures of government all his life.
He also had commissioned himself to write a history of
the Goths. He was interested to spread learning through
the state, for before leaving office he had urged Pope
Agapetus (535–536) to found a school of Christian learn-

[35] *Cassiodori Variae*, VI, v (Hodgkin).

ing at Rome, like that of Alexandria or of Nisibis in Persia.
The wars between the armies of the Emperor and of the
Goths prevented that, but now that Cassiodorus had his
own means for assisting learning he incorporated it into
the monastic life and made it an essential part of the
Church's activity by making his monastery a place for the
making and using of books as well as a place of prayer.
Benedict had said, the monk shall work with his hands;
Cassiodorus said, the monk shall work with his hands
in the copying of manuscripts and the transcribing of
——books. So he founded a *scriptorium,* or writing room, and
set the man power of his monastery to work copying the
Scriptures, the Fathers, and the works of classical literature; for they had made him, and he too well knew their
worth to leave them out. Ponder the meaning of this.
Cassiodorus' invention of the scriptorium was no less
momentously significant to his day than Gutenberg's invention of the printing press was to his. The word
designating the one who copies a manuscript is *antiquarius.*
Hear what Cassiodorus says of him, and note how deeply
moved the inventor of the Scriptorium is at the thought
of the meaning of his invention. These are his words in
the thirtieth chapter of his *De Institutione Divinarum
Litterarum,* as Mr. Hodgkin translates them. The *antiquarius* "may fill his mind with the Scriptures while copying the sayings of the Lord. With his fingers he gives life
to men and arms them against the wiles of the devil. So
many wounds does Satan receive as the *antiquarius* copies
words of Christ. What he writes in his cell will be scattered far and wide over distant Provinces. Man multiplies
the heavenly words, and by a striking figure—if I may
dare so to speak—the three fingers of his hand express
the utterances of the Holy Trinity. The fast travelling
reed writes down the holy words, and thus avenges the

malice of the Wicked One, who caused a reed to be used
to smite the Head of the Saviour." [36] To set an example the
great man himself copied the Psalter, the Prophets, and
the Epistles, and he wrote books of commentary and prepared an outline summary of the three liberal arts, grammar, rhetoric, logic, and the four sciences, arithmetic,
geometry, music, and astronomy. He also wrote for his
monks a work on orthography to teach them how to spell.
Cassiodorus was for thirty years a monk and father of
monks at Vivaria.

While these great developments were going on in Italy,
there are significant records of effort both in Spain and
in Gaul. The second synod of Toledo (527 or 531) passed
the decree, "Those who as children are dedicated to the
clerical office, shall soon after receiving the tonsure or
after admission to the office of lector, be instructed by one
set over them in a building belonging to the Church, under
the eyes of the bishop." [37] The Christian academies of
Dumium, Valclara, Toledo, Saragossa, and Seville [38] bear
witness that that canon of the council did not become a
dead letter. The fourth synod of Toledo (633) a hundred
years after the first, reaffirmed the demand of the Church
for an instructed clergy by ordering that "priests shall be
instructed in the Holy Scriptures and in the canons and
edify all by their knowledge of the faith and by the purity
of their works." [39]

In Gaul the synod of Vaison in the year 529 decreed:
"All priests in the parishes must as already is the very
wholesome custom in all Italy receive the younger unmarried readers into their houses and instruct them in

[36] Hodgkin, *The Letters of Cassiodorus,* 58.
[37] Hefele, *History of the Councils,* IV, 149.
[38] Hume, *The Spanish People,* 60.
[39] Hefele, *loc. cit.*

the singing of psalms, in the Church lessons and in the
laws of the Lord, so that they may have able successors." [40]
Gregory of Tours, whose life extended from 538 to 594,
records in the preface to his History of the Franks that
many of his time were saying: "Woe to our day, since the
pursuit of letters has perished from among us and no one
can be found among the people who can set forth the deeds
of the present on the written page." But John Fiske, the
American historian, views that time differently. "The
darkest age," he writes, "was perhaps that of the wicked
Frankish queens, Brunhild and Fredegonda; but the
career of civilization was then far more secure than it
had been a thousand years earlier, in the age of Pericles,
when all Europe except a few Greek cities, was immersed
in dense barbarism." [41] A canon of the provincial council
of Narbonne in the year 589 directed that "no ignorant
person may be ordained priest or deacon. If he is already
ordained and refuses to learn more reading and the fulfilling of his office, he must be deprived of his stipend until
he learns. If he is obstinate he is to be shut up in a
monastery." [42] Even in that age in which men "were
tamed by the ax" more commonly than by schoolmasters,
Gregory of Tours finds it proper to remind his readers of
St. Jerome's order from heaven to abstain from "Cicero's
cleverness and Virgil's lies." "And bishop of God, whoever you may be, if our Martianus [Capella] has trained
you in the seven disciplines, that is, if he has taught you
by means of grammar to read, by dialectic to apprehend
the arguments in disputes, by rhetoric to recognize the
different meters, by geometry to comprehend the measurement of the earth and of lines, by astrology to contemplate

[40] Hefele, *op. cit.*, IV, 169.
[41] Fiske, *Essays, Historical and Literary,* II, 28.
[42] Hefele, *op. cit.*, IV, 423.

the paths of the heavenly bodies, by arithmetic to understand the parts of numbers, by harmony to fit the modu-
lated voice to the sweet accents of the verse; if in all this
you are practiced so that my style will seem rude, even
so I beg of you do not efface what I have written. But if
anything in these books pleases you I do not forbid your
writing it in verse provided my work is left safe." [43]

The Church was the only institution that lived on
through that awful period of disorder. It alone undertook to and succeeded in molding the barbarians into the
form of civilization. The bishop was the guardian of his
community. Very properly could Chilperic say, "There is
no king but the bishops," for the bishop was guide,
counsellor, and defender of his people. Through wars,
pestilence, and famine his heroic work went on. He built
the churches, instructed and heartened the clergy, and
provided the schools when there were schools. It is
true that literature and theology shrank to narrow dimensions and knowledge of every kind almost disappeared;
but the Latin Bible did not cease to be read nor the
services of the Church to be performed in the Latin
tongue. That the language of France is a Romanic instead of a Germanic tongue is a proof that instruction
did not fail.

The monks of Monte Cassino are included among those
who must be accounted blessed because they have no
annals. They lived their life according to the Rule.
History does not concern itself to tell how day follows
day in uninterrupted orderliness of prayer, work, psalms,
and listening to the reading of a brother. Even the sending away of a group to found another monastery did not
at first vary their days, for Benedict founded but one

---

[43] Gregory of Tours, *History of the Franks*, transl. Ernest Brehaut
(New York: Columbia University Press, 1916), 248.

other monastery, Terracina, after coming to Monte Cassino. But there was trouble coming up the horizon. In 568 the Lombards poured through the Alps into Italy. "Albin, king of the Lombards . . . abandoned his country," says Gregory of Tours, "and set out for Italy with all the Lombard people. They put their army in motion and went with their wives and children, purposing to remain there. They entered the country and spent seven years chiefly in wandering through it, despoiling the churches, killing the bishops, and bringing the land under their control." [44]

The Lombards did not cease from plundering after seven years. In 590 a savage band of them under their Duke Zotto fell upon Monte Cassino by night and sacked it. The monks all made their escape, gathering up and taking with them the only things of value in the monastery, the copy of the Rule which Benedict had written out by his own hand, and certain other writings, a pound of bread and a measure of wine and perhaps the pallets on which they slept; they made their way to Rome and were housed by the Pope in a monastery beside the Church of St. John Lateran.

It was not until one hundred and thirty years had rolled around that a little band of monks again climbed the mountain under their leader Petronax and, by advice of Pope Gregory II, reconsecrated the ground and settled themselves as monks of St. Benedict in the spot which was to be the monastic capital of the world. If you go there today on a pious pilgrimage to one of earth's holiest places, the monks will show you some chambers in the lower basement of the monastery which were discovered a half-century ago entirely filled up with earth and ashes, and were carefully excavated and restored and decorated by artist brothers from Vienna with great

[44] Gregory of Tours, *op. cit.*, 95.

fresco scenes from the life of St. Benedict. These rooms, the monk guides will tell you, are believed to be the veritable first monastery of St. Benedict. Monte Cassino has been the mother house of the Benedictines ever since their return in 720.

But great developments took place shortly after they were driven to take up their abode at Rome. Gregory the Great (c. 540–604) was, against his will, made Pope in 590, and at once set about his work of organizing the Church throughout the world, and by missionary enterprise converting the heathen. He was a Roman of a noble house which owned great estates in Sicily. He had been carefully schooled at Rome and "was so versed in grammar, dialectic, and rhetoric that he was believed second to none in the city." [45] In 573 he filled the great office which Cassiodorus had occupied of Praefect of Rome. In that capacity he wore the Imperial purple, rode in a four-horse chariot, and presided over the Senate. Then one day he gave up all his worldly glory, put off his Imperial purple, put on the coarse dress of the Benedictines, and became a monk. He founded and endowed six Benedictine monasteries in Sicily and gave the rest of his property to the poor—all save his ancestral palace on the Coelian Hill, which he turned into a monastry dedicated to St. Andrew, and himself entered as the humblest of the brothers in it. That was perhaps in 575. For three years he led the life of religious quiet there. Bede's story of him seeing fair-haired slave boys for sale as he walked about the city and, upon being told that they were Angles, resolving to make angels of them, belongs to that period. He sought and obtained from Pope Benedict permission personally to go and convert Britain, and had advanced three days on his journey when he was overtaken and called back to Rome by messengers from the Pope. He

[45] Gregory of Tours, *op. cit.*, 227–228.

was appointed "seventh deacon" of the Church of Rome,
and in the following spring sent as *Apocrisiarius,* or Papal
ambassador, to the Imperial Court at Constantinople.
He was in residence there for some six years. In 586
he returned to Rome and was made abbot of St. Andrew's
monastery. In Constantinople he had begun, and here
he finished, his commentary on the book of Job which
goes by the name of the *Magna Moralia.* Gregory wrote
a biography of St. Benedict. So completely did he embrace the monastic life that when he became Pope he
would have none but monks and priests in his household,
and with them he led the life in common of a strictly
ascetical monastic company. He insisted upon pure
Latinity of speech on the part of all associated with him,
and employed it himself in writing that vast collection
of Letters which Hodgkin finds not far surpassed by the
great Codes of Theodosius and Justinian.[46] In energy,
spirit, and accomplishment he was the greatest of all the
Popes who have led the Church. He denied to the Metropolitan of Constantinople the title of Patriarch of all the
world and by so doing laid the foundation of an independent western hierarchy. He consciously subordinated the
civil to the churchly power and, carrying on the work of
Ambrose of Milan, he set a standard for the guidance of
Popes. He it was who made the organized Church of the
West the mighty power it was in the Middle Ages. He
mediated between the Lombards, who held almost all
Italy, and the Emperor, and though living "between
the swords of the Lombards" he persuaded them after
long effort to make peace. He is called "the defender of
Rome," "the protector of Italy," but most of all he is
the missionary to the barbarians. The Roman state did
not extend far to the west in his day. Not much of Italy

[46] *Italy and Her Invaders,* V-vi-7.

was held by the exarch who directed affairs from Ravenna; Britain had long since been given up (439); Gaul was ruled by the Merovingian descendants of Clovis, and Narbonnese Gaul and Spain by the Visigoths. The church of Spain had just three years before been persuaded from Arianism to Catholicism and had to be watchfully guided; the church of Gaul was sinking into barbarism and had to be brought to hold national and provincial councils to strengthen the faith and correct abuses; the church of Africa had to be built up after its centuries-long struggle with the heretical Donatists, and the people of England had to be converted from paganism. That was done by Gregory sending Abbot Augustine of St. Andrew's monastery and forty Benedictine monks to them; but before we speak of them let us tell of one other great matter which Gregory the Great effected: the improvement in the service of the Church. He made over the Roman Liturgy, introducing the "plain song" to take the place of the earlier Ambrosian chants, and he established and endowed two school for training in church singing, the one at the Lateran and the other at St. Peter's. He himself trained his choir and held and sometimes brought down the rod upon the backs of too inattentive youthful singers.

Gregory the Great sent two missions to Britain: Augustine and his company in 596, and Melitus, Paulinus, and their companions in 601. He had wanted to go himself and had gone, but had been called back. He cannot have been altogether heartened by the start which his deputy, Abbot Augustine, made. It seems that Augustine and his forty monks must have travelled by sea to Marseilles. There, says Bede, "they were seized with a sudden fear and began to think of returning home rather than proceed to a barbarous, fierce and unbelieving nation to

whose very language they were strangers." They sent
Augustine back "to obtain of the holy Gregory that
they should not be compelled to undertake so dangerous,
toilsome, and uncertain a journey." [47] Gregory sent him
back with a letter addressed "to the brethren going to
England" whose first sentence is: "Since it had been
better not to have begun what is good than to return
back from it when begun, you must, most beloved sons,
fulfil the good work which with the help of the Lord you
have begun." [48] They went on, and in the autumn of
597 landed upon the island of Thanet in the kingdom
of Kent, whose king was Ethelbert, a pagan, but whose
queen was Bertha, a Christian Frank. In the Teutonic
royal town, Canterbury, Augustine found a broken-down
church which had not been used for a hundred years.
He and his companions were assigned a dwelling-place
and sustenance, and immediately began the daily life of
prayer, watching, and fasting of a transplanted Italian
Benedictine monastry, which they were. King Ethelbert
and large numbers of his people were converted to Christianity, and Abbot Augustine made the long journey across
Gaul to Arles, where Bishop Virgilius, Pope Gregory's
representative, consecrated him Bishop of Canterbury.
Augustine converted Kent and founded the see of Canterbury. So great was his success that in 601 he asked for
a reinforcement and Gregory sent a second company:
Melitus, an abbot, probably of St. Andrew's monastery,
who was soon made Bishop of London; Justus, who became Bishop of Rochester; Rufinianus, the third abbot
of St. Augustine's monastery at Canterbury, and Paulinus,
who went to Northumbria in 625 and was there for eight

---

[47] Bede, *Ecclesiastical History*, I, xxiii.
[48] Gregory the Great, Epistle LI, in *Nicene and Post-Nicene Fathers,*
etc., Vol. XII.

years preaching and teaching. There were others in the second company of reinforcers, no doubt. It is important to note that these were markedly capable men.

Before the coming of Augustine—long before it, in the days when the Romans ruled in Britain—there had been some Christian churches in the land. Very little is known of those earliest British churches. Three of them were represented in the Council of Arles in 314. In 357 the British bishops protested against the introduction of an Arianizing creed. In 359 several bishops from Britain were in the Council at Rimini. After the Romans had withdrawn from Britain, Pelagius, a British monk, developed and spread the heresy that bears his name, and Germanus was twice (427 and 429) sent over to correct the clergy.[49] But for one hundred and fifty years the land of Britain was overrun by Teutonic invaders, and of those hundred and fifty years there is no history. Augustine introduced the alphabet, and records, for the Anglo-Saxons did not have them. Through him the Latin language comes back in the worship of the Church, in the writing of reports and letters and in literature; through him the organization of life, which is called civilized, with its manifold activities returns.[50] Among other benefits which King Ethelbert conferred upon his nation was this: "by the advice of wise persons he introduced judicial decrees after the Roman model; which, being written in English, are still kept and observed by them." [51]

Now, though Augustine planted the faith in Kent, he met with difficulties when he sought to bring into one administration the Celtic Christians who were beyond its

[49] The Abbe Duchesne as quoted by Cardinal Gasquet in *The Mission of St. Augustine*, 6.

[50] See Cardinal Gasquet, *The Mission of St. Augustine*.

[51] Bede, *Ecclesiastical History*, II, v.

borders. Here we come upon one of the most astonishing
facts of history. The original church of Wales, planted
in Roman days, had not been crushed out by the Anglo-
Saxon invaders—they had not as yet been able to get
so far west—but instead had been greatly strengthened
and renewed by monastic influences brought perhaps by
St. Patrick from Lérins and by others also, for that there
was a vital connection with Lérins is shown by the fact
that its abbot in 433 was the British monk Faustus.

The people of the Celtic countries lived in a tribal, not
in a city, organization of life.[52] The bishops of the Roman
Church headed the churches of cities; but among the
Celtic peoples the monastery takes the place of the
bishopric as the central organization of the faithful.
There was, therefore, in Wales and in Ireland an enormous development of monasteries, in Wales, Bangor,
Llancarvan, Llantwit, Caerleon, St. David's, etc. The
movement started in South Wales, where the monastery of
St. Illtyd on Caldey island became a great school in the
early sixth century, much like Lérins itself. Bede describes the monastery of Bangor as a place where there
were so many monks "that the monastery was divided
into seven parts, with a ruler over each, none of those
parts contained less than 300 men, who all lived by the
labor of their hands." [53]

Augustine in 603, with the assistance of King Ethelbert, "drew together to a conference the bishops, or
doctors of the next province of the Britons," at a place
called Augustine's Oak, to invite them to join in the
common labor of preaching the Gospel, and to keep the
feast of Easter at the same time as the Romans. They
said they could not depart from their ancient customs.

[52] Dawson, *The Making of Europe*, 196.
[53] Bede, *op. cit.*, II, ii.

A second meeting was held to which "seven bishops of the Britons" came, "and many most learned men" from the monastery of Bancornburg presided over by the Abbot Dinooth. Augustine was seated when they came and did not stand up. That conference did not bring about the unity of the Church. Augustine's successor, Laurentius, also tried in vain (605) to convert "the ancient inhabitants of Britain and the Scots who inhabit the island of Ireland" from their uncanonical ways.

Bishop Paulinus, who had in 625 accompanied Ethelberga, the daughter of the King of Kent, and performed her marriage ceremony to Edwin, King of Northumbria, labored long in vain there, but in 627 baptized the king and a great number of the people. Edwin was slain in battle in 633, and Paulinus and the Queen returned to Kent. There was much slaughter in Northumbria, but Oswald, "a man beloved of God," finally became King. He, "being desirous that all his nation should receive the Christian faith," sent to "the elders of the Scots" from whom he had received baptism when in banishment, for a bishop to instruct his people. Bishop Aidan was sent, and King Oswald gave him Lindisfarne for his episcopal seat, a place like an island when separated from the mainland twice a day by the tides. Here Aidan preached in the language of "the Scots," and the King himself, standing beside him, translated what was said into the language of the Angles. Aidan had been trained at Iona. Oswald was killed in battle in 642 after reigning nine years. Aidan died in 651. After him Finan and after him Colman was bishop. Under Colman a great controversy arose about the observance of Easter, since the men of Iona celebrated it on one date and the men of Rome on another. "This reached the ears of King Oswy and his son, Alfrid; for Oswy having been instructed and baptized by the Scots, and being perfectly skilled in their language, thought nothing better than what they taught. But Alfrid, having been instructed in Christianity by Wilfrid, a most learned man, who had first gone to Rome to learn the ecclesiastical doctrine, and spent much time at Lyons with Dalfin, archbishop of France, . . . rightly thought that this man's doctrine ought to be preferred before all the traditions of the Scots." [54] King Oswy, the brother of Oswald, observed that those who served God should follow the same rule of life and held a conference to listen to the arguments; the results were inconclusive, the contention grew, and King Oswy summoned the Synod of Whitby in 664 and decided that the claims of Rome were superior. The Scots gave up the struggle in England: some, like Cuthbert of Lindisfarne, accepted the new order, but most went back to Ireland.

The story of the early church of Ireland has never been adequately told, and that must be because it is too wonderful to be told, for the Irish are not lacking in power to tell such tales as can be. Ireland is an exception. It was never under Roman rule, and invaders did not harry it until 795. But it was so far outside the Roman Empire that it was not swept into the Church with the crowds that followed Constantine. There were a few Christians in Ireland from earlier days, offshoots of the first planting of Christianity in Great Britain; but the faith was firmly planted and the Church organized there, Professor Bury believes, "mainly by one man, a Roman citizen of Britain," Patrick, the son of Calpurnius, decurion of a Roman town.[55] Patrick's dates, though somewhat doubtful, are given as 389–461. Being the son of a deacon, he was taught the Scriptures. When he was

[54] Bede, *Ecclesiastical History,* III, xxv.
[55] J. B. Bury, *The Life of St. Patrick,* II, 16.

sixteen a band of Irish pirates fell upon his town and carried him off as a captive "to the ultimate places of the earth"—that is, to Ireland. There he was a slave for six years; then he ran away and got aboard a ship which landed on the coast of Gaul. He made his way to Lérins and for a few years was a monk in that great mother monastery of the West. Then he went home to his father's house in Britain and dreamed that he heard voices in Ireland, where he had been a slave, calling, "We pray thee, holy youth, to come and walk amongst us as before." Dreams, then as now, were but reëditions of the dreamers' waking thoughts. Patrick's call was clear, but first he must go back to Gaul to prepare for his mission. He went to Auxerre, was shortly made a deacon by its bishop, Amator, and spent fourteen years, most of it perhaps in study, before starting on his life work. In 429 Germanus of Auxerre was sent to England to look after the Pelagian heresy, and shortly after, Pope Celestine detailed Bishop Palladius to direct affairs in Ireland. Palladius died within a year; Germanus consecrated Patrick Bishop of Ireland, and he started to his field in 432.[56] There were no cities in Ireland; there were tribes of clansmen—that is, vast patriarchal families ruled over by kings, each tribe owning its own land. A church had to have a site, and priests land to till, in order to live; so the chief men of the tribe had to be converted, for they alone could allot land. Patrick went among the people of Ulidia, Meath, and Connaught preaching, con-

---

[56] Monsignor Gradwell holds that Martin of Tours was his uncle, and that he was at Marmoutier and Lérins from 394 to 418. He thinks he was at Auxerre from 418 to 429 with Germanus. See his *Succat; or, The Story of Sixty Years of the Life of St. Patrick* (London: Burns & Oates). See also the "Life of Patrick" in the *Lives of Saints from the Book of Lismore*. Edited by Whitley Stokes, D.C.L., in *Anecdota Oxoniensia*. Mediaeval and Modern Series, Part V.

futing the Druids, baptizing, and organizing churches.
After eight years of most successful work he went to
Rome to report to and enlist the encouragement of Pope
Leo the great. When he came back he founded the
monastery of Armagh (444). The monastery is described
as a Great House for the monks to dwell in, 27 feet
in diameter, a kitchen 17 feet and an oratory 7 feet in
diameter, all enclosed in a circular space 140 feet in
diameter, surrounded by an earthen wall.[57] This was the
metropolitan centre of Ireland. Patrick preached also in
Leinster and Munster. He says he baptized thousands
and ordained ministers of religion everywhere. Monasteries for men and for women were established. The
lands for these were given by the heads of tribes, sometimes with the understanding that the abbot should be
selected from the family assisting the foundation, but always that the monastery should care for the religious
services of the tribe and usually that it should educate
without cost the sons of tribesmen who should wish to
devote them to the life of religion. Monastic foundations
were even more important than churches for the propa-
gating of Christianity and the educating of the clergy.
Patrick made Latin the language of the Church of Ireland and made the young Church he founded a part of
the Roman Church. This is the Book of Lismore's summary of the character of Patrick "A true man, surely,
was that man from purity of nature like a patriarch. A
true pilgrim, like Abraham. Gentle, forgiving of heart,
like Moses. A praiseful psalmist, like David. A student (?) of wisdom and knowledge, like Solomon. A
chosen vessel for proclaiming righteousness, like Paul
the Apostle. A man full of grace and favour of the Holy
Spirit, like John. A fair garden with plants of virtues.

[57] Bury, *op. cit.*, 156.

A vine-branch with fruitfulness. A flashing fire with the fervour of the warming and heating of the Sons of Life, for kindling and illuminating charity. A lion for great strength and might. A dove for gentleness and simplicity. A serpent for cunning and prudence. A man mild, gentle, humble, tender to the sons of Life [but] rough, ungentle to the sons of Death. A slave in labour and service to Christ. A king in rank and might for binding and loosing, for freeing and enslaving, for quickening and killing." [58] After him that Church, shut off so far from Rome by the tumults on the Continent, fell away and developed features of its own. "Monasticism, an institution which appears to have been intensely attractive to the temper of the people, ran riot, we might say, at the expense of ecclesiastical organization." [59] When St. Patrick died the Druids seem to have made heavy and pretty successful efforts to reëstablish the old Irish religion; but a new crusade for Christianity started, help from Wales giving it power and determination. Finnian of Clonard (c. 470–548) was the master-worker of this new movement which led to the founding of that great number of monasteries which made Ireland so serviceable and so famous in the next three centuries. Finnian had fellowed with St. David and Gildas in Wales. When he came back to Ireland he founded the monastery of Clonard in 520. Three thousand monks, it is said, received instruction there. [60]

[58] Section 597, p. 166, *Lives of Saints from the Book of Lismore,* edited by Whitley Stokes, D.C.L., in Anecdota Oxoniensia, Mediaeval and Modern Series, Part V, Oxford, 1890.

[59] Bury, *op. cit.,* 183.

[60] Reversus in Clonardiam   Trium virorum millium
Ad cathedram lecturae   Sorte fit doctor humilis
Opponit delegentiam   Verbi his fudit fluvium
Ad studium scripturae   Ut fons emanans rivulis.
(Hyde, *A Literary History of Ireland,* 196.)

Clonard looked more like Pachomius' or St. Martin's original monastery than like St. Benedict's Monte Cassino. It was a collection of little huts "of clay and wattles made," surrounded by a ditch and an earthen wall. Twelve of Finnian's scholars carried on the work in which they had been schooled, so greatly that they were called the Twelve Apostles of Ireland. What was that work? The answer is almost too unexpected to be believed. The native pagan priests of Ireland cultivated learning and held an exalted place in the esteem of the people. The Christians challenged them and had to meet them on their own ground, skill for skill. Remarkable stories are told of the Druids; they were exhaustless tale-tellers who imparted their stories to their pupils with the injunction that they must never be written down. These stories were kept in their original exactness and repeated word for word by experts in menmonic proficiency. The thing was a fine art guarded and preserved by a corporation, the File which was divided into ten classes from the *Oblar,* who knew but seven stories, to the *Ollam,* who knew three hundred and fifty. The bards invented; the File never invented, it remembered. With the coming of Christianity and new practices this vast literature was in time committed to manuscripts. So numerous are those ancient Irish writings that it is estimated that about a thousand octavo volumes would be needed to publish them.[61] The Christian priests and monks did not have to master and preserve that pagan learning, but they had to offer proficiency in their own kind to win and hold their people. The standards of public opinion were high in Ireland, far higher than in the invasion-racked countries of the Continent. Even in the dreadful sixth century the study of both Greek and Latin was vigorously pursued there.

[61] Jusserand, *A Literary History of the English People,* I, 11.

In the words of Hauréau: "Until the end of the eighth
century the treasure of knowledge amassed by the pagan
and Christian Scots was preserved intact; and at a time
when the remainder of the Roman world was brutalized by
conquest to the point of forgetting the simplest elements
of Latin grammar, the schools of Ireland dwelt in peace
and flourished and famous masters instructed a multitude
of youth not only in the eloquence and poesy of the Latins
but in the grammar and philosophy of the Greeks. Bede
is a witness that if any cleric or noble Briton was anxious
to free himself from the yoke of ignorance he crossed
the straits and presented himself for study in the schools
of Ireland." [62] These schools were monasteries and monastic schools such as Patrick founded at Armagh, Finnian at Clonard. Of his twelve disciples, Kieran founded
Clonmacnoise in 541; Columba, Derry in 546; Brendan,
Clonfert in 552; Comgall, Bangor in 552; and Finnian,
the disciple, founded Moville c. 540, and Columba, Durrow c. 553; Glasnevin, Derry, Kells, Arran, Boyle,
Swords, Raphoe, Tory Island, Drumcliff are a few names
of other foundations whose total number was far beyond
any reckoning we can now make of them. Aldhelm is
responsible for the statement that ships brought legions
of students to Ireland, and like bees they flocked to the
schools of Lismore, Downpatrick, Clonfert, Clonmacnoise,
Bangor, Clonard, and Armagh.[63] Even the Franks made
an early and long-lasting connection with the schools of
Ireland.[64] At Armagh it is said that over seven thousand students were gathered, and at Clonfert three
thousand assembled. Kildare was founded c. 467 by

[62] Hauréau, *Singularités historique et littéraires,* 4.
[63] Hauréau, *op. cit.,* 6.
[64] Ozanam, *History of Civilization in the Fifth Century,* 1–33 (London,
1868).

Bridget. Its special fame was that of an early arts and crafts school which produced all kinds of church equipment, chalices, bells, shrines, etc. The Book of Durrow in Trinity College, Dublin, is thought to have been transcribed by Columba himself; the Book of Kells, one of the most beautiful manuscripts in existence, was as its name indicates made in the monastery of Kells in Meath. From Clonard there still exists St. Aileran's *Mystical Interpretation of the Ancestry of Our Lord Jesus Christ,* written before 664, found at St. Gall in Switzerland and published by the Benedictines in the seventeenth century.

The Irish have never stayed at home. In that early day they went as missionaries to nearly every country of Europe. In 563 Columba left Derry and with a band of brother monks went across the sea to the island of Iona off the coast of Scotland and there established the great monastery of Iona which was the chief powerhouse of Celtic Christianity. Columba and his monks lived on the sea, not only in the fog of "the salt main on which the sea-gulls cry," but in boats, little and big, incessantly going up and down it, for it was their highway and they were hardy sailors. They went far afield to preach, to the Orkneys and Faroes and even to Iceland. The mission to Northumbria came from Iona, and the saintly Aidan whom Bishop Lightfoot beheld as the apostle of England, the converter of the English race. Scotland was of course the special object of Columba's converting zeal. There were many monasteries that looked up to Iona as their mother. The island took on a peculiar sanctity when Columba died in 597 (the year that Augustine landed in England) and was buried in its soil. Pilgrims came to die there and through the world Iona was "the holy isle." Repeatedly it was plundered by Norse sea-rovers. In 1203 the Benedictines, taking over the remnant of the Celtic community, established a house of their order there. This again was ordered dismantled by the Convention of Estates of Scotland in 1561. In that spot "the seeds of the word of God" were sown on paper as well as in the hearts of men. "And this great favour has also been granted to this same man of blessed memory, that although he lived in this small and remote isle of the British ocean, his name has deserved to be honourably made known, not only throughout the whole of our Ireland and Britain, largest of the islands of the whole world, but to reach even as far as triangular Spain, and the Gauls, and Italy, that lies beyond the Pennine Alps, even to the City of Rome itself, which is the head of all cities." [65]

In 573 Columbanus went forth from the Irish monastery of Bangor with twelve companion monks on a missionary journey to the continent of Europe, the first of a long line of Irish missionaries to the mainland. Columbanus was born in Leinster in 543, the year St. Benedict died. Under Comgall at Bangor he not only became a fervently pious monk but learned Latin, Greek, and even, it is said, Hebrew. At the age of thirty he was ordained a priest and set forth to the mission field with twelve companion monks, landing in Gaul and going to Sigibert, King of Austrasia, who urged Columbanus to settle in his kingdom. They settled at Anagrates. Later they were given the Roman ruins at Lexovium and, moving there, established the monastery of Luxeuil. In Gaul all abbots were subject to the bishops of their diocese. In Ireland it had perhaps been the other way around. Columbanus refused to submit himself to any one; and there was strife too over the Irish tonsure which he and

[65] Adamnan, *The Life of St. Columba*, transl. W. Huyshe, 235.

his monks wore and the date on which they celebrated Easter. But Luxeuil grew; so many monks came that a new monastery had to be formed for them, Fontaines. Rules became necessary and Columbanus made them: obedience, absolute and non-resisting, to the abbot; silence; a minimum of vegetable food, cabbages, beans and bread with fish once in a while, to be eaten in the evening; poverty, and the complete renunciation of ambition and all vanity; chastity. In addition, so many psalms were to be sung—seventy-five on great festivals and thirty-six on minor ones—that ever-singing choirs seem to have been brought from Britain and instituted at Luxeuil. Other rules dealt with austerity. Every monk was to work daily at plowing, mowing, cutting wood. Every one was to fast and pray and read and study daily. There were punishments for faults too, such as Columbanus knew at Bangor, ending in flogging and solitary confinement.[66] Columbanus, an entirely upright and fearless man, corrected the unmoralities of the king, and after twenty years at Luxueil was driven into exile. With many stops and changes of plan he made his way finally to Agilulf, King of the Lombards at Milan, who, being told of Luxeuil, offered him Bobbio, a place with similar Roman ruins. In them Columbanus founded the great monastery of Bobbio. There the noble Irish civilizer died in 615; but the monasteries which he founded lived on and expanded in usefulness. Luxeuil became, Montalembert says, the monastic capital of the Gauls, the most celebrated and most frequented school of Christendom in the seventh century. The children of the Frankish and Burgundian nobles crowded it, and the cities sent their youth to it for instruction.[67] Of Bobbio it is enough to say

[66] Holmes, *The Christian Church of Gaul,* 540.
[67] Montalembert, *The Monks of the West,* II, 463 (London, 1861).

that Muratori has listed a long catalogue of manuscripts which it possessed in the tenth century.[68] Of hardly less importance was St. Gall on Lake Constance, which took the name of its founder, disciple of Columbanus and apostle to Switzerland. The monastic library of St. Gall has delivered up a manuscript of Priscian with Gaelic notes. Some two hundred manuscripts of the Irish monks, of a date earlier than 1000, still survive.[69] From Ireland came Fridolin who established a monastery on the Rhine, and St. Virgil, Bishop of Salzburg. A veritable stream of Irish missionary monks went forth to Wales, Britain, Gaul, Germany, Switzerland, and Italy, each of them an apostle of learning as well as an apostle of religion.

Eleven bishops in all owed their consecration to Augustine; six of them were Italian, five were Englishmen. Boniface of Dunwich, the last of them, died in 669, and the Gregorian mission was ended. In that same year came to England the monk Theodore of Tarsus, "a man well instructed in worldly and divine literature as also in Greek and Latin." [70] Sent by Pope Vitalian to be Archbishop of Canterbury, "this was the first archbishop whom all the English church obeyed." The Abbot Hadrian, equally skilled in Greek and Latin, came with him, "and forasmuch as both of them were . . . well read both in sacred and in secular literature, they gathered a crowd of disciples, and there daily flowed from them rivers of knowledge to water the hearts of their hearers; and together with the books of holy writ, they also taught them the arts of ecclesiastical poetry, astronomy, and arithmetic. A testimony of which is that there

[68] Drane, *Christian Schools and Scholars*, 255 (London, 1881); Tiraboschi, *Storia della Letteratura*, 1-464.
[69] Edgar, *Early Scottish Education*, 9.
[70] Bede, *Ecclesiastical History*, IV, i.

are still living at this day some of their scholars, who are
as well versed in the Greek and Latin tongues as in their
own, in which they were born. Nor were there ever
happier times since the English came into Britain; for,
their kings being brave men and good Christians, they
were a terror to all barbarous nations, and the minds
of all men were bent upon the joys of the heavenly kingdom of which they had just heard; and all who desired
to be instructed in sacred reading had masters at hand
to teach them." [71] Theodore visited all parts ordaining
bishops where they were needed. Over the see of
Rochester he placed Putta, "extraordinarily skilful in
the Roman style of Church music, which he had learned
from the disciples of the holy Pope Gregory." Others
who were familiar with Gregorian music at Rome were
at work in Britain.

A young English noble, Benedict Biscop, is first seen
in Bede's story on his way to Rome with Wilfrid, the son
of King Oswy. On his way back he spent two years at
Lérins, where he took the vow. He is present at the
synod of Heathfield, called and presided over by Archbishop Theodore in 680. This time Bede calls him "the
most reverend Abbot Biscop . . . For the said Benedict
having built a monastery in Britain, in honour of the
most blessed prince of the apostles at the mouth of the
river Were, went to Rome with Ceolfrid, his companion
and fellow-laborer in that work, who was after him abbot
of the same monastery; he had been several times before
at Rome, and was now honourably received by Pope
Agatho of blessed memory; from whom he also obtained
the confirmation of the immunities of this monastery,
being a bull of privilege signed by apostolical authority,
pursuant to what he knew to be the will and grant of

[71] Bede, *op. cit.*, IV, ii.

King Egfrid, by whose consent and gift of land he had built that monastery." [72] It is well to be as concrete and full about this monastery as we can be, for it is one of the holy places not only of the Church but of civilization. Benedict Biscop founded it in 674. Five times he made the long, hard perilous journey to Rome, bringing back manuscripts both of sacred and of secular literature for the library of the monastery he had founded. Among them was the Bible which Jerome had translated and edited. Of that Ceolfrid prepared three copies, one of which he returned as a votive offering to Pope Gregory in 716. It is now in the Laurentian Library in Florence, the oldest complete Latin codex. In 682 King Egfrid was so well pleased with the monastery of St. Peter at Wearmouth that he gave an additional grant of land for another monastery on condition that the two should be one and "no man should ever try to divide these two monasteries." [73] At a distance of about five miles from St. Peter's at Wearmouth, the monastery of St. Paul at Jarrow was built in 683. There the Father of English history, the greatest scholar in Europe of that day, a master of Latin style and all his life a quiet, careful student, spent his days and did his work. At the end of his greatest book you will find these words: "Thus much of the ecclesiastical history of Britain and more especially of the English nation, as far as I could learn either from the writings of the ancients or the traditions of our ancestors, or of my knowledge, has, with the help of God, been digested by me, Bede, the servant of God, and priest of the monastery of the blessed apostles, Peter and Paul which is at Weremouth and Jarrow; who being born in the territory of that same monastery, was given, at seven

[72] Bede, *op. cit.*, IV, xviii.
[73] Bede, *Lives of the Holy Abbots of Wearmouth and Jarrow*, 7.

DIAGRAM
to show the
CHIEF HOUSES OF THE
UNREFORMED BENEDICTINE
ORDER IN MEDIEVAL ENGLAND

From *Documents Illustrating the History of Civilization in Medieval England* (1066–1500), by R. Trevor Davies, M.A., by permission of Methuen & Co.

years of age, to be educated by the most reverend Abbot
Benedict, and afterwards by Ceolfrid; and spending all
the remaining time of my life in that monastery, I
wholly applied myself to the study of Scripture, and
amidst the observance of regular discipline, and the
daily care of singing in the church, I always took delight
in learning, teaching, and writing. In the nineteenth year
of my age, I received deacon's orders; in the thirtieth,
those of the priesthood, both of them by the ministry of
the most reverend Bishop John and by order of the Abbot
Ceolfrid. From which time, until the fifty-ninth year
of my age I have made it my business, for the use of me
and mine, to compile out of the works of the venerable
Fathers, and to interpret and explain according to their
meaning these following pieces." (Here follows a list
of some forty-five works, most of them exegetical, but
among others a book of hymns, a book of epigrams in
verse, a book on the Nature of Things, a book of the
Times, a book on the Art of Poetry, "The Ecclesiastical
History of Our Island and Nation," "The History of the
Abbots of This Monastery in Which I Rejoice to Serve
the Divine Goodness," the book of the Life and Passion
of St. Anastasius, "which was ill translated from the Greek
and worse amended by some unskilful person, I have
corrected as to the sense." Also the Life of the Holy
Father Cuthbert and a book of Orthography. Besides
there are translations into Anglo-Saxon of the Psalter
and the Gospels and a Book of Homilies which was much
used in the Middle Ages.)

Bede (c. 673–735) is the highest expression of early
Benedictine monastic learning. The conditioning of a
single greatly useful life has sometimes been so important to the history of men that, if a whole system of
instruction had done nothing more than that, it would

not be too high a price to pay for its service. The Benedictine order had done vastly more than that when it
produced the greatest of the students of its training. It
is unfair to the seventh century, Professor W. P. Ker
thinks, not to take Bede's work as representing the
learning and the intelligence of his time. That is the
sounder way to interpret all truly great men. They belong to their context and represent their context. But,
if that is true, the monasteries and the monks saved
civilization. They were microscopic colonies of peaceful men living in the midst of rapine and slaughter; they
maintained their little governments of law when all outside them was lawless. They stood for things ancient,
stable, and enduring when all beyond their abodes boiled
with turbulence and destruction; they spoke confidently
of strange matters nearly incomprehensible to Roman and
to Nordic minds, of charity, humbleness, self-denial, and
self-discipline. They made love their watchword and
peace their battle cry, and they were so terribly armed
with unyielding character that they were appalled at
nothing and by their very serenity distributed blessings.
A race of warriors, they were under a Divine Commander, a race of heroes more heroic than those of ancient song and story.

IV

CHARLES THE GREAT AND THE BENEDICTINE AGE

In the year 690 the Saxon Willibrod, who had been for twelve years a disciple of the monks of Ireland, went as a missionary and planted the Church among the Frisians. In 716 his fellow countryman Wynfrith of Wessex followed him. This man was trained in the monastery of Exeter, and he had been a teacher in the monastery of Nutshalling and had left a reputation for persistent application to literary studies in both places. In 717 he journeyed to Rome, and after some months was "sent by the most blessed Pope [Gregory II] to inspect the savage peoples of Germany: that he might consider whether the uncultivated fields of their hearts, if tilled by the gospel ploughshare, would be disposed to receive the seed of preaching." [1] He saw that the harvest was plenteous but the laborers too few, and joined himself for three years uninterruptedly to Archbishop Willibrod in Frisia. The aged Willibrod insisted upon consecrating him as his successor, but Wynfrith refused and begged instead that he be sent "back to those lands to which at first I was sent by the apostolic see." "When he had cleansed many thousand people [in Germany] from their inveterate paganism," he was summoned to Rome by the Pope,

[1] Willibald, *The Life of St. Boniface*, transl. G. W. Robinson, 51 (Cambridge, Mass.: Harvard University Press, 1915).

given a new name, Boniface, and made bishop over the people he had converted. He is henceforth known as the Apostle to the Germans.[2]

The successors of Clovis were the Merovingians. The years of their rule were full of disorder, anarchy, and slaughter. They were called sluggard kings, and earned the name. The mayors of the palace ruled for them, and local bishops who were the real rulers of the day learned to govern their territories as though they were independent. Such a state of things led to much civil war. The mayor of Austrasia fought with the mayor of Neustria, the mayor of Neustria conquered the Burgundian nobles commanded by Bishop Leger. Pepin d'Heristal, mayor of the palace of Austrasia, governed Frankland for twenty-seven years (687–714), giving himself the title of Duke of the Franks. At his death his power passed to his son Charles Martel, who had to fight with several rival claimants for it. The Merovingian king died after a shadowy reign of sixteen years, and Charles did not feel called upon to appoint a successor. Thus the government of France passed to the Carolingian line (730) though Pepin, Charles Martel's son, continued for a time the appearance of serving under a Merovingian king whom he placed on the throne. The battle of Tours was fought in 732.

In these stormy days the bishops were more accustomed to war than to prayer, for they were ordered into battle with their contingents by Charles Martel, and learned to live lives of plundering and oppression. They came to be war lords rather than spiritual leaders.

[2] As I write this, August 21, 1935, the press carries the news that, to consider the serious situation facing the Church in Germany, a great council called to assemble at Fulda has begun its sessions with a solemn devotional service in the crypt which surrounds the tomb of St. Boniface.

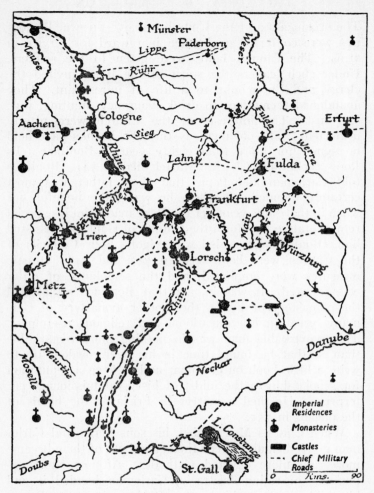

IMPERIAL RESIDENCES, MONASTERIES AND CASTLES IN THE CAROLINGIAN
PERIOD, C. A.D. 800.

From *An Historical Geography of Europe,* by Gordon East, by permission
of E. P. Dutton & Co., Inc.

The organization of the Church was overthrown. Bishoprics were conferred on laymen in reward for service in arms. The Church lands were given to the soldiers. Under such leaders the spirit of the times invited the clergy and the monks to a life of unrestraint. They abandoned themselves to drink, vagrancy, hunting, war, and lust. The interests of the Church were utterly neglected. "The old men say that the Franks have held no synod for more than eighty years," Boniface tells Pope Zacharias. Charles Martel died in 741. Boniface told Carloman and Pepin that their father was most certainly damned. Of them he was more hopeful, for when in that same year 741 the Pope made him his special representative to reform the Church of Gaul they assisted him. Boniface proceeded with vigor. Four Councils of the Church were held between 742 and 748. Drastic measures were employed, and the semblance of order was restored. It was in 744 that Boniface established the monastery of Fulda, the mother monastery of Germany, great in its educational and religious usefulness. This remarkable man was in nothing more remarkable than in that he found time in his overcrowded life to write a little book on grammar and to keep a reputation for scholarship in the midst of his great missionary enterprises. He died a martyr in Frisia at the hands of the pagans in 755.

When Charles Martel died, his sons Pepin and Carloman divided Gaul between them, and both of them became more and more devoted Catholics. After a short experience of ruling Austrasia, Carloman handed it and his children over to his brother Pepin and went to Rome, where in the Church of the Holy Apostles he took the vows of a monk. He entered a monastery which he had himself built at Mount Soracte, about fifty miles from

Rome, in 748. But his fame drew too great a throng of visitors, and to escape them he fled to Monte Cassino, where he insisted upon being the humblest brother in the monastery. His tomb is still pointed out there.

Pepin, though *de facto* king, was nominally mayor of the palace. He in time worked out a plan by which he took over the crown. In 751 an assembly of the Great Ones proclaimed him King, and Boniface, the Legate of the Holy See, consecrated and anointed him. To establish him still more securely Pope Stephen II came to Frankland (754), and in the Church of St. Denis consecrated him a second time, enjoining the nation upon pain of excommunication never to choose a king from any other family. For full measure the Pope then conferred upon Pepin and his two sons the title of Patrician of the Romans. Thus the Church made the Carolingians kings by divine right, for the Church needed their support against the Emperor at Constantinople and the Lombards in Italy. The royal house did not cease to be German, but Latin ideas were in high favor with it. A great new combined civilization was to be wrought out and the new program inspired a tremendous energy. The policy was Pepin's, but he did little to carry it out. In 768 he died, and his two sons divided the kingdom. In 771 Carloman died, and Charles reigned alone.

Gibbon has pointed out that Charlemagne alone has retained the title of "The Great" as a permanent addition to his name. He was born in 743 and died in 814. As a boy he must have seen Boniface; at any rate he grew up in a household that never tired of recounting the greatness of that great man. There was another kind of greatness which Charles valued fully as much, i.e. battle greatness. He is the joint product of **Charles Martel** and St. Boniface, a man of size and strength—

"his height was seven times the length of his own feet."
He could straighten four horseshoes joined together. He
constantly took and was very fond of physical exercise,
riding and hunting, but above all of swimming. "The
best man on earth and the bravest was Charles." Of
the high fervor of his temperament nothing more is
needed than the story of how one day, when Alcuin was
telling him of the great work of Jerome and Augustine,
his eagerness kindled and he exclaimed: "Why, why
have I not twelve such in my kingdom?" To which the
outraged Alcuin flashed back: "The Lord God of Heaven
and earth had but two such, and thou wouldst have
twelve." He loved foreigners, not as a species but
as a genus, and had so many of them about him that
Einhard says they were a burden to the kingdom. Always he wore the Frankish dress, for he disliked foreign
clothes; and always he wore a sword. His step was firm
and his bearing manly, but his voice was not so strong
as you would have expected. He was married nine times
and had twenty children. "He had such care of the up-
bringing of his sons and daughters that he never dined
without them when he was at home, and never travelled
without them," says Einhard. His daughters, we are
told, were handsome, but he kept them all at home and
would not allow them to marry, for he could not forgo
their society.

This mighty king waged wars for forty-seven years,
first against Aquitania, which he speedily conquered;
for he was a great general famous for the speed with
which he struck the enemy in surprise attacks, but even
more celebrated for the thoroughness of preparation which
made that possible, the perfection of organization, commissary, rapidity of mobilization, etc. In 772 Charles
determined to subjugate and convert the fierce Saxon

peoples dwelling on the northeast of Frankland. That undertaking proved so great that it took thirty-two years of heavy warring to complete it and perfect the work which Boniface had begun. In the next year (773) the Pope sent word that the Lombards under Desiderius were marching on Rome, and begged Charles to fulfil his father Pepin's promises and protect the Holy See. Charles forthwith called up his army; and, sending one part of it through the St. Bernard pass and leading the other over Mt. Cenis, he laid siege to Pavia and after eight months took it and made an end of the Lombard-ruled kingdom (774). While that siege was going on, Charles left his army and went to Rome. The magistrates of the city marched out thirty miles to meet him, and a great concourse of citizens, the papal army, and the school children waving palm branches, welcomed him and attended him on his way. At the doors of St. Peter's Pope Hadrian and all his clergy stood ready to receive him, chanting in loud voices: "Blessed is he that cometh in the name of the Lord." Desiderius and his wife and daughter were taken to Frankland and shut up in a monastery, perhaps that of Corbie; his son Adalgis fled to Constantinople, and Charles now signed himself "By the grace of God, King of the Franks and of the Lombards and Patrician of the Romans." In this interval the Saxons came on again, as they did each year but one for a generation. It was a terribly bloody war, and it took the energy of nearly a lifetime to bring it to a satisfactory end. But there were other wars to be fought at the same time. In 778 Charles crossed the Pyrenees to attack the Saracens. At first the enterprise turned out badly, and in the return home there was the defeat at Roncesvalles mourned in the Song of Roland. But a second time the king attacked them and fixed the limit

of their Empire. In 795–797 there were campaigns against
the Huns and the people of Bohemia, and in the last years
of his rule the Danes, the terror-spreading Normans,
dared to sail their long boats far up the rivers of Frankland.

Occupation and preoccupation enough for one lifetime!
Yes, but this constant anticipating the attacks of the
neighboring barbarian nations and striking them before they strike is only a part of the business of this
greatly energetic king. His is an ecclesiatical monarchy,
"the most fundamentally ecclesiastical government the
world has ever seen." [3] His is a church state and he is a
king-bishop. The Pope is his partner, who does obeisance
to him at Aachen while he kneels to his spiritual overlord
at the steps of St. Peter's. It is his office, but besides
that, as a man, he is as devoutly eager to support, uphold, and magnify the Church as the glorious St. Boniface was. Always he is working for the good of the
Church, improving its ritual service, taking priests and
bishops along to leave behind him when with his army he
invades and conquers a pagan country, sending the missionary priests back to their posts the very moment he
has subdued the violence of the Saxons. (One, Willehad,
had doubts that Saxony was yet safe, and asked what he
should do. "Do!" said Charles. "Go back to your diocese,
in the name of Christ.") He is ever urging the churchmen of his kingdom to greater diligence, opening schools,
and ordering all the children to attend them. These are
the things which are heaviest on his heart and on his
hands, too, for half of his legislative acts are concerned
with church discipline.

One of Charles' very first public acts was the publish-

[3] Funck-Brentano, *The National History of France: The Earliest
Times*, 346.

ing of a capitulary (769) directing that priests should not engage in the shedding of blood (i.e. go to war), "and all bishops and priests before entering upon the duties of their office shall be examined before a synod of the church, that those who shall be found incapable of performing their ministry shall be suspended from their functions until they shall have given satisfactory proof of fitness. Finally those priests who have frequently been admonished by their bishops for their ignorance and have taken no care to instruct themselves shall be removed from office and sent away from their churches because they who are ignorant of the law of God are not able to announce it to others." [4]

We do not know much about Charles's education in youth. It seems to have been good enough to make him eager to get more as long as he lived, which according to Platonic standards shows that it must have been pretty good; but no doubt he was much more painstakingly trained to be a soldier than to be a clergyman or a scholar. This very earnest king, though he was the greatest ruler of his time, was never too busy not to keep up his studies. "For his lessons in grammar he listened to the instruction of Deacon Peter of Pisa, an old man," says Einhard of him (25). Just when that master came to the court, we do not know. It seems certain that what Charles had seen in Italy strengthened his resolve to bring learning to his kingdom. Italy had two very active seminaries in that day: Bobbio and Monte Cassino. There were cities there while the rest of western Europe was farm land and forest, with here and there some villages and sometimes a fortified castle or a palace. The

---

[4] Stallaert and Van de Haegen, *De l'Instruction publique au Moyen Age,* 13 (referring to Migne, *Patrologiae Cursus Completus,* XCVII, 123–124, part 2, 14–16).

life of the Lombard towns, Milan, Pavia, and Verona, was far more than rural life. Their churches claimed that their priests were the most learned in Italy. Grammar was taught in these cities, and public theological disputations were held. Deacon Peter of Pisa became famous for refuting a Jewish rabbi in one such public discussion which the English scholar Alcuin chanced to hear in Milan.[5]

Of the other teacher and helper whom Charles got from Italy we know much more. He was Paul the Deacon, or Paul Warnefried, of a distinguished Lombard family and himself distinguished in several ways. Paul was born in Friuli about 725. He was educated probably at the court of King Ratchis by Flavianus the grammarian.[6] He training was good and even included the Greek language. For the Duchess of Benevento, Adelperga, whose tutor he seems to have been in her father Desiderius' palace at Pavia, he wrote a Roman history amplifying Eutropius and bringing the account down to the end of the Gothic kingdom in Italy. That work of his was an authoritative textbook for nearly a thousand years. Some time before 782, Paul had become a monk at Monte Cassino. When Charles's vassal, Hrodgaud, the Duke of Friuli, rebelled in 776, the king put down the insurrection and seems to have taken certain captives back to Frankland with him, among them Paul's brother, Arichis, whose widow "had to beg bread in the streets with trembling lips" for her four children. To beg the release of the prisoners the king had held for six years, Paul in 782 journeyed across the Alps to the court of the monarch, who drafted him into his service for the

[5] Migne, *Patrologiae Cursus Completus*, C (Alcuin, *Opera Omnia*), 314.
[6] *History of the Lombards*, VI, vii.

next four years. While at the palace in Frankland, perhaps in January of 783, he wrote a letter to Theudemar, the abbot of his monastery, Monte Cassino, so touchingly beautiful and informing that it deserves a place among the choicest letters of all time. This is his letter:

"To my master and father, dearest abbot Theudemar, cherished with all my heart, your humble and devoted son Paul:

"Although a great distance separates me from your companionship, a strong love for your society affects me which cannot be severed, and so great a desire for you and for my superiors and brothers torments me every moment that I cannot express it in the brief compass of a letter. For when I think of the time I devoted to holy things and the pleasant situation of my little cell; of your kindly sympathy; of the pious troop of so many champions of Christ eager in the service of God; of the shining examples of particular brothers in virtues of every kind; of our sweet converse on the excellencies of the heavenly kingdom, then a desire seizes me and I cannot keep back my tears. I live here among Catholics and good Christians. All receive me well; kindness is eagerly shown me for your sake and for that of our father Benedict; but in comparison with your cloister, the royal palace is a dungeon to me; compared with the calm of your monastery, life here is a stormy gale. This country keeps me only in my poor, weak body; with my whole soul, in which alone I am strong, I am with you. It seems to me that now I am listening to your delightful songs; now I am sitting in the refectory to be refreshed more by the reading than by the food; now I perceive the various occupations of each of you; now I see how it goes with the old and the sick; now I tread the holy threshold which is as dear to me as heaven. Believe me, my master and father, believe me, you holy and venerable band, I am kept here for a while only by a feeling of pity, only by the injunctions of love, only by the demand of the soul, and what is still more than all this, by the quiet power of our lord, the king. But as soon as I am healed and the Lord through our gracious sovereign shall take away from my prisoners the night of sorrow and the yoke of misery, I will straightway, as soon as I can obtain leave from our gracious prince, return to you without delay, and neither money, nor property, nor treasures of gold, nor the love of any man shall keep me from your company. I implore you therefore, sweetest father, and you, O dearest fathers and brothers, that our good father and teacher Benedict may procure it through his merit with Christ that I can return to you right soon. I trust indeed in our God, who never lets any one be cheated in good wishes, that he may restore me to you with fitting fruit for my toil according to the desire of my longing heart. I do not need to write to you to pray for our sovereigns and their army, since I know you are doing this unceasingly. Pray Christ also for the lord abbot, by whose special kindness according to the royal grace I live here. Your number, my beloved ones, is so great that if I wished to mention you all one by one, this whole page would not suffice for your names. Wherefore I greet you all in common and pray you not to forget me. But I ask you, my master and venerable abbot, to write me concerning your welfare and that of the brothers, and what fortunes the present year has brought, and at the same time to send the names of the brothers who have been released from earthly fetters and have gone to Christ. For I hear that many of them have died, but especially ————, who, if it is really so, has taken with him no little part of my heart. Farewell, most holy father. Deign to remember your son." [7]

There was much burlesque verse-making in the court of Charles the Great. In one of the rhymed letters which Peter of Pisa on behalf of the king addressed to Paul, he is thanked for teaching Greek to so many, particularly to the priests who are to attend the Princess Rotrud to Constantinople. That young lady was betrothed at nine years of age to the crown prince there, but the match was broken off by her father six years later. Paul did some literary odd jobs for the monarch and a really large service in helping him to prepare the collection of homilies which the king sent to the clergy of his realm in the year 788 with the statement: "Desirous as we are of improving the condition of the churches, we impose upon ourselves the task of reviving, with the utmost zeal, the study of letters, well-nigh extinguished through the neglect of our ancestors. We charge all our subjects, as far as they may be able, to cultivate the liberal arts, and we set them the example. We have already, God helping, carefully corrected the books of the Old and New Testaments, corrupted through the ignorance of transcribers. And inasmuch as the collection of homilies for the service at nocturns was full of errors . . . we have willed that these same should be revised and corrected by Paul the Deacon, our well-beloved client; and he has presented us with copies of readings, adapted to every feast day, carefully purged from error and sufficing for an entire year." [8] Paul the Deacon, at the request of the Bishop

[7] Quoted in Introduction to *History of the Langobards* by Paul the Deacon, transl. W. D. Foulke (New York: Longmans, Green, 1906), xx–xxiii.

[8] Baluze, *Capitulari Regum Francorum*, I, 203. Mullinger, *The Schools of Charles the Great,* 101.

of Metz, wrote a history of the bishops of that diocese, which dwells in detail upon the early members of the family from which Charles the Great sprang. In December, 786, Paul returned to Italy in the company which attended Charles the King. While at Rome he wrote a short life of Gregory the Great, from which he omitted the usual account of miracles, for he said they were not necessary in order to judge men. In March, Paul had the privilege of introducing Charlemagne to Monte Cassino. That must have been for him a thrilling experience, and for the monastery nearly or quite the greatest day of its existence. The king was deeply impressed by what he saw, and at once formed plans to remake the monasteries of Frankland on the model of Monte Cassino. The king went on, but Paul the monk remained at Monte Cassino, where he must at once have begun the most important labor of his life, the writing of the History of the Langobards, a great book which Mommsen valued and even Gibbon was constrained to praise. Some time about 795 the irreproachable life of this many-sided scholar and good man came to an end in the quiet peace of the monastery of St. Benedict.

But the king had other learned men about him, Paulinus of Aquileia, Theodulf, afterward Bishop of Orléans, Benedict of Aniane among them. Yet we must remember that his plan was ambitious, not to say colossal, nothing less than a forced renaissance of antiquity or, as Harnack has put it, the gaining by storm of a higher culture for the Frankish people. More men were needed; indeed, for so great a task, Charles could never have found enough. In 780 Charles inspected his government at Pavia, and by Easter he was in Rome where Pope Hadrian baptized his four-year-old son Carloman with the new name of Pepin and crowned both him and his baby brother kings, Pepin of the Lombards and the infant Lewis King of Aquitaine. In the interval between these two events he met for a second time at Parma a young English scholar, Alcuin (735–804), who twelve years before had visited his court in Frankland. It seems to have occurred at once to the king that here was the man he needed. He had always venerated the English Boniface. The same piety and learning were evident in this young churchman from the British Isles. Charles at once proposed to the Scholasticus, or Master of the School, of York that he come to Frankland, live with him in the palace, and take responsibility for the educational and religious upbuilding of the kingdom. Extraordinary inducements were offered, and Alcuin—who had come to Italy on this his second visit for the purpose of bearing the pallium from the Pope back to his senior fellow teacher, Eanbald, who had recently been made Archbishop of York—accepted, with the single reservation that his king and his archbishop should first give their assent to his departure from England. Upon his return home, the necessary sanction was secured, the archbishop urging the claims of friendship that his associate be not completely lost to his native land by this assumption of new duties, and Alcuin journeyed to Aachen and forthwith began to teach in the palace school.

It is necessary to say something of this new untitled minister of education and religion in the court of Charles the Great. No other man in the kingdom was so clearly the valued confidant and keeper of the king's conscience as this English schoolmaster became. Alcuin was a noble of Northumbria. He belonged to the monastic tradition of York. The great Bede, "the most learned man in Europe," who had died about the time he was born, was his spiritual ancestor. Egbert, the Archbishop of York from 732 to 766, received a long letter from Bede shortly after his elevation which may still be read. The relation between the two men is indicated in the first sentences of that letter: "I remember hearing you say last year when I spent a few days in your monastery for purposes of study, that you would wish, this year also when you should arrive at the same place, to have me near you to converse with, for the same purposes of study, common to us both . . . I consider it above every other thing important that you should endeavor to implant deeply in the memory of all men the Catholic faith which is contained in the Apostles' Creed and the Lord's Prayer as it is taught us in the Holy Gospel. And, indeed, there is no doubt that those who have studied the Latin language will be found to know these well; but the vulgar, that is those who know only their own language, must be made to say them and repeat them over and over again in their own tongue." [9] Archbishop Egbert, the friend and disciple of Bede, was the founder of the Cathedral School at York; Ælbert was his scholasticus and the teacher of Alcuin. When Egbert died in 766 Ælbert became archbishop and when he died in 780 Eanbald became archbishop.

As a young boy Alcuin had come into the care of Archbishop Egbert; and he seems early to have shown the love for poetry which was his through life. He was a pronounced lover of Virgil at eleven, which interfered, the stories have it, with his chanting of the Psalms. "My Master Egbert," he once wrote to Charles the Great, "often used to say to me, 'It was the wisest of men who discovered the arts, and it would be a great disgrace to allow them to perish in our day. But many are now so pusillanimous as not to care about knowing the reasons

[9] *An Epistle from Bede to Bishop Egbert,* 1, 5.

of the things the Creator has made.' Thou knowest well
how agreeable a study is arithmetic, how necessary it is
for understanding the Holy Scriptures, and how pleasant
is the knowledge of the heavenly bodies and their courses,
and yet there are few who care to know such things and
what is worse, those who seek to study them are considered blameworthy." [10]

We have another and a better means of determining
the character of the influences which played upon Alcuin
in his youth at York than that which our knowledge of
the Venerable Bede affords. It is contained in his own
account of the cathedral library which was housed at
York and of which he himself had had charge. Professor
West has reproduced the cataloguing lines as follows:

Here shines what Jerome, Ambrose, Hilary thought,
Or Athanasius and Augustine wrought.
Orosius, Leo, Gregory the Great,
Near Basil and Fulgentius coruscate,
Grave Cassiodorus and John Chrysostom
Next Master Bede and learned Aldhelm come,
While Victorinus and Boethius stand
With Pliny and Pompeius close at hand.
Wise Aristotle looks on Tully near,
Sedulius and Juvencus next appear,
Then come Albinus, Clement, Prosper too,
Paulinus and Arator, next we view
Lactantius, Fortunatus. Ranged in line
Vergilius Maro, Statius, Lucan, shine.
Donatus, Priscian, Probus, Phocas, start
The roll of masters in grammatic art.
Eutychius, Servius, Pompey, each extend
The list. Comminian brings it to an end.

[10] Quoted in West's *Alcuin,* 37.

> There shalt thou find, O reader, many more
> Famed for their style, the masters of old lore,
> Whose many volumes singly to rehearse
> Were far too tedious for our present verse.[11]

And Mullinger notes that Isidorus is not mentioned, probably because of the metrical difficulty of that name as he was well known and much prized at York. It is well to remember that in those days libraries were not kept as ornaments. The tireless searching of the earlier sons of York had increased the small stock of books and manuscripts which Theodore brought to England until the library of York in the time of Alcuin contained far more volumes than any collection of books in France or England during the twelfth century. Its considerable extent is direct evidence of the great labor which the churchmen had expended in the cause of learning and that the reputation of York as the leading school of Christendom in that age was entirely justified.

Alcuin speaks of "the pious patience" and "the maternal care and affection" with which he was treated at York. He enumerates the studies in verses that are hardly as poetical as his catalogue of the library. They were grammar and rhetoric, canon law, poetry, astronomy, natural history, arithmetic, and the study of the Scriptures. When it came to him to sit in the master's seat, he quickly achieved a reputation as a famous teacher, the best in Britain. Students like Liudger came from the Continent to study under him. Three of his Saxon pupils at York, Witzo, Fredegis, and Sigulf, were so devoted that they followed him to Frankland to continue their studies un-

---

[11] Andrew F. West's *Alcuin and the Rise of Christian Schools,* 34–35 (based on a passage in Alcuin's "Poema de Pontificibus et Sanctis Ecclesiae Eboracensis," in Migne, *op. cit.,* C̄Ī, 843). By permission of Charles Scribner's Sons.

der his instruction. That he was a poet, too, not without charm, is, I think, shown in his dialogue between Spring and Winter which is to be found in H. W. C. Davis' *Charlemagne* in this form:

VER. I am fain for the cuckoo's coming, the bird that I love the best;
And there's not a roof where the cuckoo deigns to pause in his flight and rest
And pipe glad songs from his ruddy beak but will call him a welcome guest.
HIEMS. Delay me the coming of cuckoo! The father of toils is he;
And battles he brings, and all men in the world, however weary they be,
Must rouse them from rest at his trumpet to brave land-farings and perils at sea.
VER. The note of the cuckoo brings flowers and gladdens with honey the bee.
Sends the landsman to build up his homestead, the ship to the unruffled sea,
And the nestlings are hatched by his music and the meadow glows green and the tree.[11a]

Theodulf's picture of Flaccus (Alcuin) in his poem "Ad Carolum regem" describes him as "the glory of our bards, mighty to shout forth his songs, keeping time with his lyric foot, moreover a powerful sophist, able to prove pious doctrines out of Holy Scripture, and in genial jest to propose or solve puzzles of arithmetic." [12]

The monarch welcomed the Saxon deacon in person

[11a] Davis, *Charlemagne*, 180. By permission of G. P. Putnam's Sons and Putnam & Company, Ltd. This poem in complete text and translation may be found in *Medieval Latin Lyrics* by Helen Waddell, Constable & Co., London, 1929.

[12] In Hodgkin, *Italy and Her Invaders*, VIII, 161. See the extensive "Carmina" of Alcuin, in Migne, *op. cit.*, CI, 725-848.

and established him in the palace beside himself. The
stranger was immediately installed as head of the palace
school, and the work of teaching began forthwith. The
mission of that school was the training of the sons of the
courtiers and officers of the kingdom by way of preparing them for the high offices of state and church which
the standing of their family, their race, and their ability
destined them to fill. "Charles," says the Monk of
St. Gall, "used to pick out all the best writers and readers from among the poor boys . . . and transferred them
to his chapel." This school attended the person of the
monarch as did the royal chapel, and his family, and the
families of the court. Wherever the royal court was
fixed, whether at Aachen, Frankfurt, Metz, Worms, Ingel-
heim or on campaigns with the army, there the instruction
of the palace school was given. Between the wars, or
when the army was in winter quarters and peace reigned
over the land, the great Charles himself and many of
his courtiers were in the habit of attending its sessions.
By doing that the king accomplished two things: he
satisfied his own eagerness to learn, and he set his subjects an example that they could not well overlook. Since
the greatest in the land thought it not beneath him to go
to school, what reason could other men find for neglecting
learning? "In the manner in which he thus brought his
personal influence to bear on the movement, we recognise
one all-important fact: the palace school witnessed the
first considerable innovation on the Gregorian tradition." [13]
Hitherto, since the fall of the Empire in the West, education had for the most part been regarded as a thing needed
by priests and monks, since they served the religion of
the Book. But Charles the Great put his powerful personality and kingly office to the work of demonstrating

[13] Mullinger, *op. cit.*, 69.

that it was as a secular thing necessary to government as well as a sacred thing necessary to religion.

The King of the Franks did not invent the palace school. The first Augustus had done that and thought it not unworthy of his dignity and occupation to follow the old Roman habit of teaching his own grandsons letters. Valentinian the Emperor had established such a school in the palace at Treves. Lombard kings had had such schools in their capitol at Pavia and even the Merovingian kings had had such a school. But there was something about this school which made it different from all that preceded it: it had greater scope, greater energy; it was much more of a going concern; there was more force behind it; it was meant not only for boys but also for men and was an indispensable part of a great planned national regeneration.

Alcuin taught the same subjects there that he had taught at York and perhaps in much the same way, but not to just the same sort of folks or for just the same purpose.

That the teaching of Alcuin was successful, and that his influence was wide-reaching, are best exhibited by some notice of the personnel of his students in the palace school. The most striking figure among his pupils was of course the king himself. His was a ready intellect more quick to learn than patient. He could converse in the Latin of the day as easily as in his native German, and understood spoken Greek. His former tutor, Peter of Pisa, had instructed him in grammar, but write he could not, "nor is it difficult," says Mullinger,[14] "to understand that the royal hand, stiffened with oft-wielding of the good sword 'Joyeuse,' may have refused to accommodate itself to the most painful and laborious of all the

[14] *Op. cit.*, 71.

acquirements of an ordinary education." From the former scholasticus of York the king learned the customary rhetoric, logic, arithmetic, and astronomy of the Middle Age curriculum. Beside the king his three sons sat betimes in the school: Charles, afterward King of Nuestria and Austrasia; Pepin, King of the Lombards, and Lewis, ruler of Aquitaine. Strange to relate, coeducation existed there and, much more wonderful still, the favorite sister of the monarch, Gisela, abbess of Chelles, was moved to leave her convent by the great fame of the Saxon teacher. Beside her sat Luitgarda, the queen of the realm, and near her their well beloved daughter Gisela. With them were the king's son-in-law Angilbert, afterward the distinguished abbot of St. Riquier, and the royal cousins Adelhard, Bernarius, and Wala and their sisters, Theodrada and Gundrada. There also were Riculf, Bishop of Metz, a seasoned man of the world and the king's most intimate companion, Richbod, Archbishop of Treves, Einhard the biographer, the Saxons Fredegis, Witzo, and Sigulf who had accompanied their master from York, and the poor but clever boys of the chapel. Such were some of the members of the company which gathered to his instruction.[15] Possibly no teacher ever held a more trying position; others have taught princes and the sons of power, but what other teacher has faced the greatest monarch of his time sitting in school beside the sons of his own courtiers? The cross-questioning propensity of the king was marked. He attended the classes for the purpose of having his own mental difficulties solved, not of having mental difficulties aroused within him, as did the younger pupils. There he sat "in the ardour of a long unsatisfied curiosity, propounding queries on all imaginable topics—

[15] See Migne, *op. cit.*, C 48–55; Mullinger, *op. cit.*, 72, and Guizot, *History of Civilization in Europe*, 75 (London: Cassell, 1911).

suggesting, distinguishing, disputing, objecting,—a colossal figure, gazing fixedly with bright blue eyes on his admired guest, and altogether a presence that might well have disconcerted a less assured intellect. Alcuin, however, holding fast by his Boethius, Cassiodorus, and Isidorus, is calm and self-possessed; feeling assured that, so long as he only teaches what 'Gregorius summus' and 'Baeda venerabilis' believed and taught, he cannot go very far wrong." [16] But for the fact that these men respected and were genuinely fond of each other, the position of Alcuin had been intolerable. As it was, in spite of the great labor it involved, it was agreeable rather than otherwise, for the character and reputation of the deacon of York were held in the greatest reverence at the Frankish court. As to the value of his teaching, however, it echoed the traditional formalism which the Middle Ages inherited from the Roman schools too faithfully to impress greatly one whose judgment must be made according to modern standards. Alcuin was a faithful representative of the learning of his time—one of its best representatives, in fact, "the most learned man of his time." Originality of thought was quite foreign to him. In his teaching and writing, he reproduced what he had been taught and reproduced it well; but hardly a single doubt as to its all-sufficing finality seems to have crossed his mind. Hauréau has classified him intellectually as nothing more than a grammarian, and he indeed seems to have been more famous as an instructor in the trivium than in the other divisions of knowledge. But there is danger that we may underestimate the vast services of these men. They kept the literary tradition alive. They cultivated the three arts and the four sciences, the trivium and quadrivium, as Cassidorus had arranged them. Grammar,

[16] Mullinger, *op. cit.,* pp. 71–72.

upon which they bestowed unending care and devotion, was a name for the beginnings of literature; rhetoric is more advanced instruction of the same sort; the elements are there—the analysis which separates the parts and the practice which puts them together into productions, sentences, paragraphs, or chapters. Cassiodorus, Isidorus, Donatus, Martianus Capella ("our Martianus" of Gregory of Tours), Priscian, and Bede's Prosody and Orthography were schoolbooks, yet they kept the world from sinking into darkness and utterly forgetting what Homer and Virgil, Cicero and Plato had done. Professor W. P. Ker derives the medieval taste in Latin prose writing from Apuleius, but it came through that textbook with the fantastic name and florid contents, "The Marriage of Mercury and Philology," which Martianus Capella had made, which no school or library could be without. There is study of dialectic, too, as Alcuin's theological studies and Fredegis' preference for logic prove. Boethius, Bede, Orosius, Jerome, Augustine, Gregory the Great, and the Holy Scriptures supply the substantial knowledge of the course.

Like the monks in the monasteries, Charles the Great listened to a reader during his meals: "Histories and the great deeds of men of old were read to him. He took delight also in the books of Saint Augustine, and especially in those which are entitled The City of God." [17] The book of Consolation which Boethius wrote while waiting for Theodoric's executioner to come, was a kind of universal counsel of compassion in that troubled time. It was Platonism and the last great utterance of classic purity which reached the ears of Dark Age and medieval men. It talked of order, the order which preserves the

[17] *Early Lives of Charlemagne by Eginhard and the Monk of St. Gall,* transl. A. J. Grant. 40.

stars from wrong, the universal divine order, which men
can feel and know and embody, for it is indeed that love
of God of which Augustine speaks and for which one
greater than Augustine pleaded in the New Testament.

Alcuin was seven years older than Charles the Great.
He is sometimes pictured as a sort of clerical shadow of
his master the king, a British schoolmaster but not a St.
Boniface. That judgment is pretty certainly wrong. This
Englishman had the traits of the elder missionary. He is
not afraid to speak out even very plainly about the king:
"Behold our Solomon, resplendent with the diadem of
wisdom, imitate his noble traits, cherish his virtues, but
avoid his vices." [18] On the other hand he has such strength
that the king is willing to call Alcuin master and himself
the disciple.[19] The point which is most difficult to sense
adequately is the terrible earnestness of the king in push-
ing forward the educational reform of his kingdom. Even
when Alcuin had gone to Tours and another master was
in charge of the palace school, there was no let-up in the
king's drive for satisfactory work on the part of the students. Once when he came home after a long absence he
ordered the boys of the school to bring him specimens
of their school work, compositions they had written and
verses they had composed. As was to be expected—for
expectation had no reason to be different then from expectation now—"the boys of middle or low birth presented him with writings garnished with the sweet savours
of wisdom beyond all that he could have hoped, while
those of the children of noble parents were silly and taste-
less. Then the most wise Charles, imitating the judg-

[18] Quoted in West's *Alcuin* from Migne, *Patrologiae Cursus Completus*,
CI, 649.
[19] *Early Lives of Charlemagne by Eginhard and the Monk of St. Gall*,
transl. A. J. Grant, 61.

ment of the eternal Judge, gathered together those who had done well upon his right hand and addressed them in these words: 'My children, you have found much favour with me because you have tried with all your strength to carry out my orders and win advantage for yourselves. Wherefore now study to attain to perfection; and I will give you bishoprics and splendid monasteries, and you shall be always honourable in my eyes.' Then he turned severely to those who were gathered on his left, and, smiting their consciences with the fire of his eyes, he flung at them these terrible words, which seemed thunder rather than human speech, 'You nobles, you sons of my chiefs, you superfine dandies, you have trusted to your birth and your possessions and have set at naught my orders to your own advancement: you have neglected the pursuit of learning and you have given yourselves over to luxury and sport, to idleness and profitless pastimes.' Then solemnly he raised his august head and his unconquered right hand to the heavens and thus thundered against them, 'By the King of Heaven, I take no account of your noble birth and your fine looks, though others may admire you for them. Know this for certain, that unless you make up for your former sloth by vigorous study, you will never get any favour from Charles." [20]

This is Charles as he lived on in Europe fifty years after his death. The features of his interest that were able to survive the years must have been those to which he had given greatest momentum while he lived. The materials of learning were not plentiful; but a strong enthusiasm could do much, and the enthusiasm of the king and the royal tutor knew no bounds. The teacher was not a Jerome or an Augustine (few teachers are); but "the most energetic Charles" was pleased with him, attached

[20] *Early Lives of Charlemagne, etc.*, 62–63.

him to himself, and loved him. The revenues of two monasteries—Saint Loup and Ferrières—had been assigned to him when he came to Frankland. Greater reward he was clearly earning, for the palace school was furnishing scholars of its training to fill the bishoprics of the kingdom. It was time to make more extended improvements. The music of the church service had for long been unsatisfactory. Pepin had tried to introduce the Gregorian chant but had not succeeded. In 787 Charles the Great asked Pope Hadrian to let him have two chanters from Rome, Theodore and Benedict, whom he brought back to Frankland with him and placed, one in the Cathedral of Metz to direct and reform and build up a school for Austrasia, and the other at Soissons to do a similar work for the churches of Neustria. They were commissioned to revise the Gallican Antiphonaries as well as to train the choirmasters. John the Deacon indicates that there was need for that: "The barbarous harshness of their cracked throats, when, by inflections and reverberations, they endeavoured to emit a gentle psalmody, out of a certain natural hoarseness, sent forth grating sounds like that of carts on a high road; and thus, instead of delighting the souls of their hearers, their singing, on the contrary, rather troubled them, by provoking distractions." [21] Great as this reform was, much greater undertakings mark the year 787, for it was then that the capitulary legislating a system of education for the entire realm was addressed to the monasteries and the churches of the kingdom. The copy which reached Baugulfus, Abbot of Fulda, is preserved, and Mullinger has translated it as follows:

"Charles, by the grace of God, King of the Franks and of the Lombards and Patrician of the Romans, to

[21] From the *Life of St. Gregory*, II, vii., by John the Deacon, quoted in Drane, *Christian Schools and Scholars*, I, 123.

Baugulfus, abbat, and to his whole congregation and the faithful committed to his charge:

"Be it known to your devotion, pleasing to God, that in conjunction with our faithful we have judged it to be of utility that, in the bishoprics and monasteries committed by Christ's favour to our charge, care should be taken that there shall be not only a regular manner of life and one conformable to holy religion, but also the study of letters, each to teach and learn them according to his ability and the divine assistance. For even as due observance of the rule of the house tends to good morals, so zeal on the part of the teacher and the taught imparts order and grace to sentences; and those who seek to please God by living aright should also not neglect to please Him by right speaking. It is written, 'by thine own words shalt thou be justified or condemned'; and although right doing be preferable to right speaking, yet must the knowledge of what is right precede right action. Everyone, therefore, should strive to understand what it is that he would fain accomplish; and this right understanding will be the sooner gained according as the utterances of the tongue are free from error. And if false speaking is to be shunned by all men, especially should it be shunned by those who have elected to be the servants of the truth. During past years we have often received letters from different monasteries informing us that at their sacred services the brethren offered up prayers in our behalf; and we have observed that the thoughts contained in these letters, though in themselves most just, were expressed in uncouth language, and while pious devotion dictated the sentiments, the unlettered tongue was unable to express them aright. Hence there has arisen in our minds the fear lest, if the skill to write rightly were thus lacking, so too would the power of rightly comprehending the sacred Scriptures be far less than was fitting; and we all know that though verbal errors be dangerous, errors of the understanding are yet more so. We exhort you, therefore, not only not to neglect the study of letters, but to apply yourselves thereto with perseverance and with that humility which is well pleasing to God; so that you may be able to penetrate with greater ease and certainty the mysteries of the Holy Scriptures. For as these contain images, tropes, and similar figures, it is impossible to doubt that the reader will arrive far more readily at the spiritual sense according as he is the better instructed in learning. Let there, therefore, be chosen for this work men who are both able and willing to learn, *and also desirous of instructing others;* and let them apply themselves to the work with a zeal equalling the earnestness with which we recommend it to them.

"It is our wish that you may be what it behoves the soldiers of the Church to be,—religious in heart, learned in discourse, pure in act, eloquent in speech; so that all that approach your house in order to invoke the Divine Master or to behold the excellence of the religious life, may be edified in beholding you and instructed in hearing you discourse or chant, and may return home rendering thanks to God most High.

"Fail not, as thou regardest our favour, to send a copy of this letter to all thy suffragans and to all the monasteries; and let no monk go beyond his monastery to administer justice or enter the assemblies and the voting places. Adieu." [22]

Students of this period are agreed that the hand that drafted this, "perhaps the most important document of the Middle Ages" (Mullinger), was none other than Al-

[22] Mullinger, *op. cit.*, 97–99. Baluze, *Capitularia Regum Francorum,* I, 202.

cuin's. None but a grammarian would have analyzed the need of correct speech thus, and no man of that age save a schoolmaster could have spoken so definitely and exactly of the attitude essential to the teacher.

Copies of the book of homilies prepared by Paul the Deacon and accompanied by the king's letter, already quoted, were distributed to the clergy of the kingdom in the following year. But in spite of the authority of the king's decree the desired reform of learning was not immediately accomplished. We read of an important school which was established in 787 by Gervold, Abbot of Fontenelle, and of a remarkable collection of books in the library of that monastery.[23] But the majority of the monks taking refuge in that nineteen-hundred-year-old churchman's excuse for their ignorance recounted the original simplicity of the faith and the necessity of preserving the mind of babes. Two years after the publication of the first capitulary the king was compelled to promulgate more definite instructions through another capitulary (*anno* 789) giving explicit directions to the clergy as to their private and public duties of their profession, decreeing "that candidates for the priestly office shall be taken not only from among the slave class but also from among the sons of freedmen and that schools for teaching reading should be maintained," and containing the further command: "Let every monastery and every cathedral have its school, where boys may be taught the Psalms, musical notation, singing, arithmetic and grammar and let the books which are given them be free from faults, for faulty books often lead them to address God wrongly, and let care be taken that the boys do not spoil them either when reading or writing and if the work of copying the evangels, the psalms or the missal be under-

[23] Ebert, *op. cit.*, II, 414.

taken let it be performed by men of mature mind with all diligence and care." [24] The same capitulary directs all clerics to "make themselves thoroughly familiar with the Roman method of chanting and to employ this method in the services of the church according to the decree of our father Pepin who abolished the Gallican method to be in agreement with the Apostolic see and promote the concord of the holy church of God." [25] Still another capitulary of the year 802 enjoined that "everyone should send his son to study letters, and that the child should remain at school with all diligence until he should become well instructed in learning." [26] In another capitulary of the same year which became the operative constitution of the Holy Roman Empire, the following words occur: "The secular clergy ought to lead a completely canonical life, and be educated in the episcopal palace or else in a monastery, with all diligence according to the discipline of the canon." [27] The capitularies of the year 804, 805, and 811 put the priests under still further obligation to study and in general repeated the requirements of former ordinances. Such were the edicts of Charles the Great which had for their object the educational reform of his empire. The king and his minister of education were not without powerful helpers in the movement. Theodolf, Bishop of Orléans, the intimate friend of the king who spent more time at the court than at his bishopric, but was nevertheless one of the most zealous churchmen of his time, issued in 797 a capitulary to the clergy of his diocese which served as a model for his fellow prelates equally zealous for reform,[28] men indeed, whom Charles

[24] Migne, *op. cit.*, XCVII, 177.
[25] Migne, *op. cit.*, XCVII, 180.
[26] West, *Alcuin*, 54. Pertz, *Leges*, I, 107.
[27] Baluze, *op. cit.*, I, 369, Sec. 27. Migne, *op. cit.*, XCVII, 228.
[28] Hauréau, *Singularités historiques*, 58.

had assisted to their sees because of their zeal for the improvement of learning among the people. This remarkable document was nothing short of a brief rule for the conduct of the priests under his direction. It contained many prescriptions of importance, but one article in particular upon the subject of education which read: "If any priest wishes to send his nephew or any other of his relations to school, we allow him to be sent to the church of St. Croix or to the monastery of St. Aignan, or of St. Benedict or of St. Lifard or any other monastery confided to our government." "Let the priests hold schools in the towns and villages, and if any of the faithful wish to entrust their children to them for the learning of letters, let them not refuse to receive and teach such children. Moreover, let them teach them from pure affection, remembering that it is written, 'the wise shall shine as the splendor of the firmament,' and 'they that instruct many in righteousness shall shine as the stars forever and forever.' And let them exact no price from the children for their teaching, nor receive anything from them, save what their parents may offer voluntarily, and from affection." [29] To teach to others what he himself knew became the acceptable form of a priest's charity. Theodolf had, as a worthy chief assistant in carrying out his designs, one Wulfin of Orléans, who was the master of the school of that city, and not only taught his pupils the language of Virgil but also attempted to serve the Muses in creative ways in celebrating the success with which their studies were pursued.[30] The efforts of Theodolf were crowned with a goodly measure of success.[31] Schools

[29] West, *Alcuin,* 55.

[30] Hauréau, *Singularités, historiques,* 63.

[31] Ebert, *La Littérature du Moyen Age,* II, 81 (tr. from German by Aymeric and Condamin; Paris, 1884).

which offered elementary instruction were set up in the towns and villages of their dioceses, and schools for more advanced instruction in the cathedrals and monasteries. One can find opinions of practically all degrees of variation with regard to the success which attended the educational reforms instituted by the king. There seems, however, to be little doubt that schools became quite as common as the state of the churches under which they were conducted and the insecurity of the country would permit. Professor West has called attention to the fact that the king began the organization of his system of education at the top, starting with the palace school, which served as a kind of embryonic college or advanced department of the system, and passing to the formation of what served for grammar and primary schools (in present-day nomenclature) in the monasteries and cathedrals of the bishops and in the villages. This order of procedure would hardly have been possible had the king been compelled to institute a scheme of instruction *de novo,* and it is a further witness to the reorganizing character of his efforts. The schools which were formed were thus of three indistinctly separated grades. The higher instruction which the palace school furnished in the three arts and the four sciences together with theology was frequently offered, under less famous masters perhaps, in the monastic and cathedral schools. But the larger part of their effort was devoted to imparting a more elementary instruction in the three arts, among which grammar led, while rhetoric was a distant second and dialectic received but little attention, while much of it would be classified as the work of the "first masters" under the Roman system or of primary teachers of today, differing only in the committing of the Creed, the Lord's Prayer or parts of the New Testament or the Psalms which it then involved. And such first studies of the primary school doubtless monopolized the attention of the clerics and lay brothers who conducted the public or village schools.

The king appointed the master of the palace school and was himself its board of visitation. The abbot of the monastery was *ex officio* the head of its school, reporting to his king in the case of the four imperial monasteries— in other cases to the Pope, or to the bishop of the diocese in which the monastery was situated in such cases as the local bishop had succeeded in convincing his originally co-equal fellow of his superior authority. The head of the episcopal schools was a scholasticus, or master, appointed by the bishop. The monastic schools received pupils who were not candidates for admission—a practice which the monasteries had observed irregularly from their very beginning. But the subject matter of instruction was much the same for both classes with the exception perhaps of additional emphasis upon monastic rules, practices and traditions, and church doctrine in the case of the *oblati*.

But the life Alcuin led for eight years, in constant service at the Frankish court, began to wear upon him. The persistent cross-questioning of his royal master and pupil tried, if it did not dishearten, the patient teacher; and the repeated movings of the court, together with the journeyings necessary to the care of his two monasteries, left him but little time for study and a quiet mind. Longing for an interval of peace, and regarding the work for which he had temporarily expatriated himself as accomplished, Alcuin quitted his labors in the year 790 and returned to England and the pious confines of York; but his respite was of short duration.[32] Offa, the King of

[32] Migne, *op. cit.*, C, 55 *et seq.*

Mercia, the most powerful of the Anglo-Saxon kinglets of that day, was at enmity with the Frankish king, and all forms of intercourse between the two countries had ceased. Alcuin, it is said, was commissioned as the representative of his master the Frankish king, and succeeded at length in reconciling their differences and averting war.[33] This diplomatic success made the king's confidant still more dear to him. But Alcuin's homeland was unsuited to his purposes of peaceful retirement. Instead of the quiet of his earlier recollection, he found a land in the throes of revolution. The Northumbrians had deposed their king, Osred, and had elevated Ethelred to the throne; Osred and the chiefs who were still faithful to him attempted a counter-revolution and became the prisoners of Ethelred. The deposed king was forthwith executed, and his supporters became targets for the ruthless vindictiveness of the new king. Moreover, the Northmen appeared again off the coasts of England. In the confusion of slaughter and burning which soon swept over the land, the church at Lindisfarne, one of the most revered spots in Britain, was destroyed.[34]

In the year 792, at the urgent request of the Frankish king, Alcuin left these scenes of slaughter and returned to Frankland.[35] The king had particular need of his master in theology. Adoptianism, a new form of the old Nestorian heresy, was beginning to exhibit a vigorous activity in the churches of the West. Orthodox trinitarians could not fail to be shocked by its statement that, while Jesus as the Logos was the Son of God by nature, engendered from all eternity, Jesus born of Mary was the Son of God only by adoption, being filled with the Divine

[33] Lorenz, *Life of Alcuin*, 62.
[34] Migne, *op. cit.*, C, 150.
[35] Migne, *op. cit.*, C, 58.

Spirit or the Logos not from birth but at his baptism. Such was the hateful doctrine which the Spanish bishops Felix of Urgel and Elipandus of Toledo, influenced perhaps by the Arab unitarians, were striving to propagate. The king as the ally of the Pope and champion of orthodoxy in the West and himself a devoted religionary, was full of solicitude for the purity of religion and the peace of the Church. He had already assembled two councils (Narbonne, 791, and Regensburg, 792) to hear and condemn the baneful doctrine.[36] The heretical leaders had publicly recanted, but, alas! they soon broke forth again more vigorously than ever. Church trials and legislation having failed, the king determined to attack the theologians on their own ground of controversy, and it was for this campaign that he begged his favorite theologian to return. The letters of Alcuin contain the attacks and refutations which he employed. Felix avowed that he was persuaded to orthodoxy by the Holy Spirit and the testimony of the Fathers with which Alcuin confronted him in the synod of Aachen in the year 799. The taming of Elipandus was a more difficult task, but at length the same methods availed and Adoptianism was officially dead. Meantime a still greater controversy, and one which furnishes historic proof of the high cost of ignorance to a nation, engaged him. The Seventh Ecumenical Council met at Nicaea in 757 and attempted to bring to an end a long iconoclastic controversy in the Church by adopting this definition: "That just as the figure of the precious and life-giving Cross, so also the venerable and holy images, as well in painting and mosaic as of other fit materials, should be set forth in the holy churches of God, and on the sacred vessels and on the vestments and on hangings and in pictures both in houses and by the

[36] Harnack, *History of Dogma*, V, 278.

wayside, to wit, the figure of our Lord God and Saviour Jesus Christ, of our spotless Lady, the Mother of God, of the honourable Angels, of all Saints and of all pious people. For by so much more frequently as they are seen in artistic representation, by so much more readily are men lifted up to the memory of their prototypes, and to a longing after them; and to these should be given salutation and honourable reverence, not indeed that true worship of faith which pertains alone to the divine nature; but to these, as to the figure of the precious and life-giving Cross and to the Book of the Gospels and to the other holy objects, incense and lights may be offered according to ancient pious custom. For the honour which is paid to the image passes on to that which the image represents, and he who reveres the image reveres in it the subject represented." [37]

The Council specifically distinguished between the veneration to be paid to images and the worship due to God alone. But the Council of Frankish bishops held in Frankfurt in 794 condemned "the Greek synod at Constantinople" for directing that the same adoration be rendered to the holy images as to the Trinity. This remarkable error seems to have been caused by a scribe in the Vatican having mistranslated the finding of the Ecumenical Council in the official copy which the Papal chancery sent to Charles the Great. In the light of this error, the Caroline books which it is thought Alcuin prepared for Charles the Great in 790 and all the immense confusion upon the matter in the Church of Gaul seem to have been gratuitous and unnecessary.[38]

At the Council of Frankfurt which officially condemned

[37] The Seven Ecumenical Councils, 550, in *Nicene and Post-Nicene Fathers, etc.*, Vol. XIV.

[38] Hodgkin, *Italy and Her Invaders*, VIII, 18.

Adoptianism and image worship and rejected the authority of the general council of Nicaea, Alcuin appeared in the double rôle of chief representative of the British Church and upholder of the position of the King of the Franks. He was in short the foremost theologian of the West and by far the most important of the advisers of Charles the Great. But as yet the former heir apparent to the Archbishopric of York had enjoyed but modest honors and titles in Frankland. In the year 796 his king rewarded him by making him abbot of the most venerated monastery of his realm, the very historic abbey of St. Martin of Tours. The scholasticus had expressed a desire to be free from the taxing cares of the court that he might be permitted to spend the rest of his days in serving God alone. At first the King refused to let him go; but at length his importuning prevailed, and Charles gave him his foremost monastery as a home.

Busy men not seldom retire to greater businesses. The new abbot of Tours was charged by his adoptionist adversary with being at the head of an estate which possessed twenty thousand slaves.[39] There Alcuin did two things; he reëstablished the discipline of the Benedictine Rule, and he reorganized the studies of the monastery. For the last his first great need was books. Theodore of Tarsus, Benedict Biscop, and others had been carrying them from the Continent to Britain, now they must be brought back again. To do that Alcuin asked Charles's permission to send certain of his disciples to Northumbria to bring back "the flowers of Britain, since it is fitting that the garden in which those flowers grow should be the exclusive property of York, we must strive to possess some of them at Tours upon the banks of the Loire." [40]

[39] Mullinger, *op. cit.*, 110.
[40] Migne, *op. cit.*, C, 208.

But there was no great gain in having a single manu-script of Jerome, Priscian, or Bede. Not many could read it until it became a parent manuscript and gave birth to many copies. So Alcuin must have a *scriptorium* at Tours; and, organizer that he was, he proceeded to or-ganize a great one, which was as efficient as a publish-ing house, in a day in which the need was greater. It was in that scriptorium that the famous Caroline script was perfected, and Alcuin did more for it than organize the scriptorium in which it was developed.[41] Copying was and is a fine art. At Tours it had been in part forgotten. Alcuin tells Charles that he struggles daily with Tou-rainian rusticity and begs him (800) to look after the same matters at the capital: "Let your authority so in-struct the youths at the palace that they may be able to utter with perfect elegance whatever the clear eloquence of your thought may dictate, so that wheresoever the parchment bearing the royal name shall go, it may dis-play the excellence of the royal learning."[42] The great abbot is not only scholasticus in chief at Tours but editor in chief of his vast publishing industry. He is not only a scrupulous scholar but a creative artist with the most delicate sense for beauty. Having been a copyist at York and directed the copying of the palace school he re-alizes that "the distinctions and sub-distinctions of punc-tuation give a fairer aspect to written sentences." Cas-siodorus had had the same solicitude when the scriptorium was taking form under his hand. Now it was to be found in nearly every monastery, but Alcuin's efforts raise its product to a new degree of excellence. The script of Tours became the model for the first type founders of

[41] Roger Hinks, *Carolingian Art*, 107; Rand, *A Survey of the Manu-scripts of Tours*, 38.
[42] Epistle 101 (Migne, *op. cit.*, C, 315).

France seven hundred years later. At the entrance of his scriptorium some verses were posted up which served as the by-laws of the workshop: "Here let the scribes sit who copy out the words of the Divine Law, and likewise the hallowed sayings of holy fathers. Let them beware of interspersing their own frivolities in the words they copy, nor let a trifler's hand make mistakes through haste. Let them earnestly seek out for themselves correctly written books to transcribe, that the flying pen may speed along the right path. Let them distinguish the proper sense by colons and commas, and set the points each one in its due place, and let not him who reads the words to them either read falsely or pause suddenly. It is a noble work to write out holy books, nor shall the scribe fail of his due reward. Writing books is better than planting vines, for he who plants a vine serves his belly, but he who writes a book serves his soul." [43]

This then is the picture. The monks who write out what is read to them are seated each at his own writing table. The reader, so placed that all may hear, reads to them from the manuscript which they are reproducing, slowly enough for all to take down what is read, and distinctly enough to indicate the correct punctuation. The process is a slow one, but a score or more copies may be in the making under each reader. Only monastic patience under a well administered rule could have copied enough books to save religion and learning to the world. Under Alcuin and his successor the works copied which are now in existence, Professor Rand thinks, are seven Bibles, six copies of the Gospels, two Evangelistaries, one Psalter, theological works and commentaries by St. Augustine, St. Jerome, St. John of Constantinople, and Bede, Lives and passions of the saints, works on canon and civil law, of

[43] West, *Alcuin*, 72, from Migne, *op. cit.*, CI, 745 (*Carmen* LXVII).

Tours's Liber Miraculorum and two of Alcuin's own works. Priscian is copied and studied, which means that such ancient authors are read and copied as Cicero (Orations and De Amicitia), Suetonius, Virgil, and Nonius Marcellus.[44]

When enough books were made to allow it, we may believe that Alcuin divided his monks into classes and instructed them as we find him in 796 recommending that procedure to his former pupil, Archbishop Eanbald, whom he would have keep up the school at York: "Provide masters both for your boys and for the grown-up clerks. Separate into classes those who are to study in books, those who are to practice the church music, and those who are to engage in transcribing. Have a separate master for every class, that the boys may not run about in idleness, or occupy themselves in silly play, or be given over to other follies. Consider these things most carefully, my dearest son, to the end that the fountain of all wholesome erudition may still be found flowing in the chief city of our nation."[45] From all this it will be evident what his report to the king of his occupation at St. Martin's meant: "I, your Flaccus, according to your exhortation and wise desire am applying myself to serve to certain ones under the roof of St. Martin, the honey of the Holy Scriptures, some I attempt to intoxicate with the old wine of ancient studies, some I nourish with the fruits of grammatical science, I point the eyes of others to the glittering order of the stars. . . . In the morning of my life, the time when studies flower, I sowed the seed of science in Britain. Now in its evening while my blood is cooling I have not ceased to sow in France. I desire that by the grace of God, they may develop and prosper

[44] Rand, op. cit., 1–52.
[45] Migne, op. cit., C, 224 (Letter 56).

in the one as in the other country." [46] But Alcuin prized
secular learning less in his age than in his youth. Virgil
was interdicted to the monks at Tours. "The sacred
poets are enough for you," he said; "you have no need
to sully your minds with the rank luxuriance of Virgil's
verse." [47] Yet lessons were being given at Tours by the
most celebrated teacher in Christendom, and students
came from far places—even from England and Ireland—
to sit in his classes; the wise men of the land came to
consult him, and bishops gathered to his preaching. He
was honored in his old age even as he had been in middle
age at the court of the king. Two disappointments
troubled his peace. He had left one of his three Saxon
pupils in charge of the palace school; but the king, who
loved all foreigners with a great love, had shortly after
Alcuin's withdrawal been visited by two Irish teachers
whom he found so wise and engaging that he put one of
them, Clement, into the place which Alcuin had left.
This marked change of educational policy took place but
two years after Alcuin's retirement from that post and
was undertaken entirely without his knowledge. His self-
esteem was wounded, and he did not hide his keen disappointment in a letter which he addressed to the king
shortly afterward: "Simpleton that I was and ignorant,
little dreaming that the school of the Egyptians had
gained an entrance into David's glorious palace. When I
went away, I left the Latins there; I know not who introduced the Egyptians. It is not so much that I have
been ignorant of the Memphian method of calculation, as
attached to the Roman custom; for I long ago entered
the land of promise and left the Egyptian darkness be-

[46] Migne, *op. cit.*, C, 209. Laforêt, *Histoire d'Alcuin*, 101.
[47] Migne, *op. cit.*, C, 101. Mullinger, *op. cit.*, 110.

hind." [48] The king's preferment of the Irish scholars seemed to the orthodox Latins much like the official establishing of a heresy in their midst. Nevertheless, the Irish school did not cease to lead in the educational affairs of the court during the century then opening.

The king sought to become reconciled with his offended teacher, and did so the more easily because of the absorbing character of the Adoption controversy which Alcuin was then successfully concluding. When Charles was about to set out for Rome in the year 800, to be crowned by the Pope as Emperor of the Holy Roman Empire, he begged Alcuin to accompany him; but the Abbot of Tours pleaded that his enfeebled body could not stand so long and hard a journey and claimed the privilege of his years, to spend his days instead in making preparation to go before the Eternal Judge.

The cause to which Alcuin had devoted his life did not die with him. He had sowed the seeds of knowledge in many earnest minds in Frankland. Numerous disciples strove to spread the master's teaching. His imperial patron lived for ten years more to direct and inspire his successors in carrying on the work in which Alcuin had led. The zeal of the Emperor did not wane. He set for himself the task of writing out the war songs and hero tales of his people, and he memorized them. He also began a grammar of the German language, the first in existence.[49] His last days he spent in correcting the Vulgate text of the Bible for the benefit of the clergy of his Empire. Several synods, such as Chalons, Arles, Metz, Rheims, and Tours, which were held in the last years of Charles the Great reaffirm the need for an educated clergy

[48] Migne, *op. cit.*, C, 266. Mullinger, *op. cit.*, 121–122.
[49] *Early Lives of Charlemagne, etc.*, 45.

and call upon the bishops to found schools for instruction
in the disciplines and in the expounding of Scripture.

Lewis the Pious, who succeeded Charles as Emperor,
had been a favorite pupil of Alcuin and was himself a
lover of learning, a Latin scholar, a theologian, and somewhat acquainted with the Greek language. But Lewis
was not the rounded man his father was; he was, men
said, "a crowned priest." He made a real contribution by
causing the Scriptures to be translated into some of the
dialects of Frankland. To bring about a strict observance
of the Benedictine Rule he persuaded the austere and
capable Benedict of Aniane to act as abbot of abbots of
the Empire. A council at Aachen in 816 extended to the
whole church of Gaul the regulation Chrodegang had introduced putting the secular priests under a rule, and
urged the bishops to watch with solicitude the children
and youths who frequented their schools. A capitulary
issued by the Emperor in the following year (817) detailed the observances of the monastic life and ordered
that none but monks and oblati should be taught in the
schools inside the monasteries. Henceforth the cathedral
schools were to educate the secular clergy; but the pres-
sure on the monasteries was too great, and they had to
carry on their training of pupils from the world. To do
that they organized outer schools, or schools at the gates
of the monastery. That the cause of learning did not
prosper to the satisfaction of all concerned to maintain
it, is evidenced first by a capitulary of Lewis the Pious
addressed to the bishops in the year 825, calling upon
them "not to neglect for the good of the public to establish schools in convenient places where there are none
as yet, as you promised us at Attigny and as we have enjoined you to do to the end that you should provide for
the education and complete instruction of the sons and

the ministers of the church." [50] In the spirit of Charles the Great a provincial Roman council of the year 826 adopted a canon which was in 853 reaffirmed by a council of the Church presided over by the Pope. It read: "Of certain places it is reported that there neither are teachers for the study of letters nor a care to find them. Wherefore let all bishops and the people over whom they preside, in every place in which the need arises exercise all care and diligence that masters and doctors be appointed to teach the study of letters and liberal arts, and the holy doctrines which they possess, since in them chiefly are the commands manifested and declared." [51] In the year 829 the bishops of Gaul met in Paris and petitioned the Emperor "that you, following the example of your father, will cause public schools to be established in at least three fitting places of your realm, that the labour of your father and yourself may not through neglect (which God forbid) utterly decay and perish: so shall great benefit and honour abound to God's holy church and to you a great reward and everlasting remembrance." [52]

To Charles the King all his subjects including infants over twelve years of age took an oath of fidelity. That oath was renewed by all of them after he became Emperor in 800. Charles the Great himself planted the seeds of disintegration and feudalism, first, by authorizing all "simple" free men to choose an overlord for themselves, and secondly, by dividing up his kingdom and apportioning it to his sons just as though it were a private estate. That first division, he himself made in 806. Two of the

[50] Stallaert and Van der Haegen, *op. cit.,* 27.

[51] Poole, *Illustration of the History of Medieval Thought and Learning,* 21 (London, 1885). Eichorn, *Geschichte der Kultur,* II, 450.

[52] Poole, *op. cit.,* 22.

sons died, and Lewis the Pious remained sole Emperor, but the Kingdom of the Lombards had to be detached for his nephew Bernard, the son of Pepin. Lewis divided his realm to his sons in 817. If each member of a ruling family, generation after generation, inherits a share of the kingdom, there is no end to its legal disintegration and to the wars which must be fought over it. That was feudalism. It was ordered from the top. The times begin to be times of great confusion.

During Lewis the Pious' reign the school of Tours no longer led the world, but that of the monastery of Fulda did. There Rabanus Maurus taught, a young monk who had come from Germany to study with Alcuin for a year and had pleased the master so well that he had given him the name of Benedict's favorite disciple, Maurus. He had been born in 776, studied with Alcuin in 801, was thereafter the teacher at Fulda and its abbot after 822. Sixteen tributary abbeys were under his direction. He inscribed Alcuin's admonitory rules over the door of its scriptorium and kept twelve monks engaged in copying books there. He founded a library and himself wrote several works, among them an encyclopedia of knowledge with the title *De Universo*. In it he defined grammar as "the science of interpreting the poets and historians; and the art of correct writing and speaking." The ancient classics, he frankly valued and taught. Dialectic, he made the most important of studies; with Augustine he defined it as *disciplina disciplinarum; haec docet docere, haec docet discere*. His greatest pupils were Walafrid Strabo, the poet, who was tutor to Charles the Bald and abbot of Reichenau, and Servatus Lupus, Abbot of Ferrières from 842, a great lover of the classics, and a great reader, collector, and maker of books. This man preached the refreshing but enigmatical conviction that "learning should be sought for its own sake." He is so steeped in, and so devoted to, the Latin writers of Roman days as almost to merit the title of a humanist before his time. Mullinger has compared his love of ancient letters to that of Petrarch in intensity. The Abbot of Ferrières' extreme devotion to the study of Virgil, Cicero, and Quintilian would have scandalized any Gregorian churchman. If schools declined after Charles the Great, the copying of manuscripts did not; the libraries of France have enough of them today to show a great diligence in producing them in the ninth century.

Ebert points out that, after the separation of the Germans from the Franks in the division of the Empire in 817 and finally in 843, the teaching of the German monastic schools developed in a direction different from that of the French schools west of the Rhine. In the German monasteries grammar, poetry, and religion were the chief subjects; in France, logic and theology became uppermost.[53]

Representatives of the West Frankian tendency were not wanting among Rabanus' disciples and one of them, the Saxon Gottschalk, ranks high among the troublers of the Church and exhibits the power of original thinking which the schools were beginning to impart. First he came into disfavor by requesting the abbot Rabanus to free him from the monastic obligations under which his father had placed him while but a child. He was formally unfrocked by the Synod of Metz; but upon the appeal of Rabanus that decision was set aside, and Gottschalk left Fulda to take up his residence in the monastery of Orbais. He devoted himself to a study of the works of Augustine and was so impressed by the doctrine of predestination that he came to regard it as the fundamental

[53] Ebert, *La Littérature du Moyen Age*, II, 136.

tenet of Christianity and devoted his life to that belief. He was admitted to priestly orders and travelled extensively throughout Italy and France, preaching and debating everywhere in an untiring quest for converts to his doctrine.[54] His teaching that the purposes of the immutable God could not be affected by human conduct or compliance with churchly rites, could not but be branded as a heresy by the upholders of the orthodox faith; and Rabanus put himself at the head of the opposition against his former pupil and fought him so vigorously that Gottschalk gave to all his opponents "den Spottnamen 'Rabanici.' "[55] The conflict was a bitter one. The scholarship of Gottschalk was equalled only by his earnestness. Having confounded the masters who disputed against him by citations from Augustine, he offered to prove the truth of his doctrine by submitting to the ordeal by fire. But the pious Lewis who presided at his trial declared him guilty of preaching contrary to public morals, and Gottschalk together with a number of his leading followers was condemned to be publicly whipped, after which punishment the leader was exiled from East Francia. But the fanaticism of belief was in him, and the active propaganda which he continued in the Western kingdom brought a second condemnation and scourging together with public degradation from the priestly office and a sentence of perpetual imprisonment in the monastery of Hautvilliers. But even here his spirit of controversy was unbroken, and sympathetic friends and followers, among the former the distinguished Servatus Lupus, and among the latter a number of monks and bishops, at length secured a new hearing for his doctrine. This time

[54] Ebert, *op. cit.*, II, 142.
[55] Ebert, *op. cit.*, II, 142.

he was publicly pitted against a worthier foeman, the famous Johannes Scotus Erigena, who is commonly regarded as the first of the long series of the Middle Age philosophers—the reason for whose presence in Frankland deserves consideration.

Nothing is said of Clement's direction of the palace school, and little of the Irish monks in Lewis the Pious' empire. Perhaps the king was too orthodox to think favorably of them, but they kept coming to the Continent, little bands of them, a missionary leader and twelve disciple monks. "Need I remind Ireland," wrote Eric, the biographer of St. Germanus, in 876, "that she sent troops of philosophers over land and sea to our distant shores, that her most learned sons offered their gifts of wisdom of their own free will in the service of our learned king, our Solomon [Charles the Bald]?" Servatus Lupus, who had been his tutor, describes this Emperor as "doctrinae studiosissimus"; that is, he had a superlative interest in learning. It will always add glory to his reign that he had the insight and character to give affection and hospitality to the greatest scholar of his century and one of the most original thinkers of all time in the person of Johannes Scotus Erigena. This, the most distinguished of the emigrant sons of Ireland, suddenly appears as head of the palace school at the court of Charles the Bald in the fourth decade of the ninth century. Poole suggests that he "drifted" to the court of the Emperor. Many were drifting about. The trouble with that is that this man had qualities that drifters cannot possess. He brought with him very definite proof of the advanced state of learning in his country—a knowledge of Greek vastly superior to that of any Continental scholar for centuries. So thoroughly steeped was he in Greek learning that he has been called "the belated disciple of Plato, and the last representative of the Greek spirit in the west." [56]

Throughout his life Johannes Scotus seems to have been content with the position of a layman. Like the Irish Columbanus, Johannes relied upon reason rather than upon the approved opinions of the Church and exhibited remarkable enthusiasm for Plato; [57] but his first hand knowledge of the Greek master seems to have been derived from the *Timaeus* alone and to have been supplemented by the writings of certain members of the Alexandrian, or Syrian, school, some of whom were Christians. Among these a work on the Divine Names attributed to Dionysius the Areopagite, "the first Athenian convert made by the apostle Paul," was especially interesting to the Frankish churchmen, for tradition had it that that same convert had brought Christianity to France and had founded the abbey of St. Denis, and he was revered as the patron saint of France.[58] Elaborately prepared copies of this book, or of works by this author, had been presented by Pope Paul I to Pepin in 757: by Hadrian I to Abbot Fuldrad of St. Denis and to Lewis the Pious by the Byzantine Emperor Michael the Stammerer. But no translator had been found for this work, concerning whose content the Franks were naturally quite curious. The Abbot of St. Denis had attempted to turn it into Latin but his effort had been a woeful failure. The superior knowledge of Johannes Scotus offered the means of realizing the long deferred desire to know what mysteries it contained, and the translation was accordingly made at the instance of his patron Charles the Bald. But the book on the Divine Names was of too mystical a

---

[56] Poole, *op. cit.*, 52.
[57] Hauréau, *Philosophie Scholastique* (Paris, 1872), I, 150–153.
[58] Migne, *op. cit.*, CXXII, 19.

character to be readily understood even when carefully translated, and the disappointment with which the incomprehensible Latin was read was equalled only by the admiration which the ability to translate such a work from the Greek, at all, excited.[59] The statement of the papal librarian, Anastasius, concerning Johannes' translation is too illuminating to be omitted: "The interpretation still needs an interpreter," but, he continued, "it is astonishing how this barbarian living on the confines of the world, who might reasonably have been presumed to be as ignorant of Greek as he was remote from intercourse with civilized men, could have been able to grasp such mysteries and to render them into another language." [60] We of today have almost as great difficulty in believing that "such barbarians" as dwelt in Ireland far from the traditional seats of civilization were able to grasp the mysteries which the Greek writings contained. But Johannes Scotus is an unimpeachable witness to the thoroughness of the Greek teaching of the Irish monastic schools; and that he was able to grasp such mysteries as confounded the wise men of the Continent, is convincing testimony concerning the speculative character of the Irish scholarship of his day.

But the work which he translated (which modern criticism attributes not to Dionysius the Areopagite but rather to some member of the Christian school at Edessa who lived in the fifth century, and whose doctrines Johannes in large part adopted for his own) was of entirely too pantheistic a character to escape the condemnation of the orthodox churchmen of the time. "But what astonishment, nay, even what respect, must this doctor

[59] See the *Works of Dionysius the Areopagite,* transl. Rev. John Parker (London, 1897).
[60] Migne, *op. cit.,* CXXII, 93.

inspire in us who caused so much agitation in the school and in the church, who sowed the wind and reaped the whirlwind, but knew how to brave it, who while leaving no direct inheritor of his doctrine, had at least the glory of having announced it and of preceding Bruno, Vanini, and Spinoza, the most fearless logicians who ever wandered among the trees of the academy." [61] Pope Nicholas I objected to the book and ordered the King of the Franks to send it to him for correction. The feeling of the authorities throughout the Church was that the work must be censored and the translator and upholder of the doctrines which it embodied must be branded as a heretic. But the king's friendship for his teacher (who had added to his list of services by translating for the royal study a second work of a character similar to the former one, the Greek commentary of the monk Maximus) afforded him a measure of protection and saved him from the personal violence which would doubtless have been his lot had he not dwelt in the shadow of the throne. Johannes' greatest offence consisted in proclaiming philosophy as a science equal in importance to theology and independent of it. In other words, he committed the classic sin of teaching that man's reason is as infallible a guide as revelation. The truth of revelation depends upon authority, and, when reason and what processes to be revelation conflict, not revelation but reason is sole arbiter; for reason is the source of true religion as well as of true philosophy which therefore cannot war. [62]

[61] Hauréau, *op. cit.*, 151.

[62] " 'Authority,' he says, 'emanates from reason, not reason from authority; true reason has no need to be supported by any authority. We must use reason first in our investigations and authority afterwards.'. . . The only punishment of sin, he says, is sin; there is no eternal fire; even the lost enjoy a certain happiness for they are not deprived of truth. These and a thousand equally unsound passages, raised him a crowd of adversaries all of whom he treated with that

The solitary scholar who devoted his life, as he believed, to the restoration of the Platonic wisdom and was very cordially hated, everywhere save at the court, for fostering such heresies, naturally took but little part in the public movements of his time. But the peculiar character of his studies and the superior knowledge which he possessed rendered him an indispensable ally in the Church's attempt to overthrow the heresy of Gottschalk, and the badly worsted churchmen invoked his assistance. To the Saxon monk's statement that the immutable God has caused all things from the beginning, the Irish Platonist could very easily reply that the nature of God cannot be determined according to the rules of ordinary logic or everyday habits of thought. The infinite God who transcends sense and human intelligence cannot be compressed into the categories of limitation. He is neither genus nor species nor accident, and cannot be treated under the aspect of time or finite cause. His all-inclusive being is limited only by itself, and man is therefore free in Him. Thus out of St. Augustine himself, but without invoking him as authority, he confounded the Augustinian scholar.[63] But the weapon of argument which Johannes employed in the work *De Praedestinatione,* in which the reply to Gottschalk was stated, did not meet the approval of the orthodox churchmen. They objected to its author's tone of superior learning and railed bitterly at his employment of "the trickeries of sophistic" rather

---

supercilious contempt which would seem necessarily to enter into the character of the scholastic heretic. 'They are all deceived,' he writes, 'owing to their ignorance of liberal studies; they have none of them studied Greek, and with a knowledge of the Latin language alone it is impossible for them to understand the distinctions of science.'" (Drane, *Christian Schools and Scholars,* 145.) (For these positions see the *De Praedestinatione,* particularly the paralogisms and the discussion of future punishment in Migne, *op. cit.,* CXXII, 420, 434.)

[63] Maurice, *Moral and Metaphysical Philosophy* (London, 1882), I, 480.

than the plain words of Scripture; and on the whole the
controversy was increased rather than stilled by his participation in it. Nor did a greater measure of success
crown his attempt to confute the teaching of Radbert
concerning the nature of the Sacraments—a task which
he seems to have undertaken at the instance of his
patron, Charles the Bald; and his argument, which doubtless took the form that the transcendent nature of God
is overlooked when He is conceived as reduced to the
necessity of communing with men by assuming physical
form, only brought scandal to his temporary partisans
who insisted upon making their God in their own image.
Johannes was made a target for spoken and written de-
nunciation. Two separate synods of the Church condemned his *De Praedestinatione*,[64] and thus with un-
paralleled bitterness and acrimony was philosophy introduced as ally of theology in the Western Church. Succeeding generations did not find the Irish philosopher's
work so distasteful. His books *De Divisione Naturae* were
permitted to exist and were copied. His translation of
Dionysius was widely read, as the many manuscripts
of it which exist testify, and was commented upon by
churchmen of unspotted reputation among their fellows,
although its author had to be "pardoned for some matters wherein, holding his eyes fast upon the Greeks, he
has deflected from the path of the Latins"—the only
proviso which William of Malmesbury enters against its
usefulness. A very persistent tradition of the Middle
Ages has it that after the death of Charles the Bald this
aged teacher left the inhospitable shores of France to
find a welcome at the court of the learning-lover Alfred
the Great.[65] Mr. Henry Bett thinks there is nothing un-

---

[64] Migne, *op. cit.*, CXXII, 354. Valence, 855, and Langres, 859.

[65] Poole, *op. cit.*, 78. See his Appendix II, for a discussion of the
evidence for this fact.

likely in this save the bizarre death that is said to have overtaken John. King Alfred had just beaten the Danes (878) after years of war, and the time of renewing was at hand.[66] Asser says that King Alfred "sent messengers beyond the sea to Gaul to procure teachers, and he invited from thence Grimbald, priest and monk, a venerable man and good singer, adorned with every kind of ecclesiastical discipline and good morals and most learned in holy Scripture. He also obtained from thence John, also priest and monk, a man of most energetic talents and learned in all kinds of literary science, and skilled in many other arts. By the teaching of these men the king's mind was much enlarged, and he enriched and honoured them, with much influence." [67]

In Frankland men fought a losing fight against oncoming darkness. The synod of Vern (844) ordered the bishops to provide for the instruction of the priests in the country districts. The synod of Valens, held in 855, recommended to the bishops to hold schools for the teaching of the sciences, both divine and human, and for instruction in church music—for, because of the long interruption of studies, ignorance of the faith and lack of learning had invaded many of the churches of God. The synod of Kiersy-sur-Oise (858) exhorted Charles the Bald to revive the work of the palace school. That of Savonnieres, held in the following year, spoke in favor of profane literature, which assisting divine learning had, under the protection of the Emperors, spread so much light through the Church. It appealed to the princes and bishops to encourage secular learning lest the knowledge of Scripture should be irreparably lost.[68] The synod of

---

[66] Bett, *Johannes Scotus Erigena*, 13.
[67] Asser's Life of Alfred, in Giles, *Six English Chronicles,* 70 (Bohn).
[68] Stallaert and Van der Haegen, *op. cit.*, 31.

Langres held in the same year (859) decreed that, wherever God raised up men able to teach, all suitable efforts should be made to found public schools so that the fruits of both kinds of knowledge, spiritual and secular, might grow in the Church.[69] In the year 899 Riculf, Bishop of Soissons, issued a letter to his clergy exhorting his country priests to pay attention to schools, and forbidding boys and girls to be brought together in them.[70] Such solicitation for education on the part of the churchmen indicates that ecclesiastical and parochial schools were maintained with the greatest difficulty during this period and though they did not utterly cease to exist the encroachments of a semi-barbarous age forced learning to seek refuge in the monasteries. The schools of Amand, Aniane, Condat, Corbie, Fulda, Auxerre, St. Gall, Hirsauge, Reichenau, Requier, Tours, etc., though not free from the troubles of the time, afforded it a larger encouragement in their more quiet retreats.

In the latter part of the ninth century a certain "magister" Iso doctor Nominatissimus had among his pupils at St. Gall, Notker, Tutilo, Ratpert, and Solomon who afterward became abbot, who having been thoroughly instructed in divine things "became scholars of Marcellus; who being equally versed in sacred and secular learning, taught them the seven liberal arts, but especially music," [71] in which they made great progress. The accomplishments of these three monks, as outlined by Ekkehard, the historian of St. Gall, furnish an interesting view of the monastic habits of the time. Notker, we are told, was "in ornamenting, reading and composing, assiduous; and, briefly to comprehend all his sacred endowments, he was

[69] Neander, *History of the Christian Religion and Church*, III, 427.
[70] *Loc. cit.*
[71] Maitland, *Dark Ages*, 446.

a vessel of the Holy Spirit not less eminently than any one of his time." Tutilo "was eloquent, with a fine voice, skilful in carving, and a painter. A musician like his companions; but in all kinds of stringed and wind instruments (for in a place appointed by the abbot he taught the children of the nobility to play on stringed instruments), he excelled everybody. In building and in other arts he was eminent." Ratpert had been the schoolmaster from his youth, a straightforward kind teacher, very strict in discipline, more rarely than any of his brethren putting his foot out of the cloister, and making one pair of shoes last a twelvemonth. He said that going out was destructive, and frequently admonished Tutilo, who was given to travelling, to mind what he was about. Fully occupied in the schools, he commonly neglected the services and the Mass, "for," said he, "we hear good Masses while we are teaching how they should be performed"; and although he used to say that impunity was the greatest disgrace of a monastery, yet he never came to the chapter unless sent for; because, as he observed, that most painful office of reproving and punishing was laid upon him. Such were "three of the senators of our republic."[72]   Italy, which had been instrumental in suggesting the work of educational reform to Charles the Great, and had loaned scholars to begin it, had not kept pace with France in educational development. Her simple and unpretentious schools, entrusted to the care of the communities that chose to maintain them, had but an irregular and insecure existence.[73] In the year 825 Lothaire the king issued a capitulary intended to reorganize them upon a more stable basis. "Concerning true doctrine," it read, "which on account of the care-

[72] Maitland, *Dark Ages*, 446–447.
[73] Salvioli, *L'Instruzione pubblica in Italia*, 20.

lessness and the listlessness of those in authority, has everywhere ceased to exist, we require that as it has been ordered by us so shall it be observed by all, namely that the greatest care be taken by those who have been appointed to teach others, in the places designated by us, that those entrusted to them shall become proficient scholars. And furthermore, so that neither distance nor poverty may serve as an excuse to anyone, we have fixed the localities where schools shall be conducted. Let the students assemble to the teaching in Pavia, from Milan, Brescia, Lodi, Bergamo, Novara, Vercelli, Tortona, Acqui, Genoa, Asti and Como. At Ivrea from the bishopric. Let them gather at Torino from Ventimiglia, Albenga, Alba and Vado. At Cremona those of Reggio, Piacenza, Parma and Modena shall study. The Tuscans shall go to Florence for instruction, to Fermo those of the territory of Spoleto, to Verona those of Mantua and Triento, to Vicenza those of Padua, Treviso, Feltre, Ceneda and Asolo. Other districts shall send to the school of Cividad del Friuli." [74] In the following year the decree of the Roman Council already quoted instructed the bishops "to exercise all care and diligence that masters and doctors be appointed wherever there is need to teach the study of letters and liberal arts and the holy doctrines which they possess." This canon was readopted by a council of Rome, presided over by the Pope in the year 853. Thus Church and state worked together to reform the schools; but the fact that a second council was compelled to reinstruct the clergy but twenty-seven years after the first orders were issued indicates that they had not been very zealous in performing the work enjoined upon them. The barbarity of the people, their long unfamiliarity with letters which had taught

[74] Tiraboschi, *Storia della Letteratura Italiana,* I, 461 (Milano, 1833); and Salvioli, *op. cit.,* 20.

them to hold them in little esteem and to regard them as a needless luxury, and the scarcity of books conspired to make a general educational reform impossible.[75] The laws did, however, encourage the work of the schools already in existence, and there is abundant evidence that, though the plans of the king and the bishops failed, the more humble labors of many irregular teachers continued without interruption.[76]

Under Alfred (848–900), King of Wessex—"whom men have called the 'Great' and the 'Truthteller,' whom the England of the Middle Ages named 'England's Darling,' who was 'the Warrior and the Hunter, the Deliverer and the Law-maker, the Singer and the Lover of his people,'"[77] and the creator of English prose literature—England was the scene of a revival of learning similar to that of Charles the Great in Frankland. Indeed it was more than similar: it was a part of the same revival. When but a lad of five years (853), the little prince Alfred was taken to Rome and anointed king by the Pope, who received him as his adopted son. Two years later he made a second journey to the city of the Popes, remaining there this time about one year. It is not an unwarranted supposition that the interests of his life were permanently colored by these early experiences. His long unsatisfied desire to read Latin literature and his close friendship for the Church of Rome no doubt resulted from them. On his return from Rome he lived for three months at the court of Charles the Bald. "The palace of the schools," and what he saw there and what he heard of the illustrious deeds of Charles the Great and

[75] Tiraboschi, *op. cit.*, I, 463.

[76] See the many references to their work in Tiraboschi, *op. cit.*, I, 464 and elsewhere, in Salvioli, *op. cit.*, in Ozanam, *Le Scuole e l'instruzione in Italia*, and in Giesebrecht, *De Litterarum studiis apud Italos*.

[77] Stopford A. Brooke, *King Alfred*, 1.

of the Anglo-Saxon Alcuin whose work had brought
so many blessings to the land, were a fitting propaedeutic
for the work of a king. Home influences were not wanting to keep the memory of these lessons fresh within
him and to supplement them. At his mother's knee he
learned the songs of the Saxons, receiving the book, in
which they were written down in illuminated letters, as a
reward for his interest in its contents. In addition, he
learned to read and committed certain psalms and prayers
to memory while a lad. "But sad to say! he could not
gratify his most ardent wish to learn the liberal arts, because as he said there were no good readers at that time
in all the kingdom of the West-Saxons. This he confessed with many lamentations and sighs to have been
one of his greatest difficulties and impediments in this
life, namely that when he was young and had the capacity
for learning, he could not find teachers, but when he was
more advanced in life, he was harassed by so many
diseases unknown to all the physicians of this island as
well as by internal and external anxieties of sovereignty
and by continual invasions of the pagans, and had his
teachers and writers also so much disturbed that there
was no time for reading. But yet among the impediments
of this present life from infancy up to the present time,
and as I believe until his death, he continued to feel
the same insatiable desire of knowledge, . . ." [78]

The destruction of Lindisfarne had been but the beginning of sorrows in the land. For seventy years it had
experienced "a rain of blood" at the hands of the Danish
invaders. The churches and schools were destroyed. The
monastic communities were broken up, and the few monks
who escaped death were scattered. The disorganized

[78] Asser, *op. cit.*, 32. The Jubilee Ed. of the whole works of King
Alfred the Great (Oxford and Cambridge, 1852).

clergy had almost ceased to perform its function, and the knowledge of letters was all but lost. The Danes, who had pillaged until there was little more to take, were beginning to settle in England. Such was the condition of affairs when Alfred came to the throne (871). During the first years of his reign the Danes continued their incursions, and it seemed that his kingdom must be blotted out. In the winter of 878 Alfred took refuge at Athelney and, defended by the surrounding marshes and forests, gathered and trained a host; and in the following spring he attacked the Danish army and secured the peace of Wedmore. During the succeeding years of quiet he organized his government, promulgated his laws, re-formed his army, and built a navy. When the Northmen broke forth again in the year 885, he attacked them by sea and by land and defeated them, securing a more permanent peace for his country. Plans for the educational improvement of his people had long been uppermost in his thoughts. Now he was free to carry them out. But as he looked over the land his soul sank within him at the thought of its past greatness and the low condition to which it had fallen. "There was a time," he writes, "when foreigners sought wisdom and learning in this island. Now we are compelled to seek them in foreign lands. Such was the general ignorance of the English, that there were few on this side of the Humber—and I dare say not many on the other—who could understand the service in English or translate a Latin letter into their own language, so few were they, that I do not recollect a single individual to the South of the Thames, who was able to do it when I ascended the throne." [79] His first care had been to gather around him the few English

---

[79] From the preface to the translation of Gregory's Pastoral Rule, Lingard, *The Anglo-Saxon Church*, II, 244.

scholars who might assist in the work of teaching. He found them in Werefrith, Bishop of Worcester and head of the Episcopal school there, Plegmund, the hermit of Cheshire who was made Archbishop of Canterbury, and Ethelstan and Werewulf who together with Plegmund had been trained in the school at Worcester, and were appointed royal chaplains with the duty of reading to the king whenever he had leisure whether by day or by night. These were all that England could supply; "but the king's commendable avarice could not be gratified in this," and he had to turn to the Continent and beg a return of the loan which Britain had made, wherefore he sent messengers beyond the sea to Gaul to procure teachers. He invited from thence Grimbald, Provost of St. Omer's, whom he placed in charge of the new abbey rising at Winchester. He also obtained from thence John and made him abbot of the monastery which he dedicated to God at Athelney (Malmesbury). But the king's chief assistant was Asser of St. David's monastery in Wales, who, when importuned to take up his residence at the court, was unwilling to leave his post in his native land, but when the king pleaded, "Stay with me at least six months in the year," had consented. "The king was in the habit of hearing the Scriptures read by his own countrymen . . . and he attended to it with sedulity and solicitude. His bishops too and all ecclesiastics, his earls and nobles, ministers and friends, were loved by him with wonderful affection, and their sons who were bred up in the royal household were no less dear to him than his own; he had them instructed in all kinds of good morals, and among other things never ceased to teach them letters night and day." [80] His own son Æthelwold he sent "to the schools of learning where he was in-

[80] Asser, *op. cit.*, 88.

structed along with the children of almost all the nobility
of the country, and many also who were not noble . . .
Books in both languages, namely Latin and Saxon, were
read in the school. They also learned to write so that before they were of an age to practice manly arts, namely
hunting and such pursuits as befit noblemen, they became studious and clever in the liberal arts." [81] In addition to this palace school, a school was opened at Athelney for the training of monks, and effort was made to
establish schools in the other monasteries and cathedrals
of the land. So anxious was the king to extend the
blessings of education that he even made a law requiring
every freedman possessed of two hides of land to keep
his sons at school until they were fifteen years of age,[82]
"because a man born free, who is unlettered, is to be regarded no otherwise than as a beast, having like them,
no understanding." [83] But the king's care for his people
did not stop here. When he remembered how "our fore-
fathers, who held these places before us, loved wisdom,
and through it they got wealth and left it to us," but
treasured in a foreign tongue, "wishing that there might
be the more wisdom here in the land the more we knew
of languages" and thinking that men would never "be
so careless and that learning would so fall away," and
remembered how the Law was given in the Hebrew tongue
and turned by the Greeks into their own tongue when
they learned it, and by the Romans into theirs, "therefore it seemeth better to me . . . that we also turn some
books—those which are most needful for men to know—
into the tongue which we can all understand." Then he
began "amidst other divers and manifold occupations"

---

[81] Asser, *op. cit.*, 86.
[82] Eichorn, *Geschichte der Kultur und Litteratur,* II, 209.
[83] Drane, *Christian Schools and Scholars,* 200.

of his kingdom "to turn into English the book which in Latin is named *Pastoralis* and in English *Shepherd's Book,* sometimes word for word, sometimes meaning for meaning" with the assistance of Plegmund, Asser, Grimbald, and John; and he sent a copy to each of the bishops of the kingdom, commanding that no one should remove it from the minster, for "it is unknown how long there may be such learned bishops, as now, God be thanked, are nearly everywhere." To this "well of the Lord" he added a translation of Bede's *History of the English Church,* a translation of Orosius' *History of the World,* and near the end of his life he gave to his people the ripe fruit of his wisdom, in a free translation of Boethius' *Consolation of Philosophy.* And thus having made a beginning of English prose literature and provided his people with the things most needful to be known by translating a rule of Christian life, histories of their own land and of the world, and the last feeling utterances of ancient philosophy, he is said to have undertaken other translations, among them a version of the Psalms and the *Soliloquy* of St. Augustine.

The preface to the *Soliloquy* contains a parable which reveals the personal feeling of the royal woodman of letters toward his life work better perhaps than any other passage which he wrote: "Then I gathered me darts and pillar-shafts and stead-shafts, and handles for each of the tools which I was able to work with, and 'bay timbers' and 'bolt timbers,' and for each of the works which I knew how to work, the most beautiful wood, which, felling, I could bear away. Neither came I home with an overweight; it pleased me not to bring all the wood home [even] if I could carry it all. On each tree I saw somewhat of that which I needed at home. Therefore I advise every one who may be strong enough and have many

a wain, that he go to the same wood where I cut these
pillar-shafts, and there fetch himself more, and load his
wains with branches, so that he may make many a trim
wall and many a beautiful house, and build a fair town
of them, and there may dwell joyfully and peacefully
both winter and summer as I [till] now have not yet
done. But he who taught me, to whom the wood was
pleasant, he can make me dwell more peacefully, both
in this passing dwelling on this wayfaring, while I am
in this world; and also in the eternal home which he hath
bid us hope for through St. Augustine, St. Gregory, and
St. Jerome, and many of the holy fathers; even so I
believe also that he will make (for the worthiness of
them all) both this wayfaring better than it was ere this
time; and especially enlighten the eyes of my mind, to
this end, that I may find the way to the everlasting home,
and everlasting honour, and everlasting rest which is
promised to us through the holy fathers. . . . May God
grant that I have power for both—to be useful here, and
surely to go thither." [84]
But though the king strove so mightily to restore learning to the land he did not succeed in organizing a system of institutions to carry it on after his death. In that
day the monasteries were the educational arm of the
state; and the people of England, because of the Danes,
had known so long an interruption of the established
religious life that few could be found to embrace it, for
most had learned to hold it in contempt. No worthy successor took up the educational work of the king, and his
labors speedily came to naught. A saint had to arise and
start a conflagration of religious enthusiasm before the

[84] As quoted by Stopford A. Brooke in *English Literature from the
Beginning to the Norman Conquest* (London and New York: Macmillan, 1898).

monasteries were repeopled and the schools effectually restored.

The ninth century, which had opened so auspiciously, with Charles the Great ruling over the immense territory of the Holy Roman Empire and with schools, churches, and monasteries flourishing under his beneficent protection and promising so fair a future for the state, witnessed the progressive decay of almost all the institutions which he had attempted to establish; and the close of the century ushered in a period "which for its sterility of every excellence may be denominated *iron,* for its luxuriant growth of vice, *leaden,* and for its dearth of writers, *dark.*" [85] Many causes have been assigned for the failure of the excellent establishments which the king had devoted his life to founding. They are generally of this tenor. The teachers were inapt, dry, and formal, and were not able to arouse the native curiosity of their pupils; the subjects were taught in a barbarous fashion and were indeed mere haggard skeletons of learning unfit for ornament or for use. The higher classes of society did not know even the first elements of reading and writing, and, what is worse, had no care to know them, so completely were they absorbed in the game of real or mimic war. The classics were buried and forgotten; the bishops, clergy, and monks, upon whom the care of education devolved, were without capacity. The feeling was common that religion prospered in proportion to the spread of ignorance. The churchmen feared that funds might be diverted from the churches to the schools. The Bishop of Rome was afraid of the criticism of intelligence upon the pretensions of his office, and the very "genius of the Christian system" was inimical to the learning connected with the pagan deities and "thus contributed

[85] Baronius, in Drane's *Christian Schools and Scholars,* 225.

to banish from the schools, and to consign to oblivion, those works on the study and the prevalence of which will ever depend the progress of the arts, of the sciences, and of literary taste." [86] But the teachers were not all inapt, the sciences were not worthless, kings themselves cultivated them and encouraged their subjects to do so. A goodly number of the ancient books had been preserved, and in some quarters were well known. The bishops, clerics, and monks were capable men, and their councils presided over by the Bishop of Rome pronounced again and again in favor of learning, while at least as much evidence can be brought to prove that "the genius of the Christian system" was not inimical to learning as can be produced to show that it was. What was most wanting was the sovereign soul that had created the Empire. Its partition had been the beginning of its undoing, and soon its parts passed to "the dregs of the Carlovingian race," who "no longer exhibited any symptons of virtue or power, and the ridiculous epithets of the *bald*, the *stammerer*, the *fat* and the *simple* distinguished the tame and uniform features of a crowd of kings alike deserving of oblivion." [87] It is not surprising that the half-barbarous liberty-loving Germans seized this opportunity to restore their ancient tribal system in the modified form of feudalism, and that the state became a monster with a hundred heads. What this political change meant to the Church and the schools is best told in the words of Florus, the deacon of Lyons: "A beautiful empire once flourished under a glorious crown. Then there was one prince and one people, and every town had

---

[86] Such is the summary of causes which others have assigned, offered by the Catholic writer Joseph Berington, in his *Literary History of the Middle Ages* (London, 1883), 103.

[87] Gibbon, *Decline and Fall of the Roman Empire,* chap. XLIX.

judges and laws. The word of salvation was preached to
nobles and peasants, and youth everywhere studied the
sacred Scriptures and the liberal arts . . . Now instead
of a king we see everywhere a kinglet, instead of an
Empire, its fragments. The bishops can no longer hold
their synods, there are no assemblies, no laws; and
if an embassy arrive there is no court to receive it." [88]
The monasteries and the churches disappeared, and their
schools disappeared with them. The desperate conditions
which forced each one to protect himself and so oc-
casioned the rise of feudalism caused the destruction of
many of the schools. While Lewis the Pious was still on
the throne, the Normans had appeared off the coast of
France, sailed up its rivers, and laid siege to and sacked
a dozen of the chief towns of the country. Whole provinces were devastated by them, "and not a dog was left to
bark" at the wild animals that soon prowled freely over
them. About the year 836 the Saracens attacked Marseilles and overran the South of France, possessing themselves of the district of Provence which they continued to
hold for more than a century. Near the end of the ninth
century the terrible Huns broke over the Carpathian
Mountains and pillaged the frontiers of Germany, crossed
the Alps into Lombardy, and even made inroads into
France. Not once but several times they rushed through
the land, spreading terror in advance and slaughter and
destruction behind them. Churches were plundered,
bishops and clerks were massacred, books were destroyed,
the monks driven from their monasteries, and the abbeys
burned. In this state of things it is not surprising that
the schools had but a fitful existence. The same causes
—the inroads of Saracen, Norman, and Hunnish invaders,

[88] Quoted from Florus, *Carmina Varia*, in Drane, *op. cit.*, 228.

the decay of the Empire, and the spread of civil strife—
had a similar effect upon the educational system just
then taking more definite form in Italy.

Yet even in that age so full of burning, plundering, and
bloodshed the cause of education was not entirely neglected, and the seeds which Charles the Great had
planted were cultivated in several places. Among the
disciples of Alcuin was the learned Haimon who taught
at Fulda [89] and had among his pupils Eric of Auxerre, who
afterward studied under Servatus Lupus at Ferrières and
taught in the monastery of St. Germain at Auxerre. Eric
had among his pupils the prince Lothaire, son of Charles
the Bald, Hucbald the musician and poet and director of
the monastic school of St. Amand and the cathedral school
at Rheims,[90] and Remi of Auxerre, the celebrated teacher
of grammar dialectic and music in the schools of Rheims
and Paris about the beginning of the tenth century. This
master wrote a number of religious books, a work upon
the Rule of St. Benedict, and a commentary upon Martianus Capella, Donatus, and Priscian; and like his
master Eric, who left glosses upon practically all of the
philosophical texts which were known at that time,[91]
he was very familiar with logic and gave great attention
to it in his teaching.[92] He is regarded as the restorer of
learning in France. The school which he founded in
Paris was not designed to fit monks or clerics for the
service of the Church. Independent of bishop or abbot, he
undertook to provide instruction in the liberal arts to
all who sought it, introducing the idea of learning for

[89] *Histoire Littéraire de la France*, 5–111.
[90] Ebert, *op. cit.*, II, 316. Hauréau, *Philosophie Scholastique*, I, 131.
[91] Hauréau, *op. cit.*, I, 134.
[92] Migne, *op. cit.*, CXXXIII, 52.

learning's sake. Thus he established the first "public chair" for the promotion of liberal studies in the West.[93] In his glosses on secular writings, like the pseudo-Augustine, Capella, Johannes Scotus, and his master Eric, he did not even speak of the Christian religion or its dogmas.[94] The famous first principle of Descartes, *Cogito ergo sum*, which Johannes Scotus had reproduced from St. Augustine, Remi amplified and incorporated in his writings,[95] and through him the influence of the maligned Irish teacher began to leaven the thinking of the Church.

The most famous of the pupils of Remi was Odo (879–942), who became Abbot of Cluny and reformed the monastic life of the West. Odo had the good fortune to be born in a family in which learning was appreciated. In his early youth he was put under the tuition of a priest and then placed in the household of Duke William of Aquitaine to be perfected in the discipline of knight errantry. But he wearied of these pursuits, and at the age of nineteen at his own request was admitted among the canons in the church of St. Martin at Tours. Here he applied himself to the study of grammar, and having learned all that was taught in Tours he betook himself to Paris to study under Master Remi.[96] Returning to Tours, he made a careful study of the *Moralia* of St. Gregory and wrote an epitome of it. His untiring zeal for learning is witnessed by the fact that at a time when books were hardly to be found he collected a private library of about one hundred volumes. But his zeal for the religious life was greater even than his love of books, and after

[93] Hauréau, *Singularités Historiques*, 142. *Histoire Littéraire de la France*, 6–100.

[94] Hauréau, *op. cit.*, 143.

[95] Hauréau, *Philosophie Scholastique*, I, 182.

[96] Johannes, *Vita Sancti Odonis*, Migne, *op. cit.*, CXXXIII, 52.

hunting in vain through the ruins of the monasteries of France for a community which he might join, he was about to start in despair for Italy when he heard that the brothers of Balma in Burgundy were still governed by the stern rule of Benedict of Aniane; thither he at once departed, taking his library with him. The baggage which he brought indicated to the abbot the way in which he might best serve the monastery, and he was promptly placed in charge of the cloister school. The good work of this little community served to remind men of the value of the institutions which had once been common in the land, but most of which for sixty years had been in ruins. The hope that they might be reëstablished was commonly expressed, and Duke William of Aquitaine offered the Abbot of Balma a site for a larger monastery. Here Cluny was raised, and when Berno died and Odo became abbot (927) five other houses observed the reformed rule, two of which were under his care. To Abbot Odo fell the task of perfecting the government of Cluny, restoring the ruined monasteries and extending the rule, not only in France but in Italy also, to the brotherhoods of monks still in existence, most of which had forgotten the rule which they professed to obey and were leading dissolute lives. The renovated cloisters were formed into a congregation with Odo as abbot of abbots. In the short space of one hundred and fifty years the Cluniac reform had spread through France and to Italy, England, Spain, and even Palestine; and more than three hundred churches, schools, and monasteries were under the arch-abbot's control. Every reformed monastery meant a restored school, and though the monks of Cluny preferred the "divine sciences" to classic literature they were not able to omit secular studies from their course of instruction, and their reform contributed greatly

to the restoration of learning. References to the work of
the schools are not wanting. Majolus, who refused the
papacy, became Abbot of Cluny in the year 965. He had
been trained in both kinds of literature in the school of
Lyons, and, although he discouraged the study of Virgil,
his love of such books as he believed to be beneficial was
so great that he always carried a small library with him
in his travels. His contemporary, Abbo of Fleury, applied himself diligently to the study of grammar, arithmetic and dialectic under the teachers of that monastery;
but as none of them could instruct him in the four other
arts he went to the schools of Paris and Rheims, where
he studied astronomy and dialectic. But he was compelled to go to Orléans and pay "not a little money" to
a certain cleric for instruction in music; and rhetoric
and geometry he was forced to learn without the aid of
a teacher from the ancient textbooks on these subjects. A
colony of monks from Fleury was sent over to England
and established in the monastery of Ramsey. Among
them was Abbo, to whom the task of organizing the
school of the cloister was entrusted. After two years
of distinguished service in England he was recalled to
Fleury to take the position of abbot in the year 988.
Although his official duties were peculiarly trying, he
did not cease to study, write, and dictate until the end
of his life; and he required his monks to study letters
and to exercise themselves in the work of composition as
a worthy occupation and a refuge from the temptations
of the flesh.[97] He left works on grammar, logic, astronomy,
and church history, and his influence was felt throughout the length and breadth of the Church; when to this
list are added the names of the bishops Dado of Verden
and Heraclius of Liége who attempted to establish paro-

[97] Ebert, *op. cit.*, III, 304.

chial schools in the churches under their care,[98] it will be seen that, though the tenth century was a dark age in France, schools did not cease to exist nor were men lacking who took a vigorous interest in them.

If we turn to England during this period we shall find the work which Alfred failed to make enduring taking established form under the direction of a saint who possessed the power which the king lacked of reconstructing the monasteries of the country and so providing an organization for the schools. That saint was Dunstan (924–988). He was born at Glastonbury and instructed in the school maintained by a few Irish monks who inhabited the deserted abbey and heroically continued to teach the few students who came to them, after almost all the other schools of the kingdom were closed. Here he studied so successfully and displayed such skill in grammar, theology, music, and ornamental metal work that he was introduced to the king and retained at court. But his stay there was not long, for his fellow courtiers, jealous of his ability, accused him of employing magic which they said he had learned from "the heathen." Dunstan withdrew to a hermit's cell in the neighborhood of Glastonbury until the king's successor recalled him to court, and as a reward for the service which he rendered made him Abbot of Glastonbury. The first act of the abbot was to revive the long forgotten rule of Benedict. He walled in his monastery from the outer world and proceeded to teach and discipline the monks, who came from all quarters, so that the most famous abbots and bishops of the kingdom were graduates from his cloister.[99] Among Dunstan's disciples was Æthelwold, who, after studying the religious sciences, grammar, and

[98] Drane, *op. cit.*, 253.
[99] Ebert, *op. cit.*, III, 503.

poesy at Glastonbury, "according to the king's will" re-
opened the forsaken monastery of Abingdon. Monks
were imported from France to bring the leaven of true
discipline, and the abbot was untiring in instructing the
brothers in grammar, poesy, the sacred writings, and the
works of the Fathers. Like his master Dunstan, he was
an adept in mechanical arts, restored his own abbey and
with his own hands cast the bells for its belfry. Music
and mathematics, it is said, also found a place among the
interests of this busy churchman.[100] Dunstan became
Archbishop of Canterbury and virtual ruler of England,
and Æthelwold was promoted to the see of Winchester.
With the assistance of the king, Æthelwold restored Ely,
"an event of the first importance in the history of Cambridgeshire . . . For from Ely . . . came almost certainly the first germs of our university life." [101] Next
came the restoration of Peterborough Abbey. Oswald
too, now Bishop of Worcester, who had been trained in
the monastery of Fleury, had restored the abbeys of
Pershore, Winchcombe, and St. Albans and had domi-
ciled twelve monks from Fluery, among them Abbo in the
monastery of Ramsey which he founded. Thus one by
one the monasteries were reorganized among the English people and every one of them was a school. "As
interest increased it was thought best to hold a council of
'all the authority of all Albion.' The council resulted
in the order from the king for the establishment of 'more
than forty monasteries,' and the charge of accomplishing
this was committed to Æthelwold and Oswald." [102]

The most famous representative of this revived Eng-

[100] Drane, *op. cit.*, 216.

[101] Quoted from Conybeare's *History of Cambridgeshire*, 71, in Dr.
C. L. White's *Ælfric*, 30.

[102] White, *Ælfric*, 32.

lish monastic training is Ælfric (*c.* 955–1020), one of
Æthelwold's pupils, who was educated in the Old Monastery of Winchester. The daily life of such a school, he has
described in his *Colloquium*. From Winchester he passed
to the abbey of Cernel where he devoted himself to teaching and to the preparation of books of Homilies which
he gathered from the works of approved writers of the
Church and turned from Latin into English for the benefit
of his countrymen. Here also he wrote a grammar, a compilation of Priscian and Donatus, for the use of his pupils
in order that they might "appropriate the Latin and English languages for the sake of attainment in higher
studies." From Cernel he passed to Eynsham where as
abbot he continued writing and teaching, constantly
watchful lest "holy learning grow cold and fail in our
days," and in every possible way advancing the cause
of Christian civilization until his death. But the Danes
were again in the land, and "the darkest of dark ages"
was on. After lying many years in the earth, the germs
of science planted by Dunstan, Æthelwold, Oswald, and
Ælfric bloomed in a great revival of learning, a description
of which belongs to the early history of the English Universities.

In the tenth century, while the affairs of France were
at an ebb, Germany just across the Rhine, under the
leadership of her Saxon princes, repelled the invading
Normans, Huns, and Slavs and enjoyed a period of
prosperity so marked that it is frequently said that
Germany knew no dark age. Otto (912–973), deservedly
styled the Great, having made himself master of his
kingdom by reducing his feudal lords to subjection and
having driven the Danes and Huns from his frontiers,
proceeded to Rome and was "crowned Emperor Augustus
and successor of Charles the Great" (962). The restorer

of the Holy Roman Empire, like his great predecessor
its founder, encouraged study, summoned foreign wise
men to his court at Aachen (Aix-la-Chapelle), and even
took pains to repair his own defective education by learning to read Latin. In no century, says Meiners, did
Germany possess so many virtuous and learned ecclesiastics as in the latter half of the tenth and the beginning
of the eleventh century. If the ninth century be designated the age of learned abbots, the tenth is the age of
learned bishops. Quite properly is Bruno, the brother
of Otto I, called the crown of all the German bishops.[103]
The prince Bruno had spent his youth in the school of
Utrecht studying grammar, committing to memory the
works of "the Catholic poet" Prudentius, and becoming
familiar with "Greek and Latin eloquence." [104] When
Otto came to the throne Bruno, almost his other self
through the bond of affection, was called to the post
of Arch-chaplain at the palace, and speedily collected
about him a remarkable company of learned men. Among
them were Ratherius of Liége, Luitprand of Cremona,
Racemund of Elvira, Adso of Moertier, Israel of Ireland,
and certain Greeks from Constantinople whose astonishment was great to find adorers of music among the distant
barbarians.[105] Bruno was the central figure of this group.
In learning, in power of disputation, in enthusiasm to
impart knowledge, in indefatigable energy, in kindliness
of spirit and urbanity of manner, he surpassed all. "He
restored the long ruined fabric of the seven liberal arts,"
says his biographer.[106] The renowned historians, orators,
poets, and philosophers were diligently studied, books

[103] Meiners, *Historische Vergleichung der Sitten, etc.*, II, 384.
[104] Ruotger, *Vita Brunonis*, 4.
[105] Schmid, *Geschichte der Erziehung*, II, 235.
[106] Ruotger, *Vita*, 5. *Monumenta Germaniae Historiae*, IV, Scriptorum.

were multiplied, and so highly prized were they and so indispensable a part of life that, wherever Bruno journeyed, he carried his library with him "as it had been the ark of the Lord." [107] When the people of Cologne forced him to accept the office of archbishop in their city (953), a second teaching center was organized in the cathedral there from which a crowd of disciples went forth to carry the beneficent influence of the master to the many communities included in the wide field of their labor.[108] The cathedral schools of Paderborn, Hildesheim, Magdeburg, Bremen, Liége, and Utrecht took on new life, and the revival reached Fulda, St. Gall, and Reichenau.[109] Indeed Bishop Bruno, the second *praeceptor Germaniae,* did more than restore the teaching of all seven of the liberal arts. The movement which he led waked Virgil, Horace, Ovid, Terence, Cicero, and Sallust, as it were, from the dead, and made them the culture teachers of the Germans. The esteem in which they began to be held is instanced by the fact that they were taught even by the nuns of Gandersheim and Quedlinburg. Importations of books came from Italy; Gunzo of Novara brought one hundred, among them a part of the logic of Aristotle and the *Timaeus* of Plato.[110] As a natural result, out of the new studies of a new time came a new literature.

Otto the Great intrusted the education of his son to Ekkehard, a monk of St. Gall, who was distinguished not only for his wisdom but for his political sagacity and taste for art as well. A strong culture element was introduced by the marriage of the prince to Theophano, daughter of the Greek Emperor. Otto II was himself a

---

[107] Ruotger, *Vita,* 5.
[108] Ruotger, *Praefatio Vitae.*
[109] See Specht, 301–355.
[110] Schmid, *op. cit.,* II, 235.

learned man, but he had little opportunity to encourage
learning. He was forced to spend his days upon the
battlefield to such an extent that he bears the title of
"the sanguinary." He was killed when his son and
successor Otto III was but four years old. Upon his
mother, Theophano, fell the double burden of ruling as
regent during his infancy and of carefully educating the
little Emperor. In the latter task, however, she had the
assistance of the greatest scholar of the century, Gerbert
of Aurillac, the first representative of a new learning
in Christian Europe, a thinker, inventor, schoolmaster,
tutor of two kings, abbot of one of the chief monasteries
of Christendom, and a distinguished Pope. Gerbert was
born of a humble family in Auvergne about the year
950. As a child he was placed in the Benedictine monastery of St. Gerand, where he became familiar with the
elements of grammar [111] under teachers whom he continued through life to hold in the highest esteem. When
he had reached the age of adolescence, the Count Borel
of Barcelona chanced to make a pious pilgrimage to
Aurillac, and to the abbot's inquiry whether there were
any men in Spain learned in the arts he replied that
such were to be found there. As the count was about
to depart the abbot begged him to take one of his young
scholars with him to be instructed by them. Gerbert
was chosen and placed by the count in charge of the
Bishop of Vich. Here in the shadow of the Moslem
state he studied mathematics with success (967–970).
Next he accompanied Borel on a pilgrimage to Rome
where he met the Pope, who quickly perceived his talents
and packed him off to the court of Otto to teach the
hitherto unknown subject of mathematics there. All his
life, says his biographer, Gerbert was an ardent student

[111] Picavet, *Gerbert un Pape Philosophie,* 27.

of the liberal arts. But as yet he had had no opportunity to study logic, and when Gerard the Archdeacon of Rheims, a master of that subject, came to the court on an embassy from the King of France, Gerbert prayed his royal master for permission to accompany the archdeacon to Rheims to study logic with him. His request was granted, and next we find him teaching the mathematics which he had learned in Spain and studying logic in the schools of that city made famous by the teaching of Remi.[112] Richer's account of his teaching indicates that he began with logic and explained, proposition by proposition, all the books on the subject which that age possessed. Next he initiated his scholars in rhetoric, familiarizing them with the works of Virgil, Statius, Terence, Juvenal, Persius, Horace, and Lucan. Then followed exercises in argumentation through controversies carried on by the pupils with a master. In mathematics he began with arithmetic, advanced to the study of music, and gave much attention to astronomy. At night they watched the stars, and the master constructed a system of spheres to aid the students in comprehending the subject. He also constructed an abacus, using a separate character to designate each of the nine numerals,[113] but did not employ the symbol for zero.

The fame of so enterprising a master spread through Gaul, Germany, and Italy, and students from distant parts flocked to his school.[114] He was indefatigable in his search for books. We find him writing to his archbishop for a copy of Caesar and offering in return eight books of Boethius and some remarkable geometrical figures; addressing a request to the Abbot Gisilbert for

[112] Richerus, *Historiae* in Pertz's *Monumenta Germaniae*, III, 43–45.
[113] Richerus, *ibid.*, III, 46–54.
[114] Richerus, *ibid.*, III, 55.

the medical writings of "Demosthenes the Philosopher" [115]
and begging the monks of Aurillac to send him a treatise
on the multiplication and division of numbers by Joseph
the Spaniard.[116] Gerbert composed several treatises on
mathematics, logic, rhetoric, etc., a few of which, the *De
Numerorum Divisione,* a geometry, a tract *De Rationali
et Ratione Uti,* and a theological brief *De Corpore et
Sanguine Domini,* may still be consulted. In addition he
constructed a clock which was long preserved at Magdeburg and an organ operated by means of boiling water
which was still at Rheims two centuries after his
death.[117]

So marked an innovator could not fail to make enemies
as well as friends. A crowd of them were ready to check-
mate him at every turn. With Otheric, the scholasticus
of Magdeburg, he waged a fierce dialectical tournament
at Pavia, in the presence of the Emperor Otto I and all
the learned men of the Empire, upon the subject of the
relation of mathematics and physics. The contest lasted
an entire day, and Gerbert returned to France bearing a
quantity of presents from the Emperor, who had arranged and presided over the dispute.[118] Thus right
royally was the field of scholastic chivalry dedicated.

In 983 Gerbert was made Abbot of Bobbio, whose
large library he increased; but, finding the position intolerable, he returned to Rheims in the following year.
During the remainder of his life he was deeply involved
in the political intrigues of the time. Through the same
influence in 999 he ascended the pontificial throne, taking
the title of Sylvester II. His political dimensions are

---

[115] Epistola VIII. Migne, *op. cit.,* CXXXIX, 203.

[116] Epistola XVII. Migne, *op. cit.,* CXXXIX, 205.

[117] Migne, *op. cit.,* CXXXIX, 60. Also Bell, *A History of Mathematics,* 144.

[118] Picavet, *op. cit.,* 193 *et seq.*

revealed by the fact that he at once appealed to Christendom to arm and defend the Holy Land and plotted with his pupil the Emperor Otto III for the restoration of the world empire of the Romans.[119] He died in the year 1003, before he had time to carry out his gigantic plans.

In the eyes of his contemporaries Gerbert bulked as a man of cyclopedic genius, a doer of deeds as well as a thinker of thoughts. His fame incited the fable mongers of succeeding ages. He employed magic, they said, he held converse with the evil one. He was able to call up the shades of the dead, was carried through the air by night; indeed, he had sold his soul to the Devil, hence his power.[120] But a host of scholars who had come under his influence had learned another lesson from him. To them he represented the triumphs of knowledge; fame, position, and honor had come to him through intellectual achievement, rather than as rewards of piety. They were not slow to follow his example. His success was an apple of discord thrown among the clerics, whose pride and ambition soon sent them racing after it.

The work of the lay teachers of Italy, which had not utterly ceased at any time since the fall of Rome, took on new vigor at the beginning of the eleventh century. Grammar and rhetoric had always been their chief subjects of study. Now, instead of expanding their instruction by giving greater attention to dialectics as did the Church schools on the other side of the Alps, they gradually expanded the teaching of rhetoric to include instruction in civil law, in accordance with their own peculiar social needs.[121] The schools of Rome, Pavia, and Ravenna

---

[119] Picavet, *op. cit.*, 193 *et seq.*

[120] Picavet, *op. cit.*, 197 *et seq.*

[121] See Rashdall's *Universities of Europe in the Middle Ages*, chapter "Irnerius and the Civil Law Revival," I–IV, and Giesebrecht, *De Litterarum Studiis apud Italos*, 15 *et seq.*

were famous at that period for such juristic instruction.[122]
In the same way the school of liberal arts in Bologna was
gradually being transformed into a law university. The
church at Milan boasted two schools of philosophy in
this century.[123] A successful school was conducted at
Parma. Benevento had rejoiced in the possession of
thirty-two philosophers but a little time before, and the
medical school at Salerno was at the zenith of its fame.
Schools were to be found in the monasteries and in some
of the cathedrals, and a Roman synod presided over by
Gregory VII in the year 1078 directed that all bishops
should cause the liberal arts to be taught in their
churches.[124]

Of the seventy-five or more schools sufficiently distinguished to get a place in history, which marked the
stirring of a new spirit in France during the eleventh century, it will suffice to mention four of the greatest,
Chartres, Paris, Bec, and Laon.

The school of Chartres was founded by Fulbert, who
had studied under Gerbert at Rheims. His reputation for
wisdom was so great that he became a sort of oracle to
the Church of Gaul. A great crowd of students gathered
to his teaching, and so completely was he devoted to this
phase of the work of the Church that he did not cease
to teach after his elevation to the onerous position of
bishop in the year 1007. Grammar, including the study
of some of the classics, music, dialectic, and theology were
the chief subjects of instruction, and the master who
taught them was famed for the gentle persuasion which
he employed as well as for close adherence to the ancient
doctrines of the Church. Of his pupils some rose to dis-

[122] Ricci, *I Primordi dello Studio Bolognese,* 9 *et seq.*
[123] Tiraboschi, *op. cit.,* I, 500.
[124] Tiraboschi, I, 499; Giesebrecht, 14.

tinction in the offices of the Church, some amassed wealth in the teaching profession, others became distinguished for their skill in grammar or music, and one developed so insatiable a desire for knowledge that he went from school to school and even journeyed to Spain in his search for wisdom.[125]

Fulbert died in the year 1029, and Peter of Chartres, one of his pupils, became head of the school. He was succeeded by Sigon. At the end of the century Bernard, one of the most famous humanists of the age, was in charge of the work of the school during his mastership. We are fortunate in possessing the rather detailed account of John of Salisbury, one of his intellectual grandsons. Its individuality was due to the peculiar respect for the ancients which the master sought to instil. "We are," he would say, "as dwarfs mounted on the shoulders of giants, so that we can see more and further than they; yet not by virtue of the keenness of our eyesight, nor through the tallness of our stature, but because we are raised and borne aloft upon that giant mass." [126] The pupils upon entering the school were required first to learn the principles of grammar. This done, they began the study of the classic texts, which were not only parsed but interpreted also. The master Bernard would point out how the style of prose differs from that of verse "so that what are vices in the one may even be virtues in the other." But the teacher regarded it as more important that his pupil should comprehend an author's meaning than analyze his style for the classic authors are, he said, so rich in materials that their "finished work appears in some sort an image of all arts . . . Ransack Virgil, or Lucan and whatever philosophy thou profess, thou wilt

[125] Tiraboschi, op. cit., I, 503.
[126] Joannes Saresberiensis, Metalogicus, III–LV.

find it there in its quintessence." [127] But the times were
not ripe for the spread of humanism, and devotion to logic
had to run its course through three centuries before the
revival of Bernard could flower in the Greater Renaissance.

Scholars who were neither monks nor clerics found their
way from Italy to France during this century, among them
a young student of the liberal arts and law in the rising
school of Bologna who, after teaching for a time in his
native city of Pavia, crossed the Alps and opened a school
(1040) in Avranches in Normandy.[128] After two years of
very successful teaching the master Lanfranc withdrew
from the world to the monastery of Bec. Four years after
his admission to the monastery he was detailed to its
school. "Before that time," says Odericus, in the reigns
of six dukes of Normandy, scarce any Norman applied
himself to regular studies, nor had any doctor arisen
among them till, by the providence of God, Lanfranc appeared in their province." [129] In the school of Bec he ac-
quitted himself with so much distinction that his fame
spread through Europe and students came from France,
Britain, Germany, and Rome even, to sit in his classes.[130]
The monastery became a veritable training school of
clerks and teachers in the West. In 1062 Lanfranc became abbot of the new monastery of St. Stephen at Caen,
and in 1070 he was chosen to the primacy of the Church
of England as Archbishop of Canterbury. In this capacity he served his friend and patron William the Conqueror and his successor faithfully for nineteen years.
Upon Lanfranc's withdrawal the leadership of the school

[127] Joannes Saresberiensis, *Metalogicus*, I, 24.
[128] Tiraboschi, I, 504.
[129] Quoted in Drane, 307.
[130] Tiraboschi, *op. cit.*, I, 507.

of Bec fell to his most distinguished pupil Anselm. He too was a native of Lombardy who crossed the Alps into France and because of the fame of his fellow country-man made his way to the school of Bec. Under Anselm's direction the number of its students increased, and the school became more famous even than before.[131] In the year 1093 he too was made Archbishop of Canterbury, in which trying position he served for sixteen years. But he has still better claims to fame. He represents a strikingly new spirit in the life of the Church. By attempting to prove the existence of God through the unaided reason he opened a new field of effort for the human intellect and is commonly regarded as the first of the scholastics.[132]

The school of Laon, conducted by another Anselm and his brother Raoul, was preëminent in theology. Throughout the Latin Church, Anselm the theologian was reputed *totius urbis lucerna*. Students came from France, England, Germany, and Italy to sit at his feet, and the list of alumni of the school who attained distinction in the world was long.

The reputation of distinguished masters in the capital drew crowds of students to Paris. Master Roscellin, the nominalist innovator, had dared to accuse the Christian Church of polytheism because of its belief in the Trinity. In the school of Notre Dame, William of Champeaux daily confuted the heretic with "the sound wisdom of realism." Drogo the Deaf and the famous master of mas-

[131] Migne, *op. cit.*, CLVIII, *Vita Eadmero*, 52.
[132] Anselm's argument runs as follows: God is everywhere thought of as the greatest object or being that can be conceived by man. The greatest being that can be conceived must be an existent being, else a being greater by possessing the attribute of existence could be thought of. The greatest must exist objectively as well as in the intellect of man. *Proslogion*, II (Migne, CLVIII, 228).

ters, Manegold, taught in Paris with distinction in the earlier part of the century. The wife and daughters of Manegold had even opened a school for women. The Jews had a school. Private schools flourished on the hill of St. Genevieve. The royal abbey of St. Denis and a half-dozen other Parisian monasteries were becoming distinguished as centers of learning.[133] Let these be representative of the scholastic movement of the eleventh century. At last the work of John Scotus and Gerbert was becoming effective. The human reason had been discovered. Heresies arose, and new monastic orders were formed. The great question of the Middle Ages was put, and every bishop, from the coast of Brittany to the shores of the Mediterranean, had his master of grammar and dialectics who discussed it. The monastic schools were busy with it, and private teachers did not lack for pupils, so great was the intellectual awakening.

The movement was not confined to France. Of churches there were enough in England before the Normans came; "but," says William of Malmesbury, "before this invasion, the pursuits of letters, and the practices of piety had long been relinquished. Satisfied with the slightest acquirements, churchmen could barely mutter the words of the service, and he who knew anything of grammar was regarded as a prodigy. Clothed elegantly, and observing no distinction of meats, the monks ridiculed the rules of their institutes."

The Norman invasion worked a revolution in the life of the English people. The Church was reorganized and rebuilt. Lanfranc, the scholar of Pavia and Bec, was the king's right-hand man in the reorganization of English institutions. The monastic reform which Dunstan had

---

[133] *Histoire Littéraire,* 7–104 *et seq.* McCabe, *Abelard,* 20. Michaud, *Guillaume de Champeaux,* 73 *et seq.*

attempted now became an established fact. English churchmen were gradually removed, and Norman prelates, many of whom were scholars, were placed in their stead. But little is said in the chronicles concerning any attempts to revive learning in the kingdom on the part of either of the great masters of Bec. They could hardly have overlooked so important an interest. The Continental priests who served under them certainly did not. Schools were opened, libraries were formed, and books were written, and England soon produced a crop of scholars of both races, the representatives of the five hundred and fifty-seven schools which Taine declares were established in the land between the Conquest and the death of king John.[134]

Though Germany did not share in the aesthetic and intellectual development of the Norman Age, the cause of learning had attained so great an impetus under the rule of the Ottos, and Gerbert had introduced so many of the products of Arabian science, that her schools were hardly rivalled by those of France even until the middle of the eleventh century. Under Bishop Meinverk (1009–1036) the trivium and quadrivium expanded to include the study of Virgil. Horace, Sallust and Statius, and the subject of physics were taught with great success in the school of Paderborn. Hildesheim under Bernward, Merseburg under Ditmar, and Worms under Burchard were hardly less famous. Though the monasteries of Germany were sadly in need of disciplinary reforms, their schools were not unaffected by the growing interest in the scholastic philosophy. That of St. Gall was a leader in the movement, and Notker Labeo (d. 1022) contributed German translations of Boethius' *Consolations of Philosophy* and of two books of Aristotle together with some original works

[134] Taine, *English Literature*, II, II.

on philosophical subjects. In the year 1070 a reform similar to that of Odo of Cluny, long needed in Germany, was undertaken by William of Hirschau. With the assistance of a number of his former pupils scattered through the land he succeeded in restoring discipline in more than a hundred monasteries.[135] Hirschau now took the place which Fulda had held in the ninth century, but the struggle which Henry IV waged with Hildebrand involved Germany in political wars which disorganized the Church and well-nigh destroyed the schools which it maintained.

[135] Eichorn, *Geschichte der Cultur*, II, 402.

V

INSTRUCTION AMONG THE ARABS

WHY was the capital of the Roman Empire moved from Rome to Constantinople? Was it because Rome was pagan and openly derisive of an Emperor who was a bishop of bishops, preached in the palace and kept all-night vigils in the churches, and that Church-favoring Emperor got even by moving the administration of the world to a place which pleased him better? [1] Or was it that the necessities of government required that change of headquarters? It was both. There were grave problems of state under consideration when the unfortunately timed action of the Roman mob made up the Emperor's mind for him, and Rome's day was over. It was in 330 that the new capital was dedicated. It continued to be the capital until 1453.

When Constantine moved the seat of Empire Asiaward he divided the civilized world into two parts. Human affairs thereafter pursued a dual course, that of the East for centuries being richer and fuller than that of the West. In effect the Church was divided then as well as the Empire. The busy-minded and litigious Greeks had never quite lost their occupation of perpetually canvassing and correcting the government set over them, even though they no longer set it over themselves. They had by no means pressed the questions of philosophy dry. Their eager minds were still at their perennial work, but when the new religion came along with its demand for theologi-

[1] Stanley, *History of the Eastern Church*, 215 (Everymans Library).

cal formulation they were literally in their element.

If the Western Church was a nontheological church, the Eastern Church saw to it that that reproach should not be hers. Dean Stanley illustrates the difference by saying that the first decree of an Eastern Council sought to define the relation of the members of the Holy Trinity while the first decree of the Pope at Rome forbade the marriage of the clergy.[2]

The theological battle waged fiercest over the question of the nature of Christ. The first Ecumenical Council battled over the doctrine of Arius and adopted the Athanasian creed. A hundred years after that (431), the third Ecumenical Council struggled with Nestorius' teaching that in Christ were two natures, that of the Logos and that of a man, and they coexisted without mingling. To this the Council replied: If any man shall say that the Christ is a God-bearing man and not rather very God as an only Son through nature, let him be anathema.[3] It is hard to imagine mobs rioting over such subtle distinctions; but they nevertheless did riot, and men were slain in the street tumults that broke out over them. Devoted missionaries undertook heroic campaigns among unconverted peoples to make partisans for their cause. Ibas, head of the school at Edessa, was at Ephesus as one of Nestorius' supporters. When he returned home he and his school became involved in the endless sequelae of that controversy. In 457 Barsumas, driven out of Syria, went to Persia to become Bishop of Nisibis and speedily brought over nearly the whole Church of Persia to his Nestorian belief. Barsumas had many helpers, some of whom had been driven out of Edessa with him, and others when the school of Edessa

[2] Stanley, *op. cit.*, 71.

[3] The Third Ecumenical Council—of Ephesus (431), V, in *Nicene and Post-Nicene Fathers, etc.*, XIV, 212.

was suppressed by the Roman Emperor Zeno in 489. As they were under ban of both Rome and Constantinople, they labored with incredible zeal to establish a great Nestorian Church, an independent hierarchy under its own patriarch whose seat was at Seleucia-Ctesiphon on the Tigris. A school was erected at Nisibis whose alumni with no less zeal than their master, Barsumas, hurried to sow the seed of Nestorian Christianity far beyond the limits of Persia, under the protection of whose monarchs they flourished. The missionary enthusiasm of this church was nothing short of astounding. Its bishoprics were to be found not only in Syria, Armenia, Arabia and Persia, at Halavan in Media, Merv in Khorasan, Herat, Tashkent, Samarkand, Baluk, Kashgar, but even at Peking in China and Kranganore in India. In 1265 they numbered twenty-five Asiatic provinces. Marco Polo witnesses that their churches were to be found all along the trade routes from Baghdad to Peking.[4]

The Monophysites, the upholders of the one nature of Christ, were the counterfoil of the Nestorians. The fifth and sixth centuries boiled with their conflicts and raged over their distinctions. In the prolonged and bitter war Origen was anathematized by council after council for his "idle tales," and Plato, whose wisdom he relied on, suffered in esteem also. But, to get a picture of the theological wars which the Eastern Church fought, let me quote a few sentences from the Letter of the Seventh Synod to the Emperor (787): "Having but one mind by the inbreathing of the most Holy Spirit, and being all knit together in one, and understanding the harmonious tradition of the Catholic Church, we are in perfect harmony with the symphonies set forth by the six, holy and ecumenical

[4] *Encyclopædia Britannica*, 11th ed., article, "Nestorians," by A. J. Grieve.

councils; and accordingly we have anathematised the madness of Arius, the frenzy of Macedonius, the senseless understanding of Apollinaris, the man-worship of Nestorius, the irreverent mingling of the natures devised by Eutyches and Dioscorus, and the many-headed hydra which is their companion. We have anathematised the idle tales of Origen, Didymus, and Evagrius; and the doctrine of one will held by Sergius, Honorius, Cyrus, and Pyrrhus, or rather we have anathematised their own evil will," etc.[5]

But perpetual distinguishing, classifying, proving, and disproving, the course upon which the Eastern Church had set sail with so much contentiousness, required skill in argument. The arsenal of Aristotle contained the necessary weapons, and Aristotle rose as Plato fell in the esteem of the churchmen. David, the Armenian, together with a number of his countrymen studied the logic at Athens and openly taught it in their home country. Monophysites and Nestorians both struggled to possess themselves of the texts of Aristotle's writings on logic. They studied them in Greek. But to arm their followers more powerfully Sergius, the Monophysite, translated the writings of the Stagyrite and of other Greek authors into Syriac, and the Nestorians translated them into the language of Persia. The medical works of Hippocrates and Galen were also held in great esteem in Asia. At Edessa and after 489 at Nisibis, the Nestorians devoted themselves to Aristotle's *Organon* much as did western students several centuries later at the young Universities of Paris, Oxford, and Cambridge. At Gandisapora in eastern Persia they developed a famous school of Greek medicine where of course the other sciences of Greece were taught also. The great school of the Monophysites was at Resaina. There it was that Sergius did his notable work of translating

[5] The Seven Ecumenical Councils, 572, in *Nicene and Post-Nicene Fathers, etc.*, Vol. XIV.

Greek wisdom books into Syriac. In their monastery at Kinnesrin they had another great centre of instruction, translation, and copying, from which Greek works and commentaries upon them issued.

While Greek learning was spreading far over Asia through the instrumentality of the factious Christians, and pious zealots were preaching the Gospel of the New Testament far beyond the limits of the Empire, and Jewish refugees by merely dwelling there were making known the worship of the Jewish God, a nomadic people of the Semite race dwelt in their tents in Arabia, spent their days in warring tribe against tribe, and went up annually on pilgrimage to Mecca to kiss the stone which had fallen from heaven, drink from the well of Zem Zem, and make the seven circuits around the Kaaba, in which were housed no fewer than three hundred and sixty idols. They were a wild people, an unconstructive race with just one art, poetry, which they practised with wonderful eagerness, with astonishing skill and with filigreed fineness. Horatian elegance and the rhythmical facility of Pope are comparisons which have been made to describe the perfection of their poetical art. Its favorite themes were prowess in fighting, love, the steed, the camel, the virtues of the tribe or the hospitality, courage, dependableness, and loving kindness of the poet himself or his hero of whom he sings:

> When I saw the hard earth hollowed
> By our women's flying footprints,
> And Lamís her face uncovered
> Like the full moon of the skies,
> Showing forth her hidden beauties—
> Then the matter was grim earnest:
> I engaged their chief in combat,
> Seeing help no other wise.[6]

[6] 'Amr ben Ma'díkarib in Nicholson, *A Literary History of the Arabs*, 82. By permission of the Cambridge University Press.

There were annual poetical contests at the fair of Okaz. The best of the Arabian historians, Ibn Khaldun, says that the *Book of Songs,* an anthology collected by Abu'l-Faraj about 967, "is the Register of the Arabs."[7] This and a desert dweller's knowledge of the stars, together with their language, was what the early Arabs knew in what they came to call "the days of ignorance."

In the year 569 a lad was born at Mecca to parents of the tribe of Koraish, whose duty it was to guard the Kaaba like the Levites of old. His father died when the child was scarce two months old, leaving him but a slender patrimony. His mother died when he was but six years old, leaving him an orphan to be reared by an uncle who personally held the office of guardian of the temple. His ward grew up in the shadow of the Kaaba in the metropolis of Arabia, learning neither to read nor to write but becoming wise beyond his years through association with the strangers who gathered there. He journeyed with the caravans into Syria and talked with Christian monks and Jews whom he met upon the way. He was hired to conduct the caravans of richer persons to the market towns of Syria and Arabia.

Such was the life of Mohammed until he reached the age of forty years. What he saw and heard at home and in this varied experience as a trader made a deep impression upon him. He began to dream of a religious reform which should utterly blot out the idolatry of his own people, clear away the confusion, perplexities, and doubts of the peoples "with a book," and restore the worship of the one and true God. It seemed to him that a prophet must soon come with power from on high to accomplish this change. The thought continuously recurring overwhelmed him. He dwelt upon it night and day. In the

[7] Nicholson, *op. cit.,* 32.

midst of his contemplation of the divine power, voices began to say to him, "Thou art the man." In a frenzy of doubt after seeing visions he went for consolation to his faithful wife, Kadijah, who assured him of his mission in the words: "Fear not, for joyful tidings dost Thou bring. Henceforth I shall regard Thee as the prophet of our nation. Rejoice: Allah will not suffer Thee to fall in shame. Hast Thou not been loving to Thy kinfolks, kind to Thy neighbors, charitable to the poor, and ever a defender of the truth?" [8] After days and nights of prayer and conflict on Mount Hira all doubt vanished, and the Prophet of Arabia became consecrated to his mission of preaching the threefold truth of the unity of God, the abomination of idolatry, and the necessity of humble submission to the will of Deity. "Side by side with the religion of the Jews and Christians as practiced in Arabia at least, it appeared more spiritual and more divine, and presented the truths of both religions without the blemishes. Judaism was effete, Christianity corrupt." [9] The new religion was a vigorous reaction to the older ones. But the preaching of the new doctrine to the Arabs for years met with little success. The primacy of the tribe of Koraish depended upon the maintenance of the old idolatry. At first the message of the Prophet was met with scoffing and contempt. When peaceful efforts to suppress the new teaching failed, persecution and martyrdom were invoked. After ten years of almost unavailing labor in Mecca, Mohammed withdrew (622) to another city of Arabia, Medina. The Mohammedan calendar dates its years from this *hijrah,* or flight, each year being given its number *anno Hijrah.* At first progress was slow at Medina, but in no long time the number of the faithful began to in-

[8] Arnold, *The Preaching of Islam,* 9 (1st ed.).

[9] Palmer, *Introduction to the Quran,* L.

crease mightily; and under the influence of the new religion the tribes hitherto engaged in bitter and incessant warfare with one another were brought into unity as a single nation.

The Quran was the bond of social union among them, the operative constitution of the new national life. To the Mohammedans the Quran is the inspired word of God. Noldeke has said it is "truly described as the most widely read book in existence." [10] This revelation is not like other revelations of Deity. It does not leave man to go his own way if he subscribes to a creed. This revelation remakes the entire life of men. In this religion there is no rendering to Caesar the things that are Caesar's and to God the things that are God's. All things belong to God. His Quran, or reading, voices His orders, His Prophet is His representative to execute His commands. The Divine Law, not the will of the people, determined by a consensus of the citizens, is sovereign in the Muslim state. Islam is direct government by God through His Quran, a revelation to men, a guide to the pious. There is no Church, no priests, no sacraments. Islam is the religion of "The Book." The first thing the revelation did was to make as nothing all tribal and kinship relations by sublimating them into relations of His creatures to Allah. Their political law, no less than their religious law, is revealed in The Book. It is the supreme guide in man's relations to his fellow man; the very substance of ethics is in it. In it are the choicest proverbs, parables, and legends which the Arabs know.

It is pretty certain that the Quran was the first book written down and copied out by the Arabs. Before it, memory had retained and the voice had published everything. There was a profession of reciters of poetry as well

[10] Noldeke, *Sketches from Eastern History*, 21.

as of poets among the early Arabs. They were *ráwis,* memorizers and repeaters of the production of the poets like the rhapsodes of Greece. Like the rhapsodes, they did a heavy business in their day. "I can recite to you," Hammád once said to the Caliph Walíd ben Yazíd, "for each letter of the alphabet, one hundred long poems rhyming in that letter, without taking into count the short pieces, and all that composed exclusively by poets who lived before the promulgation of Islamism." [11]

No collected edition of the Revelations had been made at the death of the Prophet. They existed in scattered fragments written upon "palm leaves, skins, blade-bones and the hearts of men." Mohammed indicated his theory of inspiration by speaking of a "Mother of the Book" (XLIII, 3) in heaven, "a well-guarded tablet" (LXXXV, 22); "The Faithful Spirit came down with it" (XXVI, 193); "The Holy Spirit brought it down from Thy Lord in truth, to stablish those who believe and for a guidance and glad tidings to those who are resigned" (XVI, 101). In another place (II, 93) Gabriel "hath revealed to Thy heart, with God's permission, confirmation of what had been before, and a guidance and glad tidings to believers." It was not sent down all at once (XXV, 33) but was received in fragments and recited by the Prophet to followers who took it down piece by piece. These revelations from heaven came intermittently to the Prophet through twenty-three years of his life. The scrappiness in which these, the first Arabic writings, must have existed can well be imagined. Some, the believers had memorized, as that was the favorite method of retaining that which was treasured. But memory, particularly the memory of the most devoted believers, was not a safe repository. After the battle of Yamama (633), Umar came to Abu Bakr,

[11] Nicholson, *op. cit.,* 132.

the Caliph, and said: "I fear that slaughter may wax hot among the Reciters on other battle fields, and that much of the Quran may be lost; so in my opinion it should be collected without delay." Abu Bakr agreed and ordered Zayd, one of those who had written out his words for the Prophet, to collect and write down the Revelations. This he did, gathering its parts "from bits of parchment, thin white stones, leafless palm-branches and the bosoms of men." Afterwards the Caliph Othman, upon being told that the Quran being read in Syria was different from that read in Iraq, and that there was danger that the Holy Book would become a subject of controversy like the Jewish and Christian Scriptures, ordered Zayd, with the help of three members of the tribe of Koraish, to prepare a revised and authoritative version.[12] Thus, what was intended to be a universally final text was made. Everything else was ordered burned; copies of the established text were sent to Damascus, Basra, Cufa, and one was kept at Medina. It is interesting to remember that Germany was ordered to restore one of these four Othman Qurans by the Treaty of Versailles.

The Quran was the source of authority in the Muslim church-state. It was supplemented, first, by the *Hadith*, or traditional sayings and practices of the Prophet (living auditors and witnesses supplied a vast collection of these in the first century of the faith); secondly, by the *Igmah*, or consensus of the highest authorities in Islam upon points concerning which neither the Quran nor the Hadith is definite; and lastly, by the reasoning of approved theological thinkers by analogy based upon the Quran, Hadith, and Igmah to cover points not decided in these writings. Such reasonings were called *Qiyas*, or Analogy.[13]

[12] Nicholson, *op. cit.*, 142.
[13] Palmer, *op. cit.*, LXVI.

The internal organization of the converted Arab tribes into the Muslim church-state had occupied the last years of the Prophet. Provinces had been marked out, and officers and religious teachers sent to the tribes inhabiting them. An army had been gathered to punish the Syrians for the murder of a Muslim envoy. At the death of Mohammed many of the recently converted tribes broke away and returned to their old tribal allegiance and activities. The restoration of the peninsula became the first work of his successor Abu Bakr. It was accomplished by Khalid. In that struggle the Muslim army came into conflict with certain border tribes of nomadic Christians who owed allegiance to Persia. Thus began a struggle which inside of ten years led to the subjugation of the Persian Empire (643). The punitive expedition sent into Syria came into conflict with the Romans. At first the Muslims were defeated, but Khalid was sent from Chaldea to Syria and utterly routed the Romans in the great battle of Yarmuk (636). One by one the Syrian cities capitulated: Damascus, Antioch, Jerusalem, and the rest of them. The year 641 witnessed the subjugation of Egypt. The advance now became more difficult, but in the year 675 the Muslim general Okba rode his horse into the Atlantic Ocean off the coast of Morocco and, raising his hands to heaven, exclaimed: "Almighty Lord! but for this sea I would have gone into remoter regions spreading the glory of Thy name and smiting Thine enemies." [14] In the year 711 Tarik crossed the straits which have ever since borne his name, at the head of 7,000 fierce Berbers, and in less than three years the victorious Muslim army camped in the shadow of the Pyrenees. On the Torre de la Vela of the Alhambra there is a marble tablet with an inscription which reads: "On this spot in the 777th year

[14] Ameer Ali, *A Short History of the Saracens*, 79.

of the Muslim dominion, in the 1492 year of the Christian era, the kingdom of Granada was surrendered by Boabdil into the hands of their Catholic Majesties, Ferdinand and Isabella." Like a scimitar, the Muslim church-state, stretching from Persia through Syria, Egypt, North Africa, and Spain, enclosed Christian Europe. That juxtaposition which was also a threat existed for a thousand years, not for quite so long in Spain but for a longer time in North Africa, Egypt, and Syria. In spite of the Crusades, Jerusalem has been a Muslim city save for short periods ever since Omar rode his horse and led his camel into it in 637. The battle line was pressed far into Christian Europe many times. Contantinople, the outpost of Empire, fell in 1453, and ever since has been a Muslim city.

So powerful a people whose life was organized about a book must have done service for education; and, close neighbors as they were to Christian Europe, they must many times have borrowed from and lent to their centuries-long antagonists.

Did the Mohammedans make their converts by the sword? If they did, they were hardly exceptional in their time or ours. When Khalid captured the city of Hirah he said to its people: "Now choose you one of these three things: either (1) accept our faith, then your rights and obligations will be the same as ours, whether you choose to go into another country or stay in your own land; or (2) pay *jizyah* (the tax for protection) or (3) war and battle." [15] When in 636 Omar took Jerusalem: "This is the favour which the servant of God, the Commander of the Faithful, grants to the people of Aelia. He gives them the assurance of the preservation of their lives and properties, their churches and crosses, of those who set up,

[15] Arnold, *The Preaching of Islam*, 51.

who display and who honour these crosses. There will be no constraint in the matter of religion, nor the least annoyance. The Jews will inhabit Aelia conjointly with

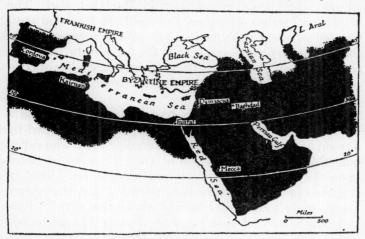

THE CONQUEST OF ISLAM, A.D. 632–945

From *An Historical Geography of Europe,* by Gordon East, by permission of E. P. Dutton & Co., Inc.

the Christians, and those who live there will require to pay the poll-tax like the inhabitants of other towns." [16]

There were great numbers of Eastern Christians that became Muslims and great numbers in the Caliph's Empire who never gave up their Christianity at all. Numbers of them were employed in the Caliph's service, some in high posts of state. There were court physicians who were Christians, and the chief of the translators in Al-Mamun's palace was a Christian. More significant evidence of religious toleration is the fact that the Nestorian patriarch moved his seat from Ctesiphon to Baghdad. Near his

[16] Muir, *The Caliphate, Rise, Decline and Fall,* 134.

palace was the Nestorian church of St. Mary. Not far from them was the Monophysite church, and about these was the Christian quarter of the city. There were other churches and even monasteries in Baghdad also. The Nestorian patriarch continued to reside at Baghdad until the fall of the Caliphate in 1258. He was regarded by the Mohammedan government as the head of the Christian community in the East. There were twenty-five metropolitans in the Caliphate, each with from six to twelve bishops under him.

The Jewish community in Baghdad had at its head a "Prince of the Captivity" who went in state, attended by a troop of cavalry with a herald preceding them who called out, "Make room for the son of David!" when he called upon the Caliph. Many rich and learned Jews lived in Baghdad, and at one time it is recorded that there were twenty-eight synagogues in and about that city.[17] Jews and Muslims lived side by side in most Muslim cities. Only under rulers of exceptional bigotry were the Jews disturbed.

Still better proof of Muslim tolerance, if it be needed, is the fact that there are still some 150,000 Nestorians in the regions where the Caliph ruled. There would have been more had not 70,000 joined the Roman Communion, some 15,000 others the Russian Church, and many the Protestant churches. The Monophysite Patriarch at Antioch directs churches with 80,000 members.[18] It must always be remembered that if the most zealous Mohammedans wished to take all men to Allah with them, the Caliph's tax gatherers hoped that large and ever larger numbers would have to pay the protection tax.

The four successors of Mohammed—Abu Bakr, 632–

[17] Bukhsh, *Studies Indian and Islamic,* 132–136.
[18] Arnold, *op. cit.,* 80.

634; Umar, 634–644; Othman, 644–656; Ali, 656–661—
are the orthodox Caliphs. The first three ruled from
Medina, the Prophet's city; Ali, from Cufa. Every Friday
they preached in the mosque, as the Founder of Islam had
done and as their generals and governors of provinces
did also. The governor of Syria, the Omayyad Muawiya,
then became Caliph, and because his rule depended upon
the Arab troops in Syria he moved the capital to
Damascus. The house of Ommayiah ruled until the house
of Abbas displaced it in 750. The Omayyad Caliphs
gave attention to the building arts. In their leisure they
employed reciters of the heroic deeds of the Arabs, and
"wasted" much money on poets and musicians. They did
not, however, encourage the more substantial forms of
learning. Of necessity the Quran came in for attention,
and the beginnings of Muslim theology and jurisprudence
were made.

When the more capable Abbasides began to rule (750),
they took learning under their special protection, and the
Golden Age of Arabic history began. These Caliphs were
of the family of Mohammed—Abbas, from whom its
members traced descent, having been the Prophet's uncle.
They found their political and military supporters in
Persia, where respect for legitimism was almost indigenous
and "The House of the Prophet!" was a cry which rallied
nearly the whole population. The seizure of the caliphate
was, like so much of the activity of that time, a bloody
business, but finally "on the old soil of the great Asiatic
Empires, another was once more set up, which at the
most was only half Arab in its character, the rest being
Persian." [19]

Al-Mansur, the second Caliph (754–775) of the house
of Abbas, determined to build a new capital on the west

[19] Noldeke, *Sketches from Eastern History*, 115.

bank of the Tigris at a place where there was a little
village called Baghdad. It is said that one reason for
choosing that spot was its comparative freedom from
mosquitoes. The name Mansur chose for the city which
he planned was Madinah-as-Salam, "The City of Welfare."
He began to build it in 762, laying the first brick himself.
One hundred thousand workmen were employed in constructing it. It was a city of palaces, mosques, government buildings, gardens, and residences, a round city
surrounded by double fortification walls with suburbs
watered by canals from the Tigris.[20] The city was ready
in 766; the wall finished in 768. It was destroyed by the
Mongols in 1258. Here, surrounded by great pomp and
magnificence, the Pontiffs of the Faith inspired a renaissance of learning, the most remarkable of all the revivals
of ancient learning. Zeal for conquest yielded to zeal for
studies. The wisdom books of five literatures, the Greek,
Hebrew, Syriac, Persian, and Indian, were translated
into Arabic.[21]

Arabic Sciences	*Foreign Sciences*
1. Quranic exegesis	1. Philosophy
2. Quranic reading and criticism	2. Geometry
	3. Astronomy
3. The science of apostolic tradition	4. Music
	5. Medicine
4. Jurisprudence	6. Magic and alchemy
5. Scholastic theology	
6. Grammar	
7. Lexicography	
8. Rhetoric	

[20] See the map of Baghdad in Muir, *The Caliphate, Rise, Decline and Fall*, p. 464.
[21] Carra de Vaux, *Avicenne*, 37.

The Muslims regard as their own all the forms of learning that they have developed about the Quran; the forms of learning which they took from other peoples, they refer to as foreign sciences.

The Arabs, who had never had a book, suddenly found themselves ruling a large part of the world by means of one. About ruling they knew next to nothing; and about city life, nothing at all. They were desert-dwelling tribesmen who had suddenly by God's will to found a state and regulate the public and religious affairs of vast populations much more advanced than themselves. To the first companions Mohammed had shown the way. The thing to do was to memorize the Revelation and carry it in one's breast and faithfully follow the practices of the Prophet. Those who were able to repeat the Quran and recite accounts of Mohammed were called Readers. They were marvellously useful men and led in supplying knowledge, but not in most cases perhaps in executing it. If God had not sent down His will in a Book, and if He had not so arranged it among men that the informed mind and the executing arm usually belong to different people, the Muslims would not have found learning necessary; they would have continued spontaneously to compose, memorize, and recite their charming poetry as in "the days of ignorance."

That the Arabs, untaught and undisciplined as they were, were the dominant race is shown by the fact that they were able to do what even the dominant Normans did not succeed in doing; that is, they made their Arabic language the language of the conquered peoples. Within about two hundred years Arabic became the language of the entire Caliphate.[22] Here then are two points in

---

[22] Bukhsh, *op. cit.*, 130.

the story: the Muslims had a Book, which was in Arabic; and that Book was directed to all men: "We have sent in every nation an apostle" (XVI, 38). "For every nation have we made rites which they observe" (XXII, 66). "We have not sent Thee save as a mercy to all created beings" (XXI, 107). "And we have not sent thee otherwise than to mankind at large, to announce and to warn" (XXXIV, 27).

Islam then is an intensely missionary religion. Its Book is intended for all men and is meant to be read by all, no matter what their rank or service. To make the Holy Book known, it had to be taught. Elementary schools were accordingly opened in the earliest times in Syria, Iraq, and other provinces.[23] They were, of course, simple affairs—usually, perhaps, only a class for children in the mosque. The Quran was read, and parts of it memorized; and the boys and girls who attended were also taught to write. The teacher was paid in kind by the parents of the children. Occupation with the Holy Book was the chief thing needful, and the children got it by heart. The Caliph Abdul Malik ordered the teacher of his sons to teach them the Quran, to instruct them in ancient poetry, to see that they acquired a faultless mode of speaking, ate nothing but meat, and mixed with neither high nor low society.[24] When a bookless people suddenly find that God Himself has sent them a book, it is perhaps but natural for them to be confused about how to use it. Holy words are apt to have magic uses. The Quran had from the first a ritual use that to a poetry-reciting people was overwhelming. It must have been an experience nearly transfiguring to have heard the Prophet recite his Quran. The Mohammedans made it an experience never

[23] Bukhsh, *op. cit.*, 104
[24] *Ibn Hamdun*, quoted in Bukhsh, *op. cit.*, 106.

to be forgotten to hear any one recite the Quran. The book is marvellous when it is pronounced. Readers of the Book of God practiced the finest and most necessary art that the Muslims knew. Of all forms of learning, the reading and reciting of the Book is uppermost. Children begin that study in their first instruction, but eternity itself is not long enough to perfect it. Nor is it difficult to understand this. Think, for example, what amount and character of training would be necessary to enable one of us to sound the call to prayer over a Muslim city as the Muezzin calls from the minaret of the Mosque five times a day: "God is great" (four times); "I bear witness that there is no God but God" (two times); "I bear witness that Mohammed is the Apostle of God" (two times); "Come hither to prayers" (two times); "Come hither to salvation" (two times); "God is Great! There is no other God but God." And in the call to the dawn prayer, the reminder, "It is better to pray than to sleep," is added. Only a voice of penetration and great carrying power can remind a sleeping city at half-past two in the morning of its duty to God. But something more is needed; that voice must be of an appealing and persuasive timbre. The public Reader in the Mosque has not so difficult a task, but he too must be trained in the use of his voice, much as opera singers are. And not only readers in the Mosque but devout men and women who read the Quran daily and some who practice the reading of it in the quietest hours of the night—all must be taught to phrase it properly, to chant it in the right manner. There were seven systems of reading the Quran, and there is a record of one student who took the course in Quranic reading eleven times to perfect himself.[25]

[25] Ribera, *La Enseñanza entre los Musulmanes españoles.*

The companions of the Prophet began the study of sounding, punctuating, and reciting the parts of the Quran which they remembered, immediately after Mohammed's death. Their studies into these matters led those of them who dwelt in Basra to invent the study of grammar. The Arabs have an informing story of how that invention came to be made. Abu-'l-Aswad who made it, "having been asked where he had acquired the science of grammar, said that he had learned the rudiments of it from 'Alí ben Abí Tálib. It is said that he never made known any of the principles which he had received from 'Alí till Ziyád sent to him the order to compose something which might serve as a guide to the public and enable them to understand The Book of God. He at first asked to be excused, but on hearing a man recite the following passage out of the Quran:

"anna 'lláha barí'un mina'l-mushrikína wa-rasúluhu

which last word the reader pronounced rasúlihi, he exclaimed, 'I never thought that things would have come to this.' He then returned to Ziyád and said: 'I will do what you have ordered.' " Mr. Nicholson, who tells this story,[26] translates the passage from the Quran (Chapter IX, verse 3) as follows: "(This is a declaration) That God is clear of the idolaters, and His Apostle likewise." With the word *rasúlihi* it means that God is clear of the idolaters and also of His Apostle.

The Arabic alphabet in the days of the Revelations must have been very imperfect. Next to nothing had been written in it. Only seventeen in the tribe of Koraish could write. All the captives taken at the battle of Badr who could write were freed without ransom.[27]

[26] *Literary History of the Arabs*, 342.
[27] Browne, *A Literary History of Persia*, 261.

It was a consonantal alphabet, but—what was worse—several consonants were written by the same symbol. It became important for the reader to know whether *b, t,* or *th* was meant. A variety of readings was possible because of imperfect spelling, also because grammatical forms were shifting, never having been anchored to a standard. Another difficulty was that the Quran, being a precious book, must according to some worshippers have a precious pronunciation. A whole machinery of vowel signs, diacritical marks, pointings, punctuation, grammatical forms, etc. had to be worked out and applied to the Quran before it became intelligible. That was the Arabic grammar which Abu'l-Aswad al-Du'ali began to construct and to teach in Basra.[28] The School of Cufa competed with Basra in that important study. It was in the time of the Omayyads that these very difficult matters were begun. The Persians added their strength to them, and the great Persian Sibawayhi (793) made a grammar which is still the basis of Arabic grammars.

Muslim theology is said to derive in part from polemical discussions carried on between Christian and Muslim theologians at the Omayyad court at Damascus. John of Damascus had a part in them. They concerned the nature of God, the origin of evil, the free will of man, etc., the stock questions of the theologians of the Eastern Church. Once introduced into Islam they became as fertile subjects of division there as they had long been among the Christians. Greek practices of analyzing, distinguishing, classifying, formulating, found eager disciples among the followers of the Prophet, and, ever since, Islam has been no more a dissensionless faith than has Christianity.

Next to the Quran in importance are the canonical and

[28] Noldeke, *op. cit.,* 54. Bukhsh, *op. cit.,* 144.

half-canonical collections of traditions of what the Prophet said, did, or did not do. This being the most authoritative guide to the interpretation of the Book, it is immensely valuable. That traditions tended to multiply beyond reason and had constantly to be cut down is indicated by the fact that Bukhárí (879) limited his collection which he called "The Genuine" to 7,000, taking them from an accumulation of 600,000.[29]

Law covers religious as well as civil matters in Islam, or rather it is at all points church-state regulation which rests throughout on the Quran and the traditions. But the traditions were various and not seldom contradictory and confusing, a quality unfortunately shared in some degree by the Quran. Of a consequence there arose in the eighth century certain masters who began to teach their disciples the master's own formulation from the whole mass of the rules of law. Four of these schools which resisted all efforts to reduce them to unity were rated as equally orthodox. These four orthodox schools of law were the Hanbalites, the Hanefites, the Shafiites, and the Malekites. But of these Mâlik ibn Anas of Medina was by far the most influential.

There was, too, an immense volume of literature in Arabic. Merely to recall the *Thousand and One Nights* is enough to remind every one of a personal indebtedness. It was but one of many; story-telling and romance weaving was a favorite literary occupation, and celebrated books of poetry and songs were not wanting. The writing of histories engaged Tabari and Maśudi, the latter being called "the Herodotus of the Arabs." Like the Father of History he travelled everywhere, collecting all manner of "curious and precious information." The Muslims too were great geographers, supplying vast bodies of in-

[29] Nicholson, *op. cit.,* 146. Bukhárí's traditions numbered 7397.

formation about their own lands. Notable among their contributions was *The Book of the Roads and Countries* of Ibn Khurdádbih, Al Farisí's *Routes of the Provinces,* and Yáqút's *Geographical Dictionary,* republished in Leipzig in 1866. There were too the *Treatises of the Brethren of Purity,* a great encyclopedia of fifty tractates on philosophy and science. These Brethren belonged to Basra in the tenth century. They held that "the Religious Law was defiled by ignorance and adulterated by errors, and that there was no means of cleansing and purifying it except philosophy which united the wisdom of faith and the profit of research. They held that a perfect result would be reached if Greek philosophy were combined with Arabian religion." [30] These tracts have been translated into German and epitomized by Professor F. Dieterici. "Great admirer as I am of European culture," writes S. Khuda Bukhsh, lecturer in the history of Islam at Calcutta University, "I set our own learning first and foremost in the curriculum of our studies. And this for obvious reasons: our own learning is the embodiment of our hopes, traditions, aspirations. It is the reflection of our civilisation, the mirror of our character. It is the monument of our achievements. I have called it, you will notice, our own learning. Though Arabic and Persian are not our own languages yet they are the two languages in which the highest achievements of Islam lie enshrined. And to us Muslims they have a priceless value; an invaluable interest; an interest which transcends the barriers of race and nationality. The tie is religion, —the unbreakable tie. Arabic is the language of the Quran. Besides, it contains a literature worthy of a great nation. The heralds and pioneers of the Middle Ages, it was left to the Muslims, amid the tumult of fallen and

[30] Quoted in Nicholson, *op. cit.,* 370.

falling things, to carry on the traditions of learning, to uphold the torch of culture." [31]

It was not piety or Mohammed, it was success that made the Muslim Empire. But Mohammed and piety had organized that success. The Arab conquerors were busy men. They were proud and disdainful. They were wholly untaught, but their responsibilities were more than they could discharge. They had to employ the services of all they could conscript to help them. In conquered Persia and among the Nestorian and Monophysite Christians of both Syria and Persia the ruling Arabs found their chief helpers. Jewish physicians were employed by them from the first. Large numbers of Jews and Christians among the conquered peoples became Mohammedans to escape the head tax. They were valuable recruits for they could be used in the offices. Here is a story from Al Fakhrì which tells how expert help was needed and was found when the wealth of the world was divided:

"In the fifteenth year of the Hijrah [A.D. 636] 'Umar who was then Caliph, seeing that the conquests proceeded without interruption and that the treasures of the Persian monarchs had been taken as spoil, and that load after load was being accumulated of gold and silver and precious jewels and splendid raiment, resolved to enrich the Muslims by distributing all this wealth among them; but he did not know how he should manage it. Now there was a Persian satrap at Medina who when he saw 'Umar's bewilderment said to him, 'O Commander of the Faithful, the Persian kings have a thing they call a *Dìwán* in which is kept the whole of their revenues and expenditures without exception; and therein those who re-

---

[31] Bukhsh, *op. cit.*, 35 (by permission of Kegan Paul, Trench, Trübner & Co., Ltd.).

ceive stipends are arranged in classes, so that no confusion occurs.' 'Umar's attention was aroused. He bade the satrap describe it and, on comprehending its nature, he drew up the registers and assigned the stipends, appointing a specified allowance for every Muslim; and he allotted fixed sums to the wives of the Apostle (on whom be God's blessing and peace!) and to his concubines and next of kin, until he exhausted the money in hand. He did not lay up a store in the treasury. Some one came to him and said: 'O Commander of the Faithful, you should have left something to provide for contingencies.' 'Umar rebuked him saying, 'The devil has put these words into your mouth. May God preserve me from their mischief! for it were a temptation to my successors. Come what may, I will provide naught except obedience to God and His Apostle. That is our provision, whereby we have gained that which we have gained." [32]

The Persians were rapidly Arabicized under the Abbasids, and Arabs and Persians both began to work with incredible zeal for the cultivation of knowledge in the Muslim Empire. The period from 750 to 900 is the age of translations. Nestorian and Monophysite Christians in the great schools of Nisibis, Gandisapora, Resaina, and the monastery of Kinnesrin had already turned many of the Greek wisdom books into Syriac and into Persian. The King of Persia, Chosroes (531–579), had made the medical center of Gandisapora outstanding in the world. He had sent his own physician to India to collect medical books which were translated from Sanskrit into the Pahlavi of Middle Persia. Sergius of Resaina had translated the Greek medical books into Syriac. From Harran too, an ancient heathen town, came Babylonian mathe-

[32] Nicholson, *op. cit.*, 187–188 (by permission of the Cambridge University Press).

matical lore mixed with Greek learning to which its people were deeply attached.

The Caliph Mansur (754–775) was the first to cause Greek scientific works to be translated into Arabic. The plans for his building of Baghdad were made by the Persian astronomer, Naubakht, and Mash a allah, a Jew. A Hindu treatise on astronomy, the *Sindhind,* was introduced to Al-Mansur's court by a learned Hindu, Manka. Abu Yahya translated books on medicine and the *Quadripartitum* of Ptolemy. The Caliph Mansur, it is said, offered rewards to such as would produce translations of works upon mathematics, astronomy, medicine, and philosophy.

Harun-al-Rashid (786–809) was not so systematic a supporter of learning as Mansur or Mamun, but no Caliph of them all had so many learned men about him: poets, jurists, grammarians, and some translators. Harun was a dilettante rather than a driver of men such as Mansur had been. Of Al-Mamun (813–833) his son, the accounts are different. He was himself a student and devoted in every way he could be to the advancement of learning. He gave himself up to its cause. He organized a vast work of translating books on mathematics, medicine, astronomy, and philosophy from the Greek into the Arabic. Agents of the Caliph collected Greek writings at Constantinople and dispatched them to Baghdad. The organized staff of translators at the palace took them in hand and converted them into Arabic. The man in charge of this staff of translators was Hunayn ben Ishaq, a Nestorian Christian of Hira. He had studied Greek in Constantinople and had mastered Arabic through years of residence and study at Baghdad and Basra. He was a physician. He—that is, the staff under his direction— translated the Septuagint Bible, the works of Hippocrates,

Galen, and Archimedes, the *Republic, Timaeus,* and *Laws* of Plato, the *Physics, Ethics,* and parts of the *Metaphysics* and *Logic* of Aristotle. Ishak, his son and chief assistant, translated the *Sophist* of Plato, the *Metaphysics* and the *Logic* of Aristotle together with the *Hermeneia* and the treatise on *Generation and Decay.*[33] Other primary works were translated by other scholars, and the works of the commentators also were turned into Arabic. The *Iliad* of Homer had to wait until 1904 for translation into Arabic verse. The Arabs drew their translated literature from Persia and India. They specialized in the wisdom literature of Greece.

As a culmination of his efforts to drive learning forward in the Arabic Empire the Caliph Al Mamun constructed the House of Wisdom at Baghdad, which included a library and an astronomical observatory. The Arabs derived their first knowledge of mathematics from the Hindus and the Greeks. It is said that the Caliph Al Mamun sent to India as well as to Constantinople for books. It seems probable that Euclid's *Elements* was the first work translated from Greek into Arabic. The Arabs put the world under an eternal debt to them by contributing the system of writing numbers which goes by their name. There is endless discussion as to whether they really invented the numerals or borrowed them from India. The numerals have a handier form among the Arabs than elsewhere, and the symbol for zero, the cipher, they seem to have invented and used two hundred and fifty years before it was known in the West. An Arabic writer of the tenth century, the author of the *Keys of Science,* says that if a power of ten is not represented, a little circle is used "to keep the rows." [34]

[33] Carra de Vaux, *Avicenne,* 58.
[34] *The Legacy of Islam,* 386.

The words cipher, algorism, and algebra witness to the part the Arabs played in developing mathematical calculation.

"Algebra" is *al-Jabr*, the adding of something to a given quantity, as *a* plus *x* equals *b*, or multiplying as *ax* equals *c*, so that two quantities become exactly equal. The Arabs solved equations of the second degree; the theory of such equations down to the sixteenth century remained as they had formulated it. The study of astronomy appealed to the Arabs in the days of learning as it had in the "days of ignorance." They set up observatories at Baghdad, Gandisapora, Cairo, and several other places. They took observations in different places and compared them, and from them constructed tables. Al-Farghani wrote a *Compendium* which was translated into Latin by Gerard of Cremona. Al-Battani calculated the appearances of the new moon, eclipses, the length of the year, etc., and made important contributions to trigonometry. Abu'l-Wafa wrote an *Almagest* with important astronomical contributions and added materially to the science of trigonometry. Omar Khayyám was as great a geometer as he was a poet. This mass of astronomical and mathematical work was done by the Arabs in a definitely scientific spirit. Their observations were as careful as they could make them. Astrology, the popular lore of the stars, they were not responsible for. It was a far more ancient Babylonian development which lived on as it still lives outside of astronomical observatories.

Arabic words like alcohol, alkali, alum, alembic, and elixir indicate that the science of chemistry has Arabic roots. Parts of the work of the man to whom the title of the first chemist is sometimes applied are in English.[35]

[35] *The Works of Geber,* transl. William Russell (London: Dent).

Geber belongs to the period of Harun-al-Rashid. His father's town is Cufa. He studied everything from the Quran to the art of war. He was a physician to the Barmecide ministers of the Caliph, and at their downfall he returned to Cufa, where he is said to have died in 813. The Egyptians are said to have tried to make gold; the Emperor Caligula tried to make gold, and every other people on the earth would have done that if they could have followed their desires. The Arabs in their turn tried to make it, tried in fact so systematically that they made something far more valuable; namely, the science of chemistry. That science, says Geber, investigates the properties and generation of minerals and substances obtained from animals and plants. "It must be taken as an absolutely rigorous principle," he writes, "that any proposition which is not supported by proofs is nothing more than an assertion which may be true or may be false. It is only when a man brings proofs of his assertion that we say your proposition is true." [36] In his preface to the *Investigation of Search of Perfection*, Geber says: "Whatsoever we saw and handled, we have compleatly described, according to the Order of Science, with Experience and certain Knowledge, which we acquired by our Scrutiny." [37]

A second chemist, even more distinguished, was Rhazes, who died about 923; that is, he lived about one hundred years later than Geber. His book, he called *The Book of the Secret of Secrets*. Rhazes practiced medicine at Baghdad and wrote a book on smallpox and an encyclopedia of Arab medicine.

Because dissection was forbidden to them by their re-

[36] Quoted in Bukhsh, *op. cit.*, 175, from Holmyard, *Chemistry to the Time of Dalton*, 18.
[37] But see *The Legacy of Islam*, 326.

ligion, Arabic medicine was limited to superficial diagnosis and pharmacological study and treatment. Botany accordingly came in for much attention, and in it the Arabs did valuable collecting and observing.

But medicine, by means of which all the other sciences had been introduced, remained the art *par excellence* among the Arabs. The sudden change from the wild life of the desert to the confined sedentary life of unhygienic cities brought its services into abnormal prominence. The title of sage, among the Arabs, usually included some knowledge of it. No matter how many other subjects he had mastered, a learned man hardly counted for much unless he had studied medicine also. The medical books of the ancients were eagerly translated and retranslated, and hundreds of titles testify how zealously Arabic writers composed books of their own on medicine. Hospitals were established in Baghdad in its early days under the Caliph Al-Muktadir (907–932). A Christian physician, Sinan Ibn Thabit, held the position of director of hospitals in Baghdad. Other towns too had hospitals. A hospital was a centre of medical study then just as it is now.[38]

Was there an Arabian philosophy? Did the Arabs produce any thinker of the first order, or did they merely study the works of the ancients and by so doing save them for the modern world? That itself was a service of the first order. They recognized their debt to the ancients and acknowledged it: "Did we not possess the books of the ancients in which their wonderful wisdom is immortalized and in which the manifold lessons of history are so dealt with that the past lives before our eyes, did we not have access to the riches of their experience which would otherwise have been barred to us, our share

[38] Bukhsh, *op. cit.,* 197.

in wisdom would be immeasurably smaller and our means of attaining a true perspective most meager." [39]

It is said that there were seventy-three kinds of Believers.[40] The Quran had contributed three controverted points: (1) Its wholesale determinism forced the question, "If Allah determines all things is He not then the author of evil?" (2) The Quran is uncreated and eternal. (3) Does God have hands and feet and sit on a throne, as the Quran says? The Persians like the Greeks were born disputers. They took eagerly the invitation to rationalism which Greek studies gave them. The Caliph Al-Mamun shared their passion to such a degree that he was called the "Commander of the Unfaithful." [41] This furious effort to combine Greek culture with a Mohammedan conscience was Arabian scholasticism. Logic was the driving force, and Aristotle the Philosopher was the chief engineer here as he was in the Church of the West three hundred years later. It was the philosophy of Aristotle that inspired the Mu'tazilites to rationalize the Quran and the traditions. The Quran is not uncreate, they said; if it were, there would be two Eternal Beings. To Mohammed's statement, "One day ye shall see your Lord as you saw the full moon at the Battle of Badr," they replied: The dead shall see by the eyes of the spirit. God is the Divine Unity. He has neither hands nor feet nor attributes of any kind. Man is free. All truth needed for salvation belongs to reason both before and after Revelation. In all times and places man should have these truths and guide

[39] Al-Jāhiz of Basra (d. 869), quoted in *The Legacy of Islam,* 239.

[40] See Asin, *Algazel,* 14, and Schmolder's "Essai sur les differentes sectes philosophiques chez les Arabes" in his *Ecoles philosophiques chez les arabes,* 88.

[41] Browne, *op. cit.,* 307.

himself by them.[42] Some Mu'tazalites even declared it was possible to write a better book than the Quran.

But reaction follows and is a part of action. The Caliph Al-Mutawakkil (847–861) was not willing like Al-Mamun to be a commander of the unfaithful; instead "he was of the number of the most excellent Caliphs for he forbade men to believe that the Quran was created." [43] The orthodox leaders, also, learned logic and found it more powerful in defence even than it was in attack, and philosophy defended dogmatism which is real scholasticism. Al-Ash'ari (born 873), a man who had been trained to their rationalism by the Mu'tazilites, backslid, renounced their doctrines, joined their enemies, and fought them till his death. He wrote an enormous number of polemical tracts and books, of which a catalogue of one hundred by title was published in Germany in 1876.[44] He was the counterfoil of the Mu'tazilite rationalists in the great theological struggle. The Brethren of Purity took a middle ground, urging that Greek Philosophy be combined with religion. "The strife between Nominalism and Realism . . . had already during the ninth and tenth centuries set in motion all the minds of the East." [45]

A singular coincidence is that scholasticism both in the West and in the East was the mother of universities. Greek mental activity as portrayed in Aristotle was so fecund that it set whole nations to mental activity. The Arabs soon learned from their Nestorian Christian guides how to make translations from the Greek themselves. Al-Mamun had set up a House of Wisdom to give perma-

---

[42] See Dozy's account of the Mu'tazilites in Browne, *op. cit.*, 286.

[43] Abu'l-Fidá quoted in Browne, *op. cit.*, 290.

[44] Spitta, *Zur Geschichte Abu'l-Hasan Al-Ash-Aris* (quoted by Browne, *op. cit.*, 291).

[45] Dieterici, *Philosophie der Araben*, 1–80.

nence to these activities which he himself cherished greatly. In 1065 Nizamu-l-Mulk, the Vizier of Alp Arslan and the friend of Omar Khayyám, founded the Nizami University at Baghdad, the first in Muslim or Christian lands and certainly the mother university of Mohammedan countries and possibly, as Professor Julian Ribera believes, the mother university of the Christians as well. There Al-Ghazali, the champion of orthodoxy, taught theology from 1091 to 1095. Other universities shortly came into being at Nishapur, Damascus, Jerusalem, Cairo, and Alexandria.[46]

To found a Madrasah, or center of studies, was a pious act acceptable to God and serviceable to the community, particularly to the religious part of it. It did something for the one who gave it. "He dies not who gives life to learning," was a Muslim saying. The founder erected the building and endowed the university to be housed in it. The buildings usually were of permanent stone construction. They included a prayer mosque or chapel and were arcades built about a court with a fountain. The endowments provided the upkeep, the salaries of the professors and assistants and sometimes even total support for the students.[47] A people whose religion is revealed to them in a book must make provision for the study and interpretation of that book. The problem of difficulty is not, How did the Muslims, the Christians, or the Jews come to develop education? (that was in each case inevitable) but How did the Greeks come to develop it? It must have been that the book which they had forced them to it too; but being a different kind of book its results were different.

In the *Missive on the Galenic Translations*, Hunayn

---

[46] *The Legacy of Islam*, 241.
[47] Bukhsh, *op. cit.*, 196.

the author tells how the *Twenty Books* of Galen were
studied at Alexandria and therefore in other Arab centres in 856. "The reading of the students of the medical
school at Alexandria was confined to these books, keeping to the order which I have followed in my list. They
were accustomed to meet daily to read and interpret one
of the standard works, as in our days our Christian
friends meet daily at the educational institutions known
as *scholē* to discuss a standard work from among the
books of the Ancients. The remainder of Galen's books
they used to read each for himself, after an introductory
study of the aforementioned books, just as our friends
today do with the explanations of the books of the Ancients." [48]

There is a concrete description of another Muslim
university (the proudest of them, it is said), the Mustanṣiriyah, founded at Baghdad in 1234. "We are told
that in outward appearance in stateliness of ornament,
and sumptuousness of furniture, in spaciousness and
in the wealth of its pious foundations, the Mustanṣiriyah
surpassed everything that had previously been seen
in Islam. It contained four separate law-schools, one
for each of the orthodox sects of the Sunnīs, with a
professor at the head of each, who had seventy-five
students in his charge, to whom he gave instruction
gratis. The four professors each received a monthly
salary, and to each of the three hundred students one gold
dīnār a month was assigned. The great kitchen of the
college further provided daily rations of bread and meat
to all the inmates. According to Ibn-al-Furāt there was
a library . . . in the Mustanṣiriyah with rare books
treating of the various sciences, so arranged that the

[48] *The Legacy of Islam,* 319 (by permission of the Clarendon Press,
Oxford).

students could easily consult them, and those who wished could copy these manuscripts, pens and paper being supplied by the establishment. Lamps for the students and a due provision of olive oil for lighting up the college are also mentioned, likewise storage places for cooling the drinking water; and in the great entrance hall . . . stood a clock . . . doubtless some form of clepsydra, announcing the appointed times of prayer, and marking the lapse of the hours by day and by night. Inside the college a bath house . . . was erected for the special use of the students, and a hospital . . . to which a physician was appointed whose duty it was to visit the place every morning, prescribing for those who were sick; and there were great store-chambers in the Madrasah provided with all requisites of food, drink and medicines." [49]

In 1258 Hulagu the Mongol put to death the last of the Caliphs, Al-Musta'sim, and sacked the capital. There were "mock caliphs" supported by the Memluks of Egypt from 1261 to 1520, then the Osmanli sultans claimed to be caliphs until their rule ended. But the holy cities remained holy, and every year the Muslim world went to Mecca on pilgrimage as it still goes two hundred thousand strong. The two industries of Mecca are caring for the pilgrims and caring for the students who go there to study the sacred sciences. They are young men from many nations: India, Egypt, China, Malaysia, Turkey, North Africa, the Sudan, Turkestan, Syria, etc. The classes sit in circles about the master in the mosque when it is not in use for religious services. As many as a dozen classes are going on at the same time in which the Arabic grammar, poetry, logic, sacred jurisprudence, theology and the advanced study of the Quran and of

---

[49] Quoted in *The Legacy of Islam*, 242, from G. Le Strange, *Baghdad During the Abbasid Caliphate* (Oxford, 1900), p. 267.

the Traditions are taught. Dr. Snouck Hurgronje, Professor of the Arabic Language in the University of Leiden, Holland, spent one year as a student in Mecca and describes the activity of that capital center of Mohammedan studies thus: "The most important lectures are delivered during the forenoon and in the evening. A walk at one of those hours, through the square and under the colonnades of the mosque, with ears opened to all sides, will enable you to get a general idea of the objects of mental exercise of this international assembly. Here you may find a sheikh of pure Arab descent explaining to his audience, composed of white Syrians or Circassians, of brown and yellow Abyssinians and Egyptians, of negroes, Chinese and Malays, the probable and improbable legal consequences of marriage contracts, not excepting those between men and genii; there a negro scholar is explaining the ontological evidence of the existence of a Creator and the logical necessity of His having twenty qualities, inseparable from, but not identical with His essence; in the midst of another circle a learned *mufti* of indeterminably mixed extraction demonstrates to his pupils from the standard work of Al-Ghazali the absolute vanity of law and doctrine to those whose hearts are not purified from every attachment to the world. Most of the branches of Mohammedan learning are represented within the walls of this temple by more or less famous scholars; and still there are a great number of private lectures delivered at home by professors who do not like to be disturbed by the unavoidable noise in the mosque, which during the whole day serves as a meeting place for friends or business men, as an exercise hall for Quran reciters, and even as a passage for people going from one part of the town to the other." [50]

[50] Hurgronje, *Mohammedanism*, 164 (by permission of G. P. Putnam's Sons).

The making of books in large quantities in early times depended upon two things, a plentiful supply of paper and the speed of the copyist. Arabic is a shorthand language, and when the Arabs conquered Egypt in 641 they came into control of the papyrus-paper industry of the world. Its chief seat was at Bura in the Delta. Improved methods in time made paper of cotton at Tehama in North Arabia. An enterprising Chinaman introduced the art of making it from flax. The center for that manufacture was Samarkand. Paper factories were soon developed in several places in the Muslim empire. It was manufactured by them in Spain and in Sicily. The paper of Xativa was famous. In the twelfth century Saracenic paper supplanted parchment in Europe. This of course made the means of learning more available. The book trade grew. Besides the mosques the book dealers set up their little booths offering for sale the copies of books which they had employed scribes to make.[51] Some of these books, particularly copies of the Quran, were wonderfully ornamented. Books were plentiful in Arabic lands, and libraries both private and public were many. Just before its destruction by the Mongols Baghdad is said to have had thirty-six. Even little towns had them. There is a vast unexplored wealth of manuscripts in the mosque libraries of Constantinople, Baghdad, Damascus, and Cairo. The Escorial collections are not yet listed. Of Spanish Islam there are treasures there.

The story of Muslim education in Spain deserves a chapter by itself. It has been written by Professor Julian Ribera of the school of Semitic studies in the University of Madrid in his volume, *La Enseñanza entre los Musulmanes Españoles*. The history of *Spanish Islam* is in Dozy's volume with that title.

[51] On this whole subject see Bukhsh, *op. cit.*, 46.

The native population fared better in Spain after the conquest of 711 than before. Its Arab masters treated the religions which they found there with tolerance, even consideration. Newly converted African tribesmen swarmed into the newly conquered lands. The Arab leaders who had brought them the faith and led in the conquest held them in check. But Spain suffered, as did every other land the Muslims conquered, from lack of unity on the part of the conquerors. To this day its official name is not Spain but the Spains, a result of the centrifugal tendency they brought with them. They were men of different countries, different civilizations in fact, and they settled in different parts of Spain and cultivated their differences. Arabs from Damascus occupied the beautiful Vega of Granada, because of its likeness to the Vega of Damascus. Egyptians were in Murcia, the Berbers in the southwest; Christians in Spain in numbers joined the new faith for a variety of reasons, not the least of which was the certainty of escaping the capitation tax by doing that.

Spain was never a part of the Abbasid Caliphate. When the house of Abbas deposed the Omayyad Caliphs of Damascus the only Omayyad to escape their wholesale slaughter was the young prince Abd-er-Rahmân, who fled to Morocco. He decided that the Omayyads should rule Spain, and the Syrians and Yemenites who were there helped him; but the Baghdad Caliphs had their partisans and agents who bitterly and with heavy bloodshed opposed Abd-er-Rahmân the Omayyad. But in 752 Abd-er-Rahmân became Emir of Spain. He was a very king of men, a great warrior, a ruler who made his own plans and kept them, a leader with backbone and engine power, in fact, a fitting antagonist for Charles the Great, whom he discomfited in the Pyrenees in 777. In 756 Abd-er-

Rahmân established his capital at Cordova, which continued to be the capital of the Emirs until 1031 and a center of government for the Almoravides and the Almohades until it was captured by the Christians in 1238. The Arabs continued to rule the Kingdom of Granada as we have seen until 1492.

Cordova was by far the most splendid city of Europe while the Emirs ruled there. It is a small city now of but some 85,000 people, then it had more than half a million inhabitants. The splendid palaces of the Caliph had intriguing names: the Palace of Damascus, the Palace of Flowers, the Palace of Contentment. The public parks of the city were the Golden Meadow, the Garden of the Waterwheel, the Meadow of the Murmuring Waters. On Mt. Olarus, about nine miles from Cordova, the Caliph built a summer palace or city, for it is referred to by both names—Al Zahra, it was called. Forty-three hundred marble columns supported its roof. Its halls were paved with marble. Its ceilings were of cedar and gold. Forty thousand persons, it is said, were assembled to look after the Caliph's court there. For centuries only broken bits of carved stone marked the spot where this great palace had stood. In recent years the Spaniards have made excavations and given the place a new name, "The Pompeii of the Arabs." This palace, unlikely as the statement is, was, it is said, more beautiful than the Alhambra. The oldest of the great cathedral churches of the world is in Cordova. It is the great mosque which Abd-er-Rahmân began in 786 and his son Hisham completed. When Cordova fell, it was converted into a Christian church just as St. Sophia was converted into a mosque in 1453. Next to St. Peter's it has the largest floor space of any church in Europe, being 420 feet in length and 370 in breadth. Its roof is supported by some 900 marble columns. It is an enduring witness of a substantial civilization.

"In the centuries from the fifth to the ninth the chief seats of learning were in the cities of Syria," says Thomas Davidson. "From the ninth to the eleventh century," says Madariaga, "the civilization of our world was Islamic." [52] "It is one of the duties of the government to make the canals necessary for the cultivation of the soil," was a principle of Arabic political science. In Spain the Arabs were devoted agriculturists. They brought in Persian, Indian and Syrian fruits and crops and began their culture there: rice, dates, oranges, peaches, apricots, lemons, sugar cane, cotton, pomegranates, medicinal plants and a wealth of flowers: roses, morning glories, etc. Both in manufacture and in merchandising the Arabs were active. They sailed the seas and sent caravans to many trading centres.*

It is sometimes said that the Arabs had state-supported schools in Spain. The statement is based upon the fact that Hisham, the second Emir, had certain of the learned men who gathered about him at his palace lecture from time to time in the mosques of Cordova. There was, however, no regularity or permanence to that arrangement. The Caliph Al-Hakam (912–961) is said to have founded public state-supported schools. What he did was done after recovering from a severe illness. As an act of piety he freed his slaves and directed that the rent from a few stalls in the market should be used as an endowment to enable certain masters to teach the faith to poor children in the city of Cordova. His act was a religious act, not the establishing of a public school policy. Others made gifts

[52] *Spain,* 28.
* See Pirenne's *Economic and Social History of Medieval Europe* (Harcourt, Brace & Co., New York, 1937).

from piety also, but no Mohammedan founded a university there, such as pious men founded in the East. It is a curious fact that the first Muslim university was founded in Spain by a Christian prince, Alfonso the Wise, from 1252 to 1284 king of Castile and León. It was modelled upon the Christian universities of Castile, Palencia, Salamanca, and Valladolid which go back to 1212 or 1214. The Arab philosopher, Abu Bequer El de Ricote, was its rector; Moors, Jews, and Christians could study in it. The king of Granada, who had been his pupil, urged Abu Bequer to come to Granada and teach his own people. He did so. A house was given him in the Vega of Granada. There he instructed the many students who came to him—some of them sent by the King—in the ancient sciences, philosophy, mathematics, etc. As philosophy, was never in favor with orthodox Muslims in Spain, his school died with him. With this exception government did not provide education in Moorish Spain. It was left wholly to private teachers to do that.

The Muslim church is not an organization apart from the body of the faithful. It has no priesthood and no hierarchy. It is a body of laymen any one of whom may be called to any office and, after discharging it, returns to his place as a lay member again. But the men who study distinguish themselves by their learning and have an unofficial preëminence and power on that account. They were recognized by emirs, kings, and people as a class to be consulted and conciliated. Of the four orthodox schools of Quranic law, one is the school of Malik ibn Anas. For the founder of this school the Omayyad Emir of Spain Hishâm, the son of Abd-er-Rahmân, came to have great regard. Mâlik ibn Anas at Medina had slighted the claims of the Abbasid Caliph at Baghdad and been bastinadoed for doing so. His preference was naturally for men of the Omayyad house. When his enthusiastic pupils from Spain told him of the regard in which the Emir at Cordova held him and sang the Emir's praises, the great Muslim sage found no difficulty in thinking Hishâm a prince beyond compare. When these Spanish students finished their course at Medina and returned to Cordova they told the Emir of the high regard in which he was held by the sage. Hishâm naturally did all he could to spread the tenets of the Medina master and urged students to go to Arabia to study with him, which they did. Then came the greatest of Mâlik's pupils to Spain in the person of Yahya ibn Yahya, a Berber who had travelled to Medina to study in Mâlik's classroom. He had made himself rarely valued there too, for one day as the professor was lecturing an elephant passed along the street and all the students rushed out to see it—all save Yahya ibn Yahya, who still sat there listening to the lecture. "Why do you not go out with the rest?" asked Mâlik. "There are no elephants in Spain." "I left my country to see you and profit by your teachings, not to gaze at an elephant," said Yahya ibn Yahya. Thereupon Mâlik gave him the title of the *akil* of Spain, which means the discerning one. He returned to Cordova to become the first of Quranic theologians.[53] Thus it was that the Mâlik sect began to dominate in Spain. It became in time a hard-hearted and tyrannical keeper of the law and morals of the people, the official Muslim church in fact if not in right. The books of other doctors were read, but only in a speculative way. Spanish Muslims were agreed that the doctrines of Mâlik ibn Anas were orthodox, and that all heretical teaching must be frowned upon and kept out. Heresy hunting, par-

[53] Dozy, *Spanish Islam*, 243 (Stokes transl., London: Chatto & Windus, 1913).

ticularly among teachers and writers on theological subjects, was pretty active. When the Emirate broke up
and the land split into little kingdoms (1031) heresy
hunting became a secondary matter. When the half-
savage Almoravides came from Morocco to rule Spain
(1085–1143), knowing next to nothing of the Quran
and the traditions of the Prophet, they made the books
of Mâlik ibn Anas their sole guide. The arbitrary intolerance of ignorant men wrecked nearly everything.
In 1143 the Almohades came and made Arabic Spain
a part of the government of Morocco. They soon
found that neither the Quran nor the Traditions determined its life and set themselves to destroy all Mâlik
books and doctrines. They appointed a commission which
formed a collection of traditions which they took from
ten books of the greatest authority and commanded all
to memorize at once. They tried to root out the Mâlik
doctrines utterly, but the teachers went on teaching the
forbidden interpretations, and, says Professor Ribera,
the last Spanish adept in Mâlik doctrines was the last
Moor in the peninsula. There was, then, very little freedom of teaching in Moorish Spain.

There is a thing that is very striking about Arabic education, i.e., the esteem in which it and those who followed it were held. If all Roman teachers had been
Catos or Augustus Caesars, teaching and teachers would
have been socially approved at Rome. But most were
Greek slaves, and it was not. In Muslim lands teaching did not start at the bottom but at the top. The companions of the Prophet, the men most closely associated
with him in blood and responsibility, were the ones who
had to teach the Revelations. They were the princes of
the land and its first teachers. That was true in Arabia
but not in Spain, which was conquered by military

chiefs who were little learned in anything, particularly in the religion which they professed. They did the conquering; others, devout and humble men, came after them who taught the precepts of religion and the Holy Book.

Spain had a Celt-Iberian-Phoencian-Roman-Visigothic population when the Arabs brought their very mixed armies into it. Its people spoke a Gothic Roman, a Gothic Latin patois. Arabic became the official language, used with complete success by only a few people among the invaders, the most of them having the languages of the localities from which they came. Spain had literally an appalling confusion of tongues, the chief of which were the Gothic Latin of the land and the Arabic of the conquerors. The native people of Spain who had not changed their religion and lived under the political rule of the Muslims, paying the capitation tax, were called Mozárabes. Their language was of course what it had been before the conquest with such modifications as the influence of Arabic had upon it. That native language was the one in most general use, the language from which the Spanish of today is derived. Spain then was bilingual. The Arabic was hard to learn and was not learned successfully save by a few, but to them it brought great advantages as it was the language of education, religion, literature and government.

In Spain Arab culture reached its highest splendor.[54] It began as in all Muslim lands with learning to read and write the Holy Book. All Muslims must acquire that knowledge when they are young, for it is, they said, the foundation of all learning, the source of religion and morality in which the young should be well grounded before the coming of adolescence. By learning to pro-

[54] Buksh, *op. cit.*. 97.

nounce the verses of the Quran one learns to pronounce Arabic correctly, and by memorizing them the memory is both properly stocked and trained. In Spain the teachers of young children taught other subjects as well: selections from poetry, examples of letter writing, and the elements of Arabic grammar. In Spain reading and writing were taught together. The pupils wrote with a reed dipped in ink upon a tablet of hard wood. When an exercise was finished they dampened the tablet with water and washed it clean and wrote again. The copies they used were from the Quran. The teacher was any one the fathers chose to employ to teach their children. All such instruction was private, and the fathers contracted with the teachers usually for twelve months and paid them each month. Discipline was not so severe in Spain as in North Africa, where the schoolmasters are thought by their severity to have made the people cowardly. Under Hakam II himself, a learned man, the primary schools were good and numerous. In Andalusia nearly every one could read and write at a time when in Christian Europe only the clergy aspired to be literate.[55]

There was no recognized and well systematized course of study. Branches were taught, not curricula. One took the studies he wanted to take, when he wanted to take them. There was no time at which one left the elementary school and passed on to the high school for there was neither high school nor elementary school. One took up more advanced studies when he could read and write. There was a great variety of them, all the "Arabic sciences" and "foreign sciences" were taught in Spain. One studied them in whatever order he pleased.

What the Prophet did and said is more concretely

[55] Dozy, *op. cit.*, 455.

determining in Muslim lands than is what Christ did among Christians. The Prophet revealed the best means of teaching. He recited his Revelations to others. As a matter of fact he did that because he could not write them down: to make them known he had to repeat them. That repeating on his part became the standard method of teaching among all Muslim peoples.

The method of learning was of course the obverse of this. The student must remember what the master told him. So memory is more heavily employed in Muslim lands than elsewhere. Astonishing feats of memorizing were performed there, much more amazing than the Homeric rhapsodes were able to perform. It was hardly exceptional to get the Quran by heart or to add to that the grammar of Sibawayhi. To memorize a poem 2,500 pages long, such as the Songs of Ispahan, was attempted and done. Whoever is in search of incredible memory feats should go among the Arabs or read Richard Burton. All manner of drugs were known for their power to stimulate the ability to remember. A literature is shaped by the purposes for which it is used. Arabic literature was used mnemonically and shaped didactically. Professor Ribera quotes Ibn Khaldûn as saying: "It is not rare to see men who have spent years and years committing many books to memory and are not capable of explaining a single scientific fact with clearness."

At first in Spain the Traditions as collected and taught by Mâlik ibn Anas of Medina were given almost exclusive attention. In time the traditions as arranged and taught by others were introduced and studied so zealously that Spain became famous for its students of the holy traditions. History, biography, and genealogy were necessary aids to, indeed almost parts of, that study. The Quran itself was basically important and received more attention than any or all other studies. Its reading and interpretation had been begun in the first schools and must be carried on in higher courses, which were so valuable that many persons repeated them over and over again. The art of reading it aloud was so fine an art that classes and even schools were established for that alone. In classes for its exegesis it was studied phrase by phrase. The authoritative, not the rational, meanings were sought for. Most of the time scholastic or rational theology was heresy in Arabic Spain.

The most popular course was Jurisprudence, Alcoranic or religious law, since it prepared for both civil and religious offices. This course was shaped, as we have seen, by Mâlik ibn Anas at all periods but the last. There were in addition to it courses on the division of inheritances and on judicial practice, both difficult and involved subjects among the Arabs. There were, too, courses on the government of states, on scholastic theology and the ascetic principles of mysticism.

The grammar of the Arabic language was diligently studied and successfully in Spain, for it was begun in the first schools and carried on vigorously in advanced classes. Arabic literature had much attention, and good Arabic writers were commoner in Spain than in other lands. Poetry of every description was produced, and professional literary men were in demand and well recompensed. Hospitals gave opportunities for the study of medicine in the eastern countries which were lacking in Spain. There one had to apprentice himself to a practicing physician and read the books on medicine. For the most part physicians grew up in physicians' families, the father training the son and the son his son in turn. The art was a thing of social heredity. The medical folk were the ones who studied botany and zoölogy. Distinguished physicians such as Abu'l Kâsim, Averroës, Avempace, and Avenzoar were produced in Spain.

Philosophy was driven into secret corners by the orthodox rigidity of the Spanish Muslims, but it flourished in the dark and never was quite without adherents and cultivators. There were times of tolerance when those who taught it were allowed to come into the open, but such times were both few and brief. Nevertheless, three great names derive from Spain, Averroës, Avempace, and Ibn Tofail.

The mathematical sciences, arithmetic, algebra, geometry, and astronomy, were all studied, and books were written upon them.

In music both vocal and instrumental, the Arabs excelled. Vocal music, they appreciated more than instrumental. Their ardent love of poetry either was a part of that appreciation or reinforced it. There was great attention to music, much employment of it on military and festival occasions, and a vast literature on musical theory, musical instruments and rich collections of songs. There was one musician whose fame outdistanced all the rest, enabling him to be a kind of social dictator and set the fashions of taste even in things remote from music such as gastronomy and dress. He was the Persian Ziryâb who came from the court of the caliph at Baghdad to Spain. His fame was so great that he was met when he landed and attended by representatives of the Emir to Cordova. Before he had heard him at all Abd-er-Rahmân II (822–852) announced to him that his salary would be 200 gold dînârs per month, with an additional grant of 3,000 gold dînârs each year, 200 bushels of barley, 100 of wheat, and the several houses which were assigned him. The Emir was so pleased when he heard him that from that day Ziryâb lived as a favorite of the court. It is said he knew the words and music of ten thousand songs. Besides, he was learned in astronomy and geography. His conversation was wonderful; as a master of fêtes or banquets he was unequalled. Indeed he was the *arbiter elegantiarum* of Arabic Spain. He not only set fashions, he established national customs.[56] This man was not only a celebrated performer but a great teacher of music and the founder of a school. The city of Seville still owes to him somewhat for her primacy in Andalusian song.

The Arabs contributed to Europe the lute, the rebec, the guitar, and a whole family of bowed instruments. Before that Europe had only the cithara and harp among stringed instruments. These were tuned by ear. On the the Arab instruments the places of the notes were marked, having been determined by measurement. Mensural music then came from the Arabs, and the "gloss" with which they adorned their melody was, it would seem, the forerunner of harmony.[57]

The teaching of young children for pay was not regarded as among the noblest of occupations even when the book which they were learning to read was the Quran. But all forms of more advanced teaching were held in honor in Arabic Spain. In the first centuries that teaching was gratuitous. In the later period it was paid for, but those who taught retained something of the pride and the high social approval that their predecessors had established. Any one who would was free to offer himself as a teacher. There was no official regulation, but the teacher had to have knowledge or he would not continue to have pupils. Teachers who came from Mecca or Medina, Baghdad or Damascus were looked up to in the earlier time, and Spanish students who had travelled to the distant East to study brought back learning from

[56] Dozy, *op. cit.*, 263.
[57] *The Legacy of Islam*, 374.

abroad and were therefore held to be superior persons. But the time came when the Muslims of Spain knew that Spain's learned men were abler than those of any other land and followed them in preference to foreign teachers from any country. There was an incredible amount of travelling from Spain to the East, and from the East to Spain. Competition in teaching between one Muslim country and another was keen. Teachers from Spain were to be found in them all, and their fame was great. There was even one bold Spaniard who vowed he would go to Basra and teach Arabic grammar where Sibawayhi had taught it and would show that a Spaniard could teach it better than any other person in the world; and he made good his boast, we are told.

A reputation for orthodoxy was necessary in order to fill one's classes, but something else was needed. Mâlik ibn Anas said: "The master should have more desire for communicating than the students for learning." That eagerness to communicate learning must have been very general, for a great industry of teaching was carried on. The Traditions ascribe that eagerness that learning should go forward to the Prophet. "To sit in the class of a master is more meritorious than to pray with a thousand prostrations, to visit a thousand sick and accompany a thousand funerals." "The angels of heaven, the fish of the sea, and the birds of the air bless the sage; even the smallest ant prays for him." "The title of greatest nobility is knowledge; the sage occupies the highest rank in the human hierarchy, since he is the heir of the prophets." These are sayings attributed to the Prophet. There were posts of honor for most who would fit themselves laboriously. The nobles had to keep up the reputation of their families in pretty vigorous competition with the ambitious and able sons of families in no wise noble. The offices were accessible to all the people, and under the better Omayyad rulers great value was placed upon learning. Education was private. The master either taught his students in his own house or gathered his class in a semicircle about him in the mosque. The mosque, when not in use for prayer, is a public meeting place for deliberative gatherings in Muslim lands. It is and always has been the general schoolroom in which most teachers of the community meet their classes, being under few regulations save the necessity of not interfering with the work of other classes meeting beside them in the same place of assembly.

"Communities," says Professor Ribera, "did not have to quarrel with each other in obtaining a decree from the king or a bull from the Pope, in order to establish a centre of studies. As masters and pupils were free they went where they pleased." They resorted to whatever city offered the most favorable conditions for study, hospitality, and support, and there an educational centre was formed. "At first when Cordova was the capital of the Empire, the natives just returned from pilgrimage to the Orient went to that city in search of an opportunity to practice their profession and make use of their knowledge. Great Oriental Masters resided there. The peace and prosperity of the provinces, the security of the highways, and the liberal policy of the government attracted an immense population and the city became a literary capital as well as the seat of government. Afterward when the Emirate ceased to exist, other cities began to dispute the leadership in matters of culture; Seville, Granada, Valencia, Saragossa, etc., all were active centres of education.

"But they tried in vain to surpass Cordova and the great Mosque continued to be the centre of instruction in Muslim Spain. What a varied spectacle must it have presented from dawn until dark in the period of its greatest splendor! Through its twenty-one gates entered a motley multitude of students of most diverse ages and most varied costumes. They penetrated that forest of columns and formed circles around the masters. Here the class of Ibn Aidz, the Tortosan, whose voice could not reach all of the thousand persons who strained their ears to hear him, occupied various naves. Students seated in convenient places took up the words of the master and passed them on to the pupils in the outermost circles. The echo of their voices died away and for a moment no other sound was heard than the scratching of the pens on the paper. Another phrase was dictated, repeated and taken down. And thus the exercise went on. Here the master of grammar explained in the Spanish dialect the canons of his art. Yonder the teacher of literature taught the separation of hemistichs and the scansion of verses of most difficult metre. In one quarter the sonorous and melodious voice of a student chanting the Quran was heard. His companions followed him, reading from tablets of wood; while in the galleries of the outer court great companies of boys might be seen repeating a hundred times the first azora of the Religious Book before the master who impatiently held the strap raised lest they should again make the oft repeated mistakes in pronouncing the lesson.

"Here and there in the galleries the circles dissolved, their exercises being finished, and other circles formed about new masters. And within those walls where so great a multitude was coming and going no officer to keep order was anywhere seen. The caretaker of the Mosque passed silently through the company and no other guardian was needed since the throngs knowing that order is the first condition necessary to the enjoyment of liberty were interested in preserving it.

"When the voice of the Muezzin announced the mid-day prayer, all work ceased and the faithful took up their devotions. In the afternoon the lessons continued until twilight when they ceased." [58]

The University of Cordova, for that is the name by which Reinhart Dozy refers to it, was in the period of Al-Hakam II one of the most renowned in the world. Its lectures were delivered in the great Mosque.[59] There were other mosques in Cordova in which the same thronging of students took place. In many private houses classes met also, and in their offices physicians taught their art. The Christian churches, which under all but the most bigoted of the Muslim rulers continued to be open and active, had their schools too for religious teaching and for the study of Virgil and the other Latin authors. The synagogues too were open and in them were classes for the study of the Law in Hebrew.

Sicily belonged to the Arabs from 902 to 1091, which is nearly two hundred years. Indeed, Arabic settlements dotted the shores of South Italy. The region pleased them and they prospered there. Then the Normans made something very like a private crusade against the Mohammedans in South Italy, and Sicily became the other island conquest of Norman invaders. Here is Malaterra's story of how it all started. "That most elegant youth, the Count of Calabria, staying with his brother the Duke of Rhegium, after the conquest of the country; hearing that Sicily was unbelieving, and seeing that it was close at hand, an extremely narrow arm of the sea being interposed; being moreover always eager after dominion, was seized with the ambition of acquiring it. He considered that a double advantage would thus accrue to himself:

[58] Ribera, *La Enseñanza entre los Musulmanes españoles.*
[59] Dozy, *op. cit.*, 455.

benefit to his soul, benefit also to his body. He would at once recall to the divine worship a nation given to idolatry [*sic*] and gain possession of the fruits and rents of a land usurped by a people unpleasing in God's sight. These fruits and rents he would himself employ in God's service." [60]

He, Roger Guiscard, thereupon entered Sicily with an army of sixty men and was of course promptly driven out. Then a disaffected Saracen governor invited him to come back, and he came with one hundred and sixty men, prowled about the land at night and got away with some booty. After a couple of generations these freebooting Northmen ruled the land. The Norman conquerors of Sicily ruled over peoples to whom they were quite foreign. They were a polyglot assortment. Christian Greeks formed the working population, Mohammedans from all the countries the ruling class; then there were a few Normans in the guard, some Italians, and more Jews. Norman dukes rule, but their court is Oriental, Byzantine and Arabic. The official records are kept in Greek, Arabic, and Latin. Their coins have Arabic inscriptions. They maintain the harem. Arabs and Jews are their physicians, Arab court poets sing to them and tell them the never-ending stories of the East. This island is set at the crossing of the sea-ways. Its vigorous and striking life was a thing for surprised comment throughout the world. Translations from Arabic and from Greek were systematically made there, books were written there, and Frederick II's Court (1198–1250) was the cradle of Italian poetry.[61]

[60] In Barlow's *A Short History of the Normans in South Europe,* 96 (London: Kegan Paul, Trench, Trübner & Co., Ltd., 1886). By permission of the publishers.

[61] Haskins, *The Renaissance of the Twelfth Century,* 59.

VI

ABELARD AND THE FOUNDING OF THE UNIVERSITIES

"THE man who, by his qualities and his defects, by the audacity of his opinions, the éclat of his life, his inborn passion for controversy, and his rare talent for instruction contributed most to increase and expand the taste for study and that intellectual movement from which the University of Paris issued in the thirteenth century was Peter Abélard." These are the words of Victor Cousin in his introduction to his edition of the works of Abélard. Was Abélard the founder of the University of Paris, the mother university of the West? What does it mean to found a human institution such as a university is? Clearly it does not mean to make it out of nothing. Human makings are not of that sort. John Ruskin has it somewhere that, though men have long tried to invent a new animal, they have never succeeded in doing more than put together in new combinations the animal parts with which Nature supplies us. To found or create, humanly speaking, is to reëdit the materials which are given, to rearrange and reassemble them in new forms.

To found a university now usually means to contribute a large sum of money for the purchase of a site, the erection of buildings, the establishing and equipping of libraries and laboratories, and the endowing of professorships. An architect must be chosen and a president selected who will in turn pick out the members of a faculty. When all is ready the doors are flung open and the students come and take their places in the classrooms. In Abélard's day the process was different. It began at the other end. University disciplines had to be wrought out. There were cathedral and monastic schools as there had been for centuries. He taught in them. Indeed he never taught in anything but them or in schools which he conceived to be like them. Yet his methods of teaching were so different from theirs that he assembled such vast crowds of students that guilds, or trade unions, of teachers were formed to instruct them after he was gone. He handled the familiar subjects of cathedral school instruction in such a way that he made new and higher studies out of them, employing in his handling of them methods of presentation and discussion which became the methods of the universities.

The University of Paris did not begin with an endowment. It grew from the work of a supreme teacher, one whose mind was so acute that he found new exciting meanings in old doctrines, whose power of insight and of systematization made him the originator of scholastic theology and whose ability to summon students to his instruction has, it would seem, never been equalled by any other master since schools began to be. Abélard did not create the conditions in which he worked. He taught old subjects in astonishing new ways. New winds of change were blowing over the world. He used the opportunities his age afforded, but he used them greatly, so greatly that vast consequences came from his use of them. To one he is the Father of Universities, to another "he is the Descartes of the twelfth century."

On the ceiling of the upper porch of Royce Hall at the University of California at Los Angeles, underneath the figure of Abélard, are these words in gold letters: "It is through doubt that we come to investigation and through investigation to the truth." That is not only the key sentence in his writings: it is the cornerstone of universities.

Peter Abélard was born at the village of Pallet in 1079. He died in 1142. "I had a father," he says, "who had won some smattering of letters before he had girded on his soldier's belt." Long afterward that father remembered his early privilege so keenly that he had each of his sons taught letters and did what he could to encourage his eldest boy's passion for learning. "So enthralled was I by that passion," says that eldest son, "that I gave up the glory of arms, my right to the inheritance and all the honours to which I was heir to arm me in the armory of logical reasoning for the battle of minds in disputation. I went wherever dialectics flourished." [1]

First he seems to have sat in the class of Jean Roscellin, Canon of Compiègne, who had been condemned for tritheism by the Council of Soissons in 1092. Roscellin speaks of him as "the smallest of my pupils" and says he was in his school "from boyhood to youth." [2] Abélard made no mention of that celebrated rationalist in his *Historia Calamitatum,* perhaps for the reason that he was an ex-heretic. His statement that he went wherever dialectics flourished indicates that he attended several schools. He could have had no difficulty in finding them, for schools were beginning to be numerous in the regions in which they had been scarce hitherto. Almost every cathedral had a teacher of the trivium, grammar, rhetoric, and dialectic. In the larger towns the four sciences of the quadrivium were added. At Chartres, Tournai,

[1] *Historia Calamitatum,* chap. i. (transl. H. A. Bellows; St. Paul, Minn.: T. A. Boyd, 1922).

[2] McCabe, *Abélard,* 9-10.

Tours, Rheims, Angers, and Laon were famous bishops' schools, and at Bec, Cluny, and Saint-Denis the monasteries had schools of more than local distinction.

After going from place to place for perhaps five or six years Abélard came to Paris and entered the most celebrated of the schools of that day, the cathedral school of Notre Dame. There William of Champeaux, "the pillar of the doctors," the outstanding teacher of logic in France, was lecturing. "With him I remained for some time, at first indeed well liked of him; but later I brought him great grief, because I undertook to refute certain of his opinions, not infrequently attacking him in disputation, and now and then in these debates I was adjudged victor." [3]

The question upon which Abélard attempted to set his master William of Champeaux right was and is a very old one, the question of universals, "the ancient question" as John of Salisbury characterized it, "in the solution of which the world has grown grey, and more time has been consumed than the Caesars gave to the conquest and dominion of the globe, more money wasted than Croesus counted in all his wealth." [4] That is in fact an under- rather than an over-statement, for the question of universals is the question of the relation of the one and the many, the relation of the individuals to the genera to which in some fashion or other they belong. Just now discussion about it rages most furiously in the field of politics: What is the nature of the state? Is it alone real and the individual of no consequence, or do individuals relating themselves in certain ways make it and unmake it at will? In Abélard's day the question raged in terms of theology. Roscellinus had used logic to examine the

---

[3] *Historia Calamitatum,* chap. ii.
[4] Quoted in McCabe's *Abélard,* 29.

doctrine of the Trinity. They are three Divine Persons, he said: their oneness is but a name; as existent Beings they are three. But the answer of Nominalism is too easy. It leaves the problem just where it was before. William of Champeaux taught the doctrine of Realism. The Trinity is a unity because one substance, God, is essentially the same in each member of the Trinity. They differ in accidental forms, but their substance is universal. Or take the general term man and men, the individuals who make up mankind. The Realist says that one identical substance is in them all. Different accidental forms adhere to the one substance and give it actuality in individuals. The universal is not in itself perceptible; only when clothed in accidents is it apparent to the senses. Particulars exist, universals are understood.

First take Abélard's own words, then an accepted rendering of them: "Erat autem in ea sententia de communitate universalium, ut eandem essentialiter rem totam simul singulis suis inesse astrueret individuis; quorum quidem nulla esset in essentia diversitas, sed sola multitudine accidentium varietas. Sic autem istam suam correxit sententiam, ut deinceps rem eandem non essentialiter sed individualiter diceret." [5] Dr. Bellows' translation of this passage runs: "Now the basis of this old concept of his regarding the reality of universal ideas was that the same quality formed the essence alike of the abstract whole and of the individuals which were its parts—in other words, that there could be no essential differences among these individuals, all being alike save for such variety as might grow out of the many accidents of existence. Thereafter, however, he corrected this opinion, no longer maintaining that the same quality was the es-

[5] *Petri Abailardi Opera nunc primum edita . . . Francisci Amboesii,* 5 (Paris: Nicolai Buon, 1616).

sence of all things, but that rather it manifested itself in them through diverse ways." [6]

It must not for a moment be forgotten that this is the time and France the place of the organizing of the First Crusade. Pope Urban II called a Great Council of the Church to assemble at Clermont in November, 1095. The city of Clermont was too small to hold the prelates, princes, and delegates that came to the Council. Tents and pavilions had to be erected in the fields to shelter them, though the winter was beginning. In the great square of Clermont after Peter the Hermit had spoken, the Pope himself addressed the vast assemblage. "Nation beloved of God," he said to them, "it is in your courage that the Christian Church has placed its hope; it is because I am well acquainted with your piety and your bravery, that I have crossed the Alps, and am come to preach the word of God in these countries. You have not forgotten that the land you inhabit has been invaded by the Saracens, and that but for the exploits of Charles Martel and Charlemagne, France would have received the laws of Mahomet. Recall, without ceasing, to your minds the danger and the glory of your fathers; led by heroes whose names should never die, they delivered your country, they saved the west from shameful slavery. More noble triumphs await you under the guidance of the God of armies; you will deliver Europe and Asia; you will save the City of Jesus Christ—that Jerusalem which was chosen by the Lord, and from whence the law is come to us." As the Pope went on, the great audience sobbed and shook under the power of his words. When he called upon them at the summons of Jesus Christ to leave father and mother, wife and children to become soldiers of the Living God, the vast company rose as one man and with

[6] Abélard, *Historia Calamitatum,* chap. ii.

a single voice shouted, "Dieu le veut." [7] The council fixed the festival of the Assumption of the next year as the time of departure for the crusade, and with one mind the whole land fell to preparing for that momentous going forth. So great a peace came over the land that differences were forgotten and even criminals ceased to be criminals. Then the immense armies in due time began their long march while the folks at home must almost have held their breath in their eagerness to hear from them. It took them years to reach the Holy Land. At daybreak on June 20, 1099, the heights of Emmaus heard their cry, "Jerusalem!" "It is the will of God!" At nightfall on July 15th the Crusaders "sobbing for excess of joy" prayed together at the Sepulchre.

Only those who have lived through a period of warfare in which their own people are engaged know the high tension to which life is keyed at such a time. This was a religious war. In it the concerns of religion were enormously heightened. Beginnings had been made which were now carried to a great development. Norman architecture which dates from 1050 flowered into Gothic, the initiating and determining of which, Ralph Adams Cram points out, consumed but fifteen years, from Bury (begun in 1125) to Saint-Denis (in 1140).

The period in which Abélard studied with William of Champeaux seems to have been after 1100 and before 1108, for it was in that year that William founded the canonry of St. Victor. In his persistent correcting of the Master he insisted upon the claims of a middle ground between Nominalism and Realism—which middle position Hauréau called Nominalism and the German, Ritter, called Realism. To Abélard himself it was Conceptu-

---

[7] Michaud's *History of the Crusades*, transl. Robson, 1–1–51 (New York: Armstrong & Son, 1881).

alism. Realism makes the one substance everything and is therefore pantheism. Nominalism at the other end has it that only individual things exist, some of which have common names. But the predicate is more than a name. If you say, "This is a horse, that is a dog, that is a man," you join a concept to a percept by an act of thinking. The predicate term, or universal, is therefore made by thinking. Knowledge, which is nothing but universals, could not exist if these universals did not stand for something which exists in nature. That something for which the universals stand is the likeness of individual substances. God, who created all things, created them as individuals after archetypal ideas in the divine mind. Universals exist therefore before things in the mind of God, they exist in things as their discernible likenesses, they exist after things as likenesses discerned by inquiring minds. The theory taught by Abélard was adopted by the Arabic philosophers and taught by St. Thomas Aquinas. The relation of the individual to the species is yet a subject for persistent investigation.

Abélard, after he had won some dialectical battles over his master, determined to set up a school of his own. With a little group of his fellow students he moved to the royal town of Melun about thirty miles from Paris. Here he lectured with such acclaim that he gathered students about him, and when William tried to suppress him some enemies that William had made, perhaps in the king's official household, gave Abélard their backing. Growing bolder, Abélard moved to Corbeil, but fifteen miles from Paris, "for there I knew there would be given more frequent chance for my assaults in our battle of disputation." His health could not stand the ordeal, and he was compelled to return to his parental home in Brittany and was cut off from France, he says, for some years. When he returned to Paris he found that William, his teacher, had entered the monastery of St. Victor and was teaching rhetoric there. Abélard immediately entered his class, "and in the course of our many arguments on various matters I compelled him by most potent reasoning first to alter his former opinion on the subject of the universals, and finally to abandon it altogether." William had placed a substitute in the chair at Notre Dame. Abélard descended upon the substitute and was by him put in charge of the class; but William, hearing of that, took matters in hand, and Abélard went to Melun and opened a school there. William went back to his monastery, and Abélard returned to Paris, pitching the camp of his school on the hill of St. Genevieve. The academic war went on for a time pretty vigorously. Then Abélard was called home by his mother, who desired to see him before entering a monastery, a thing which his father had already done.

He came back to France, intent upon studying theology. The leader in that field was Anselm of Laon. Abélard accordingly joined Anselm's school, only to be bitterly disappointed in the quality of Anselm's teaching. "He was wonderful, indeed, in the eyes of those who only listened to him but those who asked him questions perforce held him as naught. He had a miraculous flow of words, but they were contemptible in meaning and quite void of reason. When he kindled a fire, he filled his house with smoke and illumined it not at all." [8] Abélard said as much to his fellow students, who thereupon dared him to show them how lectures on Holy Scripture should be given. Abélard accepted the challenge and lectured to them the next day on Ezekiel so brilliantly that the report of his lecture brought larger crowds the next day and the

[8] *Historia Calamitatum,* transl. Bellows, chap. iii.

next. Anselm, hearing of this, had "the impudence to forbid me to carry on any further in his school the work of preparing glosses," Abélard had the bad taste to say.

Then he returned to Paris, this time to the mastership of the cathedral school of Notre Dame. There he lectured on both logic and theology with such skill that his fame spread far and wide. This period began perhaps in 1116 and lasted for several peaceful years. So great was the celebrity of the teacher that students gathered to him by thousands, from all the neighboring countries. This is the era in which Paris became what she was for long to continue to be, the chief thronging place in Europe for instruction. From early daybreak to midday the students sat on the straw of the lecture room, laboriously taking down the sentences of the book which the master read and explained to them. The verb "to lecture" means to read. Books were scarce then and had to be multiplied by the teacher dictating them. Abélard's gifts were many —the first of them, says Héloïse, "a tone of voice." Others speak of his clearness, and lightness of touch, the richness of his imagery, the sprightliness and instant penetration of his mind. He was a vivid being, highly charged with charm, interested in human concerns; with a memory that both retained and served, and a masterful familiarity with the books which were known and used in his time. Prior Fulk of Deuil in his letter to Abélard reminds him that "neither distance nor the height of mountains nor the depth of valleys, nor roads infested by brigands were sufficient to arrest the concourse of students pouring to you. Neither the sea which separates us nor the fury of its waves stayed the crowd of English students. Hearing thy name, braving every danger they flowed to you. Remote Britain sent you its *animalia* to be educated. Seeing their rudeness softened Anjou gave you hers to be civilized. The inhabitants of Poitou, the Basques, the Spaniards, the Normans, the people of Flanders, of Germany, of Suevia have not ceased to honor, to praise and extol your genius. Finally those who dwell in Paris or the countries of France near or far having a thirst for science as if you only were able to dispense it, drawn by the brilliancy of your genius, your appealing eloquence and your simple and understandable language, run to you as to the purest source of philosophy." [9]

If the Crusade had plowed up the customs of the land and raised all men's interest in the Faith to something like white heat, it was the repute of Abélard's preëminent gifts and pugnacity that assembled them to Paris in something little short of multitudes. The Master was the center of that thronging. He had both friends and enemies. Like every leader of a novel and popular enterprise, he was abnormally loved and hated. The names which his enemies gave him are a tribute to his power; "Goliath," "Herod," "Leviathan," "Serpent," "Dragon," "Hydra" are some of those drawn from the saintly Bernard by reference to him. Others spoke of him as "Prometheus," "friend of the devil," etc. It was not they but himself that wrought his downfall. When he had reached the very zenith of fame and usefulness, he sinned and suffered, as few men in history have suffered. We shall not tell that part of his story. Dejected in mind and broken in body, where could he go? "Chiefly the clerics, and above all my scholars, tortured me with their intolerable lamentations and outcries . . . What path lay open to me thereafter? How could I ever again hold up my head among men, when every finger should be pointed at me in scorn, every tongue speak my blistering shame,

[9] *Petri Abailardi Opera, etc.,* 218.

and when I should be a monstrous spectacle to all eyes?" [10]
His disgrace drove him to seek refuge in a monastery;
and the monastery of St. Denis in which he sought asylum was the least suited to his purposes of all those in
France. It was just outside Paris, rich, worldly, and
Abélard says, "Its life was scandalous." The monks of
St. Denis must have welcomed the addition of the brilliant teacher to their number. If they did, they were
disappointed, for "this intolerable state of things I often
and vehemently denounced, sometimes in private talk
and sometimes publicly, but the only result was that I
made myself detested of them all. They gladly laid hold
of the daily eagerness of my students to hear me as an
excuse whereby they might be rid of me; and finally, at
the insistent urging of the students themselves, and with
the hearty consent of the abbot and the rest of the brotherhood, I departed thence to a certain hut, there to teach
in my wonted way. To this place such a throng of students flocked that the neighborhood could not afford
shelter for them, nor the earth sufficient sustenance." [11]

The exact location of this hut or cell is not known. It
was on an estate belonging to the monastery and probably not far from Paris. Abélard says that he lectured
chiefly on theology there, but gave instruction in the secular arts to draw his students to the study of the true
philosophy just as "Origen, the greatest of all Christian
philosophers," did. The numbers of his students increased greatly. Objection soon began to be made by
Abélard's enemies that a monk should not teach secular
studies, and that this monk should not teach theology
as he had never been taught it. For the use of his students at this time Abélard wrote a book, *On the Unity and*

[10] *Historia Calamitatum,* viii. 31.
[11] *Historia Calamitatum,* transl. Bellows, viii. 34.

Trinity of God, explaining the matter in rational terms as the students requested and omitting from it meaningless phrases which the intellect could not follow. That tract was widely read, and two of Abélard's enemies from the days in which he made such vigorous objection to the teaching of Anselm in the school at Laon now came forward and in great rage summoned a Council against him. Anselm of Laon and William of Champeaux were both dead, but two of Anselm's students, Alberic and Lotulphe, carried on the war. The Council was held at Soissons in 1121. When Abélard reached Soissons he found that the clergy and people had been stirred up against him by being told that he preached the existence of three Gods. He at once took his book to the papal legate for examination, declaring if he had written anything contrary to the Catholic faith he was ready to correct it and make amends. While the book was being examined, he publicly each day discussed the Catholic faith and what he had written. Nothing was found in the book which was objectionable, Abélard says, and the Bishop of Chartres made a speech in which he reminded them that Abélard was the greatest of their teachers. "He has spread the offshoots of his vine from sea to sea . . . If, then, you are disposed to take canonical action against him, his doctrine or his writings must be brought forward as evidence, and he must have free opportunity to answer his questioners." When his accusers demurred to meeting him in open council, the Bishop of Chartres urged that Abélard's abbot take him back to St. Denis and that a full committee of learned men should study the matter and determine what should be done. But the cry was raised that that was a change of venue, that Abélard must be judged in that diocese and not in another. The accusers worked upon the legate until he agreed to con-

demn the book without further hearing. Forthwith Abélard was ushered into a solemn sitting of the Council and
ordered to throw his book into the fire and to repeat the
Athanasian creed, both of which he did. He was then
handed over to the Abbot of St. Médard for detention in
that monastery. Shortly there was a reaction of feeling
in Abélard's favor, and the very papal legate who had ordered him shut up at St. Médard ordered him sent back
to St. Denis. There Abélard's fatal facility in provoking
offence allowed him to rest in quiet only a few months.
Dionysius the Areopagite, the convert made by St. Paul
when he preached on Mars' Hill, tradition said, was the
first Bishop of Athens and later in life had travelled to
Gaul, founded the monastery that bore his name, and
suffered martyrdom on the hill which is still Mt. Martyr.
One day as Abélard was reading Bede he came across
the statement that Dionysius the Areopagite was bishop
not of Athens but of Corinth. Somewhat gleefully, perhaps, he showed that statement in the Venerable Bede to
some of his brother monks. Instantly a fury of rage
flared up against him, and Abélard was driven to flee
by night from Saint-Denis and to beg protection from
Count Theobald of Champagne, near whose estate that
hut or cell which he by his teaching had made the intellectual centre of the world, but a few weeks before, was
located. Abélard then brought every influence he could
induce to help him, to bear upon the Abbot of St. Denis
to wring from him permission to live the monastic life
wherever he could find a suitable place. After much en-
treating he was permitted to go to any solitary place he
might choose, but not to come under the rule of any other
monastery:

"Forthwith I sought out a lonely spot known to me of
old in the region of Troyes, and there, on a bit of land

which had been given to me, and with the approval of the bishop of the district, I built with reeds and stalks my first oratory in the name of the Holy Trinity. No sooner had scholars learned of my retreat than they began to flock thither from all sides, leaving their towns and castles to dwell in the wilderness. In place of their spacious houses they built themselves huts; instead of dainty fare they lived on the herbs of the field and coarse bread; their soft beds they exchanged for heaps of straw and rushes, and their tables were piles of turf. . . . Even so did my followers build their huts above the waters of the Arduzon, and as their number grew ever greater, the hardships which they gladly endured for the sake of my teaching seemed to my rivals to reflect new glory on me, and to cast new shame on themselves . . . Saying, 'Behold now, the whole world runs after him, and our persecution of him has done nought save to increase his glory. We strove to extinguish his fame, and we have but given it new brightness. Lo, in the cities scholars have at hand everything they may need, and yet, spurning the pleasures of the town, they seek out the barrenness of the desert and of their own free will accept wretchedness.'

"The thing which at that time chiefly led me to undertake the direction of a school was my intolerable poverty, for I had not strength enough to dig, and shame kept me from begging. And so, resorting once more to the art with which I was so familiar, I was compelled to substitute the service of the tongue for the labour of my hands. The students willingly provided me with whatsoever I needed in the way of food and clothing, and likewise took charge of the cultivation of the fields and paid for the erection of buildings, in order that material cares might not keep me from my studies. Since my oratory was no longer large enough to hold even a small part of their number, they found it necessary to increase its size, and in so doing they greatly improved it, building it of stone, and wood. Although this oratory had been founded in honour of the Holy Trinity, and afterward dedicated thereto, I now named it the Paraclete, mindful of how I had come there a fugitive and in despair and had breathed into my soul something of the miracle of divine consolation." [12]

As Abélard's fame spread through the world two new censors appeared in the person of Norbert of Prémontré and the great Bernard of Clairvaux. They raised a hue and cry against him, "shamelessly slandering me in every way they could . . . When the only way of escape seemed to be for me to seek refuge with Christ among the enemies of Christ," i.e. to go to Mahommedan Spain, an abbot died on the coast of Brittany and some sinister influence put it into the heart of the monks of the monastery of St. Gildas to elect Abélard as his successor in their monastery. When the new abbot took up his residence among his monks he found them living in a terrible state of monastic remissness. The rule of St. Benedict, they had not so much forgotten as utterly derided. When Abélard set about reforming their life they rebelled. Just then the monks of St. Denis dispossessed the nuns of Argenteuil of their monastery in which Héloïse was prioress, and Abélard at St. Gildas pondering their sad plight resolved to give them the Paraclete for their convent. The offer was gladly accepted, and Héloïse (then twenty-eight) and eight of her sisters in religion at once moved in and took possession of the abandoned school. Abélard came in person to arrange this transfer. The neighborhood welcomed the new owners, and after some months began making donations to the new undertaking. "In a single year," wrote Abélard, "they acquired greater pos-

[12] *Historia Calamitatum*, transl. Bellows, x. and xi. 51–55.

sessions than would have fallen into my hands had I labored a hundred on the spot." [13]

When he returned to St. Gildas the insubordination of his monks terrified him. Repeatedly they tried to kill their abbot by poison and by hiring bandits to waylay and destroy him on the road. The leaders he excommunicated, and the others tried to cut his throat with a sword. The Pope sent a legation to inquire into the condition of the monastery; but even that did not rectify it, and Abélard finally left it, perhaps in 1132. There is no record of his activities for some years. He may have been with his relatives in Brittany or living near the Paraclete or may have held a canonry at Tours, Chartres or Sens.[14] In 1136 John of Salisbury was in his classes at the hill of St. Genevieve. In 1139 William, Abbot of St. Thierry, wrote a letter to Geoffrey, Bishop of Chartres, and Bernard of Clairvaux which ran after this fashion: "Peter Abélard again begins to teach his novelties and to write them; his works cross the seas, nor are the Alps any obstacle to their progress; his wild opinions deluge the provinces; they are publicly taught and as publicly defended; it is even said that they have found admirers in the court itself of Rome. I must therefore be open with you, your silence is dangerous to yourselves and it is dangerous to the church of God. Very lately a work of this man fell into my hands; it was entitled the *Theology of Abélard*. I confess, the words excited my curiosity, I read it; and as many things therein struck me I noted them down with the reasons why I did so. These remarks I now send you, and with them the book itself. Form your own judgments . . . " [15] The Bishop of

---

[13] Berington, *The History of the Lives of Abeillard and Heloisa*, I, 242 (Basil, 1793).

[14] See Sikes' *Peter Abailard*, p. 25 (Cambridge University Press, 1932).

[15] Berington, *op. cit.*, II, 79.

Chartres did not answer, and Bernard's answer advised caution. William of St. Thierry then wrote a book renewing the attack; Bernard read the book and visited Abélard and urged him to retract certain errors which Bernard specified. Abélard did not do that. Then Bernard wrote to the Pope and to certain of the Cardinals. To one of these he sent this letter: "Abélard is a monk without a rule, is a superior without care, nor has discipline or order the least check over him. He is a man ever varying from himself, interiorly a Herod, exteriorly a Baptist, he is ambiguous as a riddle, possessing nothing of a monk, but the name and the habit. But what is this to me? Each one must answer for himself. One thing there is which I cannot dissemble; it appertains to all who love the name of Christ. He proclaims iniquity in the streets, he corrupts the integrity of faith and the purity of the church. Disputing and writing on faith, on the sacraments, and on the Trinity, he overleaps the bounds which our fathers placed; as he wills he changes, he multiplies and he diminishes. In his works and actions he proves himself the fabricator of lies and the worshipper of false doctrines; he is a heretic not in error only, but in obstinacy and in the defence of error. He knows all things in heaven and on earth, save only himself. Before the legate of the Roman see, with his work he was condemned at Soissons, but as if that sentence were not enough, again he exposes himself to censure and the last error becomes worse than the former. Secure, however, he thinks himself, because he can boast that Cardinals and Roman prelates have been his scholars; them whom he should have feared as his judges, he dares to call the protectors of his past and present errors." [16]

Bernard was twelve years younger than Abélard. He

---

[16] Bernard, Epistle 336, in Berington, *op. cit.*, II, 84.

was, according to most estimates, the most commanding man of his time; abbot of the Cistercian monastery of Clairvaux, so great was his fame that no fewer than ninety-three monasteries affiliated themselves (1130–1145) with his monastery. The contest between the rival Popes Innocent II and Anacletus II and the schism in the Church, Bernard healed. He could "create popes, command kings, and lead councils by the nose. His advice was asked by the greatest persons in Church and State; and he was even adored by the common people who fancied that he was an inspired man and endowed with the gifts of healing." [17] He was a great preacher, so great that Eugenius III procured him to preach the Second Crusade. The quality of his eloquence and his thought may be gathered from his words at Vézelay: "You cannot but know we live in a period of chastisement and ruin; the enemy of mankind has caused the breath of corruption to fly over all regions; we behold nothing but unpunished wickedness. The laws of men or the laws of religion have no longer sufficient power to check depravity of manners and the triumph of the wicked. The demon of heresy has taken possession of the chair of truth, and God has sent forth his malediction upon his sanctuary. Oh, ye who listen to me! hasten then to appease the anger of Heaven, but no longer implore his goodness by vain complaints; clothe not yourselves in sackcloth, but cover yourselves with your impenetrable bucklers; the din of arms, the dangers, the labors, the fatigues of war are the penances that God now imposes on you. Hasten then to expiate your sins by victories over the infidels, and let the deliverance of the holy places be the reward of your repentance." [18] He depopulated cities by his preaching,

[17] Justin, II, 294, quoted in Lewis' Introduction to his translation of St. Bernard's *On Consideration*, 6.
[18] Michaud, *History of the Crusades*, I, 333.

and so fervent was his faith that Heaven seemed to him to have commissioned him for the extermination of heresy. It was into the hands of this mighty man that Abélard had now fallen.

It was nearly twenty years since Abélard had been forced to burn his book *De Unitate et Trinitate Divina* at the Council of Soissons (1121). His work on Logic, *Dialectica,* was written before that time. Since then he had written the *Sic et Non* (1122–23), a very striking book in which one hundred and fifty-eight questions of a fundamental sort concerning God, the Trinity, Man's Redemption, the Sacraments, etc. are put; then Abélard searches the Church Fathers, and in one column he writes the "Yes" answers he finds to his questions in their writings, and in another column all the "No" answers. The *Sic et Non* is a book of contradictory statements, and no attempt is made in it to resolve the contradictions. "I expose these contradictions so that they may excite the susceptible minds of my readers to the search for truth and that they may render their minds more penetrating as the effect of that search." In his introduction to the *Sic et Non* Abélard suggests ways in which the opposed statements should be inspected to see whether or no they can be reconciled. They should be carefully read and in their contexts. Textual corruption should be disproven. Great care should be used to determine the real opinion of an author and to separate it from incidental statements. That no retractions are on record should be established. The facts which lead to a decision are the explanation of the decision. The reasons for an ordinance and the time at which it is passed are material to the understanding of the ordinance. Words are used in different senses which must be carefully examined. With every effort, not all contradictions can be synthesized, they must simply be taken for what they are. The book is distinctly a book for students, a textbook to teach them how to build sound theological doctrine. They must start with problems and work out conclusions. Unless they doubt, they will not investigate; and, unless they investigate, they will never reach the truth. Mr. Sikes holds that Abélard adapted the question-examining method of the canon lawyers to the study of theology.[19] The use which he made of the method was Abélard's. It was something between the Socratic method and its modern development, the case method of study. Peter Lombard, his pupil, employed it in his *Book of Sentences,* placing the learning of his master at the service of the Church. Through him Abélard's powerful method became the method of the schools; indeed, the method built the schools.

Professor Harnack calls Abélard "the great inaugurator of Mediaeval Scholasticism."[20] Bernard, he says, was *Augustinus redivivus.* It was not from Augustine that medieval men learned how to systematize.[21] Neither was it from St. Bernard. He was a preacher who relied upon impassioned words, surging from a full heart, to overpower his hearers. His instrument is sacred rhetoric. The Augustinian Neo-Platonic doctrine of God, the only substance, the all-one, whose worship could be nothing but mysticism nullifying the world and leading on to pantheism, had to be broken up, to be made articulate, to be analyzed and understood. Scholasticism, Harnack contends, is nothing but *scientific thought.* Abélard, the acutest thinker of his century, found the Socratic way of making words have meanings and taught an unheeding and perverse generation which condemned him the les-

[19] Sikes, *Peter Abailard,* 85.
[20] *History of Dogma,* VI, 42.
[21] De Wulf, *History of Mediaeval Philosophy,* 24.

sons which its children gladly learned from Aristotle in succeeding decades. Dialectic is the analyzing, the differentiating science. Abélard used it not to break down but to make clear what the Church believed. He used reasoning not to destroy belief but to make it intelligible and therefore firm. For him as for all other medieval scholars, the Bible was the chief standard, and to dissent from what it taught was to be a heretic; but what it taught could be found only by searching.

Abélard has been called the founder of the moral system of the Middle Ages.[22] His Ethics, or *Scito Teipsum*, was written in the latter part of his life, a few years before 1140. An English translation bearing the date of the year, 1935, has been made by J. Ramsay McCallum and published by Blackwell at Oxford. One of the discoveries that one makes who studies Abélard intently is that he was in fact the Socrates of Gaul. The Abbot of Cluny who gave him that name in the epitaph was speaking with exactness, not hyperbole—not that he used Socratic phrases but that he used Socratic thoughts. It is the inner man that concerns him, the conviction of the inner spirit that he seeks. That is what is meant by saying that his appeal is to individuals, that he was a Protestant long before Luther. He was, but he was a very different kind of Protestant—a Socratic Protestant, whereas Luther was a Pauline Protestant. The reason why Abélard employed the *Sic et Non* method was the identical reason that forced Socrates to employ the Socratic method.

The title of Abélard's book on Ethics, *Scito Teipsum*, announces that for him it is a science of inner experience. The human race does not share in Adam's guilt, for no man can act before he is born. Good and evil do not consist in the outward act, but in willing it. The will is

[22] Endres, in De Wulf, *op. cit.*, 165.

independent of everything save reason; God also is conditioned by reason. To will anything is to intend it. It is the intention that makes the virtue as well as the crime. Defective intention may be due to weakness of mind and body (inherited make-up) or due to ignorance. Thus far this is pure Socratism. That action is good which is in accord with the agent's own conviction. But an intention must not be called good merely because it seems good; its aim should not be mistaken. But Abélard is a devout Churchman, not a thorough going Socratic. For him sin is an act of will, an intention to set oneself against God and act in contempt of Him and His law. "When we say that we sin ignorantly, that is, do what is not seemly, we take sin of this sort to be not in real contempt, but in action only . . . This, then, is our definition of the sin of ignorance: to do without guilt, what we should not do. Sin is that which can never come about without personal guilt." [23] There are three stages in the reconciliation of the sinner to God: compunction, confession, satisfaction. Penitence is heartfelt contrition.

St. Bernard was temperamentally different from Abélard. His conception of Christianity was of a Divine mystery to be accepted, meditated upon, gloried in, but not interrogated, analyzed, or logicized; the supreme gift of God which must not be profanely inquired into or tested by the upstart intelligence of men. Christ died on the Cross to pay the debt men owe. Why talk about a Lord incarnated to teach mankind a holy way of living? It is Adam's sin that brings guilt on all. Absolution is for the priest, not the sinner. "The human mind," said St. Bernard, "the human mind usurps all, no longer leaving anything to faith. It lays hands upon what is most high. It searches that which is stronger than itself. It flings it-

[23] *Abailard's Ethics,* transl. McCallum, pp. 53, 55.

self upon divine things, it forces rather than opens the
holy places. Read if you please Peter Abélard's book
which he calls *Theology*." [24]

The lines of battle were drawn. All of France and a
large part of the Catholic world were involved in the
great contest. Then Abélard's students wrote a letter to
the Archbishop of Sens asking him to arrange a public
disputation between Abélard and the Abbot of Clairvaux.
The archbishop was arranging a great public ceremony
to translate the body of a saint into the cathedral. All
the bishops of his province and of Rheims were to be
there, and the King and his courtiers were to come. The
occasion was splendidly opportune. Abélard asked his
students to be present and support him there. The Abbot of Clairvaux at first refused to appear, saying that
the tenets of the faith are from the infallible God and
ought not to be submitted to human investigation. He
wrote to the bishops: "I am challenged as you have
heard, to a public disputation; the servant of God should
rather bear all patiently than contend. Were the cause
my own, I might place confidence in your protection,
but it is yours. I therefore entreat and admonish you to
show yourselves the friends of Christ in the day of
need." [25]

It was a day of splendor in the Church of France.
The holy relics of the saint were transported to their last
resting place through a vast concourse of awed and pious
people who gazed in wonder at the pageantry which surrounded the king and the long train of bishops and priests,
mitred abbots and monks, masters and scholars from the
schools, the learned and distinguished men of the kingdom. That night Bernard arranged a meeting with the

[24] *Petri Abailardi Opera, etc.*, 271.
[25] Bernard, Epistle 187, quoted in Berington, *op. cit.*, II, 88.

bishops and packed the jury—they voted to condemn the theological opinions of Abélard. When the great assembly met on the morrow Abélard and his supporters found that the agenda had been changed: they had not come for a disputation but for a trial. The Abbot of Clairvaux arose and said: "I am no accuser of this man, let his own words speak for him. Here they are, and these are the propositions extracted from them . . . " The reading of the charges began when suddenly Abélard rose and said, "I will not be tried thus like a criminal— I appeal to Rome," and proceeded to leave the cathedral. There was great confusion, but when it was quieted Bernard went on with his speech. The next day the bishops decided to leave the judging of Abélard to the Pope but to proceed to condemn his writings as heretical, which they did. The Abbot of Clairvaux was deputed to make report of their action to His Holiness. Meanwhile Abélard started on his long tramp to Rome to present his case before the Holy See. After proceeding but a little way on his journey he fell ill. In distress he entered the open gate of the monastery of Cluny and, making his helpless condition known to the abbot, was instantly met by Benedictine hospitality. "I am happy," said the good Peter the Venerable, "to have within these walls a man of whose abilities and virtues I have long heard so much; but tell me, from whence do you come and whither are you going?" "I come from Sens, a council has been sitting in that city. I have been charged before it with opinions which I never held, which opinions they have condemned as heretical; I have appealed to Rome and to Rome I am going." "I applaud your intention," said the Abbot of Cluny. "Rome is the asylum of the oppressed and you do well to rely upon its justice." The Abbot of Cluny urged the poor broken teacher to stay at hospitable and kindly Cluny long enough to recruit his strength before again taking up his journey, and in the calm peacefulness of that genuinely pious home of monks the sick man rested and for a while seemed to mend. The heavily importuned Pope did not wait for him to defend himself in person but somewhat too cruelly proceeded to condemn his writings and himself in the judgment: "With the advice of the bishops and cardinals of our court, we have condemned the articles which were sent to us, and all the false opinions of Peter Abélard with their author and as a heretic we have imposed perpetual silence on him." His followers, too, were cut off from communion with the faithful. He was to be confined in a monastery and his works, wherever found, were ordered burned.[26] While Abélard tarried to recover his health at Cluny, Peter the Venerable, whose goodness instigated the entire matter, says that the General of the Cistercians came to Cluny to beg Abélard to go with him to Clairvaux to talk over their differences and make peace with Bernard. Abélard went and a sincere reconciliation was worked out by Bernard and himself. When he returned to Cluny he announced to his friend the good abbot, Peter, that now he must be on his way to Rome. Then the abbot could no longer withhold the shocking news that in his absence his case had already been judged by Rome and that he had been condemned as a heretic to silence and imprisonment. That was a blow to break the spirit of a strong man, and Abélard was a worn veteran of many and great wars. The Abbot of Cluny said: "You must not leave us . . . There is not one of us here who does not long for your example and your instruction." When Abélard was able to reply to such almost supernatural kindness, he said: "Your goodness is like balm to my mind,

[26] Berington, *op. cit.*, II, 97.

and touching is the generosity of your monks. But it is not in my power to accept your too considerate offer; I have myself a monastery to which I must return if my enemies will allow it. Beside this fatal sentence has cast me out of the society of Christians, in a prison my days must be spent." "I will make your peace with Rome," replied the abbot, "and procure permission for you to remain at Cluny, if you will give your consent." [27] That was done, and in the great quiet of the second monastery of Christendom, far from "the tumultuary scenes of scholastic studies and disputation," Abélard came a little to know peace. As the horizon of his days narrowed he penned a brief apology to the Universal Church: "I may have written what should not have been said; but heaven is my witness that I have written nothing in malice, nothing from pride of heart. In the schools I spoke to thousands, but it was not surreptitiously; and what I thought might tend to the elucidation of truth, and the progress of morality, that I publicly delivered; and what I have written that I laid before the public not to make proselytes to my opinions, but that they might judge them. . ." [28] One other letter he wrote to "my Sister Heloise, once dear to me in the world, and now most dear in Christ": "Logic has brought the enmity of men upon me. For there are certain perverse caluminators, whose wisdom leads to perdition, that say I take preeminence in logic but fail egregiously in the interpretation of Paul; commending my ability, they would deny me the purity of Christian faith . . . I would not rank as a philosopher if it implied any error in faith; I would not be an Aristotle if it kept me away from Christ. For no other name is given to me under heaven in which I may find

[27] Berington, *op. cit.*, II, 112.
[28] *Petri Abailardi Opera*, etc., 330. Berington, *op. cit.*, II, 139.

salvation. I adore Christ reigning at the right hand of the Father . . . " [29]

"Never," writes the venerable Abbot Peter to Héloïse, "did I behold abjection so lowly or abstemiousness so exemplary. By my express desire he held the first place in our numerous community, but in his dress he seemed the last of all . . . His reading was almost incessant; he prayed frequently and he never interrupted his silence, unless when urged by the monks he sometimes conversed with them or in public sermons, explained to them the great principles of religion. When able he celebrated the sacred mysteries, offering to God the sacrifice of the immortal Lamb; and after his reconciliation, by my labor, to the Apostolic See, almost daily. In a word, his mind, his tongue, his hand, were ever employed in the duties of religion or in developing the truths of philosophy or in meditating upon learned things . . . Thus this good and simple man, having spent some time with us, was by my express desire sent to Châlons [to a monastery in a more healthful location]. . . . There as his strength permitted recalling his former studies he was ever engaged with books allowing no moment to pass in which he was not occupied in prayer, or reading or writing or dictating. There active in holy work the Visitor of the Lord found him, not asleep but watching, and he called him." [30] In the night the good Abbot Peter delivered his body to the Abbess Héloïse at the Paraclete.

No other life of that terribly busy century can compare with Abélard's in sampling the many features of the age. His contemporaries must have found in him the same dramatic intensification of the issues of their day that we find in him. He is the one solid scholar in history who

---

[29] *Petri Abailardi Opera, etc.,* 308. McCabe, *Peter Abélard,* 365.
[30] *Petri Abailardi Opera, etc.,* 341.

could command great multitudes. Sophists had done that, but Abelard was not a Sophist; the preachers had done that, but Abelard did not do it as a preacher. He did it by the analysis, rejection, correction, and synthesis of thinking applied to faith. The age was eager-minded in the ferment of great enterprises. "On all sides people devote themselves ardently to study," wrote Guibert de Nogent.[31]

If Abélard was by far the greatest teacher, there were many lesser ones who were some of them distinguished enough to get their names into the permanent record, Bernard of Chartres in 1117 and Gilbert de la Porrée among his students. Later than that but before 1120, William of Conches was in his classes. Thierry was master of Chartres in 1121 and taught in Paris in 1141. William of Conches was teaching in Paris in 1122. Adelard of Bath, another Paris teacher, had gone to Greece and even to Spain for knowledge, and in 1116 translated Euclid from the Arabic. William of Mortagne had come from the school of Tournai to teach philosophy and rhetoric at St. Genevieve in Paris from 1126 to 1144. Hugh taught at St. Victor from about 1125 to 1141. Richard of St. Victor, a Scotchman, taught there until his death in 1173. John of Salisbury (c. 1115–1180) had for teachers in Paris, he tells us, Abélard, Alberic, William of Conches, Gilbert de la Porrée, Adam of Petit Pont, Robert Pulleyn, and some others. Alan of Lille, Robert of Melun, Peter Lombard, and Robert de Courçon taught in Paris in the twelfth century.

Bernard of Chartres and William of Conches were lovers of the classics, teaching them as Quintilian directed, parsing them, explaining their figures, analyzing their subject matter and requiring their pupils to write copiously in the

[31] Funck-Brentano, *The Middle Ages,* 198.

manner of the authors they studied. The scholarly men
of this period knew good Latin and themselves wrote it.
John of Salisbury was a humanist and a protagonist of
humanistic rather than dialectic studies. But logic claimed
the field and reduced every other interest to the lowest
terms. The cathedral schools of other places lost ground,
but that of Paris grew inordinately. Scholars from all
Europe poured in to it, until the city had almost more
students than citizens. "Oh, Paris," cries Pierre de la
Celle in 1164, "you catch souls with lime." "It was the
fame of Abélard which first drew to the streets of Paris
the hordes of students whose presence involved that
multiplication of Masters by whom the University was
ultimately formed. In that sense and in that sense only,
the origin of the University of Paris may be connected
with the name and age of Abélard." [32]

Three things coming at the same time moved these
great beginnings forward to a tremendous revival of philosophy: (1) the recovery from the Arabs and the Greeks
of the writings of Aristotle, (2) the founding of the Universities, and (3) the organization of the Mendicant orders
by St. Francis and St. Dominic. The University of Paris
grew with the growth of the cathedral school of Notre
Dame. It is impossible to say at what moment that vast
scholastic enterprise ceased to be a cathedral school and
became in fact a university. The bishop's chancellor was
the schoolmaster usually in the cathedral schools; if not
that, he managed the schools. If other teachers than himself were required, he supervised them. When the bishop's
school became too small for the crowd of students, the
chancellor, its responsible director, issued permissions
to some of the graduates of his school to hold classes of
their own forming in its neighborhood. These classes were

[32] Rashdall, *Universities of Europe in the Middle Ages,* I, 280.

a sort of overflow of the cathedral school, and the chancellor assumed responsibility for them by authorizing certain ones to conduct them. This was the beginning of the license, *licentia docendi,* and at the same time of that teaching by masters on their own account, outside the classes of the cathedral school, and finally in opposition to it.[33] The number of students increased: "Philosophy and all clerkly knowledge flourished in Paris. The study of the seven arts was so great there, and in such authority that it was not so full or so fervent in Athens, Egypt or Rome, or in any part of the world." [34]

More and more masters with the permission of the chancellor organized classes in the neighborhood of his school. There was not space enough for them on the Island, they flowed over the Little Bridge and their classes dotted the approaches to the hill of St. Genevieve. They were men following the same occupation, all in a common neighborhood, many of them were foreigners who needed special protection in a city and country in which they had no birthright. It was an age of guilds. All men around them who followed the same occupations were organized into guilds, or trade unions. They organized themselves into a guild, or trade union of teachers or masters, to keep the chancellor from keeping the number of licensed masters small and subservient. That union was the University of Paris. No one knows just when it was formed. There is a reference in Matthew Paris' life of his teacher Johannes de Cella, which says that he became a member of the "fellowship of the elect Masters"; the date is about 1175.[35] This points to the formation of the guild of masters not long after Abélard died, perhaps as early as

[33] Funck-Brentano, *The Middle Ages,* 199.
[34] *Chronica de St. Denis,* in Funck-Brentano, *op. cit.,* 200.
[35] Rashdall, *op. cit.,* I, 294.

1150. We may be certain that some time between that date (1150) and Matthew Paris' date of guild election the University was formed. By what process did this partnership of teachers become a corporation? (1) It had to adopt written by-laws; (2) it had to be recognized or registered as having the right to sue and be sued as a legal entity; (3) it had therefore to have officers who could represent it, and (4) as evidence of that fact it had to have a common seal.

There was a town-and-gown riot in Paris in the year 1200. The servant of a foreign student was assaulted in a tavern. The students rallied and badly pounded the innkeeper. The Provost of Paris then brought up a guard of citizens to take the hostel into which the students had gathered themselves and in the mêlée several students were killed. The masters appealed to King Philip Augustus for redress. The King, evidently fearing that the masters and their students would move away from Paris, dealt harshly with the Provost, ordering him into perpetual imprisonment unless he took the ordeal by fire or water. If he did so and it convicted him, he was to be hanged. If it did not convict him, his imprisonment was to be commuted to banishment. For the future the King declared that, whenever a scholar was arrested by an officer, he must forthwith be handed over to the Church court. The citizens were required to take oath to respect the privileges of scholars, the Provost of Paris to swear to the masters in a body that he would respect those privileges. These privileges which Philip Augustus accorded were extended to masters and scholars as masters and scholars, not as members of the University, which in fact is not mentioned by the King.

But in 1210 a Bull of Pope Innocent III referred to regulations which the guild of masters had adopted, the first prescribing the wearing of a "round black cope reaching to the heels when new," the second, "the accustomed order in lectures and disputations," and the third, "attendance at the funerals of deceased masters." At about the same time the Pope authorized the guild to elect a syndic to represent it in the papal court. The reason for that was that the guild was having a bitter contest with the chancellor of Notre Dame as to whether he should continue to have the power to permit additional masters to teach, or the guild of masters should have the power to do that, the chancellor being bound to issue permission to all whom the masters recommended. More technically the question was whether the chancellor should continue to issue the license at his own discretion or should henceforth be required to issue it to all whom the masters approved for it. This was by far the most serious struggle in which the young University engaged, for the question at issue was whether the growing service of instruction was only an enlarged cathedral school or an institution of learning free and autonomous with power to determine and direct its own life and service. The chancellor represented the power of the Church, in the face of which the new organization of masters was relatively weak and helpless; but the Pope came to its aid and with characteristic wisdom cut the leading strings which restrained the young organization of great promise, by requiring the chancellor to grant the license to all candidates recommended by a majority of the masters in the higher faculties—to grant it gratuitously and without exacting any oaths of obedience whatever. But the struggle went on. Not willingly did the Bishop of Paris and his chancellor see the new organization which was coming to power separate itself from their control. The masters were charged with being a secret society engaged in conspiracy, when they passed statutes for the regulation of their own affairs without consulting the Bishop, chapter, or chancellor. Repeatedly the Pope came to the aid of the struggling masters. The chancellor was ordered to abolish his prison. The Bishop was forbidden to excommunicate the masters and scholars or their rector or proctor when acting officially for them. It was this conflict that forced the University to organize itself. It had to have officers to represent it in the papal court, and it had to find money to enable them to go to Rome and appear for it. That money it had to borrow, and a seal must be affixed to its bond.

We have been speaking of the University of Paris. They did not at first call it that: they called it a *studium*, that is, a place of higher education, in theology, law, or medicine. When the adjective *generale* was added, that meant that students from other countries were receiving instruction there. It was a place of general resort for instruction where there was a considerable number of teachers as well as of students. The word "university" means a number, an aggregation, more strictly a corporation. It was a general term for corporation and was used to designate many kinds of corporate entities. The schools were *studia*, the associated masters a university of masters. If the corporation was made up of students, as at Bologna, it was a university of students. Paris and Bologna were the two archetypes. All other universities in the West have been modelled upon them.

There were four faculties at Paris: a faculty of arts, of theology, of law, and of medicine. The last three are the superior faculties, but only in the sense that theirs is the more advanced instruction. The faculty of arts was by far the largest. Its masters were divided into nations; that organization came into being about 1220. At first the Pope did not approve it, but by 1231 it was fully recognized. The masters of arts at Paris were grouped according to nationality into four organizations, the French, the Normans, the Picards, and the English. The French nation included all masters of Latin origin; the English nation, those from Germany and all others from the north and east of Europe. The Picard nation included the Netherlanders. Perhaps in the earlier days, when the youth of the world thronged to Paris for instruction, these groups of masters were not of disproportionate size. After some decades, when universities had been planted in other countries, the French nation far outnumbered the others.

Each nation elected its own head, a proctor; and the nations together elected a common head, the rector. In the year 1245 these offices were clearly distinguished in a statute. The four proctors were to elect the rector. His was a splendid office. He was clad in silks and ermine. In public processions he took precedence over even the Archbishop of Paris. Lest such great honor should go to his head he was until 1266 elected for a term but six weeks long. After that the term was extended to three months, then to a year and even to two years. (The *rector magnificus* is still the presiding officer of the Continental universities. The adjective has respect to the historic rather than the present splendor of his office. In most cases he is elected by the faculties for one year. Until the Nazi government remodelled German education, the government of Continental universities—even in the Emperor-ruled states—had been democratic from the start. The United States, a democratic country, has universities directed by a president, appointed by a board of trustees and holding for life or good behavior. In the monarchical countries the universities have been democratic, in the democratic they have been autocratically ruled. It would be interesting to know just why this reversal of arrangements took place.)

In the early universities the power of the rector was the power of the purse. He was appointed to defend the university, to be its spokesman and champion. At the papal court he carried on the litigation in its behalf. To do that he was empowered to get the necessary funds. For his own services he was not heavily compensated. The new masters paid a fee for their gowns, which came to him, and there was a percentage on the sale of parchment which was handed him each year at the *lendit* fair when he went in state to lay in the university's stock for the coming year. The rector was elected by the proctors of the faculty of arts. He was the officer of that faculty. There were three higher faculties. Theology and arts had separate instruction in the time of Abélard; Canon Law was taught in Paris as early as 1175, and instruction in medicine belongs to the same date. The society of masters, that is, the University, included them all. The faculty of Arts being the largest and indeed including the masters of theology, medicine, and canon law as former students of Arts, and also including all their students as former students of Arts, was the first to organize itself; and when it did so it of course included all the masters and spoke for them all. Little by little the superior faculties grew within this matrix and gave themselves organizations of their own. In 1252 one, at least, of them is making written statutes for itself. Deans of the higher faculties are mentioned in 1264 and in 1270. The faculties of medicine and law have separate seals. The rector of arts is throughout the presiding officer of the whole university. The deans of the higher faculties insist upon their prerogatives, and there is a period of struggle in the defining of their separate functions, but in it the rector's right to summon all the faculties is established. The rector presided at the meetings of the entire University, the congregation, and laid the matter for consideration before them. It was then discussed by each faculty and nation separately, and the result of deliberation reported by the proctors and the deans. The rector pronounced in accordance with the majority, and his "conclusion" was binding, for all had bound themselves by oath to "obey the liberties and honest customs of the Faculty."

There are several things to be remembered about the early universities: one of them is that they were greatly valued by both Church and State; another, that they were in large part made up of strangers in a strange land; and a third, that their poverty was their strength.

The Popes regarded them as chosen instruments of faith and piety. Gregory IX in 1229 reminded the King of France that "wisdom is necessary and that wisdom is nourished by the study of letters." In 1231 he wrote to the masters and students, "Paris, Mother of sciences, city of letters . . . where as in a special factory of wisdom . . . skilful men ornament and decorate the precious stones of the Spouse of Christ." [36] A hundred years after that in 1331, John XXII writes: "We desire ardently and with all our heart that the study of letters should everywhere flourish and be increasingly developed." Just a hundred years after that in 1431 Eugenius IV says of the study of letters: "Thanks to them, the worship of God is increased; they prepare the salvation of souls." Emperors, princes, and kings were not less eager to support the great new institutions of learning. Their presence made the kingdom glorious. They brought people and wealth from foreign parts to the land, they were schools of public spirit and political loyalty, and most of

[36] Compayré, *Abélard*, 38.

all they supplied a constant body of trained men to fill
the offices and assist in the work of government. While
the Church valued the teaching of theology and canon
law, the kings were most particularly grateful for the
teaching of law, which led to the "understanding of what
is customary" and helped to distinguish what is just
from what is unjust. Of the three institutions of that
flourishing time, the cathedrals, the castles, and the universities, the universities were destined to grow beyond
the others.

Frankland was a country of personal laws. Its Salic
Franks lived according to the Salic law; its Swabians, the
Alemannic law; its Romans, the law of the Romani.
Bishop Agobard of Lyons said that if one saw five men
walking or sitting together, perhaps no one of them was
under a law which was common to him and another of
them. There was no common or uniform law. The
priests as rulers over spiritual things were accorded ex-
emptions from civic obligations which interfered with
the discharge of their holy duties. They enjoyed "benefit
of clergy," that is, exemption from the jurisdiction of the
secular courts, and were answerable to ecclesiastical courts
only. One did not have to be "in orders." "The adoption
of the clerical tonsure and dress conferred, so long as the
wearer continued celibate, the immunities and privileges
of the clerical order—exemption from the secular courts,
personal inviolability, and the like—in as ample a
measure as they could be enjoyed by the bishop or the
priest." [37] Whether in holy orders or not, the students
were always clerks. "Bishops and clerics," said Pope
Celestine III in 1198 to those residing in Paris, "have
their own judges in fact, and they have nothing in common
with the laws of the state." At Paris the members of the

[37] Rashdall, *Universities of Europe in the Middle Ages*, II, 645.

University had the right of *non trahi extra,* that is, whether as plaintiffs or as defendants their cases must be tried in the place where they were studying. The members of the University were exempt from all special assessments, all taxes, and all military service. While not compelled to do so, the University could and did many times volunteer for military service.

The University had no buildings of its own. Each master taught in the house where he lived or in a room which he rented for that purpose in the Rue du Fouarre, the Street of Straw. There were no laboratories or libraries, and no endowments tied it down. The University was footloose. That was its strength. In 1229 some students got into a brawl with an innkeeper about the amount they owed him for wine they had drunk. Near-by citizens rescued the innkeeper and beat off the students. The next day the students returned heavily reinforced by their fellows and broke all the wine jars in the inn and as many heads as they could in the neighborhood. The prior of the church in that quarter rushed to the Bishop of Paris and to the Cardinal Legate for aid. They flew to the Queen, who ordered out the Provost and the troops, who fell upon a lot of innocent students who were playing in a field and killed some of them. When word of this assault reached the masters of the University they suspended all lectures and disputations and, going in a body to the Queen, demanded that justice should be done immediately. The order of the Provisors of the University, May 27, 1229, read that, "unless satisfactory reparation is made to the whole body of masters and students for the atrocious injuries suffered by them from the Provost of Paris, his accomplices and certain others, within one month after Easter day, no one shall be permitted to remain in the city or diocese of Paris to study, either for the purpose of teaching or being taught. For a period of six years, beginning at the end of the aforesaid month no one shall teach either publicly or privately. Nor shall anyone be permitted to return at the end of six years unless satisfactory reparation is made for the aforesaid injuries. And to make this binding, we jointly attach to this charter our seals." [38]

The Queen, the Bishop, and the Cardinal Legate held out, and "that wonderful multitude, which had gathered from every region under heaven, departed. Some of them went to Rheims, some to Angers, some to Orléans, some to England, and others into Lombardy to Bologna." [39] The King of England saw a great opportunity and sent a royal letter inviting the whole body of masters and students to transfer themselves to his kingdom. The Pope at Rome was gravely concerned at this breaking up of a great institution from which the Church hoped so much. "Our beloved sons, the Masters and students of Paris have moved the University elsewhere," he said, "and by so doing they seem to have carried the key of knowledge with them and to wish to close the kingdom of Heaven for mankind." He supplicates and implores the King and the Queen-Mother to readmit these men to their grace and favor. He writes to the masters and students sojourning at Angers that he is grieved that a dissension has arisen which has caused "the study of theological learning and the principles of scholastic training" to cease in the city of Paris. He asks them forthwith to send representatives to him and copies of all the privileges that they have thus far been granted. On February 27, 1231, Pope Gregory IX sends them his findings in the celebrated

[38] In Duncalf and Krey, *Parallel Source Problems in Medieval History,* 151.
[39] *Loc. cit.*

document which defined their powers, the Bull called
Parens Scientiarum:

"Gregory, Bishop, Servant of the Servants of God, to
his dear Sons, all the Masters and Students of Paris.
Greeting and Apostolic Blessing . . .

". . . As to the status of the students and the schools,
we have decreed that the following regulations must be
observed, to wit: that whoever shall next be created
chancellor of Paris must be elected in the presence of the
bishop or at his command, in the chapter of Paris, and
two masters shall be summoned and present on this
occasion representing the whole body of students. At
his installation he shall take oath that, for the regulation
of theology and decretals [canon law], in good faith and
according to his conscience at every time and place, with
due consideration for the welfare of the city and the
honor and reputation of its faculties, he will not confer
the license unless it is deserved, and will not admit unworthy persons when the approval of persons and nations
is lacking. Indeed, before he shall license any one within
a period of three months from the time when petition is
made for the license, he shall diligently make inquiry from
all masters of theology in the city as well as from other
upright and learned men, from whom the truth can be
obtained, concerning the morality, learning, eloquence,
probable future, and all other matters which are required
on such occasions; and when he has made such inquiry,
in good faith, according to what is right and expedient,
and according to the dictates of his conscience, he shall
grant or refuse the license to the candidate seeking it.
Moreover, the masters of theology and decretals, when
they begin to teach, shall take public oath that they will
give faithful testimony regarding the matters previously
considered. The chancellor shall likewise take oath that

he will in no way reveal the advice of the masters to their prejudice, but that he will do all in his power to preserve the regulations of Paris, openly and legally (as they were in the beginning). Concerning the students of medicine, of the arts and others, the chancellor shall promise to examine the masters in good faith, and that he will not admit any who are not worthy, but will refuse the unworthy. Further, inasmuch as confusion creeps in wherever there is disorder, we grant to you the right to make prudent regulations and ordinances concerning the manner and hours of readings and discussions, concerning the prescribed dress, the burial of the dead, concerning the hours at which bachelors may teach and what they ought to teach, likewise concerning the rent and prohibition of hospices, and further grant to you the right to punish all who refuse to obey such regulations and ordinances, by expulsion from the society. If, perchance, the rating of hospices is removed from your control, or because it is not in your control, any of your people should suffer injury or wrong—namely, death or mutilation of body—unless, after due warning has been given in advance, reparation is made within fifteen days, you shall have the right to suspend teaching until satisfaction is obtained. Further, if any of your people happen to be imprisoned without just cause, if the molestation does not cease after warning has been given, you have the right to immediately suspend all teaching, if you believe that by so doing you can help matters.

". . . We command, further, that masters of arts should give one course in Priscian, and should always give one other ordinary. Those books of natural philosophy which were prohibited by the provincial council for a definite cause, shall not be used at Paris until they have been examined and purged of every suggestion of error. The masters and students of theology should strive to occupy themselves in a laudable manner in the field which they profess, and should not try to be philosophers, but should rather seek to become learned about God. They should not speak in the language of the people, and confuse the sacred language with the profane, but should discuss such questions in the schools as can be definitely settled by the theological books or the treatises of the holy fathers.

.   .   .   .

"Indeed, because the masters and students, irritated by wrongs and injuries, have bound themselves by oath and have departed from the city of Paris, thus breaking up the university, and they seem to have made it not so much an individual matter as a common affair, we, in the interest of the general Church and its well considered advantage, enjoin and command that when privileges shall have been granted to masters and students, by our dear son in Christ [Louis]—King of the Franks—and the punishment of the malefactors who injured them has been determined, they should see to it at Paris that nothing of censure should be brought forth concerning their absence or return or irregularity. No man whatsoever shall be permitted to infringe or to oppose without grave risk to himself, this our charter of provisions, constitutions, concessions, prohibitions, and inhibitions. If, moreover, any one should presume to try this he should know that he will incur the displeasure of the Almighty God and of Peter and Paul, His blessed apostles."

The right to strike, their chief asset and source of strength, was thus guaranteed to them in this, as Père Denifle calls it, the Magna Charta of the University. In 1499 King Louis XII in a mighty rage made an end to that privilege of the University. From 1231 to 1499 the strike was employed with reason and without reason upon provocations slight as well as provocations serious. An order to cease from sermons and lectures was no slight inconvenience to a church-going city, for it silenced the preachers who were M.A.'s of the University as well as the masters in their lecture halls. It took the judges off the benches and closed the courts and even stopped the physicians. Medieval universities were pretty turbulent aggregations of men at times. Bloody town-and-gown riots in which the masters accompanied by their students, as well as the students alone, took part were not uncommon. The mild punishments of the ecclesiastical law were not adequate deterrents. The privileges and immunities bred disorder. To keep its masters both regnant and non-regnant obedient to their oaths and its orders, the University used the terrible weapon of *privatio* or expulsion. When it was ordered, public notices were posted up throughout Paris denouncing the member as perjured and excommunicated or as "an arid, rotten and infamous member." [40]

As centres of educational activity the monasteries declined in the twelfth century. The cathedral schools, however, led, and their success produced the universities. The great expansion of human interests brought into being two great new religious brotherhoods, the Dominicans and the Franciscans. Dominic of Calahorra, Spain, was born in 1170 and died in 1221. He was ordained and became a canon regular in the cathedral at Osma. On a visit to Rome he was charged by Pope Innocent III to preach to the Albigensian heretics in Languedoc. He spent ten years on that mission, living in poverty, tramping barefoot from village to village, preaching, instructing, disputing, in a nearly vain effort to make converts. The rest

[40] Rashdall, *op. cit.*, I, 421.

of his life he spent in organizing, with his little band of
helpers in Languedoc as the core of it, an Order to preach
to and convert the world. When he died six years after
its founding, there were more than five hundred friars in
the eight provinces they had formed in western Europe.
In 1216 this new order of friar preachers was authorized
by the Pope. Its members took a vow not only of personal but of corporate poverty. Aside from their churches
and the monasteries in which they lived, they had nothing
save what begging and charity brought them. Their
missions went to every part of the world. "Your work is
teaching and preaching," Dominic said to them. To make
themselves invincible converters of men they diligently
cultivated learning. It was an important part of Dominic's
plan to found houses of his Order in all the great university towns. In Paris, Bologna, Padua, and Salamanca
they made themselves a power in the teaching of the Universities. Albert the Great and Thomas Aquinas were of
their company in the University of Paris.

Francis of Assisi was but a dozen years younger, his
dates being 1181 or 1182 to 1226. He seems to have been
the indulged child of a prosperous father. He was the
leader of the young men in their revels, we are told. Of a
sudden he left all that and gave himself to meditation,
prayer, and solicitude for the poor. He nursed in the
leper hospitals. He watched and prayed and heard a call
from heaven one day in the words of the lesson: "Everywhere on your road preach and say: The Kingdom of God
is at hand. Cure the sick, raise the dead, cleanse the
lepers, drive out devils. Freely have you received, freely
give. Carry neither gold nor silver nor money in your
girdles, nor bag, nor two coats, nor sandals, nor staff, for
the workman is worthy of his hire." [41] Layman though he

[41] Matthew 10: 7–10. As Francis heard them at the Portiuncula.

was, he began to preach on the streets the next day. One by one, disciples joined themselves to him until they were twelve in all; then Francis wrote out a rule, and in the year 1210 the whole company walked to Rome, where the Pope approved their Order. At first they were called the Penitents of Assisi, but Francis chose the title of Friars Minor. They were laymen with no fixed abode, who went two by two about the country, working in the fields to earn their bread and imitating in such detail as they were able the public life of Christ. Only when they could not earn their bread by the work of their hands were they to beg. They were to possess nothing, to wear mean clothes, to live in mean houses, and, ever following with the lowly, to be the guardians and heritors of Holy Poverty. St. Francis thought that but one thing is needful. "My brethren," he said, "who are being led by curiosity after learning will find their hands empty in the day of retribution. I would rather have them strengthened in the virtues so that when the times of tribulation come they may have the Lord with them in their distress. For tribulation is indeed coming wherein books shall be thrown into cupboards and hiding places as useless. He did not say this because the study of Scripture displeased him, but in order to withdraw the brethren in general from being over anxious to learn, and because he would have them all accomplished in charity rather than smatterers in research." [42]

This confraternity grew with amazing rapidity and soon numbered thousands of members scattered through the world. The utopian simplicity of the first organization was speedily changed into a monastic order in the technical sense. This development is said to have disappointed the founder. Almost at once there were a left wing, a right

[42] *The Second Life of St. Francis*, CXLVII (Howell's translation).

wing, and a great middle party of moderates. The organization which had come into being to insure pure peace to the soul broke into turbulent factions which devoted themselves to warring upon each other. The middle party encouraged the study of theology and other sciences, producing such great scholars as Alexander of Hales, Bonaventura, and Roger Bacon.

Both these orders were fishers of men, savers of souls. The Franciscans were less completely committed to intellectual training than the Dominicans, but both were committed to it. The Dominicans were champions of orthodoxy; the Franciscans, being more democratic and much more divided within themselves, experimented with new philosophies, shaped new social movements, developed fruitful new variations and new heresies. The Dominicans constructed the orthodox Aristotelian theology for the Church. The Franciscans leaned more heavily upon Plato and showed more kinship with mysticism than with Aristotelian articulateness.

When the mendicant friars first established their houses in Paris, they sent their members out to the regular University teachers for instruction. The University strike of 1229, however, changed their relation to the University. They did not want to leave Paris and they did not want to offend the King, and so they took no part in the dispersion, stayed on, and opened theological instruction of their own within their houses, which was not limited to members of their orders. The guild of masters allowed that for twenty years; then the Friars stirred up trouble for themselves by asking the Pope for a Bull enjoining the chancellor to confer the license upon as many religious as he should find qualified even if their monastic humility had kept them from asking for that honor as the chancellor's rule required. The other theological doctors in the University were not mentioned. The theologians thereupon passed a statute that "no Religious not having a College at Paris" should be admitted to the Society of Masters.[43] In 1253 there was a riot, and a University strike was ordered which three friar masters refused to join. They were expelled from the guild of masters. Then the University ordered all masters of every faculty to take an oath to obey its statutes, keep its secrets, and go on strike when ordered. All friars were expelled. They at once procured a papal Bull which suspended all the masters. The Pope by another Bull decided almost every point in the dispute in favor of the mendicants. The University refused to obey this Bull and was excommunicated entire. The war went on with increasing violence. Finally, in 1261, the patron of the Dominicans, Pope Alexander IV, died. Through his support the friars had won, but the University masters had stood together and continued to stand together until in 1318 the friars took the oath of obedience to the statutes and observed it.

The education of the European peoples had taken a great new impetus from Abélard. He had also given it a new direction. The French are a particularizing nation. In their music and painting, their literature, their government and foreign relations, things do not melt into one another; they stand out in their separateness. They are crystalline in the definiteness of their particularity. "The French are a nation of nominalists," says a great Frenchman. I should have preferred to say that they are seekers after meanings. At any rate that nation does not believe in the independent existence of genera and species. Its national philosophy is scholasticism—to this day it is scholasticism. Before Abélard it was theosophical Augustinian Neo-Platonism. It worked itself out of that

[43] Rashdall, *op. cit.*, I, 374.

fog into the clarity of dealing with discernibles through the centuries of logical disputation which engaged the masters and students at the University of Paris. "Although the Universals of Porphyry have been pretty adequately explained by him and elsewhere have been stated sufficiently in logic, metaphysics and natural and speculative philosophy, yet there is no man so well grounded as not to need in many ways to have teachers and to listen to them for a long time and to study before he knows the whole truth of the Universals. And no one with difficulty learns enough about these before death, no matter how many teachers he may have, as is clear, owing to the disagreement of all in this matter: since some maintain that these exist only in the mind, others that they exist only outside it, while still others maintain that in respect to being they are in things, but in their universal aspect they are in the mind." [44] Of St. Thomas it is said that he conducted "the emphatic theological idealism of Anselm and the Victorines into the sober channel of precise and clear concepts." [45] The scholastic method is a speculatively fruitful method, the method of the *Sic et Non*. It starts with a problem—St. Thomas built the *Summa* about 631 questions—and gathers the pros and cons which bear upon each and by balancing them reaches a solution. It lacked only the appeal to nature through experiment to make its findings complete. It was the true continuator of Greek philosophy, with problems and a motive power of its own, but problems not so unlike the Greeks' that it could escape their methods of handling them. It is well to remember too that it was strife and war that bred the tension here just as it had been at Athens. Another thing to be

---

[44] *The Opus Majus of Roger Bacon,* transl. R. B. Burke, Part I–VI–48 (Philadelphia: University of Pennsylvania Press, 1928).

[45] Grabmann, *Thomas Aquinas: His Personality and Thought,* 92.

borne in mind is that this great development like the
Socrates, Plato, Aristotle movement, was a teaching movement. St. Thomas was a teacher himself, and in his Prologue to the *Summa* that is very clearly put: "Because
the doctor of Catholic truth ought not only to teach the
proficient but also to instruct beginners . . . we purpose
in this book to treat of whatever belongs to the Christian
religion in such a way as may tend to the instruction of
beginners." [46]

The men of the Middle Ages were at work upon a vast
classification of human knowledge—a pyramid with a
base, a middle and an apex. Professor De Wulf represents it thus:

   I. Particular sciences, such as botany, zoölogy, etc.
  II. Philosophy.
      A. Theoretical
        a. Physics
        b. Mathematics
        c. Metaphysics
      B. Practical
        a. Logic
        b. Ethics
        c. Social and political philosophy
      C. Poetical
 III. Theology
      A. Doctrinal
        a. Scriptural (auctoritates)
        b. Apologetical (rationes)
      B. Mystical

The basic sciences, such as chemistry, zoölogy, and
astronomy, since they depend upon observation of the
senses, and nothing is in the intellect that was not first
in the senses, must come first. The analytic or detailed

[46] *The Summa Theologica of St. Thomas Aquinas* (London, 1920).

conception furnished by the special sciences must come
before the synthetic or total conception which is philosophy. The material is the same, the sciences differ in
their point of view. "Philosophy is simply a survey of
the world as a whole." The highest order of studies is
theology, founded upon revelation, scriptural and apolo-
getical.[47] To know is to order. Aristotle is the great
orderer, the arranger of human knowledge.

How "the Master of them that know" came back to
Europe is a long and difficult story, the details of which
are not yet fully worked out. In the time of Abélard few
of Aristotle's writings were known, the *Categories,* the
De Interpretatione. In the next generation the whole of
the *Organon* was in common use in a Latin translation
made by James of Venice. There was nothing heretical
in it, and by that time Bernard's objection to the human
mind busying itself about doctrine had been generally
forgotten. "The whole sacred text," says Roger Bacon,
"has been drawn from the Greek and Hebrew, and
philosophy has been derived from these sources and from
Arabic." From 1100, eagerness for learning drove
Christian scholars to go to Spain to get it. They had many
difficulties. The Christians had recaptured Toledo, at
that time the centre of Muslim learning, in 1085. The
Mozarab Christians whom the knowledge-eager students
from abroad met knew little Arabic and no philosophy.
A Jew is found who knows Arabic well but no Latin,
and next to no philosophy. The Jew turns the Arabic
text into the Mozarabic patois and a local Christian
painfully helps the visiting scholar to turn it into Latin.
This is Professor Singer's reconstruction of what happened when the first translations from Arabic to Latin
were attempted. No wonder Roger Bacon writes: "For

[47] De Wulf, *Philosophy and Civilization in the Middle Ages,* 85–95.

so great is the perverseness, crudity and terrible difficulty in the translated works of Aristotle that no one can understand them, but each one contradicts another, and false statements are found again and again, as is clear from a comparison of the different translators and of the texts of the different languages." [48] The first European scholar of distinction to come to Toledo was the Englishman Adelard of Bath. This man ranged the world, searching for mathematical and philosophical knowledge. About 1106 he was in southern Italy studying Greek and wrote a book *On the Unchangeable and the Changeable;* as yet he knew no Arabic. In 1126 he translated from the Arabic the trigonometrical tables of Al-Kwarizmi. Euclid's *Elements* followed.[49] Plato of Tivoli, Robert of Chester, and Hermann of Carinthia were other Christian scholars who went to Spain in order to make translations from the Arabic. Gerard of Cremona (1113–1187) was both the most famous and the most voluminous of translators. He went from his native city in Italy to Toledo expressly to learn Arabic in order to translate Ptolemy's *Almagest,* which he did in 1175. He spent all the rest of his life in making translations from the Arabic and Hebrew into the Latin, translating more than seventy native Spanish authors and translators. The Jew, Petrus Alfonsi, was born in Toledo in 1062, and after his conversion to Christianity came to England, where he was physician to King Henry I. Another learned Spanish Jew who visited England was Abraham Ben Ezra (1092–1167), a theologian, philosopher, and mathematician, who may have been the model for Browning's Rabbi Ben Ezra. The greatest of native translators was the Jew of Toledo who goes by the name Avendeath (*c.* 1090–*c.* 1165). He became converted to Christianity and

---

[48] *Opus Majus,* "Study of Tongues," 77.
[49] Charles and Dorothea Singer in *The Legacy of Israel,* 208.

mastered the Latin language and was thereby able to translate directly from the Arabic into the Latin. He had for a team fellow Dominicus Gundissalinus, Archdeacon of Segovia. Avendeath turned Avicenna's *On the Soul* into Spanish, and Gundissalinus put that into Latin. Avicebron's *Fons Vitae* and the philosophical books of Algazali, they also translated. Avendeath translated a vastly popular book, falsely attributed to Aristotle, called *The Secret of Secrets.* He also translated the mathematical works of Al-Kwarizmi, in which the Arabic method of writing numbers was introduced to Europe.

At first translations were made here and there in several places, Barcelona, Tarragona, Segovia, León, Narbonne and Marseilles; later Toledo became the chief centre for the making of them. There in the farthermost outpost of Christianity while the battle against the Arabs raged just a few miles beyond, as though to take possession of the loot of the conquest, the two Archbishops Raymond of Toledo and Rodriquez Ximines set up in the Archbishop's palace a college of translators where Englishmen, Italians, Frenchmen, Germans, and Spanish Jews and Christianized Arabs worked side by side for seventy-five years.[50]

"More of Arabic science in general," Professor Haskins thinks, "passed into Western Europe at the hands of Gerard of Cremona than in any other way." After him Roger Bacon puts Alfred the Englishman, who expounded the natural philosophy of Aristotle and in 1210 wrote a book *On the Motion of the Heart.* Michael Scot came to Toledo in 1217, translating first the work of Al-Bitrogi *On the Sphere,* and in 1220 Aristotle *On Animals.* Hermann the German about 1250 was at work on the *Ethics,* the *Poetics,* and the *Rhetoric* of Aristotle. Michael

[50] De Wulf, *op. cit.,* 80.

Scot and Hermann were both engaged on the commentaries of Averroës. "From Spain," says Professor Haskins, "came the philosophy and natural science of Aristotle and his Arabic commentators in the form which was to transform European thought in the thirteenth century." [51] Besides these known translations of the great works, the *Physics* and the *Metaphysics* and some lesser books of Aristotle came to the West about 1200, but who made the translations is not known.

In the twelfth century, translation from the Greek went on under the patronage of the Norman King of Sicily. There Aristippus, a high officer of state from 1160 to 1162, translated the *Meno* and the *Phaedo* of Plato and the fourth book of Aristotle's *Meteorology*. He was able to bring Greek manuscripts to Sicily from Constantinople. A second distinguished translator at the Norman court was Eugene the Emir, who knew both Greek and Arabic and could manage Latin also. He translated the *Optics* of Ptolemy. The *Data, Optics,* and *Catoptrics* of Euclid, the *De Motu* of Proclus, and the *Pneumatics* of Hero of Alexandria were translated there, and new translations were made of Aristotle's *Logic*. There were Italians from other parts of the peninsula who went to Constantinople, and some of them made translations.[52] "It is hard for us adequately to realize what this enrichment must have meant at that time. The great treatises of Aristotle—his *Metaphysics,* his *Physics,* his treatise *On the Soul,* works of which doctors had spoken for five hundred years, but which no Westerner had read since the days of Boethius —were brought to them from Greece and from Spain. Neo-Platonic works were added to these, principally the *Liber de Causis,* written by a compiler of Proclus, and the

---

[51] *The Renaissance of the Twelfth Century,* 289.
[52] Haskins, *The Renaissance of the Twelfth Century,* 292.

Elementa Theologiae of Proclus himself. Henceforth the
west knows the best that Greek thought has produced.
Nor is that all. Along with these works, the Parisian
doctors receive a vast number of commentaries, made by
the Arabs of Bagdad and of Spain. Finally, they also
come into possession of a large collection of Arabian and
Jewish works, having their sources in Alfarabi, Avicenna,
Averroës, Avicebron, not to mention others." [53]

This great wealth of new teaching material brought on
a burst of speculation. Free thought was unloosed.
Amalric of Bena was accused of teaching that every believer should regard himself as a member of Christ.
Amalric died before the pantheistic nature of his offence
was fully known. But a synod held in Paris in 1210 condemned the works of David of Dinant to be burned,
ordered Amalric's body to be dug up and put in un-
consecrated ground, and turned over a whole gathering
of heretics to be brought to punishment by the secular
arm. On the new books of Aristotle on natural philosophy
and his commentators, the masters were forbidden to
lecture for three years.

In 1215 the papal legate, Robert de Courçon, gave the
masters a body of statutes to regulate them. By these,
lecturing upon Aristotle's books on physics and metaphysics is again forbidden. Pope Gregory IX again in
1231 renewed that prohibition "until they shall have been
examined and purged from all heresy." In 1254 nearly
all of the Aristotelian books are required by statute to be
read as textbooks in the courses of the faculty of arts.
In 1204 the Crusaders took Constantinople, and Greek
texts and direct translations from them became more
common. About 1262 Thomas Aquinas prevailed upon his
Dominican brother William of Moerbeke to translate the

[53] De Wulf, *op. cit.*, 78.

works of Aristotle directly from the Greek. In this fashion the greater and the lesser works of Aristotle entered the University "to exercise there for several centuries an intellectual domination whose equal it would be impossible to find in the history of human thought."

The University of Paris was a guild or corporation of masters, or professors. The students were apprentice-masters, apprentice-professors. They studied to be admitted into the masters' guild, and as apprentices they must prove their proficiency by doing demonstration master work, that is, demonstration teaching. There were three grades they must surmount, the baccalaureate, the licentiate, and the mastership. One could not qualify for the mastership until he was twenty. The full course in Arts was seven years long and so most students entered perhaps at thirteen years of age. But at Paris the statutes said that one could "determine as a Bachelor" at fourteen, and those who chose to do that must have entered at a much earlier age. These University students were thus, many of them, mere schoolboys, which shows that the University was engaged in giving secondary as well as primary education. The distinction was made much later. As the lectures and books were in Latin, the ability to read, understand, and write that language was presupposed, though there were no entrance requirements to test its actuality. Ecclesiastical schools of the several sorts did not go out of existence with the coming of the universities. Most likely they multiplied in number and were stimulated by such greater educational activity. The lad who came to the University attached himself to the teacher of his choice, who thereby became his master who protected, supervised, and taught him all the subjects of his course.

The curriculum of the Dark Ages was the trivium

(grammar, rhetoric, and logic or dialectic) and the more advanced quadrivium (music, arithmetic, geometry, and astronomy). These subjects, particularly the four sciences, were taught only in skeletonized form. In the better schools there was some reading of Virgil or Ovid and of the *De Oratore* and perhaps an oration of Cicero. In the time of Abélard dialectic became the supreme subject and logic and philosophy almost constituted the course in arts. In the medieval universities the classical literature of the Greeks and Romans and the good Latin writing of Abélard and John of Salisbury were completely abandoned in favor of the books of Aristotle.

What the student must study in the course in arts is outlined for the first time in the statutes which the English Cardinal, Robert de Courçon, gave the University in 1215. In Latin grammar the "two Priscians," in logic the whole of Aristotle's *Organon* and the *Isagoge* of Porphyry are to be read *ordinarie*. Rhetoric and philosophy are to be read on festival days. In rhetoric the Barbarisms of Donatus, and the Topics of Boethius are specified. Philosophy seems to have included the Nicomachean ethics of Aristotle and some notice of the arithmetic, geometry, music, and astronomy of the quadrivium, for which study no books are indicated. The newly recovered *Metaphysics* and natural philosophy of Aristotle are forbidden.

The course as prescribed by the Statute of 1255 was the old and new Logic, the *Ethics*, the *Physics*, the *Metaphysics*, the *De Anima*, the *De Animalibus*, the *De Coelo et Mundo*, *Meteorica*, *De Generatione*, *De Sensu et Sensato*, *De Somno et Vigilia*, *De Memoria et Reminiscentia*, *De Morte et Vita*. To these authentic books of Aristotle the doubtful *De Plantis* and the *Liber de Causis* were added. In rhetoric and grammar the Six Principles of Gilbert de la Porrée, the Barbarisms of Donatus, the

Priscians and the Divisions and Topics of Boethius were indicated. The master did two things, he lectured and disputed. The student did two things: he took down the lectures of his master and thus made his own copy of the book which the master read and commented upon, and he listened to disputations until he was advanced enough to give a sample lecture and take part in some sort of disputation himself. The most informing descriptions of what takes place among men are not infrequently omitted from history. No account of the classroom instruction in logic or philosophy seems to have come down to us. Perhaps the masters at Paris read Aristotle in much the same way as Odofredus, who tells his class in Roman law at Bologna how he proposes to proceed:

"Concerning the method of teaching, the following order was kept by ancient and modern doctors and especially by my own master, which method I shall observe: First, I shall give you summaries of each title before I proceed to the text; second, I shall give you as clear and explicit a statement as I can of the purport of each law [included in the title]; third, I shall read the text with a view to correcting it; fourth, I shall briefly repeat the contents of the law; fifth, I shall solve apparent contradictions, adding any general principles of law [to be extracted from the passage], commonly called 'Brocardica,' and any distinctions or subtle and useful problems [*questiones*] arising out of the law with their solutions, as far as the Divine Providence shall enable me. And if any law shall seem deserving, by reason of its celebrity or difficulty, of a repetition, I shall reserve it for an evening repetition, for I shall dispute at least twice a year, once before Christmas and once before Easter, if you like." [54]

[54] In Charles H. Haskins, *The Rise of the Universities*, 58–59.

About the teaching of Logic, John of Salisbury has many things to say in the *Metalogicus:* "For there had to be a lore which should distinguish the true from the false and teach which reasoning holds the path of truth, which of probable truth, which of assumed truth and which should be distrusted. Otherwise truth cannot be found by reasoning . . . the rules of the art were seized and handed down finally by Aristotle. . . . For beginners in philosophy it is a prerequisite as the interpreter of words and concepts without which no item of philosophy comes precisely to light. . . . *Logica* has for its distinctive function to serve as effective instrument. . . . The exposition of every book should be such as to furnish most readily the knowledge of what is written. No occasion should be sought of introducing difficulty. Everywhere the way should be opened. That was the practice, I remember, of Abélard. . . . Thus Porphyry should be read so that the significance of the expressions in question may be retained and the sense of the words got from the surface. He will be sufficiently introductory so, and conspicuous for being quickly intelligible . . . for the text is to be searched mannerly, not bitterly racked as if it were a prisoner until it gives up what it has not taken." [55]

". . . No method as yet found out is able to compete in perfection with the sternly logical plan of the Scholastics. Two reasoners are placed face to face: one of them defends a proposition, the other attacks it. He who attacks has to prove by means of two short premisses his conclusion, i.e., the negative of the proposition which the defender maintains. The latter, admitting or waiving the least doubtful of these premisses, challenges his antagonist to prove the other; or he takes a distinction that destroys all the force of his opponent's syllogism, unless

[55] In Baldwin, *Mediaeval Rhetoric and Poetic,* 165–167.

he goes on to prove either of his premisses, *as thus distinguished*. No useless oratory, no pages of oracular obscurity, no string of questions leading one cannot tell where are allowed: from the very first you know what your adversary is aiming at and how he intends to reach it. Such was the method of public debate; such was also the method pursued by the thinker in his cell: he successively attacked and defended the same proposition, and by that means went as deep into the heart of the question as the human mind could go. And yet this, even this, method availed very little in the way of progress. Scholasticism, after the death of St. Thomas, just like Peripateticism after Aristotle's death, hardly took a single step forwards. The onward movement which, beginning with Anselm, culminated in the 'Angelic Doctor' also terminated with him. Every conclusion arrived at by the mighty Master was contested—often enough not without reason— by his successor and rival, Duns Scotus. The defect is in the method: though the best extant, it is all but worthless. We can easily see how cumbersome and awkward it becomes for practical use after the first few steps. Take any conclusion; for instance, *The soul is immortal*. This conclusion flows from two premisses. Each of these from two others. These two others proceed from two more. It is clear that, for any proposition removed from self-evidence by only ten degrees, an immense number of other propositions have to be brought forward and demonstrated. But this is not all. Supposing that each of these propositions has been proved, an assailant of the conclusion may at every step bring forward a distinction, which distinction must be borne in mind until we reach the axiom on which the whole is grounded; for if the axiom is not true in that sense, all is over. Therefore, if we suppose the above conclusion to be removed by 10 degrees from absolute certitude, 1024 axioms must be affirmed. And if it be said, to reduce this number, that many of those axioms may be identical, we must remember that at every step towards evidence they may be loaded with a new distinction—ten distinctions for each axiom! This is surely enough to differentiate them with a vengeance. Further, this work having been accomplished, the opponent comes forward and admits that his distinctions have been badly taken; but he says that this proves nothing in favour of our thesis, for he has a new set of distinctions that will overthrow the truth of our proposition. And the work is to begin anew, until the adversary is convinced that to assail us is a hopeless task. I think it may not be quite useless to point this out more clearly, by presenting the reader with a specimen of an imaginary conflict between an Idealist assailant and a Realist defender, carried on in strict Scholastic form. Most people have heard of these debates; but comparatively few, I believe, have any adequate idea of what they really are. Thus a twofold purpose will be served; for not only the defects of the Scholastic method, but also its merits, will be seen.

"The assailant having first denied that *An external world exists,* which is of course asserted by the defender, proceeds to prove his case as follows:

"No world independent of consciousness exists;
"Now, an external world is a world independent of consciousness;
" ∴ No external world exists.

"DEFENDER. At the major premiss, 'No world independent of consciousness exists,' I take a distinction. No world independent of *all* consciousness? I waive that question. No world independent of *my* consciousness exists? I deny it.—

At the minor, 'An external world is a world independent of consciousness,' I counter-distinguish. Of *all* consciousness? I deny it. Of *my* consciousness? I grant that. By this distinction your argument is out of form and inadmissible.

"ASSAILANT. But no external world independent of *my* consciousness exists; ∴ your distinction is worthless.

"DEFENDER. I deny that.

"ASSAILANT. I prove it. Nothing but a modification of myself exists; Now, a world independent of my consciousness is not a modification of myself; ∴ No world independent of my consciousness exists.

"DEFENDER. At the major, 'Nothing but a modification of myself exists,' I distinguish. Exists *as my perception?* I admit that. Exists *as the cause* of my perception? I deny it.—As for the minor, 'A world independent of my consciousness is not a modification of myself,' I grant that. So I distinguish the conclusion: 'No world independent of my consciousness exists': *as my perception?* I grant it. *As the cause* of my perception? I deny that.

"ASSAILANT. But my perception and the cause of my perception are identical; ∴ your distinction is worthless.

"DEFENDER. I deny that.

"ASSAILANT. I prove it. What is perceived by me is the cause of my perception; But my perception is what is perceived by me; ∴ My perception is the same as the cause of my perception.

"DEFENDER. 'What is perceived by me is the cause of my perception': here I distinguish. What is perceived by me *as something in myself* is the cause of my perception? That I deny. What is perceived by me *as something outside of my-self* is the cause of my perception? I grant it. —As for the minor, 'My perception is what is perceived by me,' I counter-distinguish. Is what is perceived by me *as something in my-self?* I grant it. Is what is perceived by me *as something outside of myself?* I deny that. By this distinction, your argument is out of form, and inadmissible.

"ASSAILANT. But to perceive what is outside of self is absurd; ∴ your distinction is worthless.

"DEFENDER. I deny that.

"ASSAILANT. I prove it. To have within self what is outside of self is absurd; Now to perceive what is out-side of self is to have within self what is out-side of self; ∴ To perceive what is outside of self is absurd.

"DEFENDER. I distinguish your major. To have within self *really* what is *really* outside of self is absurd? That I admit. To have within self *ideally* what is *really* outside of self is absurd? I deny it.—I counter-distinguish your minor. To per-ceive what is outside of self is to have within self *really* what is *really* outside of self? I deny it. Is to have *ideally* within self what is *really* outside of self? I admit that. By this dis-tinction your argument is out of form and in-admissible." [56]

The students in the medieval universities were ap-prentice teachers. They were in training to be masters. They sometimes played at being masters before they were of an age to be admitted to the guild. The practice which came to be known as Determination seems to have origi-

---

[56] Winterton, "The Lesson of Neo-Scholasticism," in *Mind*, No. 51 (July, 1888), pp. 397–400.

nated as a student's game. At first it was quite voluntary;
then little by little it became a fixed feature of the course
of every student who was on his way to become a master.
To determine was to maintain a thesis against an adversary. The student who undertook to do that with
a younger student opposing him was doing exactly the
thing the masters did in their disputations. In 1279 it
became obligatory to determine before one could qualify
for the chancellor's license. The masters, of course, were
interested in the public showing their students made; and,
to protect their own reputations as well as their students,
they made a rule that prospective determiners must first
hold a disputation with a master and next must be examined by examiners appointed by their nation. The successful determiner came to be called a Bachelor, and so
a student game in time supplied a university degree.

Determination was a colorful student activity. The
determiner rented his master's classroom and strove to
fill it with admiring friends and important people. Wine
was served by the determiner, and in the evening he gave
a banquet. After determining, the student went back to
his master's instruction, but in a somewhat changed status,
for now he must hold a certain number of disputations and must give one course of instruction himself.
"Cursory" lectures, they were called, commonly upon
one book of Aristotle's *Organon*.

When that student had read all the prescribed books
and reached the age of twenty years he could claim his
license at the hands of the chancellor. That Church
officer named four examiners, who must be acceptable to
the master, and who together with him inquired into the
candidate's residence, attendance at lectures, and performance of work, and gave him some sort of examination upon the books he had studied. Upon the basis of

this examination of the candidate and his record, the chancellor decided whether he should be admitted to examination by the faculty. If the faculty approved him for the license, he appeared on a set day along with other candidates in full academical dress attended by the rector, proctors, and faculty of the University, before the chancellor, and kneeling he received "the solemn license in the name of the Trinity to incept or begin to teach in The Faculty of Arts, together with the Apostolical blessing."

The ceremony of inception was his initiation into the guild of masters. A congregation of his nation must first order it. Then he must make oath to obey the rector and his own faculty and nation. In the evening of the day preceding his inception he held a solemn disputation; the next day came his ceremony of investiture. Before the faculty he gave his sample lecture or disputation, i.e., his piece of master work, and was seated in the master's chair, capped with the master's biretta; a ring was placed on his finger, an open book placed in his hands, and he was given the kiss of fellowship. Thus he *commenced* his calling as a master. In the evening there was a great inception banquet. The new master must now hold disputations continuously for forty days. Then he must stay in Paris and teach for two years; that is, he must for two years work as a regent master. Dispensation could be had from most oaths, and dispensation from that one made him a non-regent master. Many did not teach but instead went on with their studies in the higher faculties.

At the University of Paris the course in Medicine was five and one-half years for those who had been licensed in Arts, and six years for those who had not. The *Liber Tegni* of Galen, the aphorisms of Hippocrates, the works of Theophilus, were among the books studied. The regulations said that students should read the most important books twice in ordinary and once in cursory lectures. Dissection of the human cadaver was not permitted until 1300. Medical studies at Paris were not distinguished, as those of Salerno and Montpellier were. Medicine, though not scientific, was a popular study because physicians could grow rich in its practice.

The faculty of theology was regarded as superior to all the others. It was not merely a teaching organization, it was a consultative committee for the entire Church. For the most part its masters and students belonged to the great monastic orders. In 1253 there were twelve professors of Theology at Paris; nine of them taught in the monastic houses. The two books studied in Theology were the Bible and Peter Lombard's *Book of Sentences*. Peter Lombard was born at Novara, Italy, about 1100. He learned theology at Paris, was in Rome for two years, and became bishop of Paris in 1159. "When the great disciple of Abélard, Petrus Lombardus, published his Sentences, and in them fittingly placed the learning of his master at the service of the Church theology—as yet the Middle Ages had not possessed a compendium for the study of theology. . . ." [57] Peter Lombard's *Book of Sentences* is made on the model of the *Sic et Non*. It is a collection of authoritative passages for and against; but its author, unlike Abélard, gives a solution. Its matter is arranged in four books—the first on God, the second on the Creatures, the third on the virtues, and the fourth on the Sacraments. Hundreds of commentaries were written on this book, and for four hundred years it remained dominant. Albert the Great regarded it as so elemental that he declared that Mary,

[57] Harnack, *History of Dogma*, VI, 42.

the Mother of Christ, must have had a summary knowledge of the Bible and the Sentences.[58]

The student who had studied theology for six years and was twenty-five years of age could ask for his first course, i.e., to be made a bachelor. For a year he lectured upon some one book of the Bible, and in the following year, upon another book. In his ninth year he took part in a disputation which was called the Tentative. The bachelor of theology might now, after nine years of studying theology, be allowed to give a year course on the first of the four books of the Lombard's Sentences, and in the following years on the second, third, and fourth. There were formidable public disputations as well. At one of them, the Sorbonic, the bachelor of theology had to reply to the continuous fire of interrogators from six o'clock in the morning to six at night.

The bachelor of theology's *Aulatio,* or admission to the mastership, was presided over by the chancellor, who pronounced the sacred words of admission and himself placed the cap of a theological doctor upon the new professor's head. Thus theology recognized its relation to the cathedral school after the other disciplines had separated themselves more completely from their origin.

We have still to speak of one of the greatest of the renewing forces of the twelfth century—the revival of the study of law. The study of the civil and canon law in the medieval universities was a means and influence of civilization not less powerful than the study of dialectic and philosophy themselves. That great student of the processes by which laws extend themselves, Sir Henry Sumner Maine, points out that legislatures are of very recent appearance, in modern Europe. The pow-

[58] Rashall, *op. cit.,* I, 465.

erful bodies from which legislatures sometimes developed, court and national councillors, and great men advising kings, were not true legislatures. "In truth, far the most influential cause of the extension of particular laws and of particular systems of law over new areas was the approval of them by literate classes, by clergymen and lawyers, and the acquiescence of the rest of the community in the opinion of these classes." [59] In the early universities Law signified the Roman civil law and the Church or canon law. It used to be thought that, with the overthrow of Roman government in the West by the barbarians, the Roman law had been blotted out, too. Until 1806 Roman government, going by that name, was never utterly abolished, and "the Roman Law, on the other hand, was practically everywhere, and its tendency was, not to decay, but to extend its area and enlarge its authority . . . A barbarous system of law is always scanty, and if it be contiguous to a larger and more extensive system, the temptation in practitioners to borrow from this is irresistible." [60] Barbarian Europe in every part had an almost superstitious reverence for the Roman Law. It was felt to be law absolute in the presence of which feudal customs were mere makeshifts. In Italy it had never altogether ceased to be taught and used in the courts. The great battle between the Papacy and the Empire became a war of long drawn-out arguments. Both sides searched their foundations, and as a consequence there grew a vigorous interest in Roman Law which brought together teachers and students of it at Pavia and Ravenna in considerable numbers in the eleventh century. Bologna had, it would seem, long been a place where rhetoric and grammar were taught. It at-

[59] Maine, *International Law*, 19.
[60] Maine, *op. cit.*, 17–18.

tained celebrity by adding to them instruction in *Dicta-men,* or the art of preparing legal documents such as no-taries compose and the public business requires. The *Digest* of Justinian is mentioned there in a legal docu-ment of 1076. In the battle between the Pope and the Emperor the Countess Matilda is said to have requested Irnerius to renew the books of the Laws as they had been compiled by Justinian. That account is probably correct. At any rate a great teacher of law appeared at Bologna in the person of Irnerius, and under his leadership the study of the Roman law soon took on the proportions and the organization of a university.

Bologna is the oldest of European universities. In 1888 it celebrated its eight hundredth birthday, but to do so it had to go back to a somewhat uncertain date of beginning. Rashdall believes that Irnerius taught there perhaps in the period 1100–1130. What Bologna stands for in law is: (1) the reinstatement of the *Digest,* as fundamental to the re-creation of legal knowledge as the recovery of the works of Aristotle and their persistent study were for the renewal of logic and philosophy; (2) the Irnerian revival of close, critical, and textual study of the Roman sources of law; (3) leadership in the thorough systematization and organization of the laws; (4) elevation of the study of the law an under-taking so vast and so worthy that it could not be re-garded as merely a part of general education.[61]

But there was another body of law and another book, made on the model of the *Sic et Non* of Abélard, which had to be studied: the canon law in the *Decretum* of Gratian. Canon law is Church or ecclesiastical law. In every country of Europe, Christianity was first a mis-sionary religion, then a voluntary society, and after that

[61] Rashdall, *op. cit.,* I, 122.

a national church with its laws and regulations, its tri-
bunals and executives. With Hildebrand (Pope, 1073–
1085) the consolidated Catholic Church took on great
power. It insisted not only that its spiritual machinery
should be free from secular control, but that secular affairs
should be under its control. To consolidate its claims and
make them strong, codifications of Church laws were undertaken. The sources of Church law are the Holy Scriptures and the canons of Church councils, the regulations
of archbishops and bishops. But there was no universal
form of ecclesiastical law, and so in each nation the details of the relation of Church and State varied from
those of other nations. Collections of canons were made
by several churchmen. Ivo of Chartres made one, using
the *Corpus Juris* of Justinian. Then Gratian produced
his *Decretum* about 1151. These books were not codes
but collections of Church laws.[62]

Gratian was a monk living in a monastery at Bologna.
The prevailing activity of the city of his residence stirred
him to make a textbook of the Church's law. He made it
after the manner of Abélard's famous arrangement of
scholastic arguments, putting down faithfully the points
in favor and the points opposed, upon every disputed
question. Not only was this a model textbook of scholastic method; it was arranged in two parts, the first containing the discussion of the law, the second, hypotheti-
cal cases for solution. The law of the Church had grown
out of the Roman law, and its formulation and teaching
were inspired by the civil law. The work of Gratian
separated the teaching of canon law from the teaching
of theology and made it a part of the function of the
faculty of law, but a distinct part separated from the
civil law. The civil law had been formulated by Jus-

[62] Stubbs, *Lectures on Early English History,* 93.

tinian, but the canon law was a growing body, for every act of the Pope and the councils added to it.

There seems to have been a corporation of teachers of law at Bologna as early as 1158, when the Emperor Frederick I issued his charter, but the University of Bologna takes its place in history as a student-university. The teachers at Bologna were not as at Paris the authorized agents of the cathedral. They were private adventurers who offered their wares of instruction where there happened to be a market for them. The students at Bologna were perhaps older men than those who came to Paris. They came from other parts of Italy and other places in Europe and were strangers in a medieval city whose citizenship was hereditary, and whose laws did not protect the foreigner. So the students banded themselves together for their protection and to carry out the purpose for which they came. The Roman law recognized *collegia,* or de facto corporations of three or more persons without express authorization of local government. The foreign students, availing themselves of that right, formed student clubs or guilds which coalesced into the University, or rather (from 1244) into the two universities, an ultramontane university formed of students from beyond the Alps, and a cismontane university; the former was made up of fourteen nations, the latter of three; the Romans, the Tuscans, and the Lombards. Each of these universities elected its own rector, who held office for two years and must be a secular clerk, unmarried, of five years' standing in the study of law and not less than twenty-four years of age. A good deal of pageantry and no little expense was attached to that office. The professors were hired and regulated by the students. Naturally they did not like that arrangement and protested that a guild could not be made out of apprentices only, that it must have master workers in it. But the masters in the days when the University took form were citizens of Bologna, and the students were not and had to make their organization to protect themselves, sometimes against the citizens, sometimes against the professors. The University was stronger than the professors and stronger than the citizens. If a professor offended, he could be boycotted; and if the citizen and their town government mistreated the University in any way, it was so footloose that it could pick up and move into another town almost on the instant. By means of the boycott the professors were constrained to take the oath of obedience to the rectors and to accept the *salaria* which the student-university fixed for them. The government and citizens of Bologna did not of course like the University's free way of moving off to another place on provocation, but could do nothing to prevent it seceding when it resolved to. In 1204 the students, because of difficulties with the townsmen, moved to Vicenza; in 1215, to Arezzo; and in 1222 a great migration founded the University of Padua. In 1321 another "wrong" done the University led to the founding of the University of Siena. The University of Bologna was a secular rather than a Church university such as Paris was, but the Church extended a helping hand in need and assumed a kind of guardianship and protectorate over the students. The Magna Charta of the University was the *Habita* issued by Frederick Barbarossa in 1158, in which the Emperor said: "We will that the students, and above all the professors of divine and sacred laws, may be able to establish themselves and dwell in entire security in the cities where the study of letters is practised. It is fitting that we should shelter them from all harm. Who would not have compassion on these men who exile themselves through love of learning, who expose themselves to a thousand dangers, and who, far from their kindred and their families, remain defenceless among persons who are sometimes of the vilest? . . . If any person, for any cause whatsoever, wishes to bring action against students, he must cite them, according to their own choice, before their professor or before the Bishop of the city." The congregation, the whole body of students, exercised the supreme power of the University. The lectures were in hired rooms or in the professor's house. Great University occasions were celebrated in the Cathedral.

There were two kinds of lectures, ordinary and extraordinary. The first, being the regular and more important ones, were given in the morning; the others, in the afternoon. The *Code* and the first part of the *Digest* of Justinian were the ordinary books. The other two parts of the *Digest,* and certain smaller books of Justinian, and the *Liber Feudorum* of the Lombards were read in the extraordinary hours. In the teaching of canon law, the *Decretum* of Gratian and five books of *Decretals* published by Gregory IX were ordinary, while lectures on the *Clementines* and *Extravagants* were extraordinary. Ordinary lectures could be given by doctors only. After a student had studied the civil law for five years, he could be admitted by the rector to lecture on a single title of the civil or canon law; and after six years of study, to lecture on a whole book. By giving either course the student became a bachelor. To attain the rank and privilege of a doctor of the civil law, one must qualify as a bachelor and have studied at least seven years. To become a doctor of the canon law one must have studied it for six years; and to become a doctor of both laws, ten years of study of them was necessary. When the doctors of law at Bologna admitted students to the doctorate, they raised up competitors for their own very profitable business, a thing which they were naturally not too anxious to do. At that point the Church stepped in, by Honorius III in 1219 enjoining that no promotion to the doctorate should take place without the approval of the Archdeacon of Bologna. Doctors of law thus became not merely members of a local guild of law professors but approved legal representatives of the entire Catholic Church. Explicit acknowledgment of that fact was recorded in a papal bull of Nicholas IV, 1292, which conferred upon all doctors licensed by the Archdeacon of Bologna the right to teach throughout the entire world.[63]

The process by which one became a doctor of law at Bologna was elaborate. First the consiliarius of his nation presented him to the rector who administered the necessary oaths. Next the candidate's doctor must present him with his own guarantee of the candidate's eligibility, to the Archdeacon. Then he must attend a mass of the Holy Ghost and appear before the assembled college and be publicly assigned by one of the doctors two passages of law, which he was permitted to study until summoned by the Archdeacon in the afternoon to a conclave where he took some more oaths and gave his sample lecture on the passages which were assigned him in the morning. He was then examined by two doctors upon those passages of the Law, and the votes of the doctors present were taken. If a majority of the ballots favored him, the Archdeacon announced that, and he became a licentiate and proceeded to the public examination, which was a costly and colorful ceremony. Before the day of the *Conventus* he rode up and down the city in state, preceded by the beadles of the Archdeacon and his promot-

[63] Rashdall, *op. cit.*, I, 224.

ers inviting city and University officials and such friends as he wished to have present to take part in his commencement. On the day, his presenting doctor and his fellow-students attended him to the Cathedral. There he delivered an address and defended a thesis against antagonists selected from the students, and was presented by his promoter to the Archdeacon, who welcomed him and solemnly conferred the license to teach one or both laws in the name of the Holy Trinity. The new doctor was then invested with the symbolic implements of his craft. He was seated in the master's chair, the open book was placed in his hands, a ring was put on his finger, the master's cap was put on his head and the kiss of peace given him. After the benediction he was escorted in triumph through the town. That evening he must give a great banquet at his own expense to his rejoicing University friends.

Sometimes the new doctor stayed on in Bologna and taught in the University. Usually he went elsewhere, for jurisconsults from Bologna were in demand everywhere in Europe. They formed a privileged caste in the Church, in the offices of state, and in the universities. Theirs was a favored profession. Theology and canon law were the road to Church preferment. The civil lawyers found more favor with princes. The Church sometimes regarded the civil law as the enemy of God. Pope Honorius III in a Bull of 1220 says: "Although Holy Church does not reject the docile coöperation of the secular laws, yet, as in France and other provinces, the laity do not use the laws of the Roman Emperors; and as moreover, ecclesiastical suits are seldom met with which may not be settled by the rules of canon law alone, we forbid under pain of excommunication, both at Paris and in the neighboring towns and cities, any person to employ him-

self in teaching or learning civil law." [64] The Pope in his
Bull severely arraigned the civil lawyers for their wealth
and ostentation and forbade bishops to consider them
for ecclesiastical preferment. By formal interdict he prohibited all teaching of the civil law in France, England,
Scotland, Flanders, Spain, and Hungary. But he added
the phrase, "if, however, the heads of the state permit."
But the prohibition of the teaching of the civil law in
France by the Pope seems to have been ineffective. Roger
Bacon complains that the jurists so dominate princes
and prelates "that they monopolize all places and favors
at their disposal . . . The civil lawyers alone are honored and enriched." "Our Frenchmen," says Crevier,
"went to Bologna to gain a knowledge of Justinian law
and brought it back from there to Angers, Orléans, and
Paris." [65] These, together with Montpellier, were the
chief universities for legal study in France.

The proper housing of its students is a problem of
large dimensions for every modern university. Universities at the beginning took no thought for that at all.
The fourteen-year-old student who went to Paris to
study arts was as free to live where he could as the ma-
turest student in the University. Groups of students
soon got together and hired houses, the rent of which
in time was fixed by a duly constituted board made up
in part by masters and in part by citizens. These students' boarding houses, or *hospitia,* as was inevitable,
appointed either a resident student or an outsider to
look after the undertaking. At first that principal was
not a master but perhaps most commonly an older student. Some houses fared better by including a master
as their principal, and that practice grew. Rich students

[64] Compayré, *Abélard,* 217.
[65] In Compayré, *Abélard,* 224.

preferred to live in their own houses with their own servants, perhaps a tutor among them. The poorest students
lived where and as they could. The student hospice with
a master to head it established itself as the acceptable
arrangement. It grew up democratically, the students
themselves choosing and inviting the master to head their
household. Little by little, however, the democratic head
became a monarch, and the boarding hospice, a Pedagog-
ium. The College was at first only an endowed boarding
house. The founder put a master in charge of it to administer the endowment which he had made. The founder
provided board and lodging for poor scholars. There was
always a master in charge of the foundation, but his responsibility did not include the giving of lessons inside
the house. Lessons were given at the University, and
the students who roomed and boarded under the master's
care in the college went out for their lessons.

The first college at Paris was endowed by a man from
London, "dominus Jocius," who on his way back from
Jerusalem bought a room in the "Hospital of the Blessed
Mary of Paris" and appropriated it perpetually for the
support of "eighteen scholar-clerks." This endowment
was made in the year 1180. Other foundations were
made from time to time. The several monastic orders,
stimulated by the active part which the Dominicans and
the Franciscans were taking at Paris in the life and benefits of the University, established colleges, that is, monasteries whose rules were modified to meet academic opportunities. About the year 1257 Robert de Sorbon, chaplain
of Louis, the Saint King of France, founded an endowed
college to support sixteen masters of arts, four from
each nation, who were entering upon their studies in the
theological faculty; added provision soon raised that
number to thirty-six. The house was the responsibility

of a board made up of the chancellor, the doctors of
theology, the deans of medicine and law, and the rector
and proctors of the University. The executive under this
board was a provisor not a member of the college. In succeeding centuries the endowments shrank, and membership in the Sorbonne became an honor to which members of the theological faculty were admitted. The College of Navarre was founded by Joanna, Queen of
Navarre, in 1304. Provision was made in it for twenty
students in grammar, thirty in arts, and twenty in theology. Each group had quarters and a master of its own,
the theological master being head over all. The grammar master gave all the instruction which his scholars
received. The others went out to the University. But
repetitions were given in the college, and from that beginning other instruction and instructors were added until shortly the students had all their instruction inside the
College. The same thing happened in the Pedagogies.
In 1445 a petition presented to the King declared that
"almost the whole University resides in the Colleges."
By 1500 a degree could have been earned from college
lectures alone and after Ramus' time there were no
lectures in the Street of Straw.[66]

We add here as a kind of amplification of this great
story Compayré's historic table of the founding of the
universities:

Twelfth Century

1158, Bologna

Thirteenth Century

1200, Paris; privilege granted by Philip Augustus.

12—, Oxford; whose university constituted itself without any
official sanction; the first royal recognition, a charter
from Henry III, is dated 1258.

[66] Rashdall, *op. cit.*, I, 478–500.

12—, Cambridge; which sprang from Oxford, and developed spontaneously like Oxford; letters-patent from Henry III in 1217 and 1231; a bull from Pope John XXII in 1318.

12—, Arezzo; which likewise dates from the first half of the thirteenth century; imperial recognition from Charles IV in 1355.

1212, Palencia; in Spain, founded by Alfonso VIII, King of Castile.

1222, Padua; which arose from an emigration of Bolognese professors.

1224, Naples; Frederick II, Holy Roman Emperor.

1224–1228, Vercelli; which arose from an emigration of Professors from Padua.

1229, Toulouse; Pope Gregory IX.

1243, Salamanca; Ferdinand III, King of Castile and León; confirmation in 1254 from Pope Alexander IV.

1244, Curia Romana; Pope Innocent IV; this school followed the Popes to Avignon.

1245, Valencia; in Spain; James I, King of Aragon.

1248, Plaisance; in Italy; Innocent IV; the Duke of Milan, Gian Galeazzo, in 1398 confirms its privileges.

1254, Seville; Alfonso X, the Wise, King of Castile and León.

1288, Lisbon; Denis, King of Portugal; Pope Nicholas IV transferred it to Coimbra in 1308.

1289, Montpellier; Pope Nicholas IV.

1289, Gray; Otho IV, Count of Burgundy; transferred to Dôle in 1423 by Philip the Good.

1293, Alcalá; Sancho IV, King of Aragon.

1295, Pamiers; Pope Boniface VIII.

Fourteenth Century

1300, Lérida; James II, King of Aragon and Sicily.

1303, Rome; Pope Boniface VIII.

1303, Avignon; Pope Boniface VIII.

1306, Orléans; Pope Clement V; in 1312, King Philip the Fair.

1307, Perouse; Clement V; in 1355, the Emperor Charles IV.

1308, Coimbra, already organized toward the close of the thirteenth century, in 1279; successor to the University of Lisbon.

1310, Dublin; Pope Clement V.

1332, Cahors; Pope John XXII.

1339, Grenoble; the Dauphin, Humbert II; Pope Benedict XII.

1343, Pisa; Pope Clement VI.

1346, Valladolid; Pope Clement VI.

1347, Prague; Pope Clement VI; in 1348, the Emperor Charles IV.

1349, Florence; confirmed in 1364 by Charles IV.

1349, Perpignan; Peter IV, King of Aragon; confirmed in 1379 by Clement VII.

1354, Huesca; Peter IV, King of Aragon; reëstablished in 1464 by Pope Paul II.

1357, Siena; from 1321, emigration to Siena of professors from Bologna; privileges conceded, 1357, by the Emperor Charles IV.

1361, Pavia; Charles IV; in 1389, Boniface IX.

1365, Vienna; the Emperor Rudolph IV; Pope Urban V.

1365, Geneva; the Emperor Charles IV.

1365, Orange; Charles IV.

1365, Cracovia; Casimir III, King of Poland; Urban V.

1367, Fünfkirchen, in Hungary; Urban V.

1367, Angers; Louis I, Duke of Anjou.

1379, Erfurt; Pope Clement VII.

1385, Cologne; Pope Urban VI.

1385, Heidelberg; Pope Urban VI.

1389, Ofen; Boniface IX.

1391, Ferrara; Boniface IX; this university had been established by muncipal statutes since 1263.

Fifteenth Century

Würzburg, 1403; Turin, 1405; Aix, in Provence, 1409; Leipzig, 1409; St. Andrews, Scotland, 1412; Rostock, 1419; Dôle, 1423; Louvain, 1426; Poitiers, 1431; Caen, 1436; Bordeaux, 1441; Catana, 1445; Valence, in France, 1452;

Treves, Glasgow, 1454; Freiburg, Greifswald, 1456; Basel, 1459; Nantes, 1460; Besançon, 1464; Bourges, 1469; Ingolstadt, 1472; Saragossa, 1474; Copenhagen, 1475; Upsala, 1476; Tübingen, Mayence, 1477; Parma, 1482.

Sixteenth Century

Aberdeen, 1506; Königsberg, 1542; Jena, 1552; Leyden, 1575; Edinburgh, 1582; etc.

VII

PETRARCH AND THE GREATER
RENAISSANCE

"This therefore will be a fitting order of learning: First, let the young be instructed in Logic, since Logic gives the method of all Philosophy. Secondly, they are to be taught mathematics, which neither demand experience nor transcend imagination.

"Thirdly, in Natural Philosophy; which although not exceeding sense and imagination, nevertheless needs experience.

"Fourthly, in Moral Science; which demands experience and a soul free from passions.

"Fifthly, in things wise and divine (*sapientalibus et divinis*); which transcend imagination and demand a strong intelligence." [1]

In the renaissance which is commonly called the lesser, but which may in fact have been the greater, the Christian Church appropriated what it found of Greek learning among the Arabs and the Jews and then what it could come upon in purer form among the Greeks themselves. For it Greek learning meant the works of Aristotle in Latin translations, the medical works of Hippocrates and Galen; the writings of the Church Fathers, and the law books of Justinian—a rather formidable addition to the instruc-

[1] From St. Thomas Aquinas, *In Libros Ethicorum ad Nicomachum,* VI–7, quoted in McNabb's *The Catholic Church and Philosophy,* 62.

tion material of the western world, and so diligently
studied that it became part of the structure of the time.
But antiquity had other lessons as well as these, and
there came a time when other men set about studying
them.

Francesco Petrarca (1304–1374) is the prime mover of
the Renaissance, but before him is a servant of humanity whose work of colossal proportions portrays actual
happenings on earth under the guise of an Inferno, the
repenting of and forgiveness of sins in the Purgatorio,
and the beatific vision of the blessed saints in the Para-
diso. Dante's *Divine Comedy* is the supreme glorification
of scholastic and mystic learning. "I judged that Philosophy was a thing supreme, and I conceived her after
the fashion of a gentle lady, and I might not conceive
her in any attitude save that of compassion; wherefore the sense for truth so loved to gaze upon her that
I could scarce turn it away from her; and impelled by
this imagination of her, I began to go where she was in
very truth revealed, to wit to the schools of the religious
orders, and to the disputations of the philosophers; so
that in a short time, I suppose some thirty months, I began to feel so much of her sweetness that the love of her
expelled and destroyed every other thought." [2]

Dante began the *Commedia* in Latin but soon turned
to the Italian language, in which he wrote every one of
his books save only his defence of the imperial government, the *De Monarchia*. He defended his abandon-
ing of the historic and sacred language of Rome and his
employment of the modern speech in outline in the *Convivio* and more at length in his book *De Vulgari Eloquio*.
The Italian, he said, is understood both by the unlettered and by the lettered; it is more plastic than the Latin

[2] Convivio, II–XIII (Temple Classics).

and "I was moved thereto by the natural love of my own tongue." By his use of the Italian language he became the founder of Italian literature, and by breaking the monopoly of Latin he opened the way for all the modern languages. Dante was a layman, not a priest or monk. His interest in learning is that of a man not of the Church, but of the world. Pagan lore and Christian lore mingle in him, but the pagan serves the Christian. In a peculiar sense he stands with one foot in the Middle Ages, the other in the new world. He sings the Divine Wisdom, but the poet Virgil, personifying human reason, guides him in his course. "While I was hurrying downward toward those depths, there presented himself before mine eyes one who seemed enfeebled by long silence. When I beheld this being in the wide wilderness, 'Have compassion on me,' I exclaimed to him, 'whatsoe'er Thou art, whether a spirit or very man.' 'Not a man,' he replied to me; 'I was once a man, and my parents were Lombards, both of them from Mantua as their fatherland. Under Julius was I born, though late in time, and I lived at Rome beneath the good Augustus' sway, in the days of the false and spurious gods. A poet I was, and I sang of Anchises' son the just, who came from Troy after proud Ilion was consumed by fire. But why art thou returning to so dread annoy? Why dost Thou not ascend the gladsome mountain, which is the origin and source of all joy?' 'Say, art Thou that Virgil, that fountain-head whence flows so copious a stream of speech?' Thus with reverent brow did I make answer to him. 'Thou glory and light of all other poets, may the long study and ardent love avail me, which hath caused me closely to con thy volume. Thou art my master and my authority: Thou and Thou only art he from whom I derived the fair style which has won me honour."

After the long and painful journey through Hell and Purgatory, when at last the Lady "crowned with olive over a white vail, and wearing beneath a green mantle a robe of the colour of living flame" appears, then "so soon as the sublime power, which even before I emerged from boyhood had pierced me through and through, smote me on the face, I turned me leftward with that confidence, wherewith a young child hastes to its mother when assailed by fear or grief, to say to Virgil: 'To the last drop my blood is quivering; I recognize the tokens of my ancient flame.' But Virgil had left us bereaved of his presence, Virgil my most tender father, Virgil, to whom for my salvation I surrendered myself; nor did all the joys which our first mother lost avail to prevent my cheeks, which had been cleansed with dew, from being once more stained with tears." [3]

To Dante, Virgil is both human reason and the greatest of Roman poets, and Beatrice is the woman of his lifelong love as well as the personification of heavenly intelligence. "From that time forward Love quite governed my soul . . . and albeit her image that was with me always was an exultation of Love to subdue me, it was yet of so perfect a quality that it never allowed me to be overruled by love without the faithful counsel of reason whensoever such counsel was useful to be heard." [4] "That blessed Beatrice who liveth in heaven with the angels and on earth with my soul. This lady the most perfect in the human generation, but more than most perfect, in so far as she receives of the divine excellence beyond the due of humanity." [5]

Petrarch's passion for Laura was not so overweighted

[3] *Hell*, I, 61–87, *Purgatory*, XXX, 31–54 (transl. H. F. Tozer).
[4] *The Vita Nuova*, Rossetti, *Dante and His Circle*, 31.
[5] *Convivio*, II, 2; III, 6.

with heavenly consideration, while Boccaccio's relation to Fiammetta was blasphemously carnal, but human love was the theme of each of them.

Collections, such as D. G. Rossetti made, show that there was a vast industry of love making and poetry writing in Lombard Italy in and before Dante's day. Strangely enough, though the Church abode at Rome, Italy was secularized far beyond France, England, Germany, or any other country of Europe. The reason was the free cities of Italy, which dared to think of themselves as second Romes and to stand out against Pope and Emperor and in that long struggle to shrewdly play the game of the balance of power. The second Rome had need of Virgils of its own and reborn Ciceros to carry on the work of the men of old.

Petrarch is and always will be best known for his amatory poetry, in which only his contemporary Dante surpassed him. These sonnets of his youth are in Italian and are so perfectly wrought that even Petrarch himself expressed his inability to improve them for in them: "I think I have reached the highest perfection I can attain." [6] Lyric poetry is notoriously difficult to translate from one language to another. Petrarch's sonnets depend so completely upon their form, metre, assonances, and Italian rhymes that it is said they cannot be translated, no matter whose the effort. In spite of his matchless perfection in Italian rhyme, Petrarch set greater store by his Latin epic poem, *Africa,* in which he celebrates the works and days of Scipio Africanus. That poem, though he talked much of it, he never finished; and accordingly he became sensitive about having it referred to. Like Erasmus and Thomas Jefferson, Petrarch was an incessant letter writer. On one fatal day in 1359

[6] In Foulke, *Some Love Songs of Petrarch,* 9.

he burned a thousand or more papers. A "few" lying in a corner escaped destruction. Them he divided into twenty-four books of prose letters dedicated to that friend whom he called Socrates (Lewis of Campinia), and three books of poetic letters dedicated to Marco Barbato. These letters of Petrarch were many of them Latin essays, sometimes of considerable length on the subject of which they treated. Most interesting among them are his letters to dead authors, and the world cannot be thankful enough that his particular form of vanity caused him very thoughtfully to write a long letter to Posterity which should, if it could, be reproduced entire but must, that Petrarch may be allowed to tell his own story, be outlined:

"Francesco Petrarca to Posterity—Greeting, It is possible that some word of me may have come to you, though even this is doubtful, since an insignificant and obscure name will scarcely penetrate far in either time or space. If, however, you have heard of me, you may desire to know what manner of man I was, or what was the outcome of my labours, . . . I was in truth a poor mortal like yourself, neither very exalted in my origin, nor, on the other hand, of the most humble birth, but belonging as Augustus Caesar says of himself, to an ancient family. I was not naturally perverse or wanting in modesty. . . . My youth was gone before I realized it; I was carried away by the strength of manhood; but a riper age brought me to my senses and taught me by experience the truth I had long before read in books, that youth and pleasure are vanity . . . In my prime I was blessed with a quick and active body, although not exceptionally strong; and while I do not lay claim to remarkable beauty, I was comely enough in my best days . . .

"My parents were honourable folk, Florentine in their origin, of medium fortune, or I may as well admit it, in a condition verging upon poverty. They had been expelled from their native city [on the same day that Dante was driven into exile in 1302], and consequently I was born in exile at Arezzo, in the year 1304 of this latter age which begins with Christ's birth, July the twentieth, on a Monday, at dawn. I have always possessed an extreme contempt for wealth; not that riches are not desirable in themselves, but because I hate the anxiety and care, which are invariably associated with them. I certainly do not wish to be able to give gorgeous banquets. I have on the contrary led a happier existence with plain living and ordinary fare than all the followers of Apicius with their elaborate dainties. . . . On the other hand, the pleasure of dining with one's friends is so great that none has ever given me more delight than their unexpected arrival, nor have I ever willingly sat down to table without a companion.

"I struggled in my younger days with a keen but constant and pure attachment, and would have struggled with it longer had not the sinking flame been extinguished by death—premature and bitter but salutary. I should be glad to be able to say that I had always been entirely free from irregular desires, but I should lie if I did so . . .

"I have taken pride in others, never in myself, and however insignificant I may have been, I have always been still less important in my own judgment . . . I have always been most desirous of honourable friendships, and have faithfully cherished them . . . In my familiar association with kings and princes, and in my friendship with noble personages, my good fortune has been such as to excite envy . . . The greatest kings of this age have loved and courted me. They may know why; I certainly do not. With some of them I was on such terms that they seemed in a certain sense my guests rather than I theirs; . . . I possessed a well-balanced rather than a keen intellect, one prone to all kinds of good and wholesome study, but especially inclined to moral philosophy and the art of poetry. The latter, indeed, I neglected as time went on, and took delight in sacred literature . . . Among the many subjects which interested me, I dwelt especially upon antiquity, for our own age has always repelled me, so that had it not been for the love of those dear to me, I should have preferred to have been born at any other period than our own. In order to forget my own time I have constantly striven to place myself in spirit in other ages. . . . My life up to the present has, either through fate or my own choice, fallen into the following divisions. A part only of my first year was spent at Arezzo, where I first saw the light. The six following years were, owing to the recall of my mother from exile, spent upon my father's estate at Ancisa, about fourteen miles from Florence. I passed my eighth year at Pisa, the ninth and following years at Farther Gaul, at Avignon, on the left bank of the Rhone, where the Roman Pontiff holds and has long held the Church of Christ in shameful exile . . .

"On the windy banks of the river Rhone I spent my boyhood, guided by my parents, and then guided by my own fancies, the whole of my youth. Yet there were long intervals spent elsewhere, for I first passed four years at the little town of Carpentras, somewhat to the east of Avignon: in these two places I learned as much of grammar, logic and rhetoric as my age permitted, or rather, as much as it is customary to teach in school: how little that is, dear reader, thou knowest. I then set out for Montpellier to study law, and spent four years there, then three at Bologna. I heard the whole body of the Civil Law, and would, as many thought, have distinguished myself later, had I but continued my studies. I gave up the subject altogether, however, as soon as it was no longer necessary to consult the wishes of my parents. My reason was that, although the dignity of the law, which is doubtless very great, and especially the numerous references it contains to Roman antiquity, did not fail to delight me, I felt it to be habitually degraded by those who practise it. It went against me painfully to acquire an art which I would not practise dishonestly, and could hardly hope to exercise otherwise. Had I made the latter attempt my scrupulousness would doubtless have been ascribed to simplicity.

"So at the age of two and twenty I returned home. I call my place of exile home, Avignon, where I had been since childhood; for habit has almost the potency of nature itself. I had already begun to be known there, and my friendship was sought by prominent men; wherefore I cannot say. I confess this is now a source of surprise to me, although it seemed natural enough at an age when we are used to regard ourselves as worthy of the highest respect. I was courted first and foremost by that very distinguished and noble family, the Colonnesi, who, at that period, adorned the Roman Curia with their presence. However it might be now, I was at that time certainly quite unworthy of the esteem in which I was held by them. I was especially honoured by the incomparable Giacomo Colonna, then bishop of Lombez, whose peer I know not whether I have ever seen or ever shall see, and was taken by him to Gascony; there I spent such a divine summer among the foothills of the Pyrenees in happy intercourse with my master and the members of our company, that I can never recall the experience without a sigh of regret. Returning thence I passed many years in the house of Giacomo's brother, Cardinal Giovanni Colonna, not as if he were my lord and master, but rather my father, or better, a most affectionate brother—nay, it was as if I were in my own home. About this time, a youthful desire impelled me to visit France and Germany. While I invented certain reasons to satisfy my elders of the propriety of the journey, the real explanation was a great inclination and longing to see new sights. I first visited Paris, as I was anxious to discover what was true and what fabulous in the accounts I had heard of that city. On my return from this journey, I went to Rome, which I had since my infancy ardently desired to visit. There I soon came to venerate Stephano, the noble head of the family of the Colonnesi, like some ancient hero, and was in turn treated by him in every respect like a son. The love and good will of this excellent man toward me remained constant to the end of his life, and lives in me still, nor will it cease until I myself pass away.

"On my return, since I experienced a deep-seated and innate repugnance to town life, especially in that disgusting city of Avignon which I heartily abhorred, I sought some means of escape. I fortunately discovered, about fifteen miles from Avignon, a delightful valley, narrow and secluded, called Vaucluse, where the Sorgue, the prince of streams, takes its rise. Captivated by the charms of the place, I transferred thither myself and my books. Were I to describe what I did there during many years it would prove a long story. Indeed, almost every bit of writing which I have put forth was either accomplished or begun, or at least conceived there, and my undertakings have been so numerous that they still continue to vex and weary me." [7]

There are few spots of earth more worth seeing than the place where the Sorgue rushes out from the base of a mighty cliff and at once shapes itself within its banks into a fat little river—"the prince of streams," but a playful boy prince. It was there where the river gushes forth from the rock that Petrarch planted his garden and kept his house. While he was a schoolboy at Carpentras his father had taken him one day on an excursion to that celebrated place. "I remember as though it had happened today how I was moved by the strange beauty of the spot and how I spoke my boyish thoughts to myself as well as I could, to this effect: Here is the place which best suits with my temper, and which, if ever I have the chance, I will prefer before great cities." And now at the age of thirty-three he makes his home there. He is away some of the time on long journeys to Italy, stopping for weeks and months at Padua, Parma, Verona, Florence, Rome, and Arezzo. In 1350 he meets Boccaccio at Florence, and Francesco di Nello Rinucai and Jacopo da Castiglionchio. With each of them he has already been in correspondence about their common studies. He is in Avignon from time to time, but only when compelled to go there. The Sorgue is his place and he returns to it with great gladness. "Here the only sounds are the occasional lowing of cattle and bleating of sheep, the songs of the birds, and the ceaseless murmur of the stream . . . My herdsman's bread is often enough for me, and I even enjoy it . . . Grapes, figs, nuts and almonds are my delicacies. And I thoroughly enjoy the little fish which abound in this river, especially the catching of them, a

[7] In Robinson and Rolfe, *Petrarch*, 59 *et seq.* Foulke, *Some Love Songs of Petrarch*, 216. Reeve, *Petrarch*, 17.

pursuit in which I am most diligent, and very fond of handling both hook and net. What shall I tell you of my clothes and shoes? They are changed from top to toe. Not such was my old fashion . . . Now you would take me for a ploughman or a shepherd . . . And what can I tell you of my dwelling? You might take it for the house of Cato or Fabricius. There I live with a single dog and only two servants . . . It is a place to fire the soul to study, and I think not unlike the little court where Cicero used to declaim his speeches, except that his place had no Sorgue flowing by it. Under this grotto, then, I sit at noon, my morning is spent on the hills, my evening in the meadows or in that wilder little garden, close to the source where design has embellished nature . . . I might well spend my life here, if it were not at once so far from Italy and so near to Avignon." [8]

"By my bailiff's death yesterday not only does my farm run the risk of neglect, but my library, which is my adopted daughter, has lost her guardian . . . I think earth never bore a more loyal creature . . . And so I had given into his charge myself, my property, and all the books which I have in Gaul; and whereas my shelves contain every sort and size of volume, mixed big and little together, and I myself have often been absent for long periods, never once on my return have I found a single volume missing, or even moved from its proper place. Though unlettered himself, he had a devotion to letters, and he took special pains with the books he knew I valued most. Much handling of them had by this time taught him to know the works of the ancients by name, and to distinguish my own small treatises from them. He would beam with delight whenever I gave him a book to hold, and would clasp it to his bosom with a sigh.

[8] In Hollway-Calthrop, *Petrarch: His Life and Times*, 161.

Sometimes under his breath he would call upon its author by name, and strange as it may sound, the mere touch of the books gave him an enjoyable feeling of advancement in learning. And now I have lost this excellent guardian of my property, with whom for fifteen years I have been wont to share all my troubles, who was to me, so to speak, as a priest of Ceres, and whose house served me for a temple of fidelity." [9]

At Vaucluse, Petrarch carried on his studies and his incessant writing. Writing, he indicates, was nearly an obsession with him. "Strangely enough I long to write, but do not know what or to whom. This inexorable passion has such a hold upon me that pen, ink, and paper, and work prolonged far into the night, are more to my liking than repose and sleep. In short, I find myself always in a sad and languishing state when I am not writing, and anomalous though it seems, I labor when I rest, and find rest in labor. . . . Is it then true that this disease of writing, like other malignant disorders, is, as the Satirist claims, incurable, and as I begin to fear, contagious as well? How many, do you reckon, have caught it from me? Within our memory it was rare enough for people to write verses. But now there is no one who does not write them; few indeed write anything else. Some think that the fault, so far as our contemporaries are concerned, is largely mine . . . I am now at last suddenly awakened . . . to a consciousness that this may perhaps be true . . . Our sons formerly employed themselves in preparing such papers as might be useful to themselves or their friends, relating to family affairs, business, or the wordy din of the courts. Now we are all engaged in the same occupation, and it is literally true, as Horace says, 'learned or unlearned, we are all writ-

[9] In Hollway-Calthrop, *op. cit.,* 165.

ing verses alike.' It is after all but a poor consolation
to have companions in misery. I should prefer to be ill
by myself. Now I am involved in others' ill-fortune as
well as in my own, and am hardly given time to take
breath. For every day letters and poems from every
corner of our land come showering down upon my devoted
head. Nor does this satisfy my foreign friends. I am
overwhelmed by floods of missives, no longer from France
alone, but from Greece, from Germany, from England. I
am unable to judge even my own work, and yet I am
called upon to be the universal critic of others. Were
I to answer the requests in detail I should be the busiest
of mortals . . . But all this would be nothing if, incredible as it may seem, this subtle poison had not just now
begun to show its effects in the Roman Curia itself.
What do you think the lawyers and doctors are up to?
Justinian and Aesculapius have palled upon them. The
sick and the litigious cry in vain for their help, for they
are deafened by the thunder of Homer's and Virgil's
names, and wander oblivious in the woody valleys of
Cirrha, by the purling waters of the Aonian fountain.
But it is hardly necessary to speak of these lesser prodigies. Even carpenters, fullers, and ploughmen leave the
implements of their calling to talk of Apollo and the
Muses. I cannot say how far the plague, which lately
was confined to a few, has now spread." [10]

Petrarch was aflame for honor. In his Ode to Fame
he is more than sufficiently frank about that.

> A lady fairer far than is the day,
> And brighter than the sun, and just as old,
>   With face of rarest mould,
> Won me in youth to join her bright array.

[10] In Robinson and Rolfe, *Petrarch,* 162.

In thought and word and action did she go
　In stately majesty
Ever before me (rare it was to see!)
On all the thousand paths that men do know.
　For her I ceased to be
What I had been, and soon as I could bear
To look upon her presence, for her love
I did devote my life to toil and care.
Now if I win the port whereto I move,
　By her sweet guidance led,
Long do I hope to live, after men deem me dead.[11]

It chanced—not altogether without Petrarch's com-
plicity, it is said—that on one and the same day (September 1, 1340) letters came to him from the Senate at
Rome and from the chancellor of the University of Paris,
asking him to come, the one to Rome, the other to Paris,
to receive at their hands the poet's crown of laurel.
Petrarch debated with himself and with his friend, Cardinal Giovanni Colonna, perhaps for no long time, and
finally "recognized the claims of Rome as superior to
all others." Off he went forthwith from Vaucluse to
claim the coveted honor. To miss no glory by the way,
he decided to stop at Naples for some public preliminaries
involving King Robert, whose reputation for taste and
culture could not but add lustre to Petrarch's enterprise.
After the King had talked over Petrarch's accomplishments with him he was so moved that he offered to
laureate him forthwith himself. This did not fit in with
Petrarch's more ambitious plans, but King Robert made
another proposal which did, i.e., that he should stage a
public examination of Petrarch's fitness to receive the
crown, there in the royal court. That pleased Petrarch
entirely, and the King made proclamation of the great

[11] CXIX, in Foulke, *Some Love Songs of Petrarch*, 106.

event and gathered his entire court about him. Placing
Petrarch in their midst, he consumed two and a half
days in questioning him on every then known form of
human learning. Two and a half days of public questioning sounds like an ordeal, but we may believe that
this was no ordeal but a house party, rather. At its end
the King pronounced him worthy to receive the poet's
crown and, giving him his own purple robe to wear at the
ceremony and a deputy to attend him, sped him on his
way to Rome to receive it. In a less pretentious time
these things would be known for what they were, publicity efforts. They were publicity efforts then, and they
succeeded in their purpose. The only mishap that marred
the splendid ceremony at Rome was that King Robert's
personal deputy fell into the hands of bandits on the
way and did not get away from them until some days
after the date on which Petrarch had to be crowned,
for no day would do for that save Easter morning. Accordingly, on April 8, 1341, the people of Rome were
assembled by the sound of the trumpet. "Twelve boys
arrayed in scarlet, each fifteen years old, and all sons
of distinguished nobles and citizens, declaimed many
verses composed by Petrarch in praise of the Roman
people. After them came six citizens dressed in green
cloth, and wearing wreaths of flowers of various kinds.
Then the Senator (Orso del Anguillara) strode forward,
his head decorated with a laurel wreath, and after he
had seated himself on the chair in the Hall of the As-
settamento, Francesco Petrarca was summoned by trumpet and fife, and advanced clothed in a long garment and
cried three times, 'Long live the Roman people, long
live its Senators, and God maintain it in its freedom,'
and then he kneeled before the Senator, who said, 'I first
crown merit,' and took the wreath from his own head

and put it on that of Master Francesco, who declaimed
a beautiful sonnet in praise of the brave old Romans,
and the festival was ended with great praise of the poet,
since the whole people cried, 'Long live the Capitol and
the poet!' " [12]

This was a civic, not an ecclesiastical, ceremony—a
Roman custom revived.

From Rome, Petrarch went to his friend Azzo di Cor-
reggio at Parma, with whom he remained about a year.
The election of a new Pope called him back to Avignon
in 1342. The Pope sent him from Vaucluse to Naples
on a diplomatic mission in 1345. On his way back he
found at Verona a codex of Cicero's *Letters*. In 1347
he was so greatly interested in Cola di Rienzo's restoration of the ancient republican government of Rome that
he set out to join him; but that enterprise failed before
he had gone farther than Genoa, and Petrarch instead
of going on to Rome went to Parma, where his welcome
by the Visconti lord of the city was so engaging that he
built a house and planted an orchard. The plague robbed
him of his patron, and next we find him at Padua, welcomed, he says, by its ruler as the blessed are in heaven.
In 1350 he saw Florence for the first time, met Boccaccio face to face, and was offered a professorship in the
newly founded university, which he declined. In 1351
he was again at Vaucluse. In 1353 he left that region forever and scandalized his friends by going to live with the
Visconti, lords of Milan, who supplied him money for the
purchase and copying of books and used him on diplomatic missions. The plague drove him away from Milan
in 1361, and the people of Venice gave him a house in
return for his undertaking to leave his library to their

[12] A contemporary account in Koerting, *Petrarca's Leben und Werke*,
quoted in Foulke, *op. cit.*, 41.

city. After five years there he moved to Padua to live with Francesco di Carrara. But the palace was too noisy, and a quiet retreat was found for him at Arqua, about twelve miles from Padua, where he spent the last four years of his life and on the morning of July 18, 1374, was found dead crumpled down over the book which he had been reading.

Such was the father of humanism, the prime mover of the Renaissance. He never lectured in a university or taught a class in a school, yet he was the teacher preeminent, in literal truth the preceptor of the world. While but a boy he had been charmed by the sound of Cicero's words when read aloud. They continued to charm him. "In this susceptibility to the melodies of rhetorical prose, in this special cult of Cicero, in the passion for collecting manuscripts and in the intuition that the future of scholarship depended upon the resuscitation of Greek studies, Petrarch initiated the four most important momenta of the classical Renaissance," says John Addington Symonds.[12a]

"You are well aware that from early boyhood of all the writers of all ages and of all races the one author whom I most admire and love is Cicero . . . Christ is my God; Cicero, on the other hand, is the prince of the language I use."[13]

"O Thou great father of Roman eloquence! Not only I but all who take delight in the elegance of the Latin tongue render thee great thanks. Thou art the fountainhead from which we draw the vivifying waters for our meadows. We frankly confess that we have been guided by thee, assisted by thy judgments, enlightened by thy radiance; and, finally, that it was under thy auspices, so

[12a] *The Revival of Learning*, 53.
[13] In Cosenza, *Petrarch's Letters to Classical Authors*, 18.

to speak, that I have gained this ability as a writer (such as it is), and that I have attained my purpose.

"For the realms of poetry, however, there was at hand a second guide. The nature of the case demanded that there should be two leaders—one whom I might follow in the unencumbered ways of prose, and the other in the more restricted paths of poetry . . . Thou wilt know the man at once, if Thou art merely reminded of his name. It is Publius Vergilius Maro, a citizen of Mantua, of whom Thou didst prophesy such great things. For we have read that when Thou, then advanced in years, hadst admired some youthful effort of his, Thou didst inquire its author's name, and that having seen the young man, Thou didst express Thy great delight. And then, drawing on Thy unexhausted fount of eloquence, Thou didst pronounce upon him a judgment which, though mingled with self-praise, was nevertheless both honorable and splendid for him: 'Rome's other hope and stay.' " [14]

Petrarch was always travelling, incessantly going back and forth from France to Italy and from one to another of the cities of the peninsula. Sometimes he went farther afield. "Whenever I took a far journey," he says, "I would turn aside to any old monasteries that I chanced to see in the distance, saying: 'Who knows whether some scrap of the writings I covet may not lie here?' Thus about the twenty-fifth year of my age, in the course of a hurried journey among the Belgians and Swiss, I came to Liége, and hearing that there was a good quantity of books there, I stayed and detained my companions while I copied out one of Cicero's speeches with my own hand and another by the hand of a friend, which I afterward published throughout Italy. And to give you a

[14] Cosenza, *op. cit.*, 22.

laugh, I may tell you that in this fine barbaric city it was a hard matter to find a drop of ink, and what we did get was exactly the color of saffron." [15] An ardent desire to recover that which was lost made him hunt without ceasing for all the works of Cicero, of Quintilian, and every other bit of Roman literature that he could in any way come upon. Some success attended his efforts, but his greatest service was not in finding much himself but in causing many others to enlist in the same search for the neglected writings of antiquity.

The fourth and perhaps the greatest of the activities which Petrarch initiated was the study of Greek. In spite of all the effort which his great eagerness to read that language caused him to put forth, he was not able to accomplish that in his own person. He left it as an obligation to those who came after him. In January of 1354, the Greek general, Nicholas Sygerus, sent him a manuscript copy of Homer's poems in Greek. "From the extremity of Europe," Petrarch writes in acknowledging this gift, "you have sent me a present, the worthiest of yourself, the most acceptable to me, the noblest in intrinsic value that it was possible for you to send . . . What gift could come more appropriately from a man of your talent and eloquence than the very fountain-head of all talent and eloquence? So you have given me Homer whom Ambrose and Macrobius have well named the fount and origin of all divine imagination . . . Your gift would be complete indeed, if only you could give me your own presence together with Homer's so that under your guidance I might enter on the strait path of a foreign language and enjoy your gift in the happy fulfilment of my own wish . . . Your voice, if only I could hear it, would both excite and assuage the thirst of learning that pos-

[15] Hollway-Calthrop, *op. cit.*, 43.

sesses me; but it reaches not my ears, and without it your Homer is dumb to me, or rather I am deaf to him. Nevertheless, I rejoice in the mere sight of him; often I clasp him to my bosom and exclaim with a sigh, 'Oh, great man! How do I long to understand thy speech!' . . . Take then my thanks for your exceeding bounty. Strange to say, Plato, the prince of the philosophers, was already in my house, sent to me from the west . . . Now through your generosity the Greek prince of poets joins the prince of philosophers." [16]

Long before that gift came, in 1339 in fact, Barlaam of Calabria, who at the time was abbot of the monastery of St. Salvator at Constantinople had come to Avignon on a mission from the Emperor to do something to reunite the churches. In 1342 Barlaam was again at Avignon as a refugee, and Petrarch arranged to give him Latin lessons in exchange for instruction in Greek. But before that had gone far the bishop of Gerace in Calabria died, and Petrarch urged the Pope to appoint Barlaam to the vacant bishopric—which was done, thus bringing an end to Petrarch's Greek studies. Petrarch had one further adventure with Greek. In 1363 Boccaccio came to spend three months in his house at Venice and brought another Calabrian Greek, Leontius Pilatus, who claimed to be a pupil of Barlaam. This seemingly insufficiently qualified scholar Boccaccio had already (1360) caused to be appointed Professor of Greek at the University of Florence. Petrarch and Boccaccio had some time before put Leontius Pilatus to translating the manuscript Homer which Nicholas Sygerus had sent. The work was, it would seem, hardly well done, but such as it was, the translation gave Petrarch infinite delight. In his letter to Homer, Petrarch tells him that there are five

[16] Hollway-Calthrop, *op. cit.*, 185.

men in Florence, that "city so given over to mammon," who are faithful to him, and six scattered through other cities of Italy. "As to these barbarians by whom we are encircled they have not heard of thy name."

These were his interests; more literally, these were his passions. Near the end of a long life spent in stirring other minds in papal and courtly circles, and indeed wherever he could come upon them, to eagerness similar to his own, Petrarch could say as he did in 1372: "I read, I write, I think, this is my life, this is my delight, just as it has been ever since the days of my youth." To Boccaccio he wrote: ". . . You say in praise of me that throughout Italy, and very likely beyond Italy, too, I have stirred up the wits of many to engage in these studies of ours, which were neglected for so many centuries; and this credit I do not disclaim, for I am older than nearly all those who are now working at these subjects in our country . . . I am not fit for other labors; but this of reading and writing, in which you bid me slacken, is light toil, nay rather 'tis a pleasant rest and breeds forgetfulness of heavy labors. There is no nimbler or more delightful burden than the pen; other pleasures flee away, and do you a mischief even while they soothe you; your pen soothes you in the taking up, and delights you in the laying down of it; and it works profit not only to its master but to many besides, often to the absent, and sometimes to posterity after thousands of years. I think I speak absolute truth when I say that of all earthly delights, as there is none more honorable than literature, so there is none more lasting or sweeter or more constant; none which plays the comrade to its possessor with so easily gotten an equipment or with so total a lack of irksomeness . . . This do I desire for myself, that when death overtakes me he may find me either reading or writing, or, if Christ so will it, praying and in tears." [17]

Of Petrarch's spiritual sons who carried on the enterprise which the master started the chief responsibility fell to Boccaccio, whom Petrarch had saved for literature when, possessed by a baneful dream, he was all but terrified into abjuring it. Giovanni Boccaccio, who always insisted he was Petrarch's pupil, was but a little younger than Petrarch, having been born at Certaldo in 1313 and dying there in 1375. That little town is but twenty miles from Florence. Boccaccio, the third of that second greatest trinity of men that the world has produced, is by blood, accomplishment, and most of the desires of his heart, one of the other two. In his old age he met a Franciscan monk in Naples who said to him: "God has been moved to compassion for the Italian name . . . For in our days great men have descended from heaven, unless I am mistaken, gifted with great souls, who have brought back poetry from exile to her ancient throne." [18] Boccaccio's own conception of poetry, though he was the creative artist who fixed the prose style of Italy, was that poetry includes all that is weighty in argument, deep in doctrine, and vivid in imagination that conscious art may produce in prose or verse. Poetry is instruction through allegory and fiction.[19]

It was with difficulty that he came to his life work. His father, a banker, designed his son for a commercial life and put him to clerking in an office. Of Boccaccio's struggle and its outcome Filippo Villani has this account: "After wandering through many lands, now here, now there, for a long space of time, when he had reached his

[17] Hollway-Calthrop, *op. cit.*, 294, 300.
[18] Edward Hutton, *Giovanni Boccaccio*, 221.
[19] Symonds, *The Revival of Learning*, 69.

twenty-eighth year, Boccaccio, at his father's bidding, took up his abode in Naples in the Pergola. There it chanced one day that he walked forth alone for pleasure and came to the place where Virgil's dust lies buried. At the sight of this sepulchre, he fell into long musing admiration of the man whose bones it covered, brooding with meditative soul upon the poet's fame, until his thoughts found vent in lamentations over his own envious fortunes, whereby he was compelled against his will to give himself to things of commerce that he loathed. A sudden love of the Pierian Muses smote his heart, and turning homeward, he abandoned trade, devoting himself with fervent study to poetry; wherein very shortly, aided alike by his noble genius and his burning desire, he made marvellous progress. This when his father noted, and perceived the heavenly inspiration was more powerful within his son than the paternal will, he at last consented to his studies, and helped him as best he could, although at first he tried to make him turn his talents to the canon law." [20]

Edward Hutton says of Boccaccio that of the great trinity who opened literature to the modern world he was perhaps the most significant member, for his concern was this human world alone and it was his mission to oppose to the Divine Comedy the Human Comedy, the *Decameron*, which was to exert a shaping influence upon all literature for three hundred years. That, together with his active partnership with Petrarch, is our concern with him. As a creative artist, Boccaccio far surpassed Petrarch, who won him away from producing literature in Italian to producing works of scholarship like the *De Genealogiis Deorum* in Latin. That was certainly a doubtful service to the Muses, for Boccaccio succeeded in being but an

[20] In Symonds, *op. cit.*, 64.

indifferent scholar in the things which Petrarch most valued; but for Petrarch himself his adoration was extreme. To him, Petrarch was the marvel and glory of his time, "a man descended from heaven to restore to poetry her throne." Of him he writes in a letter to Jacopo Pizzinghe: "The illustrious Francesco neglecting the precepts of certain writers who scarcely attain to the threshold of poetry, began to take the way to antiquity with so much force of character, with such enthusiasm and perspicacity, that no obstacle would arrest him, nor could ridicule turn him from his way. Far from that, breaking through and tearing way the brambles and bushes with which by the negligence of men the road was covered, and remaking a solid road of the rocks heaped up and made impassable by inundations, he opened a passage for himself and for those who would come after him . . ." [21]

Boccaccio and Petrarch met in Florence for the first time in 1350. In the following year the government of Florence sent Boccaccio on a special embassy to Petrarch at Padua with a letter which read: "No long time since, seeing our city deprived of learning and study, we wisely decided that henceforth the arts must flourish and ought to be cultivated among us, and that it would be necessary to introduce studies of every sort into our city so that by their help our Republic, like Rome of old, should be glorious above the other cities of Italy and grow always more happy and more illustrious. Now our fatherland believes you are the one and only man by whom this result can be attained. The Republic prays you, then, as warmly as it may, to give yourself to these studies and to make them flourish." [22]

[21] Edward Hutton, *op. cit.*, 229.
[22] Hutton, *op. cit.*, 158.

But Petrarch was not persuaded. That time Boccaccio stayed with him some days making copies for himself of Petrarch's writings. In 1359 he began his four years' study of Greek with Leontius Pilatus, and some time after 1365 he was at last able to send Petrarch the Latin version of the *Iliad* and *Odyssey* which he and Leontius Pilatus had made. Boccaccio spent his whole life in writing, studying, and acting as ambassador for his fellow Florentines. He copied books, collected manuscripts, and read all the books of antiquity he could come upon. In the summer of 1373, when Boccaccio was sixty years old, some citizens of Florence petitioned the Signoria to appoint "a worthy and learned man well versed in the knowledge of the poems . . . to read the book which is commonly called *El Dante* in the city of Florence, to all such as shall be desirous of hearing him . . ." Boccaccio was appointed to do that. On Sunday October 23, 1373, he gave the first of his year's course of lectures in the Church of S. Stefano della Badia. That first, most devoted, and most eminent of the professors of modern literature not only copied out the *Divina Commedia* for Petrarch with his own hand, he also painstakingly composed a Life of Dante which is the most authoritative in existence.

Boccaccio, like Petrarch and every other humanist, was a collector of books and manuscripts. Benvenuto da Imola gives his master's account of one of his expeditions in search of them. "He said that when he was in Apulia, attracted by the celebrity of the convent, he paid a visit to Monte Cassino, whereof Dante speaks. Desirous of seeing the collection of books, which he understood to be a very choice one, he modestly asked a monk—for he was always most courteous in manners—to open the library, as a favor, for him. The monk an-

swered stiffly, pointing to a steep staircase, 'Go up; it
is open.' Boccaccio went up gladly; but he found that
the place which held so great a treasure, was without or
door or key. He entered and saw grass sprouting on the
windows, and all the books and benches thick with dust.
In his astonishment he began to open and turn the leaves
of first one tome and then another, and found many and
divers volumes of ancient and foreign works. Some of
them had lost several sheets; others were snipped and
pared all round the text, and mutilated in various ways. At
length, lamenting that the toil and study of so many illustrious men should have passed into the hands of most abandoned wretches, he departed with tears and sighs. Coming to the cloister, he asked a monk whom he met, why
those valuable books had been so disgracefully mangled.
He answered that the monks, seeking to gain a few *soldi,*
were in the habit of cutting off sheets and making psalters
which they sold to boys. The margins too they manufactured into charms, and sold to women. So then, O man
of study, go to and rack your brains; make books that
you may come to this!" [23]

John of Ravenna was even more active in spreading
Petrarch's influence. In 1365 Petrarch wrote a letter
from Pavia to Boccaccio in which he describes him.
"A year after your departure I had the good fortune to
secure the services of a fine, generous, young lad, whom
I am sorry you do not know. . . . The lad's own family and fortune are humble. But he is well endowed
nevertheless. He has a force of character and a power
of self-control that would be praiseworthy even in old
age; and a mind that is keen and flexible; and a memory
that is rapacious, and capacious, and best of all, tena-
cious. My bucolics, which are divided off into twelve

[23] Symonds, *op. cit.,* 97.

eclogues, as you know, he committed to memory within
eleven days, reciting one section to me each evening and
two the last time, repeating them without a single hitch,
as if he had the book before his eyes. Besides that, he
has himself a great deal of invention—a rare thing in
these days—and a fine enthusiasm, and a heart that
loves the Muses; and he is already, as Maro hath it,
making new songs of his own. . . . The lad has a decided leaning toward poetry; and if he perseveres in his
efforts, till in due time he learns to think clearly and
vigorously, he will compel your wonder and congratula-
tions . . . I am confident that he will develop vigor of
thought and expression, and work out as the result of
his experiments a style of his own, and learn to avoid
imitation or better to conceal it, so as to give the impression not of copying but rather of bringing to Italy
from the writers of old something new. Now, however,
imitation is his greatest joy, as is usual at his time of
life . . . The strongest of all these admirations is for
Virgil. It is marvellously strong. He thinks very many
of our poets worthy of praise but Virgil worthy almost of
worship . . ." [24]

After a time the secretary grew restless and ran away
to try his fortunes in the world. He did not succeed well
and penitently went back to Petrarch. Again he was
forced to leave home to make his own career. For a time
he was chancellor of Carrara; but that did not satisfy,
and he left it to take up the career of a wandering professor. Like the Sophists of old he went from town to
town of Italy lecturing to such as he could interest in
Cicero, Virgil, and the other Roman poets, spreading the
fire he had caught from Petrarch. The scholars of the
next generation were his pupils, almost all of them: Fran-

[24] Robinson and Rolfe, *Petrarch*, 287.

cesco Barbaro, Palla degli Strozzi, Roberto de' Rossi, Francesco Filelfo, Carlo Marsuppini, Poggio Bracciolini, Lionardo Bruni, Vittorino da Feltre, and the rest. It was through John of Ravenna that humanism was successfully planted among the governing groups of the Italian cities.

Petrarch laid his hands upon the head of another young Italian and gave him a mission. This time it was a young monk he sent forth, Luigi Marsigli, and the mission he gave him was to defend Christianity against the Averroists. That had become a common name for all sorts of antireligious thinkers. "There has arisen of late a set of dialecticians, who are not only ignorant but demented. Like a black army of ants from some old rotten log, they swarm forth from their hiding-places and devastate the fields of sound learning. They condemn Plato and Aristotle, and laugh at Socrates and Pythagoras. And, good God! under what silly and incompetent leaders these opinions are put forth! . . . Recently one of these philosophers of the modern stamp happened to be in my library. He did not, like the others, wear a religious habit, but after all Christianity is not a matter of clothes. He was one of those who think they live in vain unless they are constantly snarling at Christ or his divine teachings. When I cited some passage or other from the Holy Scriptures, he exploded with wrath, and with his face, naturally ugly, still further disfigured by anger and contempt, he exclaimed: 'You are welcome to your twopenny church fathers; as for me I know the man for me to follow, *for I know him whom I have believed!*' 'You,' I replied, 'use the words of the Apostle. I would that you would take them to heart!' 'Your Apostle,' he answered, 'was a sower of words and a lunatic.' 'You reply like a good philosopher,' I said. 'The first of your accusations was brought against him by other philosophers, and the second to his face by Festus, Governor of Syria. He did indeed sow the word, and with such success that cultivated by the beneficent plough of his successors and watered by the holy blood of the martyrs, it has borne such an abundant harvest of faith as we all behold.' At this he burst forth into a sickening roar of laughter. 'Well, be a "good Christian"! As for me I put no faith in all that stuff. Your Paul and your Augustine and all the rest of the crowd you preach were a set of babblers. If you could but stomach Averroës you would quickly see how much superior he was to these empty-headed fellows of yours . . . ' " [25]

The reverence which attached to the infallible Stagyrite had come to be shared with his great Arab interpreter. Petrarch urged Luigi Marsigli to fight against this rising tide of unbelief with the weapons of scholarship. Marsigli accordingly made his monastery of Santo Spirito a centre of learning—a sort of headquarters where students of the new studies gathered regularly to discuss the subjects of their interest. Maestro Luigi Marsigli says Vespasiano was a poet, a theologian and also very learned in "astrology, geometry, and arithmetic."

In the person of Coluccio Salutato, humanistic learning entered into government, as through Marsigli it had made a place for itself in the Church. Born in 1330, Salutato had sent his poems to Petrarch and had been commended for them. He was trained in the notary's art at Bologna, and in 1375 became cancellarius, or secretary, of the Republic of Florence. For thirty years the state papers of his draughting went to the other governments and were received by them as stylistic models of what diplomatic usage required. At his death in 1400 Salutato

[25] Robinson and Rolfe, *Petrarch*, 210.

was given a public funeral and crowned with laurel in his coffin.

John Addington Symonds has divided the Renaissance in Italy into four periods, each with a characteristic activity of its own. The first begins with Petrarch and includes the men he influenced. It is the age of inspiration. The second is the age of organization. In it the Greek classics are translated into Latin and the first libraries are founded. The third is the age of academies. The fourth is the age of puristic overrefinement.

The most significant event after Petrarch's initiation of the Renaissance was the coming of Manuel Chrysoloras to Italy in 1394 and 1399. Chrysoloras came on a mission from the Emperor Palaeologus to persuade the states of the West to arm against the Turks. He landed in Venice and was soon welcomed by two Florentines, Roberto de' Rossi and Giacomo d'Angelo da Scarparia. It soon appeared that his mission could not accomplish its purpose, and he and his companion Demetrios Kydonios returned to Constantinople; but Giacomoda Scarparia went with him, while Roberto de' Rossi went back to Florence and urged his fellow citizens to bring Chrysoloras back to teach Greek at their university. The Signoria was of a mind to do that, and a salary of 150 golden florins, afterward 250, was arranged for him. "This engagement," says Symonds, "secured the future of Greek erudition in Europe." Vespasiano declares that Palla degli Strozzi was the man who determined to raise the knowledge of Greek to a level with the knowledge of Latin: "Wherefore he brought into Italy Manuello Grisolora, a Greek, and paid the greater part of his charges. As Grisolora had no books, Messer Palla bought a number of Greek texts for him; the *Cosmographia di Tolomeo,* the Lives of Plutarch, the works of Plato and many more . . . Through Palla's introduction of Manuello Lionardo d'Arezzo, Guerino of Verona, Friar Ambrogio, Antonio Corbinegli, Roberto dei Rossi, Lionardo Gustini, Francesco Barbero, Piero Pagolo Vergerio, and Ser Filippo di Ser Ugolino, one of the finest Latin scholars of the time, became Manuello's pupils." [26]

What the coming of Chrysoloras to Florence meant to one student of this number he has himself told. "Then first came a knowledge of Greek, which had not been in use among us for seven hundred years. Chrysoloras the Byzantine, a man of noble birth and well versed in Greek letters, brought Greek learning to us. When his country was invaded by the Turks, he came by sea, first to Venice. The report of him soon spread, and he was cordially invited and besought and promised a public stipend, to come to Florence and open his store of riches to the youth. I was then studying the Civil Law, but . . . I burned with love of academic studies and had spent no little pains on dialectic and rhetoric. At the coming of Chrysoloras I was torn in mind, deeming it shameful to desert the law, and yet a crime to lose such a chance of studying Greek literature; and often with youthful impulse I would say to myself: 'Thou when it is permitted thee to gaze on Homer, Plato and Demosthenes, and the other poets, philosophers, orators of whom such glorious things are spread abroad, and speak with them and be instructed in their admirable teaching, wilt thou desert and rob thyself? Wilt thou neglect this opportunity so divinely offered? For seven hundred years no one in Italy has possessed Greek letters; and yet we confess that all knowledge is derived from them. How great advantage to your knowledge, enhancement of your fame, increase of your pleasure, will come from an understanding of this

[26] *The Vespasiano Memoirs,* transl. Waters, 235.

tongue? There are doctors of civil law everywhere; and the chance of learning will not fail thee. But if this one and only doctor of Greek letters disappears, no one can be found to teach thee.' Overcome at length by these reasons, I gave myself to Chrysoloras, with such zeal to learn, that what through the wakeful day I gathered, I followed after in the night, even when asleep." [27]

Lionardo d'Arezzo was for many years secretary of the Papal Curia, and after that was a member of the Signoria at Florence. Vespasiano lists among the translations he made from Aristotle the *Ethics,* the *Politics,* and the *Economics;* from Plato, the *Phaedo,* the *Phaedrus,* the *Georgics,* the *Crito,* the *Apology,* and the *Letters.* He translated six of Plutarch's *Lives* and besides wrote a *History of Florence,* and many other works.

Chrysoloras taught at the University of Florence. Other universities were no more tolerant of new studies then than they are today. A humanist might get a foothold sometimes as professor of rhetoric. Grammarians and rhetoricians "who had not studied in any Faculty" were objected to at Paris. The fact is, humanism was an anti-university movement. Petrarch turned away from the study of law, and abhorred dialectic as taught in the universities. In his letter about Logicians he says: "The most implacable in contests with the tongue will not resort to the pen . . . It is foolhardy to accept an engagement with these fellows upon their own terms. It is indeed from the fighting itself that they derive their chief pleasure; their object is not to discover the truth, but to prolong the argument . . . This is what I would impress upon you, my friend; if you are seeking virtue or truth,

[27] From Leonardus Aretinus (of Arezzo) called Bruni *Commentarius rerum suo Tempore in Italia gestarum,* in Taylor's *Thought and Expression in the Sixteenth Century,* I, 36.

avoid persons of that stripe altogether . . . These logicians seek to cover their teachings with the splendor of Aristotle's name; they claim that Aristotle was wont to argue in the same way . . . Aristotle was a man of the most exalted genius, who not only discussed but wrote upon themes of the very highest importance . . . Why is not the name of Aristotelians a source of shame to them rather than of satisfaction, for no one could be more utterly different from that great philosopher than a man who writes nothing, knows but little, and constantly indulges in much vain declamation?" [28]

The time came when the new studies swept the field, but in the first two centuries they made their home not in the universities but at the courts of princes, the houses of prosperous citizens, the papal offices, and the governmental headquarters of the republics. The humanist teacher, when he was not so fortunate as to be employed in "the good school of instruction" which Palla Strozzi organized for Florence, gave his lessons where he could, dictating the Greek or Latin grammar and the text of Cicero, Virgil, or Plato to students who took it down word by word and listened to his explanation of it, for only so could books be handed on to students before the invention of printing.

Anyone who will take the trouble to turn over the leaves of the book of *The Lives of the Illustrious Men of the XVth Century* which Vespasiano da Bisticci, the bookseller of Florence, wrote, will quickly become convinced that there were a great many of them. For a second time it fell to the lot of a free city to lead the world. Just why a democratic people should bloom as the second of the world's republics of culture is no easier to explain than the coming of the first one. It must have

[28] Robinson and Rolfe, *Petrarch,* 217.

been that men set problems for each other, that they breathed an expanding air, and individually thought so well of themselves that they really believed they could accomplish anything. The eminence of the Florentines was personal, was of achievement, not of birth. They were not divided into castes but were all citizens of one proud city, and all guild members vaunting themselves on their ability to perform the undertakings which were theirs.

Their leaders were not unvalued men whose greatness belonged to a distant past like the Roman aristocrats with many statues in their halls, but new men with their way still to make. They struggled for distinction, and in the new achievements they found their opportunity to reinforce political power with learning, and wealth with civic utilities. Florence was a boiling pot of rival enterprises. He who would be greatest there had to produce benefactions of learning and of art to establish his claim to the suffrages of his fellow men. The truly astonishing thing is that the leaders of Florentine enterprise were themselves the leading scholars. That must have been due to the competitions in making verses on my lady's eyes out of which came Dante's highest art of song and Petrarch's discontent with all the achievements of his time and his infectious determination to know and fellow with the worthier men of old—in which fellowing he and Boccaccio led the way. The richest fruit of their planting was the desire in the young men which brought Chrysoloras to Florence and gave his instruction such abounding welcome there.

The name of Palla degli Strozzi must never be omitted from the account of the causative factors of modern culture. The phrase "at that time the city was full of learned men" recurs in Vespasiano's pages, but of all of them it is clear that Palla degli Strozzi had more influence than any other. " 'In all the gifts, mental and physical, which made for human happiness he was more richly endowed than any other man of his time.' He was a fine scholar in Greek and Latin; he had marvellous ability and great personal beauty, so that if anyone who did not know him chanced to meet him, he would straightway exclaim: 'This must be Messer Palla.'. . . . Thus Messer Palla spent his life, prosecuting his studies, giving counsel to the republic, going as ambassador or serving with the Ten of the Balia whenever the state had need of his services. Florence had long been at peace, the people lived easy and opulent lives, and they soon began to desire to extend their boundaries, and hence arose the attempt against Lucca which led to the gravest political discords. The best and wisest of the leaders were opposed to it . . . " [29]

In the turbulence which developed Cosimo di' Medici and his friend Palla degli Strozzi and many others were exiled. After a time Cosimo was permitted to come back to Florence, but Palla degli Strozzi's first sentence of banishment for ten years was followed by a second and at its close by a third, of ten years more in each case, so that he died in exile at Padua at the age of ninety-two years. All his time he spent there in study. He engaged at a liberal salary John Argyropulus to read Greek with him, and another Greek scholar as well. With Argyropulus he read Aristotle's *Natural History;* and the other Greek read certain other works he selected. He wasted no time, but undertook the translation of Chrysostom into Latin." [30]

Cosimo de' Medici was more fortunate. Florence was a manufacturing and trading city, the centre of the world's wool trade and the making of woolen cloth. Her weavers

[29] *The Vespasiano Memoirs*, 235, 239.
[30] *The Vespasiano Memoirs*, 243.

knew and employed a secret process of dyeing it so successfully that other countries sent their cloth to be dyed
at Florence. When in 1298 the Florentines decided to
have a cathedral larger than any then in existence, the
guild of the wool merchants was given the responsibility
for building it. From the year 1282 the citizens of Florence had been organized in twenty-one guilds, the seven
"greater" ones being (1) the wool merchants, (2) the
dyers of foreign cloth, (3) the silk merchants, (4) the
furriers, (5) the bankers, (6) the judges and lawyers,
(7) the doctors and apothecaries.

The fourteen "lesser guilds" were the craftsmen of the
different trades.[31] The Signoria was composed of the
priors of the twenty-one guilds. Its president was the
Gonfalonier of Justice. The Balia was an assembly of all
the citizens who came together when the great bell in the
high tower of the Palazzo della Signoria summoned them.
The Florentines had suffered so greatly at the hands of
the Emperors of the Holy Roman Empire and at the
hands of their own Guelph nobles that when they fought
themselves free from Pope and Emperor they were more
jealous of their freedom than any other people on earth.
No noble could be a member of the Signoria. Florence
was rich. G. F. Young quotes Macaulay's statement that
the revenue of the Republic amounted to 300,000 florins
or more than 600,000 pounds sterling, a sum larger than
England and Ireland paid into the treasury of Elizabeth.
The Medici were bankers. The family name appears as
early as 1201. From the first it was a family of bankers,
the Medici of each generation being bred up to that
business. The wool, silk, and leather of Florence went
to many parts of the world and money was needed to
move them. Under Giovanni de' Medici the business of

---

[31] Young, *The Medici*, I, 36.

the house grew until it reached Constantinople on the east, and France and England on the north and west. Most of the Florentines owed his bank, and it is said that it was in his power to bring on a crisis in any part of Italy if he wanted to. Giovanni de' Medici was prior of the bankers' guild in 1402 and 1408 and 1411, and accordingly a member of the Signoria. In 1421 he held the highest office in the Republic, that of Gonfalonier of Justice. It was in the early years of the fifteenth century that public commissions for art began to be given. The plague came back in 1401, and the Signoria and the merchants' guild of the Florentines determined to ward it off by a votive offering of two bronze doors for their ancient chief church, that of San Giovanni Battista, commonly called the Baptistery. An international competition was announced, and the commission to make the votive doors was awarded in 1403, to Lorenzo Ghiberti, then a youth of twenty-three. He did not finish his task until 1452. In 1412, while this work was going forward, the wool merchant completed their church, Or San Michele, and resolved to place statues of the Apostles and the Saints upon its outer walls, a statue to be provided by each of the greater guilds, which contended to see which guild should furnish the best statue. In 1412 Donatello finished a statue of St. Peter, and in 1413, of St. Mark. In 1414 Ghiberti finished his St. John the Baptist, and in 1415, his St. Stephen. In 1416 Donatello was ready to install his St. George, and in 1418 Ghiberti offered his St. Matthew. In 1410 Giovanni de' Medici employed Brunelleschi to construct for him the Ospedale degli Innocenti, and in 1426 he was successful against great opposition in reforming the unfair methods of taxation by the *catasto*, which substituted a regular property tax of one-half florin on every hundred possessed for a hitherto irregular poll tax which left the rich relatively untouched but bore down cruelly upon the less well-provided people. By this reform he became the protector of the people, and through it the Medici established that relation with the lesser guilds which enabled them to lead in the affairs of Florence. Giovanni de' Medici handed on his wealth and his undertakings to his sons Cosimo (1389–1464) and Lorenzo (1395–1440). When he was on his deathbed he called them to him and said: "I die content because I leave you rich, in sound health, and so circumstanced that, following in my footsteps, you may dwell in Florence well esteemed and honoured by all. Nothing helps so much to make me die happy as the consciousness that I have never harmed any man but on the contrary, so far as I could, have been kind to all; and so I pray you also to be. If you would live in safety take only that share in the Government which the laws and your fellow-citizens award you. This will never expose you to envy or danger, since it is what a man arrogates to himself, not what is freely given him, that makes him hated. And you will find that those who covet what is another's commonly lose what is their own, and even before losing it live in perpetual trouble and anxiety. It has been by observing these methods that, among so many enemies and so many disputes, I have not only kept but increased my credit in this city. You too will maintain and increase it if you tread in my footsteps."[32]

Cosimo, says Machiavelli, added to that inheritance both of fortune and of qualities of mind. He was forty years old when his father left him the head of the house, and at once began to take a bolder part in public affairs, not attacking the government but seeking to be of service to all men. In the bitterly divided city, after the mis-

[32] Machiavelli, *The Florentine History,* transl. Thomson, I, 250.

carriage of the war against Lucca, the party which called itself the party of the Nobles, determined to drive Cosimo de' Medici, the chief stay of the opposition party of the people, out of the city. The reasons assigned for that action are interesting: "The things done by Cosimo which render him suspected are that he assists everyone with money, not only private men but the community itself, and not Florentines only but also foreign Condottieri; that he favours this or the other citizen who seeks office; that by the credit he enjoys with the body of the people he advances this or that friend to higher preferment. Are we then to allege as reasons for expelling him that he is compassionate, generous, helpful to his friends, and beloved by all?" [33] Nevertheless, on the pretext that unity could be secured only by crushing Cosimo, he was banished to Padua in 1433. In the following year, 1434, he was recalled from exile, and for thirty years, "for one who did not rest on armed support, Cosimo was the greatest and most famous citizen whom, not Florence only, but any city of which we have record, ever had,—excelling all of his time not merely in authority and wealth, but also in bounty and prudence . . . Though not learned he was most eloquent, and abounded in natural shrewdness; he was full of good offices toward his friends, charitable to the poor, instructive in his conversation, cautious in planning, prompt in executing, pungent and weighty in his sayings and rejoinders . . . His generosity was better seen after his death, when Piero, his son, sought to realize his estate; for there was no one of any importance in the city to whom Cosimo had not advanced large sums of money. Frequently too, when he knew a man of good standing to be in difficulties, he would come unasked to his relief. His munificence was shown in the many build-

[33] Machiavelli, *op. cit.*, I, 273.

ings he erected. For the convents and churches of San
Marco and San Lorenzo, the monastery of Santa Ver-
diana in Florence, the monastery of San Girolamo and
the Badia on the hill of Fiesole, and also a convent of the
Minor Friars in the Mugello, were not merely endowed,
but were built by him from their very foundations. Moreover, in the churches of Santa Croce, of the Servi, of the
Angioli, and of San Miniato he caused the most splendid
altars and chapels to be erected. And not only did he
build these churches and chapels, but supplied them with
suitable furniture, and with all else needed for the seem-
liness of divine worship. In addition to which sacred edi-
fices must be mentioned his private dwellings, one within
the city of a grandeur suited to so great a citizen, and
four in the country, at Carregi, Fiesole, Cafaggiuolo and
Trebbio, each of them more like a royal palace than the
residence of a private citizen. Nor was it enough for
him to be known for the magnificence of his buildings in
Italy alone; in Jerusalem he erected an hospital for sick
and poor pilgrims." [34]

Such was the great patron of the arts and learning. He
had church walls to be supplied with religious frescoes
and sacred statues, palaces for pictures, rich hangings,
and jewel cabinets, and library shelves for books. He
collected manuscripts, gems, coins. His system of branch
banks could get for him what he wanted in many places at
the same time. Perhaps his greatest contribution to the
renaissance of learning was in the libraries which he
founded and helped to found. Not only did he build the
monastery of San Marco, he added the Marcian library.

Nicolao Nicoli, who was brought up by his father in
trade but who gave himself entirely to scholarship after
his father died, studying Greek with Chrysoloras and

[34] Machiavelli, *op. cit.*, II, 155, 158.

theology with Luigi Marsigli, was a great collector of books. As he was always searching for rare books and manuscripts, he collected a fine library. If he heard of students going to Greece, France, or elsewhere he would give them the names of books which were not to be found in Florence and employ them to get them for him. Books that he could not get otherwise, he would copy with his own hand. His books he put at the service of his friends; the young men of Florence came to him for instruction, and "he cared for the needs of all who wanted books or teachers." On books he spent all that he had. His friend Cosimo de' Medici, learning that he was in want, opened an unlimited credit for him at the Medicean bank. When he died he left eight hundred Greek and Latin volumes and a will saying that forty citizens who were named therein should see to it that they should be made a public library to be consulted by anyone who cared to use them. Cosimo de' Medici, who paid his debts, was given these volumes to be placed in the monastery of San Marco. One who wrote of Nicolao Nicoli said that he had done more than Plato, Aristotle, or Theophrastus had done, for they did not will their books to the public to use.

When Cosimo had built the Badia of Fiesole he determined to collect a suitable lot of books for it. "One day when I was with him," says Vespasiano, "he said: 'What plan can you suggest for the formation of this library?' I replied that if the books were to be bought, it would be impossible, for the reason that they could not be found. . . . 'Then tell me what you would do in the matter.' I said it would be necessary to have the books transcribed, whereupon he wanted to know whether I would undertake the task. I said that I would, whereupon he replied that I might begin when I liked, that he left everything to me, and that as for the money for daily costs, he would order Don Archangelo, the prior, to present the cheques at the bank where they would be duly paid. He was anxious that I should use all possible despatch, and, after fhe library was begun, as there was no lack of money, I engaged forty-five scribes and completed two hundred volumes in twenty-two months . . . First came the Bibles and concordances with comments ancient and modern. The first of the commentators was Origen, who showed the way to all his followers. He wrote in Greek, and a portion of his work, *On the Five Books of Moses,* was translated by Jerome. There were the works of S. Ignatius, the martyr, who also wrote in Greek, and was a pupil of S. John the Evangelist, most zealous for Christianity as a writer and a preacher; those of S. Basil of Cappadocia, a Greek; those of S. Gregory Nazianzen, of Gregory of Nice, his brother, of S. John Chrysostom, of S. Athanasius of Alexandria, of S. Ephrem the monk, of Giovanni Climaco, a Greek, and of all the Greek doctors which are translated into Latin, and after these came all the sacred works of the Latin doctors beginning with Lactantius." [35]

Another great library builder who came under Florentine influence was Tommaso da Sarzana (1398–1455), who became Pope Nicholas V. He was a poor boy of Pisa who possessed a great eagerness for learning which took him to the University of Bologna, where he became a master of arts at the early age of eighteen. He went to Florence and was employed as a tutor for a year by Rinaldo Albizzi and for another year by Palla degli Strozzi. Then he returned to Bologna to become a doctor of theology. He accompanied the Bishop of Bologna to Rome and attended him when as Cardinal of Santa Croce he was

[35] *The Vespasiano Memoirs,* 221.

sent as peacemaker of the Church to France and England
and again to make peace between the Venetians and the
Florentines. When Pope Eugenius fled to Florence he
took the Cardinal of Santo Croce and his priest Tommaso with him. There the priest fell in with the younger
humanists and joined in their discussions. He attended
the Pope at the great Council of the churches and was a
large figure there, greatly befriended by Cosimo de' Medici. He used to say that if he had the money for them
he would do two things, he would buy books and build
houses; and he did both. He went as apostolic legate into
France and Germany, and on his way back found a cardinal's hat waiting for him at Viterbo. Shortly after, Pope
Eugenius died and Tommaso da Sarzana became Pope.
The Bookseller of Florence says that when he did homage
to him in the Vatican, the Pope said to him: "Vespasiano,
would the people of Florence have believed that a priest,
fit for nothing but to ring a bell, should have been made
Sovereign Pontiff?" He forthwith began to build, and to
collect Latin and Greek books without regard to price,
and to organize a staff of coypists, and to assemble scholars to make translations from the Greek. The Bible, the
Iliad, Herodotus, Thucydides, Polybius, Xenophon, Diodorus, Strabo, Philo, Plato's *Republic* and *Laws,* the
works of Aristotle and many of the Church Fathers, were
translated into Latin by the great company of learned
men he assembled and paid liberally for that work. He
established the Vatican Library with a collection of some
5,000 volumes.

Cosimo de' Medici was surrounded by a group of
learned men whose undertakings he assisted at all times,
and much of the time directed. Nicolao Nicoli was one
of the foremost; Lionardo Bruni, the translator of the
Politics of Aristotle and the secretary and historian of

Florence; Carlo Aretino, Matteo Palmieri, Giannozzo
Manetti, Ambrogio Traversari were among them. All of
these vied with one another in their support of Greek.
Cosimo brought John Argyropulus to teach Greek at the
University of Florence from 1456 to 1471. When, in
1423, Giovanni Aurispa came back from the East with
empty pockets and 238 manuscripts—including the whole
of Plato, Proclus, Plotinus, Lucian, Xenophon, Arrian,
Dio Cassius, Diodorus Siculus and Strabo—Ambrogio
Traversari advanced him fifty florins, but Cosimo and
Lorenzo de' Medici gave them to him. With Francesco
Filelfo, who had married the daughter of Chrysoloras
and had spent seven years in Constantinople, returning
to Italy in 1427 with a vast number of manuscripts he
had collected, he did not at all times get on so well.
Filelfo was even accused of conspiring against the life
of Cosimo. That seems not to have been too unusual
a crime not to be forgiven, for Filelfo lived to receive
many favors from him and died in Florence at the ripe
age of eighty-three. Poggio Bracciolini, the great hunter
after manuscripts, who spent most of his life at Rome as
secretary of the Papal Curia, has left this witness of
Cosimo's interest in learning: "You have shown such
humanity, and moderation in dispensing the gifts of
fortune, that they seem to have been rather the reward
of your virtues and merits, than conceded by her bounty.
Devoted to the study of letters from your early years, you
have by your example given additional splendour to science itself. Although involved in the weightier concerns
of state, and unable to devote a great part of your time
to books, yet you have found a constant satisfaction in
the society of those learned men who have always frequented your house." [36] An even more adequate char-

[36] Quoted in Roscoe's *Lorenzo de' Medici*, I, 24, from *Poggii Opera*, 312
(Basel, 1538).

acterization is that of Flavio Blondo, who describes
Cosimo de' Medici as "a citizen, who, whilst he excels in
wealth every other citizen of Europe, is rendered much
more illustrious by his prudence, his humanity, his lib-
erality, and what is more to our present purpose, by his
knowledge of useful literature, and particularly of history." [37]

The fateful year 1453 drew near; the Turks were
heavily threatening Constantinople, and there was division in the Church of the West. A general Council of the
whole Christian Church at the invitation and expense of
the Pope was assembled at Ferrara to see if Christendom
could not unite. The Emperor of the East, John Palaeologus, was there with his officers of state, his theologians,
and his patriarch and metropolitans. Pope Eugenius IV
was there with eight cardinals, two patriarchs, eight archbishops, fifty-two bishops, and forty-five abbots. But the
plague broke out at Ferrara, and the council had to be
transferred to Florence. Cosimo de' Medici for the second
time in his life was Gonfalonier of Justice, and as chief
officer of Florence welcomed and entertained the conclave.
Four questions had divided the churches: (1) the use of
unleavened bread in the Communion of Christ's body;
(2) the nature of purgatory; (3) the supremacy of the
Pope; and (4) the procession of the Holy Ghost from
the Father as the Eastern Church believed, or from the
Father and the Son, as the Church of the West held.
The Council sat for nine months, and twenty-five sessions
were held. Benches were erected in the Church of Santa
Maria Novella for the Council. "The Pope was placed on
the side where the Gospel is read, together with the Cardinals and Prelates of the Roman Church, and on the
other side the Emperor of Constantinople with all the

[37] Quoted in Roscoe, *op. cit.*, I, 25, from Tiraboschi, *Storia della Letteratura Italiana*, V, VI, p. 1–27.

Greek Bishops and Archbishops." All were in full canonicals. "All Florence was there to witness this noble function." The sessions began with the reading of the Gospel in both the Greek and the Latin tongue. For conducting the important debates each party selected six of its most eminent men as disputants. When the Greeks spoke, Nicolo Secondino from Negroponte explained in Latin *de verbo ad verbum* what they had said, and when the Latins spoke he instantly interpreted what they had said in Greek. Here was the thing that young Florentines had for a century longed for most ardently, in living reality in their midst. Mark of Ephesus, and Bessarion, John Argyropulus, George of Trebizond and Theodore Gaza were the bold and able leaders of the Greeks, but another of their men made a more lasting impression— George Gemisthus Pletho, who had been the teacher of Chrysoloras, an old man who had spent a life in the study of the Platonic philosophy. He discoursed of Plato so movingly in Cosimo de' Medici's presence that Cosimo determined to reëstablish the Platonic Academy at Florence in order to cultivate the philosophy of Plato. To be the leader of that revival Cosimo chose Marsilio Ficino (1433–1499), the son of his favorite physician. Marsilio says he was then only a boy but was thereafter specifically trained to restore the Platonic philosophy. "Melchisedec, that great high priest, had but one father and one mother. I, the least of priests, have had two fathers, Ficino, the Medico, and Cosimo de' Medici. Of the one was I born, of the other I have been born again . . . I had for more than twelve years, philosophic conversation with Cosimo and he was as acute in disputation as he was wise and vigorous in action. I owe Plato much; to Cosimo I owe no less. He showed me in practice those virtues which Plato presented to my mind. After he had occupied himself with philosophy all his life, and in the midst of the gravest matters, he, following the example of Solon, devoted himself more than ever to it in the days when he was passing from darkness into light. For, as you know who were present shortly before his departure, he still read with me Plato's book on 'the Highest Good,' as though he would in reality now go to enjoy that good which he had tasted in conversation." [38] Cosimo bought a house for Ficino—a house in Florence, and a farm at Careggi. In 1477 Marsilio Ficino completed his celebrated translation of Plato, on which he had worked nearly twenty years. It was printed in 1482.

Meantime Ficino led the discussions of the Platonic Academy, which was the first non-ecclesiastical learned society, formed solely for the pursuit of knowledge, in Western Europe. It was a group of friends who gathered about Ficino to share in his studies and discuss the questions which Plato makes the themes of his dialogues. It is not certain that the Academy had a hard and fast organization. It held its perhaps most formal meeting of each year on Plato's birthday, November 7th, when its members gathered at a banquet to honor their great master. Some of the group were artists, some were writers, and others, leaders in the civic and commercial life of Florence. A few were philosophers,—Leon Battista Alberti, Christoforo Landino, Peregrino Aglio, Francesco Cattani, and Pico della Mirandola. As a sample of Ficino's teaching we borrow this translation of one of his letters by Dr. Nesca A. Robb: "Know thyself, O divine race clothed in mortal raiment; strip thyself, I beseech thee, in so far as thou canst; nay more, I say, with thine utmost endeavor separate the soul from the

[38] Quoted in Horsburgh, *Lorenzo the Magnificent*, 89–90.

body, and reason from the affections of the senses. Then straightway thou shalt see the pure gold freed from the defilements of earth, thou shalt see the clear air when the clouds are dispersed; then, believe me, thou shalt reflect thyself as a sempiternal ray of the divine sun. Neither shalt thou henceforth dare either to think or to attempt any base or evil thing in thine own presence. . . . Yet thou believest thyself to be in the lowest part of the world, because thou seest not thyself soaring above the heavens, but only thy shadow, the body, in a lowly place. It is as if a boy, standing by a well, should think himself to be at the bottom, while he gazes at himself, but sees afar off his own shadow as it were in the depths. Or as if a bird, flying through the air, should think itself on earth while it sees its shadow flying on the ground. Therefore, forsaking these shadows, return unto thyself, for thus shalt thou return unto greatness." [39]

To Cosimo in his last days Ficino read Plato on the Good. At one of the banquet meetings of the Academy he read the *Symposium*. In one of Lorenzo's poems he begs Marsilio to tell him wherein felicity consists, and Marsilio expounds Plato's doctrine of happiness. The never ending theme of the poets of the Academy is beauty and Platonic love. Their poetry is religious rather than passionate.

> The world doth all things visible display,
> Nor were they, till through God they had their birth.
> Lofty and deep He is, and so men say
> That he who wrought a work of might and worth
> Having beside Himself no archetype
> In likeness of Himself did bring it forth. [40]

[39] Robb, *Neoplatonism of the Italian Renaissance*, 70, 87.
[40] Robb, *op. cit.*, 147, 282.

The Greek doctors who had become known to the
Italian scholars at the meeting of the Great Council
shortly got into a furious literary battle over the question of the relative merits of Plato and Aristotle. First
Pletho published a book on the difference between them,
in which Aristotle did not show to advantage. George of
Trebizond made a translation of Plato's Laws for Nicholas V in which Bessarion found unpardonable errors
that he exposed. George of Trebizond replied with his
somewhat savage *Comparatio Platonis et Aristotlis,* in
which the reputation of Plato suffered. That gave Bessarion an opportunity to present a sober study of the superior claims of Plato, who taught that mind is the creator
of all things while Aristotle taught that the world is
eternal; that Providence rules yet leaves the will of man
free; that the soul is deathless and exists before the body.
Plato in short was the expounder of Christianity before
Christ, a divine forerunner, and Aristotle, but a pagan
sage. Thus at long last the scales were rectified and Plato
once again became the philosopher of the Church.

Cosimo was no less interested in art than in learning.
It was for him that Donatello executed his *David* and Fra
Angelico painted his *Adoration of the Kings* on the walls
of San Marco. In him Masaccio found his champion and
protector. The monumental house which Brunelleschi
had modelled for him he would not have, employing
Michelozzo to build a simpler one. For him Filippo
Lippi painted his *Coronation of the Virgin.* "He was,"
says Vespasiano, "especially inclined toward sculpture
and showed great favour to all worthy craftsmen, being a good friend to Donatello and all sculptors and
painters . . ." Cosimo died on August 1, 1464, and
was buried as he desired, without pomp, at San Lorenzo.
The Signoria by vote conferred upon him the title

Pater Patriae and ordered it inscribed upon his tomb.

Cosimo de' Medici was succeeded by his son Piero il Gottoso, Piero the Gouty, (1416–1469). He was a man of remarkable clemency in that day of harshness. After defeating the conspirators who made civil war in Florence, he set them free. Piero carried on all his father's interests in art and learning with a knowledge that profited from his father's and an eagerness that was its equal. He was himself a scholar who knew books better than Cosimo, and collected, multiplied, and used them as every one of the greater Medici did. The artists of Cosimo's generation—Masaccio, Brunelleschi, Ghiberti, Fra Angelico—had, one by one, been taken away by death, and in their stead a new corps of master-workmen carried on their undertaking: Luca della Robbia, Leon Battista Alberti, Piero della Francesca, Benozzo Gozzoli, and Sandro Botticelli. In the Uffizi gallery is the picture of the family of the Medici which Botticelli painted, perhaps to mark their gratitude to God that they escaped destruction in the Pitti conspiracy. In it Piero il Gottoso kneels in the centre, the young Lorenzo carries a sword, Cosimo Pater Patriae embraces the feet of the Child, and Marsilio Ficino, Cristoforo Landino, the Pulcis, and other scholars and artists lend support.

Piero died in December, 1469, and the leadership of the family and of Florence fell to Lorenzo de'Medici, then a youth of twenty-one. "The second day" after his father's death, he writes in his diary (*Ricordi*), "the principal men of the City and of the State came to our house to express their grief at what had happened and to comfort me. They requested that I would undertake the care of the City and the State as my father and grandfather had done." Lorenzo then was not a self-appointed dictator. What had his father and grandfather done? What part had they taken in the government of Florence? In the days of Victorian calm when peace seemed for a generation or two to be the natural condition of man, the Medici were judged unfairly, for the fact of the incessant warfare in the midst of which they managed to live and to keep their city alive was overlooked. Now that the natural condition of man has reasserted itself, it is possible to judge them more justly. The political strength of their house goes back to Giovanni de' Medici's *catasto* which took the burdens of arbitrary taxation off the shoulders of the members of the lesser guilds and made the Medicis the defenders and allies of the *popolani*. Cosimo de' Medici was in the position of a powerful political leader who had the votes of the most numerous party of Florentine citizens. In their behalf he fought the power of the greater guilds. He was as ruthless as political leaders in his day were and not much more ruthless than political leaders in our day of blood and iron are. "I know the humors of this city," he said; "fifty years will not pass before we are driven out; but the buildings will remain." Vespasiano writes: "I once heard Cosimo say that the great mistake of his life was that he did not begin to spend his wealth ten years earlier." Lorenzo in his *Ricordi* puts down the sum expended in public buildings, works of benevolence, and contributions to the public funds from 1434 to 1471, as 663,755 florins, or some 330,000 pounds sterling, with a purchasing power equivalent to perhaps 1,500,000 pounds when Britain was on a gold basis (and perhaps twice as much now). "Though many may think it better to have some of this in hand," said Lorenzo, "I consider such an expense to be a great honour to our position. The money is well placed, and I am quite content." [41]

[41] Horsburgh, *Lorenzo the Magnificent,* 81. Roscoe, *op. cit.,* I, 134.

A Balia after Cosimo's return from exile elected the officers of government for five years and fixed five years as their term thereafter. Cosimo with the support of the lesser guilds, the majority in the state, could and did thus control the Signoria. In time this relation of majority leader became more frankly acknowledged and open. The Signoria sent its measures to the head of the Medici family for preliminary approval. Remember that the opposition party, which called itself the Nobles, never slept but ceaselessly tried to break up the relations of the lesser guilds to the Medicis and to draw in outside princes and kings and Popes to fight its battles. Lorenzo, who was the ablest member of the Medicean family, continued to direct affairs as a private citizen. He held no office and had no armed force at his disposal. Whatever power he had depended on the good will of Florentine citizens. He was a party chief. "It is ill living in Florence without the control of the government," he said. When wars threatened to overthrow the state in 1486, a Council of seventy citizens was created who held office for life. At first it was announced that this Council should last for but five years; as a matter of fact it became permanent. Of its seventy members, thirty were named by the Signoria; and these thirty chose forty more. Each member must be forty years old or over. Three-fourths were to be from the greater guilds, one-fourth from the lesser. The Council controlled appointments to the Signoria. It was divided into two sections of thirty-five each; each section acted alone for twelve months while the other rested. The Council created two executive committees: one of eight of its members, the *Otto di Pratica,* chosen every six months, and its members not reëligible, whose business was to control foreign affairs; and the other of *twelve Procurators of the Commune* chosen for the same period and with the same limitation, who looked after home government.

Lorenzo the Magnificent was one of the world's very few many-sided men. In point of versatility he was not behind Aristotle and Lionardo da Vinci. He was a statesman, a poet, a scholar, a critic of all the arts of his time, a financier, and a farmer of distinction. Besides, he deserves some credit as a general, and from his youth he was a brave man. But of all these his services to learning and to art were greatest. Walter Scaife has estimated Lorenzo's annual expenditure for books at from 65,000 to 75,000 pounds sterling. The Turks had taken Constantinople in 1453, and libraries and collections of manuscripts were broken up and scattered there. Lorenzo sent Giovanni Lascaris twice to the East with a commission to find and purchase manuscripts. On his second trip he brought back two hundred, eighty of which had not been known in Italy before that.[42] "The destruction of Constantinople," says Roscoe, "may be said to have transfered to Italy all that remained of eastern science." [43] Lorenzo's messengers "are dispersed throughout every part of the earth for the purpose of collecting books on every science," writes Niccolo Leoniceno to Poliziano; "I well remember the glorious expression of Lorenzo, which you repeated to me, that he wished the diligence of Pico and yourself would afford him such opportunities of purchasing books, that his fortune proving insufficient he might pledge even his furniture to possess them." [44]

In 1472 Lorenzo founded the University of Pisa, going himself to inaugurate its instruction. It was to be a

---

[42] Young, *The Medici*, 197. Roscoe, *op. cit.*, II, 64.

[43] Roscoe, *op. cit.*, II, 62.

[44] Roscoe, *op. cit.*, II, 63.

centre of Latin studies. The Florentine state contributed 6,000 florins each year to maintain this university,
and Lorenzo is said to have subsidized it with more
than twice as much. The centre of Greek instruction was
the chair that Boccaccio had persuaded the Florentines
to set up for Leontius Pilatus in their University. Chrysoloras had filled it with supreme distinction. John Argyropulus taught Greek there for fifteen years, having
Poliziano and Reuchlin in his classes. Theodore Gaza,
and after him Demetrius Chalcondyles, next held that
important post. It was the return home of his student
Reuchlin to Germany that caused Argyropulus to exclaim "Now is Greece flown beyond the Alps." There
were Englishmen there too: Grocyn, who was afterward
to teach Greek at Oxford, spent two years at Florence
studying with Chalcondyles and Poliziano; and Thomas
Linacre was so outstanding at Florence that Lorenzo
de'Medici invited him to share the lessons which his sons
received from Poliziano. This centre of Greek studies
has been called a Trojan horse since so many champions
of Greek letters poured out from it. It was the means
by which the knowledge of the Greek tongue went to all
Italy and to France, Spain, Germany, and England, for
young men from those countries went there for instruction and returned home to teach their own people what
they had learned in study.[45]

Nothing was more significant or more clearly a carrying out of the best precepts of antiquity than the care
with which the Renaissance leaders brought up their
children. In 1457 Cristoforo Landino was made professor of poetry and rhetoric in the University of Florence.
Not long after Piero de' Medici made him responsible for
the instruction of his two sons, Lorenzo and Giuliano. In

[45] Roscoe, *op. cit.*, II, 82.

Greek, in dialectic and in ethics, Argyropulus was their teacher; and Marsilio Ficino taught them the philosophy of Plato. Nor is Lorenzo an unworthy product of such supreme teaching. The taste that gave directions to the artists of the *Cinquecento* had profited from the best that had been thought and said in the world. In some sense, Ficino continued to be not the keeper of the conscience but the keeper of the consciousness of Lorenzo as long as he lived. Their relations were close and cordial, their common study of the *summum bonum* was never abandoned. Ficino once dared to attempt an outline of the doctrines of Plato for his friend, in prose. Lorenzo undertook to do the same thing in verse. The echoes of their discussions are not even yet completely stilled. One hardly expects to find them in the daily press of our day, yet here is a poem by Lorenzo which I took from the *Boston Transcript* of May 17, 1916.

O God, O highest good, am I so blind?
Since Thee I ever seek, and never find.
Alas! I make my search, now here; now there;
And always do I seek for Thee, sweet Lord.
All things indeed through Thee are good and fair,
And my desire with Thee doth seek accord;
I know full well that Thou art everywhere,
And yet in no place Thee I ever find.

While my sad spirit seeks for Thee in vain,
The day afflicts me, nor does night bring rest:
Alas, the more I seek, the more my pain,
While for repose I make my fruitless quest.
Where dost Thou hide? Oh, tell and make me blest:
Speak, Lord, e'en now, to this so weary mind.[46]

[46] From the Laude of Lorenzo de' Medici, translated by William J. Mann.

The Platonic Academy flourished greatly under Lorenzo's patronage. The birthday of the philosopher was celebrated with the pomp which Florentines loved. Each November 7th, the distinguished scholars of Italy assembled at the villa of Careggi. Lorenzo himself presided. After dining together, a leader proposed certain passages from the works of Plato which the members of the company were required to discuss. Lorenzo was the *arbiter litterarum* of his age. What Cosimo had planted flowered in him. For four generations Plato was glorified by them, and philosophy and letters promoted as in a forcing house. Roscoe reports Negri as listing upward of two thousand writers as coming from Tuscany in that period.

There were two men, who had been lifelong partners of Lorenzo, at his deathbed. One was Poliziano, the other Pico della Mirandola. Angelo Poliziano (1454–1494) was sent by his father from Montepulciano to the protection of the Medici when he was ten years old. He studied at the University of Florence, and when he was sixteen sent Lorenzo a translation of the second book of the *Iliad* so good that forthwith he was made to live in the Medici palace. There he wrote his *Orfeo* when he was eighteen and his *Giostra* perhaps at twenty. He edited Catullus. He was the most finished scholar of the Italian Renaissance. "The spirit of Roman literature," said John Addington Symonds, "lived again in Poliziano. If he cannot be compared with the Augustan authors, he will pass muster at least with the poets of the silver age . . . Of his Greek elegiacs only a few specimens survive. These, in spite of certain licenses not justified by pure Greek prosody, might claim a place in the 'Anthology,' among the epigrams of Agathias and Paulus Silentiarius . . . those who have studied them know that the 'Orfeo,' the 'Stanze' and the 'Rime' justify Poliziano's claim to the middle place of honour between Petrarch and Ariosto." [47]

To this friendly paragon of learning, Lorenzo entrusted the instruction of his sons, Piero, Giovanni, and Giuliano. "If," said he to Poliziano, "we esteem those who contribute to the prosperity of the state, we ought to place in the first rank the tutors of our children, whose labours are to influence posterity, and on whose precepts and exertions the dignity of our family, and of our country in a great measure, depends." [48] To protect his family from outbreaks such as that of the Pazzi, Lorenzo sent them to live at Pistoia. Poliziano went along with them. He was much like an elder brother, for he had grown up with them. He writes to their father about his pupils: "Piero attends to his studies with tolerable diligence. We daily make excursions through the neighborhood, we visit the gardens with which this city abounds, and sometimes look into the library of Maestro Zamboni, where I have found some good pieces, both in Greek and Latin. Giovanni rides out on horseback and the people follow him in crowds." When it rains they have childish sports indoors, he says. In another place he complains that Giovanni's mother "employs him in reading the Psalter, which I by no means commend. Whilst she declined interfering with him, it is astonishing how rapidly he improved, insomuch that he read without any assistance." [49]

In 1484 a young man of twenty joined the group which gathered at Lorenzo's palace about whom praise had to be unlimited. "He was," wrote Poliziano, "a man or

[47] Symonds, *Revival of Learning*, 252, 251. By permission of Henry Holt and John Murray.
[48] Quoted in Roscoe, *op. cit.*, II, 129.
[49] Roscoe, *op. cit.*, II, 130.

rather a hero, on whom nature had lavished all the endowments both of body and mind; erect and elegant in his person, there was something in his appearance almost divine. Of an acute mind, a wonderful memory, indefatigable in study, distinct and eloquent in speech, it seems doubtful whether he was more conspicuous for his talents or for his virtues. Intimately conversant with every department of philosophy, the master of many languages and of every honourable science, it may truly be said that no commendation is equal to his praise." [50] This was Giovanni Pico, Count of Mirandola. For seven years he had studied at Bologna and at Paris. It was said that he knew twenty-two languages, among them Hebrew, Arabic, and Chaldaic. At Rome he had nailed up nine hundred theses upon which he offered to dispute. When these were examined by the Roman churchmen, thirteen they found to be heretical, and they took steps to bring Giovanni Pico to trial. At that point he betook himself to Lorenzo de' Medici. To harmonize the Christian and the classical tradition, he said, was his life work. He became interested in the Cabbala, and his mysticism grew somewhat fantastical. While he lived, he was the most distinguished of Marsilio Ficino's disciples and made upon his fellow men the impression of a spirit invincibly ardent in the cause of humanity. And when he died much too soon at thirty-one, such genuinely good men as Savonarola and St. Thomas More believed him to have been a saint.

Never was any man but he served by such a company of artists as Lorenzo gathered about him. Verrocchio was his sculptor. Botticelli, Ghirlandajo, and Filippino Lippi were his painters. Lionardo da Vinci he picked out to labor for Ludovico il Moro at Milan. And in a school

[50] Roscoe, *op. cit.*, II, 98.

of sculpture which he encouraged in his garden, the young sculptors Lorenzo di Credi and Michelangelo worked.

What is called a classical education comes from the Renaissance. That phrase has changed its meaning, and not for the better, with the years. At first it meant a study of the great writings of the past in order to master their content and make oneself into the likeness of the worthy men therein described. As the years went on, the heart was lost out of that enterprise and it came to be thought and even taught that occupation with certain ancient texts, no matter what one learned of their message, was of itself educative. Not so did the humanists overlook the words of life in Cicero, Seneca, Homer, Plato, and Plutarch when first they called them back from the dead. They would not have said that their effort was to so master the Latin and Greek tongues that they could speak and write them as the great writers of the past wrote them, though in their best representatives they did both these things. They insisted with unanimity at the first that the great value of these studies was that they were practical, that they brought messages of incalculable value to the heart of man, that their content imparted nobility of attitude, reliability of judgment, and wise counsel to action. The world had found a new wellspring of human existence. In the words of the men of old, men could learn to live now the rich and beautiful life that the men of old had shaped for themselves and in their writings had shared with their fellows. Humanism differed from supernaturalism in this, that it taught that the business of man is to learn to live now and here and that by so doing he will fit himself most worthily to live hereafter; whereas supernaturalism insisted that the eyes must be fixed on the hereafter, which is different from this world, and for which life even the most triumphant cannot

be a promising first stage. There was danger in the
humanists' determination to make earth and heaven continuous, for to many of them the claims of earth had an
obviousness that the claims of heaven lacked. In its best
exponents that was not so. But less serious minds came
to find such charm in art and literature and such absorption in pagan indifference to what is beyond, that the
counsels of Christianity were more and more overlooked
by them and morality somewhat gave place to immorality.

It could not be otherwise than that what passionately
absorbed the efforts of the leading men of the time should
constitute the studies of the young. Their parents strove
to bring them up in their own image or if not that in the
image of the more accomplished and successful men of
that age. What is remarkable is the thorough-goingness
with which they did that and the high quality of the
teachers they found for them. Piero de' Medici was content with no one short of Marsilio Ficino to teach his
boys, and Lorenzo must have the great Poliziano to be
house tutor for his. There were two very distinguished
professional schoolmasters who laid the foundations and
set the standards for this new kind of education of the
young in schools of their own forming which became the
models of the best educational practice for several centuries to come. They were Guarino da Verona (1374–
1460), and Vittorino da Feltre (1378–1446). They belonged to the earlier part of the Revival of Learning, and
neither one was a Florentine. Guarino was born at Verona
in the year that Petrarch died. He was the son of a metal
worker who died when he was twelve, leaving him to a
pious mother to rear. He learned Latin after the Middle
Age fashion, and in time made his way to Padua, where he
came to know Giovanni Conversino who had lived with
Petrarch and was professor of rhetoric at the University

of Padua. Paulus Vergerius was there too, whose interest is shown by the fact that he studied Greek with the boys in Chrysoloras' class when he himself was fifty. Studying and teaching there and in Milan, Guarino at length came to Florence, where he was employed to assist the teacher Corbinelli, one of those who were instrumental in bringing Chrysoloras to Italy. In 1403 Guarino had an opportunity to go to Greece with a Venetian merchant. He stayed there nearly five years, living a part of that time in the home of Chrysoloras, who had just returned from Italy. For two years he studied Greek there with Chrysoloras' son. At thirty-four he returned to Italy. Again to Florence he went, but this time welcomed as the most learned in Greek of the men of that city, he fellowed with the enthusiasts for Greek who gathered about Nicolao Niccoli and was named by the Signoria in 1412 to fill the chair which Chrysoloras had held in their University. But Niccoli and he did not get on, and Francesco Barbaro carried him off to Venice, where he opened a school for the teaching of Greek and had Vittorino da Feltre among his students. There he not only taught but studied, chiefly Cicero and Quintilian, and made a beginning of his own Greek and Latin grammar. In 1418 he went home to Verona, which city made him its professor of rhetoric. He admitted boarders into his large household of twelve or more children and made humanists of all of them. In 1429 the Marquis Niccolo d'Este took him to Ferrara to be tutor to his son. Other young men of Ferrara were admitted to his instruction, and when the young d'Este married, Guarino took a house of his own in 1436 and gathered boarding students with such success that the town organized a University and made Guarino its professor of rhetoric. There he wrote and taught until death claimed him at eighty-six in 1460.

Antiquity was always his subject. He had studied it on its own ground, and he could impart a knowledge of it as no other could. He trained humanists and sent them into the Church and the world to practice their profession. In the mornings he lectured to his university classes. In the afternoons and evenings he taught the student boarders in his own house. "We worked until midnight," says one of them. "Youths were sent to study at Ferrara," says Vespasiano, "and to learn under Guarino, not only literature but also good manners and conduct, for he was scrupulously honest and most particular in his view of life." He translated Plutarch *On Education,* some of the *Lives,* the *Geography* of Strabo, and three works by Lucian.

What did he teach and how? Professor Woodward, whose account we follow, says there were three stages to Guarino's teaching, an elementary, a grammatical, and a rhetorical stage. In the elementary, or beginning, stage one learned to read both with the understanding and with the voice, seemingly both Latin and Italian. "When you read," said Guarino, "do not chew your words, but pronounce them with a clear voice; for this not only aids digestion but serves to impress what you are reading upon the mind." There seems to have been a beginning of study of the changes which nouns and verbs undergo to express relations, person, and time. For this beginning with declensions and conjugations Guarino used an abbreviated Donatus which he called the *Janua* or gate. In the grammar stage (stage, not school as yet) Guarino used a book which he himself had prepared called the *Regulae.* This was distinctly a book which he had made for learners, a textbook, not a treatise for scholars. Its parts as Professor Woodward has reproduced them were these and in this order: the four parts of grammar; the definition of the eight parts of speech, the classes of verbs; impersonal verbs; construction of ideas of place; supines, gerunds, and participles; "Figurae"; prolepsis, zeugma, etc.; patronymics; forms of the verb; relative pronouns; *quis* and *uter* and their compounds; heteroclite nouns in mnemonic verses; the construction of three verbs: *solvo, nubo, lateo*. Latin was to be spoken. It was therefore spoken in the class and the rules which were learned were intended to assist that conversational use of it. "In addressing one person," he tells his students, "you will write, 'Te oro,' not 'Vos oro,' because *one* is singular in number, and because all Latin authors follow this rule." Prosody was taught by precepts, but for its actuality Virgil was gotten by heart. Some of Guarino's pupils even memorized all that that poet wrote. The use of epistolary Latin was taught from Cicero's *Letters*. The students built their own dictionaries and collected choice passages from the ancient writers in their notebooks. Their books of reference they had to make for themselves.

"It is an essential note of an educated man to be familiar with the language and literature of Greece . . . without a knowledge of Greek, Latin scholarship is in the true sense impossible," is a sentence which Professor Woodward takes from Battista Guarino in 1459. It might have been taken from Quintilian, for such sentiments are to be found in him; but the humanists were as beholden to the Greeks as the Romans were, in fact much more so. Latin was the learned language which they had to use, but Greek was the language of learning which held the poetry, science, history, and philosophy of which they had to possess themselves. They studied the Latin language to acquire the language: they studied the Greek to unlock the wisdom it contained. To speak and write Latin as Cicero spoke and wrote it and to read the Greek authors at sight was the ideal that beckoned them on.

To do that the forms of Greek nouns and verbs must be as well known as the Latin grammatical forms are. And the vocabulary must be copious and familiar. Practice in reading must make it almost second nature. The two languages reinforce each other if a Latin author is translated into Greek, for nothing else will make the distinctness and fitness of the Latin writer's style so evident. Virgil was supreme among Latin authors, but Statius, Ovid, Seneca, Lucan, Juvenal, and Plautus must also be studied. Next to Cicero's *Letters,* Terence was most important in humanist instruction. Guarino made his students know Homer, Aeschylus, Sophocles, Euripides, Plutarch, Aristotle, Theocritus, Aulus Gellius, Macrobius, and St. Augustine.

The third stage of his instruction was rhetoric. Cicero and Quintilian were the authors to be mastered. The *De Officiis* was read as a text on duty, and the *Tusculan Disputations* for their wisdom of many kinds. Plato and Aristotle supplied ethical standards. Guarino never minimized the claims of religion, and the *City of God* of St. Augustine claimed the same attention that he gave to the pagan writers.

Four Englishmen made their way to his classes: Robert Fleming, John Free, John Gunthorp, and William Gray. Vespasiano says that Gray spent several years in study at Ferrara, that he caused a great number of books in the classics, philosophy, and theology to be transcribed for him and collected books in every place he visited so that when he returned to England he took a noble library with him.

The other archetypal school of humanism was that of Vittorino da Feltre at Mantua. He studied and taught for nearly twenty years at Padua, where he came under the influence of Barzizza, the distinguished Latin scholar. Then he studied Greek with Guarino at Venice. When forty-six he was invited in 1423 by the Marquis of Mantua, Gianfrancesco Gonzaga, to undertake the training of his sons. The casino in the grounds of the Castle was turned into a school building. It had been called the Pleasure House; Vittorino renamed it La Casa Giocosa, the Joyful House. There he lived and worked with the children of the Marquis, children from the household and neighborhood, and some children of poorer parents who were selected by Vittorino for free board and schooling there with the others in order that ability might not lack opportunity. The number of such leavening students was once as high as seventy.

Vittorino left upon his own time the impression of a deeply Christian spirit. "He recited the office every day," Vespasiano says. "He fasted on all prescribed vigils, and directed those of his pupils who were under discipline to do the same. When he went to table he said the benediction like a priest and returned thanks afterwards and all the rest did the same. During the meal some one read aloud that silence might be kept. He practised confession and wished all his scholars to use this same habit. His house was a sacrarium of deeds and words." [51] He anticipated Lorenzo de Medici's conviction that the teacher of the young performs a service to God and the state. He conducted his school at Mantua for twenty-two years. With the difference that his nature was more considerate than that of Guarino, their schools were much alike. The same classical studies were taught, in much the same way. But Professor Woodward tells us that their aims were different. Guarino sought to fit men to perform a work,

[51] *The Vespasiano Memoirs*, 411.

Vittorino sought to make them men. This is an old quarrel which educators maintain among themselves. It does not seem to us to be a real one. All instruction is given that it may have consequences. Some of the consequences of instruction heal the sick, right wrongs, reclaim the wicked—we call those forms of instruction medicine, law, and the ministry, and say they are professions—while certain other forms of instruction fit us only to be helpful to our fellows and to live with ourselves. These latter, it is said, produce character, and the others skill. But is not character a kind of skill? Did not Socrates discover for the world that it was that?

Vittorino taught "a liberal education" and is in part responsible for having wished the confusion of that question-begging notion upon the world. "Not everyone," he said, "is called to be a lawyer, a physician, a philosopher, to live in the public eye, nor has everyone outstanding gifts of natural capacity, but all of us are created for the life of social duty, all are responsible for the personal influence which goes forth from us." For a complete training one had to go from Mantua to Bologna for law or Padua for medicine or Ferrara for the maximum of training in humanistic Greek or Latin. Mantua was not a finishing school. It did not offer final instruction in anything. It was a preparatory school, a secondary school, and a good one. It defined and illustrated that function so perfectly that European and after it American education shaped itself upon Vittorino's model. This is a good place to notice that the educational system which has developed through the years began at the top. The University took form first; after it, the secondary school, and last of all, the elementary school. It is also time to call attention very specially to the fact that the first book on education which the Renaissance teachers who were groping for a guide came upon was Quintilian's *Institutes of Oratory*. They swallowed it whole and made the modern education which they were shaping by their practices to consist in the arts of expression, that is to be linguistic, preferring the form to the substance of knowledge. What the world required was an improved scholasticism. It did not get it from the grammar study of the Renaissance.

Prose composition in Latin and Greek, Virgil and after him the author of the *Pharsala,* but other Roman poets with care for tender minds that may be corrupted,—Livy for Roman history, Pliny for natural history, Cicero for his letters as well as for his matchless oratory, Plutarch to tell about men—was the course of study. Greek was not in a second place, for both George of Trebizond and Theodore Gaza taught it while they learned Latin at Mantua. Music had something of the place Plato had claimed for it. And physical education was not slighted. Diet, clothing, and exercise were all thought about and regulated with care. Military training in knightly arts was given. The object was *bearing;* Vespasiano always tells us about the bearing of the men he describes. Classical literature, a Christian spirit, and the passion of the Greeks for perfecting the body—this was the stuff out of which Vittorino da Feltre made Renaissance secondary education.

It is said that when Benjamin Franklin visited the room in which Gutenberg printed the first book, he went in on his knees, "for the place is holy ground; here human liberty was born." There are two striking things about that invention: it came at the moment it was most needed and at any other time would have had nothing to work upon; and the highest quality of printing that was ever done was done at the first. But the humanists did not welcome that invention. It interfered with the vested

interests of the copyists and made an end to those priceless works of art that rarely exquisite coypists and minia-
ture painters could sometimes produce. The great Duke of
Urbino, Vespasiano says, always employed thirty or forty
scribes. "He took the only way to make a fine library . . .
by beginning with the Latin poets, with any comments on
the same which might seem merited; next the orators, with
the works of Tully and all Latin writers and grammarians
of merit; so that not one of the leading writers in this
faculty should be wanted. He sought also all the known
works on history in Latin, and not only those, but likewise the histories of Greek writers done into Latin, and the
orators as well. The Duke also desired to have every work
on moral and natural philosophy in Latin, or in Latin
translations from Greek. As to the sacred Doctors in
Latin, he had the works of all four, and what a noble
set of letters and writings we have here; bought without
regard to cost. After the four Doctors, he was set on
having the works of S. Bernard and of all the Doctors
of old without exception . . . There were all the works
of modern writers . . . He added to the books written
by ancient and modern doctors on all the faculties all the
books known in Greek . . . In this library all the books
are superlatively good, and written with the pen, and had
there been one printed volume it would have been ashamed
in such company." [52]

But it did not take the printing press long to get to
Italy. In 1465 two Germans, Sweynheym and Pannartz,
who had worked under Fust at Mainz, set up a press in
the German monastery at Subiaco and printed the *De
Oratore* of Cicero. They next went to Rome, where they
printed Cicero's Letters and a number of other Latin
works. At Venice, John of Spires printed Pliny in 1469.

[52] *The Vespasiano Memoirs*, 102.

In Florence an Italian made his own type and printed the commentary of Servius on Virgil in 1471–72. The press had met a need and by 1500 as many as 5,000 books had been published in Italy—about 300 in Florence and Bologna, more than 600 in Milan, more than 900 in Rome and 2835 in Venice—while presses had been set up at least for a time in as many as 50 other places.[53] Most of these were Latin books. Only a dozen Greek books were printed in Italy before 1495. It is striking that, as the first Latin book to be printed was a schoolbook, the *De Oratore,* so the first Greek book was a textbook also, the grammar of Lascaris (Milan, 1476). Homer was printed in Florence in 1488. Though Greek had been slow in starting, it was to catch up. In 1495 Aldus Manutius began to bring out his *editio princeps* of Aristotle. In 1490 he had matured a plan to establish a Greek press and print the entire extant body of Greek literature. The Aldine press did that, and besides it printed much of the Latin literature and many Italian books. Aldus seems to have been inspired in some measure by Pico della Mirandola. In writing to Poliziano he speaks of their mutual friend Mirandola as "the most learned man of the age." [54] Aldus established his press at Venice in order not to be troubled by the incessant wars of the Italian states. His workmen were many of them Greeks. His house became a Greek colony; there were some thirty-three persons who lived together there. Greek was the language of the place, and the orders were issued in Greek. The Greek type used was made in the house upon models supplied by Marcus Musurus, a distinguished Cretan who assisted Aldus. The ink they used, Aldus made in his own house. The binding, too, was done there. Their paper,

[53] Sandys, *A History of Classical Scholarship,* II, 97.
[54] Finniu-Didot, *Alde Manuce,* 7.

which even yet is not discolored, was made at the mills of Fabriano. Aldus Manutius was a great scholar who wrote in Greek the prefaces to the Greek works he published. That practice of his seems to indicate that the ability to read Greek was at that time fairly common in Italy. He was a fervent missionary, a missionary of culture. What joy it is, he exclaimed, to see these volumes of the ancients rescued from book buriers and given freely to the world! His undertaking bears marks of being thought the greatest of his time. All the scholars of Europe seem to have made a point of looking in on him. Thomas Linacre could not return to England without seeing Aldus. Erasmus lived with him to see one of his books through the press. Ulrich von Hutten writes Erasmus of his delightful visit to the great publisher. Already in 1500 Aldus had formed his coadjutors and associates into the Aldine academy or Neaccademia, as he called it. The constitution of that body of learned men was in Greek.[55] It forbade the members when assembled to converse in any language but Greek. A list of thirty-two of these who belonged to that celebrated company has been reproduced by M. Didot.

[55] See it in Appendice I of Ambroise Firmin-Didot's *Alde Manuce*.

VIII

LUTHER AND THE REFORMATION

THE revival of the spirit of antiquity changed everything. It set Copernicus to studying the motions of the
planets, Columbus to sailing westward to get to India,
and Galileo to proving Aristotle wrong by dropping weights
from the tower of Pisa. Before it came to England crime
was described as repulsive, dirty, and loathsome. The
Renaissance pictured it as adventuresome, calculating,
well-dressed, and sometimes attractive. Everywhere men
stood up and pushed the immediate past aside, because
their study of antiquity taught them to put trust in themselves and to do that. The year 1492, it has been said, saw
the world turn over. It was in that year that Ferdinand
and Isabella took Granada, an event which so enlarged
the heart of the Queen that she was willing to lend encouragement to the fantastic dream of the one-ideaed
sailor who stood in the crowd outside the wall and saw
the banner of Boabdil pass into the hands of their Catholic
Majesties. On that day the world changed for the 150,000
Jews who were in the Spains as well as for the great body
of Moors whose government of 777 years ended there.
It was in 1492 that Lorenzo de' Medici died at Careggi,
and in 1494 the French King, Charles VIII, "conquered
Italy with a piece of chalk."

It is not necessary to ask the protagonists of the Reformation what the government of the Church was like then.

There is a description of the papal court by Guicciardini which reads as follows: "Having raised themselves to earthly power on this basis, and by these methods, the popes gradually lost sight of the salvation of souls and divine precepts; and, bending their thoughts to worldly grandeur, and making use of their spiritual authority solely as an instrument and tool to advance their temporal, they began to lay aside the appearance of bishops, and assumed the state of secular princes. Their concern was no longer to maintain sanctity of life, to promote religion, or to shew charity to mankind; but to accumulate treasures, to raise armies, to wage wars against Christians. The sacred mysteries were celebrated with thoughts and hands stained with blood; and, with the view of drawing money from every quarter, new edicts were issued, new arts invented, new stratagems laid, spiritual censures were fulminated, and all things, sacred and profane, sold without distinction and without shame. The immense riches amassed in this way, and scattered among the courtiers, were followed by pomp, luxury, licentiousness, and the vilest and most abominable lusts. No care was taken to maintain the dignity of the pontificate; no thought bestowed on the character of those who should succeed to it: the reigning pope sought only how he might raise his sons, nephews, and other relations to immoderate wealth, and even to principalities and kingdoms; and, instead of conferring ecclesiastical dignities and emoluments on the virtuous and deserving, he either sold them to the best bidder, or lavished them on those who promised to be most subservient to his ambition, avarice, and voluptuousness. Though these things had eradicated from the minds of men all that reverence which was once felt for the popes, yet their authority was still sustained to a certain degree by the imposing and potent influence of the name of religion,

together with the means which they possessed of gratifying
princes and their courtiers, by bestowing on them dignities
and other ecclesiastical favours. Presuming on the respect
which men entertained for their office—aware that any
prince who took up arms against them incurred general
odium, and exposed himself to the attack of other powers,
and knowing that, if victorious, they could make their own
terms, and, if vanquished, they would escape on easy
conditions—the pontiffs abandoned themselves to their
ruling passion of aggrandising their friends, and proved,
for a long time, the instruments of exciting wars, and
spreading conflagrations over the whole of Italy." [1]

The *Ricordi* of Lorenzo de' Medici contains this entry:
"On the nineteenth day of May, 1483, we received intelligence that the King of France had on his own motion
presented to my son Giovanni, the abbey of Fonte-dolce.
On the thirty-first, we heard from Rome, that the Pope
had confirmed the grant, and had rendered him capable of
holding a benefice, he being now seven years of age." [2]
On the eighth day of June of the same year a courier came
with the news that the King of France had conferred upon
Messer Giovanni the Archbishopric of Aix. This action
of the King proved to be a bit premature, not because
Messer Giovanni was found to be too young, but because it developed that the Archbishop of that see was not
dead. On March 1, 1484, the Abbot of Passignano died,
and the abbey was given to Messer Giovanni. Lorenzo,
Giovanni's "provident father," had destined him for the
offices of the Church, even before his birth. In 1488 that
"provident father" as Poliziano calls him, began im-

---

[1] Guicciardini, *Paralipomena, ex autographo Florentino recensita,*
46–48 (Amstel, 1663), quoted in Thomas M'Crie, *History of the Progress*
and *Suppression of the Reformation in Italy,* 21 (Edinburgh & London:
Blackwood, 1856).

[2] Roscoe, *Leo X,* I, 14.

portuning Pope Innocent VIII to make his son Giovanni de' Medici, then twelve years of age, a Cardinal. The Pope, who had solemnly promised on his election not to raise anyone to the dignity of a Cardinal who was under thirty years of age, was overborne and, when Giovanni had reached the ripe age of thirteen years, named him a Cardinal with the stipulation that he should not assume the insignia of his office for three years but should spend that time in study. Giovanni thereupon went to the University of Pisa, and after three years to Rome to his great office in the Church. That he might not go astray, his provident father wrote him a long letter of advice which we transcribe in full:

"Lorenzo de' Medici, To Giovanni de' Medici, Cardinal. You, and all of us who are interested in your welfare, ought to esteem ourselves highly favoured by providence, not only for the many honours and benefits bestowed on our house, but more particularly for having conferred upon us, in your person, the greatest dignity we have ever enjoyed. This favour, in itself so important, is rendered still more so by the circumstances with which it is accompanied, and especially by the consideration of your youth, and of our situation in the world. The first thing that I would therefore suggest to you is, that you ought to be grateful to God, and continually to recollect that it is not through your merits, your prudence, or your solicitude, that this event has taken place, but through his favour, which you can only repay by a pious, chaste, and exemplary life; and that your obligations to the performance of these duties are so much the greater, as in your early years you have given some reasonable expectation that your riper age may produce such fruits. It would indeed he highly disgraceful, and as contrary to your duty as to my hopes, at a time when others display a greater share of

reason and adopt a better mode of life, you should forget
the precepts of your youth, and forsake the path in which
you have hitherto trodden. Endeavour therefore to allevi-
ate the burden of your early dignity, by the regularity of
your life, and by your perseverance in those studies which
are suitable to your profession. It gave me great satisfaction to learn that, in the course of the past year, you had
frequently, of your own accord, gone to communion and
confession; nor do I conceive that there is any better way
of obtaining the favour of heaven, than by habituating
yourself to a performance of these and similar duties.
This appears to me to be the most suitable and useful advice which, in the first instance, I can possibly give you.

"I well know that, as you are now to reside at Rome,
that sink of all iniquity, the difficulty of conducting yourself by these admonitions will be increased. The influence
of example is itself prevalent; but you will probably meet
with those who will particularly endeavour to corrupt
and incite you to vice; because, as you may yourself
perceive, your early attainment to so great a dignity is not
observed without envy, and those who could not prevent
your receiving that honour, will secretly endeavour to
diminish it, by inducing you to forfeit the good estimation
of the public; thereby precipitating you into that gulf into
which they have themselves fallen; in which attempt the
consideration of your youth will give them a confidence
of success. To these difficulties you ought to oppose yourself with the greater firmness, as there is at present less
virtue amongst your brethren of the college. I acknowledge indeed that several of them are good and learned
men, whose lives are exemplary, and whom I would
recommend to you as patterns of your conduct. By
emulating them you will be so much the more known and
esteemed, in proportion as your age, and the peculiarity

of your situation, will distinguish you from your colleagues. Avoid however, as you would Scylla or Charybdis, the imputation of hypocrisy; guard against all ostentation, either in your conduct or your discourse; affect not austerity, nor even appear too serious. This advice you will, I hope, in time understand and practise better than I can express it.

"You are not unacquainted with the great importance of the character which you have to sustain, for you well know that all the Christian world would prosper if the cardinals were what they ought to be; because in such a case there would always be a good pope, upon which the tranquillity of Christendom so materially depends. Endeavour then to render yourself such, that if all the rest resembled you, we might expect this universal blessing. To give you particular directions as to your behaviour and conversation, would be a matter of no small difficulty. I shall therefore only recommend, that in your intercourse with the cardinals, and other men of rank, your language be unassuming and respectful, guiding yourself however by your own reason, and not submitting to be impelled by the passions of others, who, actuated by improper motives, may pervert the use of their reason. Let it satisfy your conscience that your conversation is without intentional offence; and if, through impetuosity of temper, any one should be offended, as his enmity is without just cause, so it will not be very lasting. On this your first visit to Rome, it will however be more advisable for you to listen to others than to speak much yourself.

"You are now devoted to God and the church, on which account you ought to aim at being a good ecclesiastic and to shew that you prefer the honour and state of the church, and of the Apostolic See, to every other consideration. Nor, while you keep this in view, will it be difficult for you to favour your family, and your native place. On the contrary, you should be the link to bind this city closer to the church, and our family with the city; and although it be impossible to foresee what accidents may happen, yet I doubt not but this may be done with equal advantage to all; observing, however, that you are always to prefer the interests of the church.

"You are not only the youngest cardinal in the college, but the youngest person that ever was raised to that rank, and you ought therefore to be the most vigilant and unassuming, not giving others occasion to wait for you either in the chapel, the consistory, or upon deputations. You will soon get a sufficient insight into the manners of your brethren. With those of less respectable character, converse not with too much intimacy; not merely on account of the circumstance in itself, but for the sake of public opinion. Converse on general topics with all. On public occasions let your equipage and dress be rather below than above mediocrity. A handsome house and a well-ordered family, will be preferable to a great retinue and a splendid residence. Endeavour to live with regularity, and gradually to bring your expenses within those bounds which in a new establishment cannot perhaps be expected. Silk and jewels are not suitable for persons in your station. Your taste will be better shewn in the acquisition of a few elegant remains of antiquity, or in the collecting of handsome books, and by your attendants being learned and well-bred rather than numerous. Invite others to your house oftener than you receive invitations. Practise neither too frequently. Let your own food be plain, and take sufficient exercise, for those who wear your habit, are soon liable, without great caution, to contract infirmities. The station of a cardinal is not less

secure than elevated, on which account those who arrive
at it too frequently become negligent, conceiving that
their object is attained, and that they can preserve it with
little trouble. This idea is often injurious to the life and
character of those who entertain it. Be attentive therefore to your conduct, and confide in others too little rather
than too much. There is one rule which I would recommend to your attention in preference to all others. Rise
early in the morning. This will not only contribute to
your health, but will enable you to arrange and expedite
the business of the day; and as there are various duties
incident to your station, such as the performance of divine service, studying, giving audience, etc., you will find
the observance of this admonition productive of the greatest utility. Another very necessary precaution, particularly on your entrance into public life, is to deliberate
every evening on what you have to perform the following day, that you may not be unprepared for whatever
may happen. With respect to your speaking in the consistory, it will be most becoming for you at present to
refer the matters in debate to the judgment of His Holiness, alleging as a reason your own youth and inexperi-
ence. You will probably be desired to intercede for the
favours of the pope on particular occasions. Be cautious
however that you trouble him not too often; for his temper leads him to be most liberal to those who weary him
least with their solicitations. This you must observe, lest
you should give him offence, remembering also at times
to converse with him on more agreeable topics; and if
you should be obliged to request some kindness from him,
let it be done with that modesty and humility which are
so pleasing to his disposition. Farewell." [3]

In 1513 Julius II died and after a deliberation of

[3] Roscoe, *Lorenzo de' Medici*, II, 150–155.

seven days the College of Cardinals elected Cardinal
Giovanni de' Medici Pope. He took the name of Leo X.
One of his first acts was to restore the University of
Rome by bringing from different parts men to the number
of a hundred or more who were distinguished in every
branch of learning. He encouraged the study of Greek by
putting Giovanni Lascaris in charge of it. He wrote to
Marcus Musurus at Venice: "I request that you will
take the trouble of inviting from Greece ten young men,
or as many more as you may think proper, of good
education and virtuous disposition, who may compose a
seminary of liberal studies, and from whom the Italians
may derive the proper use and knowledge of the Greek
tongue." [4] Under Leo X, Rome became first in learning
of every sort. The Italian Renaissance culminated there.
The greatest scholars, the greatest artists, the greatest
undertakings under the rich subsidies of the Church, all
radiated about Leo X. He was a most princely collector
of antiquities, a most discriminating lover of books. No
other Pope who ever sat upon the papal throne could
compare with him in devotion to learning and the extreme
favor he showed to learned men. Erasmus tells him that
he "outshines the glory of his Medicean ancestors." He
was a man of great affability and benevolence, yet no
other Pope was so badly treated by his Cardinals, for
some of those who surrounded Pope Leo X formed a
conspiracy to poison him. Three Cardinals were publicly degraded, and one at least of them, Cardinal Pe-
trucci, was found guilty and executed for that crime.
Two other Cardinals pleaded guilty, and after being heavily fined retired from Rome. By way of repairing this
breach and restoring the dignity of the Church, Pope Leo
on one and the same day (June 26, 1517) created thirty-

[4] Roscoe, *Leo X,* II, 84.

one Cardinals. On December 1, 1521, Pope Leo died, as report said, of poison.

The conclave which followed was long. Regretfully the Cardinals present concluded that no one of them could be elected. "Take," said the Cardinal Medici, "Cardinal Tortosa, a venerable and aged man, who is universally regarded as a saint." That advice was acceptable, and Adrian of Utrecht, professor of theology at Louvain and formerly the tutor of Charles V, was elected. Pope Adrian VI, a genuinely good man, did not continue the lavish splendor with which Leo X had surrounded himself. He lived in the Vatican in much the same way that he had lived as a professor at Louvain. He was a scholastic who still carried on his studies, but he was not without interest in the new learning. He opposed all that savored of heathenism and set about restoring Christianity. To his Nuncio Francisco Chieregato, whom he sent to the diet in Germany, he gave these instructions: "We know that for a considerable time many abominable things have found a place near the holy chair, abuses in spiritual things, exorbitant straining of prerogatives, everything turned to evil. The disease has spread from the head to the limbs, from the pope to the prelates: we are all gone astray, there is none that has done rightly, no not one." [5]

From 1493 the Emperor of the Holy Roman Empire was merely a German monarch, and even in Germany his power was by no means assured. He was the nominal leader of a sort of confederation of states whose real rulers were the dukes, counts, and margraves who headed them. The prince-electors had chosen Maximilian King of the Romans in 1486. His reign was one long series of struggles with the Estates to gain some form of ac-

[5] Ranke, *History of the Popes,* III, 43 (Philadelphia, 1844).

knowledged mastery over them. Diet after diet was convoked to work out a constitution under which local independence and imperial unity could go hand in hand. The problem proved to be insoluble. The Emperor would not be limited by a federal senate, and the states would not allow him to be an old-time autocratic sole ruler. The time was full of turmoil. The theory of the Empire was that the Emperor was the authentic successor of the Caesars, "Regent of the true religion." When Pope Leo III crowned Charles the Great on Christmas Day in the year 800 in the basilica of St. Peter which Constantine had erected, his purpose was to undo the work of Constantine in moving the Capital to Constantinople and to restore it to Rome. By this act it was held that Charles the Great became the true successor of Augustus, or more literally of Constantine, the protector of the Church. Emperor and Pope were both agents of God in the government of His world. The theocracy was one, the souls they governed were the same. One wielded the secular, the other the spiritual arm. The Church excommunicated and handed its recusants to the State for punishment. The trouble with the plan was that there were two heads as well as two arms, and the two heads could not work together. The Church is necessary, von Ranke points out, to keep men constantly mindful that they are born and must die, that their neighbors and the men of other nations are of like helplessness. Without its perpetual ministry of compassion, the State would harden into tyranny and inveterate intolerance and unmeasured conceit of self. And without the wear and tear of social undertakings, the thrust and counter-thrust of doubt and assent, the reinvigoration of new needs and fresh knowledge, the dialectic of growth would not minister to religion and it would become formal, paralyzed, and dead. Thus the Church and the State are the warp and the woof which must interweave to fashion existence. Without the aid of both it can take no enduring pattern. The Church and the State are equally indispensable; the problem of each is to support without thwarting the other. That function the Empire and the Papacy never learned to perform. Even the first Emperor, Charles the Great, protested against the clergy encroaching upon the secular power. The relation could not be adjusted, the war was endless, the Popes sought to dominate the Empire, the Empire fought the Popes. But the Emperors always came off second best. The spiritual arm was the more powerful. Through annates, pallia, and other exactions, the revenues of the Church far exceeded the income of the Empire. Maximilian I said they were a hundred times greater. The annates, about half the annual value of a benefice, were collected at every new appointment to a Church office. Whenever a new priest was sent to a parish, or a new bishop or archbishop entered upon his see, the parish or diocese had to raise those fees for the Papal Curia. The banking house of the Fuggers collected them and took, it is said, 50 per cent for doing so. The pallium, the archbishop's symbol, a collar of white lamb's wool with two bands hanging at the front and back of the wearer and six black crosses decorating it, came high. Mainz had to pay 20,000 gulden for one, and in three and eight years for others. It is estimated a sum of 300,000 gulden flowed to Rome each year. The barefoot friars are thought to have collected a million gulden annually. Benefices passed to the use of Rome. Plurality, or the holding of several livings by one churchman, was a burden. Abbacies and bishoprics were given to cardinals to support them. When Albert of Brandenburg, but twenty-three years of age, was elected Archbishop of Magdeburg and administrator of the bishopric of Halberstadt, though the double office was contrary to the canon law, the Pope confirmed him for a sufficient sum of money. In the next year, 1514, he was elected Archbishop and Elector of Mainz and Primate of Germany, thus holding, before he was old enough to be a bishop, three of the greatest bishoprics in the Empire. The Roman Curia confirmed him for ten thousand ducats, or fifty thousand dollars. The "holy trade" in indulgences was the most profitable of all the forms of extracting money from the faithful. Its roots were in the promises of the popes to the soldiers of the crusades that their sins would all be forgiven them. In 1145 that pardon was extended to all who provided money to fit out a crusading soldier, and in 1300 to all who came on pilgrimage to Rome. In 1393 Boniface IX sent out agents to sell letters of pardon and to confess and absolve those who bought them. The privilege of buying them for the dead was established in 1457. The theory of their sale was that the merits of Christ and the saints far outweighed divine requirement and there existed a surplusage which the representative of Christ on earth could apply to the needs of men as he chose; that is, there was a treasury of merit in the keeping of the Church. By the year 1500 the trade in indulgences, or pardon tickets, was well established. In 1514 the banking house of the Fuggers of Augsburg undertook its management in return for one-half the net receipts. The Medici Pope Leo X, needed money for his great expenditures and particularly for the building of St. Peter's Church and bethought him to proclaim a universal remission of sins in return for the purchase of pardon tickets. The sale was to run for eight years from March 31, 1515, and the young

Archbishop and Elector of Mainz who had paid such a large sum for the privilege of holding three bishoprics was named to superintend the traffic of a region of Germany and to receive half the proceeds as compensation for his services. He made John Tetzel, a Dominican prior and money raiser of great preaching power, his agent in chief. A sales staff was soon organized. Myconius, who as a schoolboy of thirteen stood in the crowd which gathered at the town of Annaberg when the indulgence-seller came there, left this description of what happened: When "the Commissary or Indulgence-seller approached a town, the Bull [announcing the indulgence] was carried before him on a cloth of velvet or gold, and all the priests and monks, the council, the schoolmasters and the scholars, all the men and women went out to meet him with banners and candles and songs, forming a grand procession; then, all the bells ringing and all the organs playing, they accompanied him to the principal church; a red cross was set up in the midst of the church, and the Pope's banner was displayed; in short, one might think they were receiving God Himself." [6]

Archbishop Albert of Brandenburg made large and appealing claims for the efficacy of the pardon tickets which were being sold under his direction. He used his high office to make it clear that an easy way to atonement had been opened. "The first grace," he said, "is a plenary remission of all sins, than which one might say no grace could be greater, because a sinner deprived of grace, through it achieves perfect remission of sin and the grace of God anew. By which grace . . . the pains of purgatory are completely wiped out. The second grace for sale is a confessional letter allowing the penitent to

[6] Lindsay, *Luther and the German Reformation*, 54. By permission of T. and T. Clark.

choose his own confessor; the third is the participation in the merits of the saints. The fourth grace is for the souls in purgatory, a plenary remission of all sins . . . Nor is it necessary for those who contribute to the fund for this purpose to be contrite or to confess." [7]

Something more should be said of the reason assigned for raising these funds, the rebuilding of St. Peter's. Julius II was a warrior Pope who set about restoring the temporal power to the fullest extent. Like other conquering rulers, he was a great builder. He determined to remake Rome, and employed Bramante to design his buildings. The old St. Peter's which Constantine had built, he ordered replaced by a grander one and on April 18, 1506, he laid the foundation-stone for it and sent word through the world that it had been begun. Bramante worked on it for eight years, tearing out the old church as the building of the new progressed. In this operation many tombs and priceless ecclesiastical relics were destroyed. Raphael was made sole architect by Leo X. In 1535 Michael Angelo was put in charge of the building. It was not completed until 1626, when Urban VIII consecrated it. Its cost has been reckoned at 50,000,000 scudi. (The nominal value of the scudo being given at four shillings, that means something like $50,000,000.) The building of this material structure involved the collapse of the Catholic Church in Northern Europe.

Universities were late in developing in Germany, but German students went abroad in numbers to study in those of other lands. One hundred and fifty years after the University of Paris took form, the Emperor Charles IV in 1348 established the first German university, in

[7] Preserved Smith, *Martin Luther*, 39. By permission of Houghton Mifflin Company.

Prague, "so that," as he said in its charter, "our faithful subjects who are ever hungry for the fruit of science will find in their own country a table for the meal, and will think it unnecessary to travel around the world for the purpose of seeking knowledge, to visit strange nations, and go begging in foreign countries." Then came Vienna in 1365 (to be reëstablished in 1385), and Erfurt in 1379; Heidelberg in 1385, Cologne in 1385. The next century saw many founded: Leipzig in 1409, Rostock in 1419, Greifswald in 1456, Freiburg in 1456, Basel in 1459, Ingolstadt in 1472, Trier in 1473, Mainz and Tübingen in 1477. The University of Wittenberg was founded in 1502. These universities were ecclesiastical institutions. They had the four faculties; but theology led, and the studies in arts were a preparation for it. Though both the canon and the civil law were taught, the canon law was the more important. The great University of Paris was the mother, the German universities were her children and her grandchildren. They reproduce her features, the endless controversy over Realism and Nominalism, the public disputations of the schoolmen, Aristotle worship, the overmastering concern with theology to which all else is secondary and acknowledges its subordination. Their theology had been wrought out at Paris, too. The doctrine of the Seven Sacraments was formulated by Peter Lombard. They were: (1) Baptism, (2) Confirmation, (3) the Eucharist, (4) Penance, (5), Extreme Unction, (6) Holy Orders, (7) Matrimony. The doctrine of transubstantiation did not mature in the creed until the Lateran confession of faith in the year 1215. With it the doctrine of the priesthood took on invincibility. Duly ordained, the priest alone had the power to perform the sacrament of the altar in which the bread and the wine became the real, but unapparent, body and blood of the Lord. The priest then, as St. Thomas affirmed, was set as a medium between God and the people. He acted in the person of Christ. "It is not in the participation of the faithful but solely in the consecration of the elements that the perfection of the sacrament lies," St. Thomas declared.[8] As the priest alone could perform the miracle, so the priest alone could prepare the sinner to receive it. This he did through confession, penance, and absolution. Above the priest was the hierarchy with the priest of priests, the Pope, at its head. To the bishops was given the power of ordination in apostolic succession, and to the supreme priest the power of the keys. The doctrine of infallibility not yet having been conceded, appeal could be taken to a Council of the Church, but Pius II, in 1460, forbade such appeal under penalty of damnation.

The *Sentences* of Peter Lombard was, as at Paris, the chief book of instruction in the theological faculty. The bachelor in theology had to lecture upon them three semesters before beginning to lecture upon the Scriptures. That the Bible was postponed until after the *Sentences* was read does not mean it was banished, only that the scholastic formulations of Christian doctrine which were interpretations of the Bible, seemed to be more serviceable arrangements. There is of course a great difference between the doctrine that God saves men through his Church and that which contends that salvation is through Christ alone. And one incidence of this difference is the different perspectives which the Bible takes in the two schemes of salvation. It is of course basic in both. But in the one it contains everything. In the other it tells only of the beginning. The

---

[8] *Summa,* Pars. III, Questio 80 (Art. I, Reply to Objection 1; Art. 12, Reply to Objection 2).

development of the Church is a no less important part of the account. So the Bible was always valued, but not always exclusively valued. There were, it is said, no fewer than one hundred editions of the Vulgate Bible published before 1500.[9] The Roman Catholic historian, Janssen, declares that as many as fourteen complete versions of the whole Bible in High German and five in Low German appeared before 1519.[10] There were three theological foundations at the University of Wittenberg: one for lectures on Thomas Aquinas; one, on the works of the Nominalist, Gabriel Biel, the much valued Erfurt professor who had but recently died; and the third, on the Bible. The works of the Fathers had always been important. The scholastic doctors had given formulation to them, and their summaries and rationalizations had long seemed supremely though not exclusively important. Now Bible study as well was coming into favor. Some professors of theology held that the Biblical writers had greater authority than the schoolmen; but others insisted that everything of value in the Bible was to be found in the writings of the scholastic professors of theology, and that the appeal which began to be made to the Bible was certain to be a means of strife and confusion.[11] The lessons from the Bible were read in the church service. There was no discouragement of its being read freely by anyone who would, but the daily and household reading of it was not prescribed as a religious duty as it soon came to be under Protestantism.

The scholastic scheme of distinctions and practices dominated every phase of education, from the alphabet-school to the university; and the creative arts, which

[9] Preserved Smith, *Luther,* 14.
[10] Lindsay, *op. cit.,* 143.
[11] McGiffert, *Martin Luther,* 35.

exist to give sensible form to the ideas which dominate
their period, had nothing to body forth save the monop-
olistic absorption in the conceptions of the Church.
Miracle working shrines and images were to be met
everywhere. Relics innumerable were collected. Amu-
lets were worn. Confraternities of pious people were
formed to assist one another in mutual fasts, prayers,
and pilgrimages. They bought spiritual benefits from
the Pope and, for fees of money or attendance at Masses,
repetitions of the Psalms, paternosters, Ave Marias, and
other such holy works, transferred them to their members. The Church was organized as a vast factory of
machinery of observances for the salvation of souls.

But the Renaissance was breaking in on Scholasticism.
The revival of the learning of antiquity brought in the
Greek Testament, the Septuagint, and the Hebrew Bible,
to take the place of the Vulgate in the concern of learned
men. The skeletonized and meatless textbooks of the
scholastics could not hold their own against the works of
Plato, Aristotle, and the Fathers in the original languages. Scholastic domination was little by little battered
down by the spirit of independent investigation which
men were learning from the Greeks. The Revival of
Learning did not lead to the Reformation in Italy, because the Church was Italian and grew out of the Italian
temperament. Its interest in religion was not primarily
ethical. Moreover, the humanists of Italy were too completely absorbed in taking possession of the new learning
to follow its consequences into application. Galileo was
to do that in one department later on. But in the first
centuries the work of domesticating and perfecting the
new learning was as much as they could do.

There was at Deventer in Holland an association
whose members took no lifelong vows and lived sim-

ply, earning their bread by teaching children and copying books. They were the Brethren of the Common
Life. Gerard Groot who was born there in 1340 was
their founder. They were .a society of ascetics whose
object was the good life. Thomas à Kempis was of their
company. Six of his pupils in the schools of the Brethren of the Common Life he advised to go to Italy for
instruction which he could not give them. They were
Rudolf Lange, Count Moritz von Spiegelberg, Rudolf
Agricola, Alexander Hegius, Ludwig Dringenberg, and
Antonius Liber.[12] Only the first three were able to follow their teacher's advice. In Italy, Agricola met Johann
von Dalberg, later on to be Bishop of Worms and Curator
of the University of Heidelberg, who in 1482 invited him
to introduce the new learning to Heidelberg. The theology which he had learned from Thomas à Kempis remained his chief interest. His fellow pupil, Dringenberg,
founded the great school of Schlettstadt in 1450 which
was a centre for the dissemination of the new learning
in the Upper Rhine country. It enrolled some nine
hundred students. Rudolf Lange had another such school
at Münster. Antonius Liber taught at Amsterdam, Kem-
pen, and Alkmaar, and in 1481 Alexander Hegius directed
the great school at Deventer and taught Erasmus in it.
The German universities founded after 1450 were raised
into existence to be centres of Greek and Latin teaching.
The old learning had its place in them but the new learning had a firm foothold beside it. A new literature came
into being with the *Ship of Fools* of Sebastian Brant,
Reynard the Fox (*Reineke Fuchs*), and the *Fastnachts-
spiele* of Hans Rosenplüt. Its object was to bring the
Church into contempt. Conrad Peutinger, who had studied in Italy and was the friend of Poliziano, was secre-

[12] Beard, *The Hibbert Lectures of 1883*, 46.

tary of the city of Augsburg. Willibald Pirkheimer, a
great German humanist who had been for years in Italy,
made converts to the new learning at Nürnberg. Abbot
Trithemius of the monastery of Spanheim remained firm
in the faith but collected a library of two thousand
Greek, Latin, and Hebrew volumes. There were travelling scholars in Germany, just as there had been in Italy.
Ulrich von Hutten was the most distinguished of them.

The humanists were an active company. Except in
point of numbers and entrenched position the Scholastics were no match for them. Academic and ecclesiastical war between them was certain. It broke out over
the person of Johann Reuchlin, the student of whom
Argyropulus had said that in him Greece had flown across
the Alps. Reuchlin was born at Pforzheim in 1455. He
studied Latin in the monastery school of his home town
and went to the University of Freiburg for a little time,
but became a scholar through his good fortune in being
sent by the Margrave of Baden to accompany his son
to the University of Paris. Greek had been taught in
Paris from 1470, and during his year there Reuchlin
began to study it. From Paris he went with a learned
Frenchman, Jean Heynlin, to the young University of
Basel, where in 1477 he became a master and lectured
on Latin and the Greek Aristotle, at the same time continuing his study of Greek and preparing a Latin lexicon.
He returned from Basel to Paris for further study of
Greek with Georgius Hieronymus. Deciding to make law
his profession, he went to Orléans and finally to Poitiers,
where he became a licentiate. Next he went to Tübingen,
intending to become a professor in the University. Instead he was engaged to go to Italy in 1482 with Count
Eberhard of Württemberg, as his interpreter. He spent
some months in Florence and Rome and made the ac-

quaintance of the Italian humanists, particularly of those in the Platonic academy at Florence. He returned to Germany and was employed at Count Eberhard's Court. Having no children of his own, he took his sister's grandson, Melanchthon, as a foster son. In 1490 he was in Italy again and saw Pico della Mirandola, whose interest in Hebrew learning was great. In 1492 Reuchlin was sent on an embassy to the Emperor Frederick at Linz, and while there he studied Hebrew with the Emperor's Jewish physician, Jakob ben Jehiel Loans. On his third visit to Rome in 1498 he continued that study under Obadja Sforno of Cesena. In 1496 Eberhard of Württemberg died, and enemies caused Reuchlin to flee to the protection of Johann von Dalberg at Heidelberg. Here he was appointed to make translations from the Greek authors, and while he was not permitted to lecture at the University he was nevertheless the moving spirit in Greek and Hebrew learning in Germany. In 1500 Reuchlin was given a post of high judicial responsibility in the Swabian League, which he held for twelve years. He had at every opportunity gathered Hebrew books, and made use of every possible means to perfect his knowledge of that language. In 1506 he published the first authoritative Hebrew grammar and lexicon, the *De Rudimentis Hebraicis*. He had long shared with Pico della Mirandola a lively interest in Cabbalistic learning and had written two books on that subject: the *De verbo Mirifico*, 1494, and the *De Arte Cabbalistica*, 1517. Orthodox scholastic churchmen did not like his concern for Hebrew learning. In 1510 a converted Jew, Johann Pfefferkorn, called upon Reuchlin and showed him an order from the Emperor Maximilian requiring all Jews within the Empire to bring their books to the town halls to be inspected by Pfefferkorn and assistants whom he

should choose; if they were found to contain any insults
to the Christian religion, they were forthwith to be burned.
Reuchlin was asked to aid in this inquisition of the books
of the Jews. Its purpose was to convert the Jews to
Christianity by first taking away their books. The first
Hebrew scholar in Europe and judge of international
cases could not lend himself to such an unholy proceeding. But the Dominicans of Cologne clamored for it.
Before the end of 1510 the Archbishop of Mainz summoned Reuchlin by imperial order to give his opinion
on the confiscation and burning of all the Jewish books
except the Old Testament. To this he replied in a
memoir dated at Stuttgart, October 6, 1510, in which he
divided the Jewish writings into seven classes, of which
only one was worthy of the fire, while the others either
were necessary in their Jewish worship which was licensed by both papal and imperial law, or contained
matter of value to scholarship. "The Jews' books should
not be burned, but with reasonable debate they should,
by God's help, be gently and kindly brought over to our
faith." To that end the Emperor should order that for
ten years there should be two chairs of Hebrew in every
German university, the Jews to furnish books for their
use. Then a furious pamphleteers' war followed, and
the chief Inquisitor stepped in and ordered Reuchlin to
stand trial for heresy. Reuchlin appealed to Rome, where
a Theological Commission gave judgment in his favor.
Pope Leo X, instead of confirming that judgment, issued a mandate in 1516 enjoining silence upon both parties. The aged scholar taught Greek and Hebrew for one
year at Ingolstadt and at Tübingen for another, and
died in 1522.

The letters from the scholars of Germany under the
title *Clarorum Virorum Epistolae ad Johannem Reuchlin*

appeared in 1514. If illustrious men supported their champion, why should not the other side be supported too? The opportunity was inviting, and so the celebrated pasquinade, the *Epistolae Obscurorum Virorum* was put forth in 1515.

Reuchlin and Erasmus were called "the two eyes of Germany." When Reuchlin died Erasmus wrote a dialogue which he called "The Canonization of John Reuchlin" and printed it in the third edition of his *Colloquies*. His estimate of the great teacher is in these words: "That which Satan did formerly by the Scribes and Pharisees against the Lord Jesus, he continues still to do by pharisaical men against good men, who have deserved well from the world by their studies. He now reaps the blessed harvest of the seed he has been sowing. In the meantime it will be our duty to preserve his memory sacred, to honour his name, and to address him often in some such manner as follows: 'Oh holy soul, be thou propitious to languages, and to those that cultivate them: favour the holy tongues, and destroy evil tongues that are infected with the poison of hell.' " [13]

Of Erasmus himself there is no need that we should give so full an account. Few books tell a connected story of Reuchlin, but many describe the work of Erasmus. He is the peerless Northern scholar, the unequalled humanist of his time and one of the greatest writers of all time. He was born at Rotterdam on October 27, 1466(?). As a little lad he attended a school at Gouda, but as he did poorly there he was sent to be choir boy at Utrecht. At nine he entered the school of the Brothers of the Common Life at Deventer, where for six and a half years he studied logic, physics, metaphysics, and morals, got

[13] *The Familiar Colloquies of Erasmus,* III (transl. Nathan Bailey; London, 1877).

Horace and Terence by heart, and began the study of Greek. Then he entered the Augustinian monastery of Steyn. Here he studied, wrote, and painted some pictures. In 1492 he was ordained a priest and became secretary to the Bishop of Cambrai, who procured for him a scholarship in the College of Montaigu of the University of Paris. Here he devoted himself to Greek literature. A wealthy young Englishman, William Blunt, who had come to Paris for study, employed Erasmus as his tutor, which relation led to his being invited to England in 1499. There he met and made lifelong friends of Colet, More, Warham, Fisher, and many others. Erasmus went to the Augustinian house at Oxford and was received as a celebrated scholar. In 1500 he was back in Paris, writing and bringing out his *Adagia*. In 1504 he published the *Enchiridion* and in 1505 was with his friends in England again. In 1506 he was sent to Italy with the boys of Henry VIII's court physician. He came to Italy, he says, "most especially for the sake of Greek, but here and now studies are cold and wars are hot." The distinctive contribution of Erasmus to his age and to all time was to divert the immense interest in ancient learning to find its objective and chief uses in developing Christianity. "I brought it about that humanism, which among the Italians and especially among the Romans savored of nothing but pure paganism, began nobly to celebrate Christ, in whom, if we are true Christians, we ought to boast as the one author of both wisdom and happiness." [14] In 1508 he was with Aldus at Venice, engaged in bringing out the great third edition of his *Adagia*. The first edition had contained but 800; this one had 3,260 and a new title, *Chiliades Adagiorum* or

[14] Erasmus' letter to Maldonato, March 30, 1527, in Preserved Smith, *Erasmus*, 358.

Thousands of Adages. In 1509 Erasmus went to Rome and spent some months in being honored by the Cardinals and other learned men in the papal city. By the end of the year he was again in England living with Thomas More and writing his *Praise of Folly,* which astonished his friends and brought discredit to its author, but sold greatly. Next he went to Cambridge to teach Greek. In 1512 the Archbishop of Canterbury appointed him rector of the parish of Aldington. But though "a man of the most consummate achievement in Latin and Greek . . . although in theology and in every other kind of science he is most learned, yet because he was unable to propound the word of God in English to his parishioners, or to converse with them in their own vernacular speech," this benefice was converted into a pension.[15] He left England in 1514 and returned to the Continent. He was in truth a wandering scholar, always going from one country to another. Having learned friends in all of them, he was in fact a sort of common denominator of the learning of his time. On this occasion he went to Basel and worked upon his edition of *St. Jerome* and his *New Testament.* His Greek New Testament was first published in 1516 under the title *Novum instrumentum.* It was reprinted sixty-nine times by the year 1536.[16] In the exhortation to the study of the Christian Philosophy which forms the preface to his New Testament, in the first edition of 1516 and the third of 1522, are these and some other sentences:

"I utterly dissent from those who are unwilling that the sacred Scriptures should be read by the unlearned translated into the vulgar tongue; as though Christ had taught such subtleties that they can scarcely be under-

[15] Mangan, *Life, Character and Influence of Erasmus,* I, 341.
[16] Preserved Smith, *Erasmus,* 163.

stood by a few theologians, or as though the strength of the Christian religion consisted in men's ignorance of it. The mysteries of kings it may be safer to conceal, but Christ wished His mysteries to be published as openly as possible. I wish that even the weakest woman should read the Gospels, should read the Epistles of Paul; and I wish they were translated into all languages so that they might be read and understood not only by Scots and Irishmen, but also by Turks and Saracens. I long that the husbandman should sing portions of them to himself as he follows the plough, that the weaver should hum them to the tune of his shuttle, that the traveller should beguile with their stories the tedium of his journey."

The great universities of Germany were branches of the intellectual workshop at Paris, the theological faculty, "that brilliant star from which everything received light and life," led them.

A vast number of holy places, sacred images, relics, doctrines, a multitude of rules and priestly agents, monks, and scholastic doctors built up the system of Rome.

There was bitter protest on the part of rulers against the cumulation of benefices in the hands of the Cardinals and Popes who could not be deposed though their lives were sometimes stained with vice. The people made bitter protest against the annates, or first fruits paid to bishops, abbots, and holders of benefices. Religious begging was a heavy drain. The privileges of clergy were burdensome to the people. There was common disapprobation of the Church and disapproval of the prevailing state of things. The priests were attacked in the popular literature of the day for their ignorance, greed, and licentiousness. Then came Erasmus and put the Greek New Testament into the hands of the studi-

ous, 1516, and Reuchlin who opened the Old Testament
to scholarly inquirers.

The prime mover of the Reformation was Martin
Luther (1483–1546). "I am a peasant's son," he loved
to say. "My father, grandfather, and ancestors were
genuine peasants; afterwards my father removed to
Mansfeld, and became a miner; that is my native place."
He was born at Eisleben. When he was six months old
his family moved to Mansfeld, so that his father might
get employment in the copper mines. Little is known
of his childhood save that there was no sparing of the
rod by mother, father, or schoolmaster. The mother
flogged him until the blood came over the matter of a
single nut; his father punished him so severely that
he was in terror of him; and in school he was once
whipped fifteen times in one forenoon. No wonder he
agreed with the Goths, who would not send their boys
to the Roman schools. "Where such fear enters a man
in childhood it can hardly be rooted out again as long
as he lives. As he once trembled at every word of his
father and mother, to the end of his life he is afraid of
a rustling leaf." [17] But these incidents not only tell about
the time and Hans and Margarethe Luther, they tell about
the boy himself. He was the kind of lad who earned many
whippings. The schools of his boyhood were "hell and
purgatory," he said. He attended the priest's school at
Mansfeld, where as elsewhere the choristers were taught
their part in the church service and to read, write, and
cipher. As the service was in Latin, a beginning of that
study was made. It was for inability to repeat declensions that he had never been taught that he received the
fifteen floggings in one forenoon. At thirteen he was
sent away to the school of the Brothers of the Common

[17] In McGiffert's *Martin Luther*, 8.

Life at Magdeburg. He had tried his hand at mining copper, but something had led his father to select another career for him. The next year he was in the high school of the parish of St. George at Eisenach, where as at Magdeburg he sang in the streets for his food. It was at Eisenach that Frau Cotta took pity on him as he went about begging and made him a member of her good home. At Eisenach the teaching was inspiring, too. Trebonius, the master, invariably saluted his scholars "for," he said, "future burgomasters, chancellors, doctors, and magistrates are among those boys." Here he made an acquaintance with humanistic learning and progressed so encouragingly that his father, who was now able to do so, sent him at seventeen to the University of Erfurt. It was a famous place—as celebrated as Paris, the Germans thought, for Trutvetter taught philosophy and Maternus humanism. Luther went in for philosophy, that is, for dialectic, rhetoric, music, physics, astronomy, etc., the scholastic course of study. The Nominalists had the field, and William of Occam's interpretations caused Luther to call him his "dear master." The humanistic studies charmed him, but he was more interested in their content than in their language. In 1502 he took his bachelor's degree, and in 1505 he graduated as a master of arts, standing second in his class. His proud father's thought for him was that he should at once take up the study of law, which he did. But as he was returning from his home to the University a terrific thunderstorm broke upon him and, in terror of death as the lightnings played about him, he fell to the ground calling upon the miner's protectress, "Help, dear Saint Anna! I will become a monk."

At once he sold the law books his father had bought him, took farewell of his friends and entered the Au-

gustinian monastery at Erfurt. "This," says Dr. McGiffert, "was the most momentous event in Luther's career."
The change from leadership in the University to the menial and sometimes meaningless tasks in which the monks
tested the obedience of this eager-hearted boy of twenty-
two did not fail to make an impression upon him. The
Augustinians were a mendicant order founded in the
thirteenth century. Once more Luther hung a sack around
his neck and begged bread from house to house. He took
part in all the prayers and fasts, kept all the vows. "If
ever a monk got to heaven by monkish life and practices,
I resolved that I would enter there." His was a deeply
brooding nature, terribly troubled by his sins and unable to find peace and the assurance of salvation. An
old Augustinian brother pointed his attention to Romans 3:28. "Therefore we conclude that a man is justified by faith without the deeds of the law." The contrast affected him deeply. He brooded upon the saying:
"The just shall live by faith." He read Augustine's interpretation of that passage. "Then was I glad, for I
learned and saw that God's righteousness is his mercy
by which he accounts and holds us justified; thus I reconciled justice with justification and felt assured that I
was in the true faith." After his novitiate he had in due
course taken the threefold vow of poverty, chastity, and
obedience. In 1508 von Staupitz, the provincial of the
Augustinians, assigned him to the young University of
Wittenberg to teach Aristotelian logic and ethics. But
he no longer relished philosophy, as he had at Erfurt.
His interest was in theology—"that theology, namely,
which explores the kernel of the nut, the heart of the
wheat, and the marrow of the bone." In 1511 the provincial of his order sent him to Rome to transact some business for the monastery. He visited the Roman churches

and performed the customary acts of devotion. This
journey gave him a perspective of the actuality of the
Church; it did not make him a reformer. That was due
to other causes. In the same year he was made a professor of divinity at Wittenberg, and in 1512 took his
degree of doctor in divinity, and began to lecture on the
Bible. He lectured on the Psalms and on Romans.
While he was engaged in that, Erasmus' Greek Testament came out, and Luther at once made it the basis of
his study. In his commentary on Romans he registers
his opposition to the scholastic theory of salvation, in
which a man of his own power can love God and do the
works of the law unaided by grace. His distrust of
Aristotle grew until on September 4, 1517, he published
ninety-seven theses calling in question the value of the
Aristotelian textbooks. To John Lang at Erfurt he sent
these theses and with them this letter under date of
February 8, 1517: "Greeting. I enclose a letter, dear
Father, for the excellent Trutvetter, containing propositions directed against logic, philosophy, and theology, i.e.,
slander and malediction of Aristotle, Porphyry, and the
Sentences, the wretched studies of our age. The men who
interpret them are bound to keep silence, not for five
years, as did the Pythagoreans, but forever and ever, like
the dead; they must believe all, obey always; nor may
they ever, even for practice in argument, skirmish with
their master, nor mutter a syllable against him. What
will they not believe who have credited that ridiculous
and injurious blasphemer Aristotle? His propositions
are so absurd that an ass or a stone would cry out at
them . . . My soul longs for nothing so ardently as to
expose and publicly shame that Greek buffoon, who like
a spectre has befooled the Church . . . If Aristotle had
not lived in the flesh I should not hesitate to call him a

devil. The greatest part of my cross is to be forced to see brothers with brilliant minds, born for useful studies, compelled to spend their lives and waste their labor in these follies. The universities do not cease to condemn good books and publish bad ones, or rather talk in their sleep about those already published . . ." He succeeded in driving Aristotle from Wittenberg, for on May 18, 1517, he wrote again to Lang: "Our theology and St. Augustine prosper and reign here, by God's help. Aristotle is gradually tottering to a fall from which he will hardly rise again, and the lectures on the *Sentences* are wonderfully disrelished. No professor can hope for students unless he offers courses in the new theology, that is on the Bible or St. Augustine or some other ecclesiastical authority." [18]

Luther was the central figure at Wittenberg. He had been ordained a priest in 1509. In a letter of 1516 he writes: "I am convent preacher, the reader at meals, am asked to deliver a sermon daily in the parish church, am district vicar (that is eleven times prior), business manager of our fish-farm at Litzkau, attorney in our case versus the Hertzbergers now pending at Torgau, lecturer on St. Paul, assistant lecturer on the Psalter, besides having my correspondence which . . . occupies most of my time." [19] Wittenberg through the influence of Luther was to be a capital of learning. It was an insignificant town when Frederick the Wise gave it its University in 1502. That University opened with 416 students. It had only 179 when Luther began to lecture there in 1508. A student in 1521 says, "There are more than 1,500 students here, nearly all of whom . . . carry their Bibles about with them." They came from

[18] Both letters quoted in Preserved Smith, *Martin Luther,* 26.
[19] Letter to John Lang in Preserved Smith, *Martin Luther,* 32.

many countries. Melanchthon, who taught Greek at Wittenberg from 1518, tells a correspondent, "At my table today were spoken eleven languages." [20]

In January, 1517, John Tetzel, the seller of papal pardon tickets, came so near to Wittenberg that the Augustinian monk finally determined to invite a debate upon the value of indulgences, and on the night of October 31, 1517, nailed ninety-five theses on the church door at Wittenberg. These challenges to debate made a much greater stir than the ninety-seven theses against Aristotle of the month before. Luther had printed those; he did not go to the trouble of printing these. Others did that for him, for they were at once in the greatest demand and were printed at Nürnberg in both Latin and German on the instant. A long but not complete list of them will be found in Preserved Smith's *Martin Luther*. Here are some samples of them:

1. Our Lord and Master Jesus Christ in saying "Penitentiam agite" meant that the whole life of the faithful should be repentance.

2. And these words cannot refer to penance—that is confession and satisfaction.

28. It is certain that avarice is fostered by the money chinking in the chest, but to answer the prayers of the Church is in the power of God alone.

30. None is sure of the sincerity of his contrition, much less of his full pardon.

31. They who believe themselves made sure of salvation by papal letters will be eternally damned along with their teachers.

36. Every Christian truly repentant has full remission of guilt and penalty even without letters of pardon.

37. Every true Christian, alive or dead, participates in all the goods of Christ and the Church without letters of pardon. . . .

[20] Beard, *op. cit.*, 92.

38. Nevertheless papal pardons are not to be despised.

43. Christians are to be taught that he who gives to the poor or lends to one in need does better than he who buys indulgences.

50. Christians are to be taught that if the Pope knew the exactions of the preachers of indulgences he would rather have St. Peter's Church in ashes than have it built with the flesh and bones of his sheep.

62. The true treasure of the Church is the holy gospel of the glory and grace of God.

The ninety-five theses were "propositions for debate," a challenge for an academic disputation. They proved to be a flame which set the world on fire. Luther wrote a defence of them, dedicating it to Leo X. He sent it to the Pope with a letter asking:

"Now what shall I do? I cannot recall my Theses and yet I see that great hatred is kindled against me by their popularity. I come unwillingly before the precarious and divided judgment of the public, I, who am untaught, stupid and destitute of learning, before an age so fertile in literary genius that it would force into a corner even Cicero, no mean follower of fame and popularity in his day."

"But when I expected a benediction from Rome, there came thunder and lightning instead . . ."

Wittenberg's rival, Frankfort on the Oder, gave Tetzel the degree of Doctor of Theology, and the Dominicans rallied in strength to celebrate his triumph. Tetzel used the occasion to publish some counter-theses which the students of Wittenberg demonstratively burned. Luther went quietly about his work. In the following May the Augustinians held the triennial convention of their order at Heidelberg. Despite the entreaties of his friends Luther went to it. He led the disputation upon Pauline

Theology. It was in the fall of that year that his chief helper appeared at the University in the person of its young professor of Greek, Melanchthon. Meanwhile the Dominicans were busy, and in August he was ordered to appear at Rome within sixty days to answer the charge of heresy. This order was quickly changed into a demand upon the Elector Frederick that he be at once arrested and turned over to the papal legate, Cardinal Cajetan, at Augsburg. Frederick of Saxony, a powerful ruler whose good will was indispensable to both the Emperor and the Pope—for he was an imperial elector, and a successor to Maximilian must soon be elected—was unwilling that violence be done to the leading professor of his University and insisted that Luther should not appear before a safe-conduct from the Emperor had been issued to him. It was issued, and Luther appeared before Cajetan at Augsburg. The legate bade him recant his errors. Luther did not recant. Cajetan having failed, a special nuncio, Charles von Miltitz, was sent armed with a ban against Luther and an interdict against the Church of Saxony. Instead of using them he employed the weapon of persuasion. Luther was to go to Rome and make his peace there. But just then the Emperor Maximilian died, and the Pope had other business for quite a time. Then came the great debate with John Eck at Leipzig. There "discord and mutual dislike" were born. Luther's answers to Eck's questioning showed that his theology was irreconcilable with that of the Roman Catholic Church. Revolt from Rome was clearly inevitable. The German people had long wanted a man who could free them from the impositions of the Church. Now they knew they had found him. Luther was the "man of Germany." Luther went back to Wittenberg and, taking his pen in hand, defined his position in the three tracts: *To the Christian*

Nobility of the German Nation, Respecting the Reformation of the Christian Estate; On the Babylonian Captivity of the Church of God; and *On the Freedom of a Christian Man.* The reformation, he decided, must be fought for with the pen and the printing press. Dr. Lindsay cites the archevist, Burkhardt, to the effect that it was Luther who started the book trade in Germany. From 1480 to 1490 the number of books printed in the German language in Germany did not exceed 40 each year. In the first ten years of the sixteenth century the number was not greater. In 1513 it was 35; in 1514, 47; in 1515, 46; in 1516, 55; in 1517, 37; in 1518, 71, of which 20 were from Luther's pen; in 1519, 111, of which 50 were Luther's. In 1520 there were 208, of which 133 were Luther's. In 1523 the whole number was 498, of which Luther contributed 183.[21]

Luther sought to break the medieval unity in government. Church and State had long been one. The Romanists had built three walls about themselves: First, they asserted that the temporal power had no authority over the spiritual power, but the spiritual power had authority over the temporal; second, no one except the Pope can interpret the Scriptures, and third, only the Pope can summon a Council of the Church. In addressing the German nobles, Luther called into the struggle the natural leaders of his people. He tied his religious reform into the rapidly accelerating movement for nationalism. What did he ask the nobles to do? The list is long; here are some sample statements:

1. Let every prince, nobleman, and city forbid and abolish the annates.

2. Let them also see that no more benefices pass to the use of Rome.

[21] Lindsay, *Luther and the German Reformation,* 91.

3. Let an imperial edict prohibit bishops and other dignitaries from going to Rome for their installation; and forbid appeals to Rome in controversies; for now bishops and archbishops have no real power, but only the Pope.

4. Prohibit the carrying of civil suits to Rome . . .

8. Let the bishop no longer take those oaths that bind him to the Curia, and let the Kaiser resume the right of investiture.

12. Let pilgrimages to Rome be abolished, not as evil in themselves, but because it is not well for pilgrims to see the wickedness of Rome. Pilgrimages after all are questionable; it is better for a man to attend to his duties at home.

23. Have done with papal dispensations and indulgences.

25. Reform the universities, where there is too much Aristotle and too little Christ. Throw out Aristotle's *Physics, Metaphysics* and the rest of him, except his *Logic, Rhetoric,* and *Poetics,* which in condensed form might be kept for elementary discipline. Maintain Latin, Greek and Hebrew, with mathematics and history. I leave it to the physicians to reform their faculty; but with regard to jurisprudence it were well to omit the Canon Law, especially the Decretals. There is enough in the Bible. As for our secular law, God help us, it is a jumble of territorial law and custom, and imperial law. For the Theologians, I say, let them give up the Sentences for the Bible, and reduce the number of treatises. Let the Bible be read in the schools.[22]

The second book of 1520 was *On the Babylonian Captivity.* It was written in Latin and intended for the learned, but against Luther's will was at once translated into German. It had to do with the sacraments of the Church and dealt so severely with them that King Henry VIII of far-away England was moved to write a book in answer to it. "Now that I have read the most subtile subtilties . . . not being unteachable in such

[22] In Taylor's *Thought and Expression in the Sixteenth Century,* I, 209.

matters I have learned and am certain that the papacy is the kingdom of Babylon . . . Giving the cup to the laity is enjoined by the Bible and forbidden by the Pope." Neither the Pope nor a general council can make new articles of faith. The Eucharist is held captive first by being withheld from the laity, secondly by the doctrine of transubstantiation, and thirdly by teaching that the Mass is a sacrifice and a good work, whereas it is only a commemoration. "I deny that the sacraments are seven in number, and assert that there are only three, baptism, penance and the Lord's Supper . . . Howbeit, should I wish to speak according to the usage of Scripture, I should say that there was only one sacrament and three sacramental signs." He who believes and is baptized will be saved, but baptism is taken captive by formal prayers and gifts. The sacraments are signs. Unless what they symbolize is believed, they are no help."

The third and most informing of all these booklets of 1520 was *On the Freedom of a Christian Man:*

"A Christian man is the most free lord of all, subject to none. A Christian man is the dutiful servant of all, subject to every one. These statements seem to conflict, but when they are found to agree they will edify us. For both are contained in that saying of Paul's [I Cor. 9:19], 'For though I be free from all men, yet have I made myself servant unto all.' . . . You owe nothing but to love one another, for true love, by its nature, is dutiful and obedient to what it loves. Thus also Christ, although Lord of all, yet was made a man under the law, free and a servant, at the same time in the form of God and in that of a slave.

.   .   .   .

"One thing only is needful to a good life and Christian liberty, the gospel of Christ . . . Faith is the sole salutary and efficacious use of God's Word, for the Word is not to be grasped or nourished with any works, but with faith only. One incomparable grace of faith is that it joins the soul to Christ as the bride to the bridegroom, by which mystery as the Apostle teaches, Christ and the soul are made one flesh . . . Let us not despise good works, but rather teach and encourage them, only guarding against the false opinion that they make a man just. We conclude, therefore, that a Christian does not live to himself, but to Christ and his neighbor, to Christ by faith, to his neighbor by love." [23]

The theology of the Reformation is very difficult to understand and very easy to state. It is all of it in the above paragraph. In the *Commentary on Galatians* which was translated anonymously and published in London in 1575, the same thought is put in slightly different words: "All the law is fully comprehended in this one saying: Thou shall love thy neighbor as thyself. God delighteth not in the observation of the ceremonies of the law, neither hath he any need of them. The only thing that he requireth at your hands is this, that ye believe in Christ whom he hath sent, in whom ye are made perfect and have all things." (Folio 255.)

"Wherefore let us learne to advance and extoll the majesty and authority of God's Word. For it is no small trifle (as brain-sick heads surmise at this day;) but every title thereof is greater than heaven and earth. Wherefore in this respect we have no regard of Christian charity or concord, but we sit as it were on the judgment seate, that is to say, we curse and condemne all men, which in the least point doe deface or corrupt the majesty of

[23] In Preserved Smith, *Martin Luther*, 92.

God's Word: *'For a little leaven maketh sowre the whole lumpe.'* But if they leave us God's Word entire and sound, we are not only ready to keep charity and peace with them: but also we offer our selves to be their servants, and to doe for them whatsoever we are able: If not let them perish and be cast downe into hell: and not only they, but even the whole world also, so that God and his pure word do remaine. For as long as he remaineth, life, salvation, and the faithful shall also remaine." (Folio 251.)

Luther was not a humanist. He was not a Latin stylist and often acknowledged the barbarity of his written Latin. Greek he studied with Melanchthon, but only for the Bible's sake. Melanchthon was his ally and adviser in all his struggles. "The little Greek outdoes me even in theology." Melanchthon championed the principles of Protestant theology in a little book which he published in 1519. The Scripture, he wrote, is not to be expounded according to the Fathers, but they are to be expounded according to the sense of Scripture. The expositions of even the greatest of the Fathers are erroneous in many places. The same is true of the Councils: their authority is of no consequence in comparison with that of the Scriptures. Much in the theologians, he believed, could never be reconciled with the Bible. When he tried the central doctrines of the Church, the priesthood, and the sacrament of the altar by that test he found them lacking.

There were other humanists who helped powerfully. One of them was Ulrich von Hutten; another was Erasmus, who did not make war on Luther but rather aided him at the first; yet on the whole he kept himself uncompromised, in order, as he said, to aid the revival of learning.

A long time was taken by Rome in preparing a Bull to excommunicate Luther. At length on June 15, 1520, Pope Leo signed it. It gave him sixty days to recant. The next step was to secure his condemnation by the Empire. But the Elector Frederick of Saxony was active in behalf of his subject. He asked Erasmus if Luther had erred. "Yes," said the humanist, "he has erred in two points, in attacking the crown of the Pope and the bellies of the monks." Erasmus suggested that the matter be submitted to a tribunal of learned men. The Elector Frederick insisted that that be done. At the end of the time allowed him to recant, instead of doing what he had been called upon to do, Luther, attended by the whole University and much of the town of Wittenberg, publicly burned the Bull of the Pope and the book of Canon Law just outside the wall of the town. On May 6, 1521, the Bull excommunicating the heretic was published at Worms. Luther was summoned by the Emperor Charles V to appear before the imperial Diet to recant. He asked for a safe-conduct. It was granted him. Still his going to Worms was not without peril, for Huss had been burned though he had an imperial safe-conduct. Yet Luther resolved to go, telling his friends: "I shall enter Worms in the face of the gates of hell and the princes of the air." On April 16th he was called before the great princes of the realm. His books were lying on a table before him. He was asked two questions, whether the books were his and whether he stood by them or recanted part of what he had published in them. He said they were his but asked for time "for deliberation, that I may answer without injury to the Divine Word or peril to my soul." He was granted one day more. His final answer was: "Unless I am convicted by Scripture or by right reason (for I trust neither in Popes nor in Councils, since they have often erred and contradicted themselves)—unless I am thus convinced, I am bound by the texts of the Bible, my conscience is captive to the Word of God, I neither can nor will recant anything, since it is neither right nor safe to act against conscience. God help me. Amen."

On April 26th he left Worms to return home under his safe-conduct. On May 4th, as he was journeying with two companions through the forest, some masked riders seized him and bore him off to the Wartburg, in which castle the Elector of Saxony kept him for his own protection until March 1, 1522. "I am reading the Greek and Hebrew Bible, I have put off my old garments and dress like a knight, letting hair and beard grow so that you would not know me," he tells a friend in a letter. Wherever he was, Luther wrote incessantly. In the Wartburg he made his translation of the New Testament into German. It was published in September of 1522. It was the Greek New Testament of Erasmus, edition of 1519, that Luther translated. In doing that his service to religion was incalculable, and his service to the German language was hardly less. The land was so given over to dialects that people who lived but a few miles apart could hardly understand one another's speech. There was a formal language of the many governments which made diplomatic interchange possible. Luther used that, putting it into less stilted colloquial form and adopting into its vocabulary great numbers of the common people's words. Thus he made a common German language which all might understand. Immediately after finishing the New Testament, with the help of Melanchthon, Aurogallus, and Rörer, he began to translate the Old Testament from the Hebrew text of Gerson Ben Mosheh, published at Brescia in 1494. It was published part by part as the translation of each part was completed. On March 16, 1532, the final part appeared. Luther's scholarship was equal to this great task, and the style of his German Bible is said even to surpass that of the great King James version in English.[24]

Erasmus, who lived for the new learning, wrote to Luther in 1524: "I observe a decline of literature and the sciences." In 1527 he expressed himself more definitely: "I abhor the Evangelicals for various reasons, one of which is that it is through them that literature is declining in every place, being entertained with coldness and contempt so that now it is on the point of perishing." [25] Humanism was peacefully penetrating the German universities when the storm of the Reformation broke. The universities were arms of the Roman Church. When their courses no longer led to clerical livings, their students fell away. In the ten years from 1525 their numbers were reduced to but a fourth of what they had been. Luther himself in his letter of 1524 to the Mayors and Aldermen, says:

"We see how the schools are deteriorating throughout Germany. The universities are becoming weak . . . through the Gospel. For through the word of God the unchristian and sensual character of these institutions is becoming known. And because selfish parents see that they can no longer place their children upon the bounty of monasteries and cathedrals, they refuse to educate them. 'Why should we educate our children,' they say, 'if they are not to become priests, monks, and nuns, and thus earn a support?'. . . Therefore I beg you all, in the name of God and of our neglected youth, not to think of this subject lightly, as many do who see not

[24] Preserved Smith, *Martin Luther*, 265.
[25] In Mangan, *Life, Character and Influence of Erasmus*, II, 239, 288.

what the Prince of this world intends. For the right
instruction of youth is a matter in which Christ and all
the world are concerned. Thereby are we all aided. And
consider that great Christian zeal is needed to overcome
the silent, secret, and artful machinations of the devil.
If we must annually expend large sums on muskets, roads,
bridges, dams, and the like, in order that the city may
have temporal peace and comfort, why should we not
apply as much to our poor, neglected youth, in order that
we may have a skillful school-master or two?

"There is one consideration that should move every
citizen, with devout gratitude to God, to contribute a part
of his means to the support of schools—the consideration
that if divine grace had not released him from exaction
and robbery, he would still have to give large sums of
money for indulgences, masses, vigils, endowments, anni-
versaries, mendicant friars, brotherhoods, and other similar impositions . . . For Almighty God had truly granted
us Germans a gracious visitation, and favored us with
a golden opportunity. We now have excellent and learned
young men, adorned with every science and art, who if
they were employed, could be of great service as teachers. Is it not well known that a boy can now be so instructed in three years, that at the age of fifteen or
eighteen he knows more than all the universities and convents have known heretofore? . . . I believe Germany
has never heard so much of the Word of God as at the
present time; history reveals no similar period . . . In
my judgment there is no other outward offense that in
the sight of God so heavily burdens the world, and deserves such heavy chastisement, as the neglect to educate
children . . . But all that, you say, is addressed to parents; what does it concern the members of the council
and the mayors? That is true; but how if parents neglect it? Who shall attend to it then? Shall we there-

fore let it alone, and suffer the children to be neglected? How will the mayors and council excuse themselves and prove that such a duty does not belong to them? Parents neglect this duty from various causes. There are some who are so lacking in piety and uprightness that they would not do it if they could . . . In the second place, the great majority of parents are unqualified for it, and do not understand how children should be brought up and taught . . . In order to teach and train children thoroughly, a separate class is needed. In the third place, even if parents were qualified and willing to do it themselves, yet on account of other employments and household duties they have no time for it, so that necessity requires us to have teachers for public schools, unless each parent employ a private instructor. But that would be too expensive for persons of ordinary means, and many a bright boy, on account of poverty, would be neglected . . . Therefore it will be the duty of mayors and council to exercise the greatest care over the young. For since the happiness, honor, and life of the city are committed to their hands, they would be held recreant before God and the world, if they did not, day and night, with all their power, seek its welfare and improvement. Now the welfare of a city does not consist alone in great treasures, firm walls, beautiful houses, and munitions of war; indeed, where all these are found, and reckless fools come into power, the city sustains the greater injury. But the highest welfare, safety, and power of a city consists in able, learned, wise, upright, cultivated citizens who can secure, preserve, and utilize every treasure and advantage . . .

"But, you say again, if we shall and must have schools, what is the use to teach Latin, Greek, Hebrew, and the other liberal arts? Is it not enough to teach the Scriptures, which are necessary to salvation, in the mother tongue? . . . Let this be kept in mind, that we will not preserve the Gospel without the languages. The languages are the scabbard in which the word of God is sheathed . . . Since, then, it behooves Christians at all times to use the Bible as their only book and to be thoroughly acquainted with it, especially is it a disgrace and sin at the present day not to learn the languages, when God provides every facility, incites us to study, and wishes to have His Word known.

"Even if there were no soul, and men did not need the languages for the sake of Christianity and the Scriptures, still, for the establishment of the best schools everywhere, both for boys and girls, this consideration is of itself sufficient, namely, that society for the maintenance of civil order and the proper regulation of the household, needs accomplished and well-trained men and women. Now such men are to come from boys, and such women from girls; hence it is necessary that boys and girls be properly taught and brought up . . . If I had children and were able, I would have them learn not only the languages and history, but also singing, instrumental music, and the whole course of mathematics . . . My idea is that boys should spend an hour or two a day in school, and the rest of the time work at home, learn some trade and do whatever is desired, so that study and work may go on together while the children are young and can attend to both . . . In like manner, a girl has time to go to school an hour a day, and yet attend to her work at home . . . But the brightest pupils, who give promise of becoming accomplished teachers, preachers, and workers, should be kept longer at school, or set apart wholly for study . . . No cost or pains should be spared to procure good libraries in suitable buildings, especially in the large cities . . . In the first place, a library should contain the Holy Scrip-

tures in Latin, Greek, Hebrew, German, and other languages. Then the best and most ancient commentators
in Greek, Hebrew, and Latin. Secondly, such books as
are useful in acquiring the languages, as the poets and
orators, without considering whether they are heathen
or Christian, Greek or Latin. For it is from such works
that grammar must be learned. Thirdly, books treating
of all the arts and sciences. Lastly, books on jurisprudence and medicine, though here discrimination is necessary. A prominent place should be given to chronicles
and histories in whatever languages they may be obtained; for they are wonderfully useful in understanding and regulating the course of the world, and in dis-
closing the marvelous works of God . . . Since God has
so graciously and abundantly provided us with art, scholars, and books, it is time for us to reap the harvest and
gather for future use the treasures of these golden
years." [26]

There was an alarming disorganization of life when
the Church was broken down in Germany. The Peasants' War was one of the expressions of disorder. In
the transition to Protestantism everything for a time
seemed doomed. Luther writes to the Elector of Saxony in 1525, "Unless Your Grace makes a strict law
and undertakes to give proper support to the parishes
and preaching places, there will soon be no parsonages
or schools or pupils, and thus God's Word and Christian
Worship will be destroyed." He tells him too that "if
we are to continue to have a university here [at Witten-
berg] we must take prompt action. It were a pity if
such a school, from which the Gospel has gone out into
all the world, were to go down, and if, when men are

[26] From the translation by F. V. N. Painter in Eby's *Early Protestant
Educators*, 45 *et seq.* (New York: McGraw-Hill).

needed everywhere, nothing were done to educate them."

A plan of Protestant education had taken definite form in his mind when in July, 1529, he wrote to the Margrave of Brandenburg: "It would be good if in your Grace's principality your Grace would establish one or two universities where not only the Holy Scriptures, but law and all the sciences would be taught. From these schools learned men could be got as preachers, pastors, secretaries, councillors, etc., for the whole principality. To this purpose the income of the monasteries and foundations could be applied so that scholars could be maintained in the schools at proper salaries, i.e., two theologians, two jurists, one professor of medicine, one mathematician, and for logic, rhetoric, etc., four or five men.

"It is well that in all towns and villages good primary schools should be established out of which could be picked those who are fit for the universities, out of which the men can be taken who are to serve your land and people."

It was to Melanchthon, Luther's younger partner, chiefly that the organization of the German school system was due. So powerfully did he shape the universities and high schools that he was called "Praeceptor Germaniae." He was a humanist as well as a leader of the Reformation in religion. "The truths of religion and moral duty cannot be rightly perceived except by minds soundly prepared by a training based upon the practice of past ages," he said in his inaugural address at Wittenberg. For ten years while he was a professor there he maintained a private boarding school for boys in his own house. It was a sort of model Latin school. Latin was spoken. The rudiments of Greek were taught, but whatever of religion, mathematics, and physics was learned was in Latin. Melanchthon wrote the textbooks.

IX

LOYOLA AND THE COUNTER–REFORMATION

THERE never were braver men or more devoted or better organized or more compelling than the members of the Society of Jesus. The Roman Church had seen the revival of antiquity sap its foundations in Italy; it had seen Martin Luther withdraw the Church of Germany and Northern Europe from its communion, Henry VIII detach the Church of England from the papal jurisdiction, John Calvin sow the seeds of revolt in Switzerland, France, and the Netherlands, and John Knox separate Scotland from the Catholic fold. The Roman religion needed a restorer and defender. It found him in the person of Ignatius Loyola. The Counter-Reformation was his handiwork.

Ignatius Loyola was a Spaniard, perhaps the greatest of all Spaniards. The Catholicism of Spain was and is different from that of every other country because of the centuries of religious warfare that her people waged against the Mohammedans. Crusading for the faith was the supreme Spanish industry for the better part of the seven hundred and seventy-seven years of the Moorish occupation. The Catholic Church of Spain had at no time lost its vigor or its cross-carrying militancy. The exaggerated deeds of knighthood still filled and directed the popular mind and shaped the religious no less than the literary imagination of the Spanish leaders.

Don Iñigo López de Recalde, the son of Don Beltran, was a warrior in his youth; and a warrior he remained until death claimed him. His father was a Basque nobleman, sufficiently distinguished to be summoned to the court of the King by a special writ. The castle of Loyola in which Don Iñigo was born in 1493 is still standing, near the little town of Azpeitia. "Up to my six-and twentieth year, I was entirely given to the vanities of the world. Above all I found pleasure in the management of arms, and felt a keen and empty craving to excel." A relative, Don Juan Velásquez de Cuellar, took the little seven-year-old Iñigo into his household as a page. Don Juan was governor of King Ferdinand's fortresses at Arevalo and Truxillo, chief of the household of Queen Isabella, and royal treasurer of Castile. His wife, Doña María, was lady in waiting to the Queen. When Isabella the Catholic died, King Ferdinand married the French princess, Germaine de Foix. The life of the court immediately became much less austere, and Doña María Velásquez de Cuellar, whom the page Iñigo served, became a close friend and confidante of the new Queen. The little Iñigo basked in the sunshine of royalty. When in due course he became a knight and must name a "queen of hearts," he chose to carry the colors of no less a person than the Queen of Aragon. Chivalry had a large place in his thoughts. He read the books which Don Quixote read, and was no less absorbed in contemplation of deeds of knightly valor. His protectress, Doña María de Cuellar, lost the favor of the Queen, and Don Iñigo's day of glory came to an end. He joined the guard of the Duke of Najera, viceroy of Navarre. Here in the border fortress of Pamplona he found warfare of a grimness very different from the jousting of the court. After four years of drilling and standing guard in that bleak country, a French army came and shut up the little Spanish garrison in the fortress of Pamplona. The defenders thought that they were too few and should surrender without a battle, but the youngest officer there would not yield so easily. He reminded them that they were hidalgos of Spain and must die rather than disgrace their arms. He rallied the defence in the thick of the fighting, and when the French broke in they found that brave young officer, Don Iñigo de Loyola, lying on the bloody bastion with a shattered leg.

Then came the long months in the castle of Loyola and the discovery that the leg had been set so badly that the bones must be broken again. Even then the bone protruded and had to be cut off by the surgeon's saw. Convalescence was slow. In looking for something to read, two books were found for him in the castle: Ludolphus of Saxony's *Life of Christ* and *The Flowers of the Saints*. These must at first have seemed poor things to a knight hungering to read of the unrivalled deeds of Amadis of Gaul; but not for long did they prove unsatisfactory. As Don Iñigo read the account of St. Dominic and St. Francis, it began to seem to him that they were more wonderful than any knight-at-arms of whom he had ever heard. They were champions of the Faith— incomparable champions of the Faith. And he, why should he not be a champion of the Faith? As he brooded on these great matters of the Faith, he saw it all as a warfare between the hosts of Satan and the armies of the Lord. He knew to which army he belonged, and he took a vow to be an ever faithful soldier. As soon as he was able he set out for Montserrat to begin his spiritual knighthood. "And arriving at a big town before he got to Montserrat, he wanted to buy there the clothing which he had determined to wear to Jerusalem. And so he bought cloth of the sort they used in making sacks, of a kind which is very prickly, and ordered a garment made of it reaching to his feet. And he took up his journey for Montserrat thinking, as was his wont, about the deeds he had to do for the love of God. And as his mind was filled with ideas from Amadis of Gaul and other books of chivalry, things came into his head like them. And so he made up his mind to watch over his arms all one night without sitting or lying down, but now standing and now kneeling before the altar of Our Lady of Montserrat, where he decided to leave his garments and clothe himself with the arms of Christ." [1]

At Montserrat, the first thing he did after praying in the church was to make a confession covering his whole previous life to the hermit of St. Damas. It took him three days to write it out. Then he hung up his sword and his dagger at the altar of Our Lady, and, marching up and down in front of them, he passed the whole night and started off to Barcelona at dawn the next morning. At Manresa, a little town on the way, not far from Montserrat, the "new soldier of Christ" tarried for eight months, every day begging alms in the streets and spending seven hours in prayer and aside from these aiding souls that came to him for help and meditating on the things of God. He fasted much, macerated his body, and had extraordinary visions. He passed from the depths of despair to the heights of spiritual exaltation and back, repeatedly. In January, 1523, he set out for the Holy Land, carrying the pilgrim's staff and the beginnings of the book of *Spiritual Exercises*. The journey was long and hard, but visions of Christ kept Ignatius to his undertaking. The Franciscans of Jerusalem told him that their

[1] Loyola's Autobiography, quoted in Paul Van Dyke, *Ignatius Loyola*, 35.

ecclesiastical authority there was complete, and that he could not stay. He forthwith took ship at Jaffa, and in January, 1524, was back in Venice. His disappointment in not being allowed to convert the Mohammedans led him to embark on a new career. Though he was twenty-nine and largely untaught, he now began a twelve-year course of schooling. At Barcelona he studied grammar for two years with a master named Ardebalo. At first he could not put his mind on his lessons—there came instead spiritual insights; but Ignatius invited his teacher to go with him to the Church of Holy Mary of the Sea, and there he said to him: "I promise you never to fail to listen to you for two years if I can find in Barcelona bread and water to sustain life." At the end of two years the master told him he was prepared to begin the liberal arts at the University of Alcalá. "He studied in Alcalá about a year and a half . . . dialectics in Soto, physics in Albertus and theology in the Master of the Sentences. And while he was at Alcalá he gave spiritual exercises and explained Christian doctrine and from this he gathered fruit for God. And there were many persons who grew in understanding of spiritual things and in liking for them." [2]

This informal preaching and teaching of Loyola and his four associates caused the Inquisition several times to investigate what they were doing. Indeed, Ignatius was put into jail for a few days and then told to dress as the other students did and not to talk about things of the Faith until he had studied four years longer, since he did not yet know the liberal arts. He thereupon left Alcalá, and after counselling with the Archbishop of Toledo he followed his comrades to the University of Salamanca. Within ten or twelve days of his arrival there, the Do-

[2] Loyola's Autobiography, quoted in Van Dyke, *op. cit.*, 58.

minican friars invited him to their house and questioned
him very closely about what it was he said to people in
his familiar talks to them about God. At the end of
three days he was put into jail, and his manuscript of
the *Exercises* was taken for examination. He was questioned before a board of judges, and after twenty-two
days in prison was told that no error had been found in
their doctrine and no evil in their life and that they could
go on talking about the things of God "without however
defining at any time this is a mortal sin or that is a venial
sin, until they had studied for four years more." Ignatius
said he would obey the command but could not accept
the sentence because "they closed his lips so that he
could not help his neighbors so far as he was able." So
he made up his mind to leave Salamanca and go to Paris
to study.

In this activity of Ignatius and his little band at Alcalá
and Salamanca there is something very significant. It was
very much like the procedure in later days of the early
Methodists and the Salvation Army. It grew from a conviction that Christianity must go everywhere and must
above all be a lay movement to the unchurched, saving
souls one by one.

Ignatius was at the University of Paris for seven years.
There were forty-nine colleges in the University of Paris
then. Ignatius entered the Collège de Montaigu as a gram-
mar-school scholar and studied the humanities, for he
found that his grammar training in Latin at Barcelona
had not sufficiently grounded him. Thoroughness was a
virtue he both cultivated and prescribed. The Collège
de Montaigu was famous for its discipline. Ignatius always valued discipline. Montaigu had able students.
Erasmus and Calvin had been in its classes. Work began there at five A.M. and went to eight P.M. It seems

to have been a place where men and boys were starved, flogged, and allowed to sicken and die in an inhuman fashion. Ignatius, it is thought, wrote consideration for health into the constitution of the Jesuit schools because of the inconsiderateness he saw there. When he first came, he lived in an inn; but a fellow Spaniard to whom he had entrusted his money for safe keeping spent it, and Loyola had to move to free lodgings in the hospital of St. Jacques, and to beg for his food. Begging took so much of his time that it nearly defeated his plan to get an education, and when he came to write rules for the Jesuit colleges, one of them was that no students of the company should beg their bread. A friar whom he met suggested to him that he should go to Flanders and beg from the rich Spanish merchants there. He did so twice. In the third year he went to England to raise the money for his education.

In the summer of 1529 he transferred to the Collège Sainte-Barbe. Religious thoughts beginning to intrude unwarrantably upon his studies, he went to the master and vowed to him never to fail to attend the course as long as he had bread and water. At the end of three and a half years Ignatius was admitted to the mastership, and thereupon began the course in theology. There was no street preaching during his seven years in Paris, only a resolute attempt to make himself an educated man and his associations with a few intimates who shared his religious zeal, and for whose salvation he was unmeasuredly solicitous. His purpose had not changed: he existed for nothing but the service of souls. But Ignatius had concluded from what he saw in Italy of the undoing of faith by the Renaissance and what he heard and knew of the overthrow of the Church by the Reformation that the effective ministry to souls must henceforth be a learned ministry. The preaching friars were sufficient for the conditions three hundred years earlier, but for his day and troubled time a new order was needed—an order of vastly better trained men who should combine with completeness of devotion the strength and dexterity of unmistakable scholarship. Early in his course in Paris he began to find here and there among his fellow students men who he felt could be brought to like mind with himself, and he quietly proceeded to bring them.

In 1529 he met Pierre Lefèvre, a Swiss peasant's son, deeply sensitive to the claims of religion, who had come to Paris for education some four years before and had dedicated his life to God and taken a vow of perpetual chastity. Lefèvre had an intimate friend, a fellow-student, Francis Xavier, the son of a Basque noble of Spanish Navarre, whose estate had suffered in the wars. These two were more advanced students in the Collège Sainte-Barbe. They took Loyola to room with them, and Lefèvre was assigned by their master, Peña, to tutor him. Lefèvre was twenty-three, Loyola thirty-four. The young man tutored the older one in philosophy, but the older took over responsibility for his tutor's religious life. At the end of four years he gave him the spiritual exercises, he made him one with himself. Xavier was more worldly-minded, much harder to win. He was an exuberant individual, the fleetest runner in the University, a social favorite who loved the company of his fellow men no less than they loved him, well-known to the taverns of the Latin Quarter, and cherishing as his chief ambition the obtaining of a fat living somewhere in his native Navarre. He regarded Ignatius as a gloomy bigot. But one day, while he was expansively describing his prospects, Loyola flashed at him the ancient question: What shall it profit a man if he gain the whole world and lose his own soul?

The words became a burr in his mind. He began to listen more attentively to what Loyola was saying, asked for instruction, and in due course became the devoted companion, who led the great mission to India and Japan. A poet he was of an extraordinary fervor:

> At such love, my love I kindle.
> Were there no heaven, still must I love!
> Were there no hell, sin would I shun!
> Were heaven and hell to pass away,
> With their rewards and punishments,
> In me would love for love endure!

Diego Laínez and his close friend Alfonso Salmerón came from the University of Alcalá to Paris and were quickly gathered into the little company of devotees. They were gifted in learning. Loyola soon gave them the spiritual exercises. The fifth companion was Simon Rodriguez from Portugal, who went to Paris on a royal scholarship. The holy zeal of Ignatius swept him into the company. The sixth recruit was Nicolás Alfonso, more commonly called Bobadilla from the town in Spain from which he came.

At daybreak of August 15, 1534, Loyola and these six companions walked from the Latin Quarter across Paris and beyond the walls to the deserted little chapel of St. Denis on the hill of Montmartre. Lefèvre, the only priest among them, said Mass; then, as he turned and held the Host up before them, each of the six advanced and, falling on his knees, took the vows of chastity and poverty, and communed. This was the first meeting of all the members of the little band. Their plans for the future were not clear. Loyola was a Spanish warrior and had gone to Jerusalem to convert the infidel. That was what Christianity had meant for so many centuries in Spain that its militant form was uppermost in the thoughts of all in that little Iberic company. The recent successes of the Turks in taking Rhodes and dominating the Mediterranean made it doubtful whether they could get to Palestine; but they were resolved, if it was at all possible, to go and support the Faith by converting the infidels there.

We have spoken repeatedly of the spiritual exercises. It is time to consider more definitely what they were. It has been said that the book which contained them made the Jesuits. Loyola was a visualizer. His imagination worked by clearly defined picturing. At Montserrat he seems to have studied the *Exercises of the Spiritual Life* of García de Cisneros, a former abbot of the monastery. In the cave of Manresa he began to formulate his own *Exercises*. He did not compose his book all at once. He worked on it for twenty years. "When anything resulting from my own experience seemed to be likely to be of use to others I took note of it." The *Exercises* are in four parts, a first week, a second week, a third, and a fourth; but the week is not a week of seven days but a week of exercises, the first ones to come first and the others in their order. "By this name of *Spiritual Exercises*," says Loyola, "is meant any method of examining one's conscience, of meditating, contemplating, praying aloud or to oneself, or performing any other spiritual operations. For, just as sauntering, walking briskly, and running, are corporal exercises, so spiritual exercises are any method at all that prepares and disposes the soul to cast away all inordinate affections, and after it shall cast them off, to seek and find the Will of God as to the ordering of one's life and the salvation of one's soul."

The purpose of the first week is purgative, to reform the sinner by "searing upon the soul a hatred of sin by

terror." Its meditations are upon sin and hell, to which
meditations upon death and the last judgment may be
added. The meditations of the second week are upon the
life of Christ, the warfare for the kingdom, the battles
under the two standards, etc. The third meditations are
on the passion and suffering of Christ, and the fourth, on
Christ's glory.

The full title of the book is *Spiritual Exercises to Conquer Self and Regulate One's Life and to Avoid Coming
to a Determination Through Any Inordinate Affection*.
The novices make the exercises in a retreat of thirty days
upon entering the order. First comes a preparatory meditation on the object of human life, whose principle and
foundation the *Exercises* state is that "man is created to
praise, reverence and serve God, Our Lord, and through
this to save his soul." After this preparatory meditation
comes a twofold examination of himself, the first particular, the second general. The particular examination has
three parts: On rising in the morning one must determine
to guard against the sin which is his, and which he seeks
to root out. After the midday meal he should go over
each hour since he made his resolve and carefully note
down in a book the times he has committed that sin.
After supper he is to examine his hours one by one since
the midday. He is to do this day by day and week by
week and compare one hour's, one day's, and one week's
record with those of other hours, days, and weeks. This
is the particular or private examination of conscience.

The general examination begins by the director pointing out that our thoughts have three sources: ourselves,
the good spirit, and the evil spirit. Sins are venial and
mortal. There are sins of words and of deeds. To prepare for the general examination, five acts are advised:
(1) to give thanks to God for benefits received; (2) to

pray for grace to know one's sins; (3) to demand an accounting from one's soul from the hour of rising until the present moment; (4) to ask pardon of God for those misdeeds, and (5) to put aside opposition to His Grace.

After this preparation, a general confession covering one's life up to this moment is to be made to a priest other than the priest directing the exercises, and the receiver of the confession gives the exercitant the Communion.

Now comes the exercise proper. It opens with a prayer. It begins with a preamble, that of composition, seeing the place. On the effort to meditate on whatever is visible the composition will be the act of seeing in imagination the physical surroundings in which the thing takes place which one seeks to contemplate. In case the contemplation is of invisible things, such as sins, the composition will be to see in imagination and to consider "my soul imprisoned in this corruptible body and everything surrounding it in this valley, as banished among brute beasts."

The second preamble is "to demand of God what I wish and desire . . . If the meditation is on the Passion, to demand pains, tears and to experience the torments which tormented Christ." Then come the three points of the meditation, each employing one of the faculties of the soul. In contemplating sin the exercitant will trace that of the fallen angels, "considering that while they went to hell for one sin, I have deserved it for many sins." Secondly, he will recall the sin of Adam and Eve, "bringing to mind how great corruption came by it upon the human race, so many men going towards hell"; thirdly, the particular sin of some definite person who has gone to hell for it, and many others without number who have gone to hell for fewer sins than the exercitant has committed.

The exercise or meditation upon sin ends with a colloquy. Imagining Christ our Savior stretched upon the Cross, the exercitant is to ask Him how He came to become man and to die for his sins; and then to ask himself, "What have I done for Christ, what am I doing for Christ, what ought I to do for Christ?"

The steps in each of the exercises are the same as in this first one. Each exercise is to be gone through first in the middle of the night, and again on rising in the morning, a third time before or after Mass, a fourth time at the hour of Vespers and a fifth time before supper.

It will help the understanding of this activity to summarize it in the words of Henry Dwight Sedgwick: "The duties of the novice in the course of a day during the first week, are roughly as follows: He is to rise from his bed at midnight and pray to God that 'all his intentions, actions and operations may be ordained purely to the service and praise of His Divine Majesty.' Then he is to frame before his mind's eye some scriptural picture, say of Christ, at Bethany, with all the physical surroundings just as they were in life, bringing himself into the presence of the living Christ. With his imagination upon this picture, he is to pray for shame and confusion at the thought of his wrongdoings, and of the eternal damnation he deserves. After these preliminaries he is to think of sin: first, the sin by which the angels fell, then Adam's sin, and third, any definite mortal sin. These sins are, as it were, to be handled, touched and weighed, as if gross and palpable to the senses, by means of will and imagination. After an hour spent in such contemplation, there follows an imaginary dialogue. The novice, bowed beneath an overpowering sense of treason against Infinite Goodness, must imagine Christ before him nailed to the cross, must talk to Him and ask Him how it could be that He, God the Creator, had taken upon Himself death for man's sake; and then he is to turn and ask himself what he has done for Christ, what he is doing, and what he ought to do. This colloquy is to be conducted as if a servant were talking to his master, or a friend to a friend, and ends with a *pater noster*." [3]

The meditation on the two standards is the work of a warrior and is particularly impressive. "The Captain of the enemies of God" has his camp in the country round Babylon. He is horrible in figure and countenance, his throne is a chair of fire and smoke, an omnipresent legion of devils obeys him. He is forever disguising himself as an angel of light and lures by snares and temptations sinners without ceasing. Christ the King marshals the armies of the Lord round about Jerusalem. He sends his recruiting officers into all the world. He bids them "lead men to a spiritual affection for poverty." The "composition" requires the novice first to see the place and the embattled hosts, then to image an earthly king and to hear him say: "My will is to conquer all the lands of the infidels. Whoever chooses to come with me must be content to eat as I eat, drink as I drink, be clad as I am clad. He must work as I work in the day and watch as I watch at night, that he may share with me the victory as he has shared the labor . . ." Much more compelling is the summons of the King Eternal. Before the universe he calls each and every individual and says: "It is my will to conquer the whole world and all the enemies and so enter into the glory of my Father. He who would go with

[3] Sedgwick, *Ignatius Loyola*, 128. By permission of The Macmillan Company.

me must work with me, for following me in pain he shall reap glory." [4]

And he who hears will say: "O Thou Supreme King and Lord of all things, I, though most unworthy, yet relying on Thy grace and help, offer myself altogether to Thee, and submit all that is mine to Thee."

Loyola's health did not allow him to finish his course in theology in Paris. Early in 1535 he left his companions with Pierre Lefèvre to direct them and returned to his home in Spain. There he insisted upon begging his own food and spent his days in teaching children and talking and preaching to older people. He drew up ordinances for the relief of the poor in Azpeitia and journeyed to the home of each of his Spanish comrades in his little company of seven to visit with and reassure their parents. Then he went to Valencia and took ship for Genoa, thence on foot to Bologna and from Bologna to Venice, which he reached about January 1, 1536. Thereupon he waited about a year, as their agreement was, for his companions to finish their course at the University of Paris and join him. At Venice, Loyola nursed and prayed with the sick in the Hospital for Incurables and made the acquaintance of, and talked with, two Spanish pilgrims on their way back from the Holy Land, Diego and Estevan de Eguía and a young Spaniard from Malaga, Diego Hoces, all of whom joined his company. On January 6, 1537, the companions from Paris reached Venice after a seven weeks' journey on foot. Loyola sent them three by three on different roads to Rome. Pope Paul III received them kindly, heard them discuss a point in theology, gave them permission to go on pilgrimage to Jerusalem, made a contribution to the expense of their journey, and granted them priests' orders without requiring them

[4] *Exercicios de S. Ignacio* (Madrid: Casa Editorial Saturnino), 84.

to assume the duties of a parish. Having attained their object, they went back to Venice to take ship for the Holy Land.

The Venetians were at war with the Turks, and no ships could set forth. The Companions were ordained as priests, and before saying their first Mass they under-took a retreat of forty days as holy preparation. They had resolved to wait one year for an opportunity to carry out their plan to go to Jerusalem and now determined to spend the time of waiting in street preaching in the near-by towns. They made Vicenza their headquarters and came together from time to time to report their work. As the months passed and no opportunity came to start for Jerusalem, it became evident to them that they must give up their first project and offer their service to the Pope instead. Loyola, Laínez, and Lefèvre started to Rome, the others two by two, to Padua, Ferrara, Bologna, Siena, preaching in the streets. On the way, Loyola at the village of Storta had a vision in which the Heavenly Father commended Ignatius and his companions to the Son, and Jesus said to Ignatius: "I will be a friend to you at Rome." This approval by Christ Himself, Ignatius held directed them to name themselves the Company of Jesus. At Rome they passed through a period of "rough maltreatment." They applied for permission to preach and hear confession, and it was given them. But a report went round that aroused objection to their character and their doctrine. They summoned the persons who had maligned them before the Legate and the Governor. They were vindicated and insisted on having the judgment in writing. It was so long in coming that Ignatius finally took the matter to the Pope.

Since their original plan of going to convert the infidels had failed, at length in Lent of 1539 they began to be

ready to apply for a charter that would determine their
future. That was a grave matter, for in the papal grant
of powers the character of the organization had to be
outlined. They met every evening to deliberate, and after
prayer and the sacrifice of the Mass each one had to declare his opinion and the reason for it in proper order.
Then they voted, and the majority prevailed. First they
asked, Shall this small band of men stay together or
break up? The answer to that was not difficult. What
should their vows be? Poverty and chastity, they already
had accepted. Should they put themselves under a vow
of obedience as well? One imagines that Loyola's military training may have been determining at that point.
The matter was discussed in many meetings. They resolved to go counter to self-love, and voted unanimously
for a general and a vow of obedience. They determined
to surpass all other orders in that virtue. They forthwith took that third vow "to do all that is commanded
them by the Pope, for the time being, to go forthwith into
every country, among Turks, pagans, or heretics, where-
ever he should send them, without objection and without
condition or reward."

As a company of soldiers takes its name from its captain they resolved to be the Company of Jesus. After
about two months more they laid before the Pope this
outline of their organization:

"Whoever wishes to be a warrior of God under the
banner of the cross in our Company, which we call by the
name of Jesus, and to serve only God and his Vicar on
earth, must keep in his mind after he has taken the vow
of perpetual chastity that he is part of a community
founded chiefly to aid souls in Christian living and
Christian doctrine, to spread the word of God by preaching, by spiritual exercises, by deeds of neighborly kind-

ness and especially by the instruction of children and the ignorant in Christianity.

"He must always have God before his eyes and strive with all his might towards the goal shown him by God, keeping always before him those rules which are in a manner a way to God. The decision about the place or position in service which belongs to every man must rest entirely in the hands of the prepositus to be chosen by us. This prepositus shall have power to make statutes with the advice of the brothers in concilium when the majority shall always decide. The executive power and the power to give orders belong only to the prepositus [general].

"All members, so long as life lasts, shall every day bethink themselves of the fact that this Company and all in it are under the command of our holy master Paul III and his successors, so that we are bound to give him something more than the obedience of ordinary clergymen. We are bound by special oath to do whatever he orders us to do; whether he sends us to the Turks or to the new world, or to the Lutherans, or to any other believers or unbelievers.

"Every member shall promise obedience to the general in all things concerning the rule. He on his side must be always mindful of the goodness, the gentleness and love of Christ. Both shall lay it on their hearts to instruct children and the ignorant in Christian doctrine, in the ten commandments and other elementary things.

"We have learned by experience that a way of living as far from greed and as near to evangelic poverty as possible is more edifying to our neighbours and that Christ will provide for his servants. We cannot hold any legal right to any income or real property, but must be content with the simple use of things necessary to life by the consent of the owners.

"All ordained members are to say the breviary according to the rites of the Church, not however all together in choir, in order that they may not be turned aside from the duties of neighbourly love. They shall not use in divine service either the organ or chanting. For these things, which adorn the divine worship of other orders, we have found by experience to be no small hindrance to us; since we devote a great part of the day and night to the bodily and spiritual care of the sick.

"We make this sketch of what we do and propose in order to warn our successors against falling into two errors we have escaped. First, no one shall ever enjoin upon the members of our company fasts, scourgings, going barefooted or bareheaded, fixed colours of dress and fixed foods, hair shirts or other ascetic observances. We do not forbid these things because we condemn them, but because we do not wish our brethren to find in them an excuse for withdrawing themselves from the duties we have undertaken.

"The second error to be avoided is this. No one can be received into the company unless he has been very thoroughly tested for a long time." [5]

It was in 1540 that Pope Paul III wrote the words *Digitus Dei est Hic* (Here is the finger of God) upon the new order's application for a charter, and on September 27, 1540, the Bull of confirmation was issued. The next step in the formation of the order was the election of a general. The election was held at Rome in April, 1541. Already Rodriguez and Xavier were in Portugal on their way to India, and Lefèvre had begun his work in Germany. They had left their ballots. Only six were pres-

[5] Van Dyke, *op. cit.*, 134–136.

ent. On every ballot except his own, the name Ignatius
was written. He protested that he was not able to govern
himself and could not govern others, and asked them to
commend themselves to God and consider further. In
four days they came together again, and once more elected
Loyola. He resolved to be guided by his confessor and
made a confession covering his entire life. The confessor sent a positive answer to the Society.[6]

Then the little company went to each of the seven
churches for pilgrims and in the last of them, St. Paul
Outside the Walls, Loyola said Mass, and, turning to
the others with the Blessed Sacrament in his hand, he
uttered these words: "I, Ignatius Loyola, vow to God
Almighty, and to the Supreme Pontiff, His vicar on
earth, in the presence of the Virgin His Mother and the
whole Court of Heaven and in the presence of the Company, perpetual poverty, chastity and obedience, in accordance with the provisions of the Bull confirming the
Company of Our Lord Jesus and contained in the constitution as drawn or to be drawn. Moreover, I vow obedience in particular to the Supreme Pontiff concerning
missions as set forth in the Bull. And I further vow that
I will teach boys in the principles of the faith, according to the Bull and the constitution."[7] Ignatius as General directed the Society until his death in 1556.

The next step was the preparation of a constitution.[8]
The members of the Company left that to the two who
remained in Rome, the General and Father Coduri.
Shortly afterward Father Coduri died, and Ignatius'
health and the burden of work upon him made the drafting of the constitution for the Order a slow business. It

[6] See Ribadeneyra, *Vida del S. Ignacio*, 4–1.
[7] Sedgwick, *op. cit.*, 215.
[8] See Dudon, *Saint Ignace de Loyola*, 383.

was not finished until 1550, and was further revised and ordered in 1552.

The constitution states that "the object of this Society is to labor not only for the salvation and perfection of our own souls, by the help of God's grace, but also by the same help, to devote ourselves zealously to the salvation and perfection of our neighbors."

The outward form of life is not marked by difference from that of ordinary men; penances and bodily chastisement are not prescribed, but may be employed by individual members with the consent of their Superior. Admission to the Society is gained only through a novitiate of two years. After it is satisfactorily completed, those who are adjudged worthy take the three vows in the famous oath: "I promise to Almighty God, before his Virgin Mother and the whole heavenly host, and to all standing by; and to thee, Reverend Father, General of the Society of Jesus holding the place of God, and to thy successors, perpetual poverty, chastity, and obedience; and according to it a peculiar care in the education of boys according to the form of life contained in the Apostolic Letters of the Society of Jesus and in its Constitutions."

The Company includes all who live under obedience to the General: (1) novices, (2) approved scholars, (3) coadjutors, (4) professed of the three vows, (5) professed of the four vows. It belongs to the General to admit to probation; this power he may entrust to others. There are certain positive disqualifications. The candidate must not be married or be a slave. He must not be insane or threatened with insanity. He must never have worn a monastic dress. He must never have committed a major crime. He must never have denied the faith among infidels or been a schismatic or been found guilty of heresy. Other disqualifications, not quite so final until investigated, are strong passions, bad habits, worldly motives, inconstancy of character, devotions of a fantastic and erroneous nature, lack of education and of mental capacity, obstinacy, debts, and social obligations. For twelve or more days at the beginning the postulant is a guest with a room of his own. During this period he is examined thoroughly. If he is unsatisfactory, he is sent away; if satisfactory, he is admitted to the common house and the probation of two years. He may leave at any time, and, unless he is promising, no effort will be made to retain him; or he may be dismissed at any time. The novices are to take the spiritual exercises for a month, to serve in a hospital for a month, to travel for a month without money, begging their food from door to door; to perform menial services in a house of the Society, to teach the catechism to children, and hold themselves ready to preach and hear confession. For the care of their souls and their advancement in virtue, "it is very necessary for the novices to avoid all communication which might chill their purpose; they must not go out of the house except at the time prescribed, and with an appointed companion, and while in the house converse only with those whom the Superior shall designate; they shall keep watch and ward over eyes, ears and tongues; they should speak in words apt for edification, wear modest looks, walk with unhurried gait and never a gesture showing pride or impatience; they should in all matters leave the better things to others, look upon themselves as inferior, and treat every one with the respect due to his station; indeed each should see in every other an image of God. And it is of the first importance for spiritual progress that all shall give themselves over to a perfect obedience, looking upon the Superior as in the place of Christ, and performing not only in outward act but with inward reverence and love, what he shall command, however hard, *integre, prompte, fortiter,* with due humility, without a murmur, without an excuse. Novices shall love poverty like a mother; they shall strive after righteousness, and learn to divest themselves, as much as may be possible, of love of all creatures in order to turn all their affection toward the Creator." [9]

The Constitution had sections "on the manner of instructing those who remain in the Society, in liberal studies and other things that serve to help our neighbors." The chapters are: (1) On the gratitude to be shown towards Founders and Benefactors of Colleges; (2) On the property of Colleges; (3) On the students to be matriculated therein; (4) On dealing with the students who have been admitted; (5) On studies. These shall consist of grammar, rhetoric, languages, logic, natural and moral philosophy, metaphysics, theology, both scholastic and positive, and the Holy Scriptures. As a rule Latin is to be spoken. These textbooks are prescribed: in Theology, the Old and New Testaments; in Scholastic doctrine, St. Thomas Aquinas; in positive theology, part of the canon law and decisions of Councils; in logic, metaphysics, natural and moral philosophy, the works of Aristotle. In Greek and Latin literature care is to be taken in the choice of books, unless they have been expurgated. These directions of the Constitution of the Society as to studies were later amplified in the *Ratio Studiorum*.

The highest grade in the Society is the professed of the four vows. It constitutes the very core of the Society, from which its chief officers are taken. As a usual thing membership in this grade can be reached only after a

[9] In Sedgwick, *Ignatius Loyola,* 219.

long probation of thirty-one years from the time of entrance into the Society, requiring an age of fifty-four years. The number of these Fathers is small. To the three vows of poverty, chastity, and obedience already taken they add a fourth vow; "Moreover, I promise the special obedience to the Sovereign Pontiff concerning missions, as is contained in the same Apostolic Letter and Constitutions." The approved scholars pass into the grade of coadjutors, or professed of the three vows. The coadjutors are of two kinds, spiritual and temporal, the former to become priests, the latter to be assistants in temporal matters.

One chapter of the Constitution is on Obedience. All must observe it. "Dropping every occupation, leaving unfinished the letter we have begun, and banding all our strength and purpose in the Lord to that end, so that holy obedience be perfect in us in every respect, in execution, in will, and in understanding; obedience in execution consists in doing what is ordered; obedience in will, in having no other will than his from whom we receive the order; obedience in understanding, in thinking as the Superior thinks, and in believing what he ordains is rightly ordained. Otherwise obedience is imperfect. We are to do whatever shall be commanded us, with great promptitude, and spiritual joy and steadfastness; persuading ourselves that all commands are righteous; and laying aside in blind obedience our own opinion to the contrary; yea, in everything prescribed by the Superior—where it cannot definitely be shown that some kind of sin is involved. Let every one convince himself that those who live under Obedience should be led and governed by Divine Providence through their Superiors, *perinde ac si cadaver essent,* as a corpse would be, that allows itself to be carried here or there, and handled after any fashion; or like an old man's staff, which suffers itself to be used everywhere, and in any way, that he who holds it wishes." [10]

A member of the Company may not take a parish, as he must continually be free to go wherever his Superior would send him. He must avoid secular affairs. He takes certain supplementary vows after taking the three vows of poverty, chastity, and obedience: (1) that he will never act nor consent that the provisions of the Constitution concerning poverty be changed; (2) that he will not directly or indirectly procure election or promotion for himself to any prelacy or dignity in the Society; (3) that he will not accept or consent to his election to any dignity or prelacy outside the Society unless forced thereto by obedience; (4) that if others do these things he will denounce them to the Superiors; (5) that if elected to a bishopric he will not refuse to hear the advice of the General,. and will follow it if he judges it better than his own opinion. Unity is necessary and difficult to maintain among members scattered through the world. "Whoever is seen to be the cause of division among those who dwell together . . . ought to be separated from that congregation like a pestilence which can spread its contagion if a remedy is not at once applied . . . The chief bond for the union of the members with each other and their head is the love of God . . . The principal enemy of that union is self-love which can be combated by charity and by every goodness and virtue and also by contempt for temporal things . . . The sending of letters missive, by which through the efforts of the provincials and the General, news of the entire Company reaches every part of it, is a very especial aid for consolation and mutual edification in Our Lord." The separate detachments must

[10] In Sedgwick, *Ignatius Loyola,* 221.

be in touch with one another and with the commander-in-chief "so that the same spirit, the same aim, and the same endeavors may prevail throughout." The Society requires a corporate organization, based on obedience, that it may not lose its fighting power. The work of its members is in the world. They have no home, the whole earth is their parish. They are to be the light cavalry of the Church, to go wherever the Pope or the General shall send them. The whole world is divided into provinces supervised by a provincial appointed by the General. The "professed houses" are governed by Superiors, and the colleges by heads appointed by the General. The General lives in Rome and is informed by reports minute, frequent, regular and irregular, official and private, of the doings of every member of the Society. The Superiors report on those under them, but the subordinates are obligated to report the irregularities of their Superiors to headquarters.

The Society of Jesus is an army which fights in extended order through the world. What of the General? He should "be closely united to God and very familiar with the use of prayer," one "whose example in all the virtues will help those in the Company. Especially must he shine with the light of charity to all his neighbors and particularly to those of the Company, and that true humility which will make him beloved by God and men." He should be strong and of good courage, "being always entirely ready to suffer death if it is necessary for the good of the Company in the service of Jesus Christ." Understanding, judgment, caution, enterprise, tenacity, health, appearance, a proper age, and fair fame outside the Company are enumerated as qualities desired in him. "And if some of the qualities mentioned are lacking in him, at least there must not be lacking great goodness and love for the Company and good judgment accompanied by a good education."

The General is elected by the Congregation of the Society.[11]

Once elected, the General is by no means the autocratic ruler that his title would indicate. A consultative council is sent to live beside him at Rome, made up of Assistants, one from each of the various nations. He is given a *socius* or "admonisher," as he is sometimes called, to warn him of mistakes, and a confessor. The services of both of these he is required to employ. It is within the power of the Company to depose a general and even to expel him from the Society for specified causes "(which it is hoped in the divine goodness will never occur) as for example mortal sin, such as licentiousness, wounding, peculation or heresy."[12]

The vow which the first General, Loyola, took in the Church of St. Paul Outside the Walls had in it the words: "Moreover, I vow obedience in particular to the Supreme Pontiff concerning missions as set forth in the Bull [i.e. the charter]." The General of the Society of Jesus is not independent of the Pope. The Society is a part of the organized Church and is subject to the orders of the Pope as head of the Church. The papal office chartered and

[11] 1. The following are entitled to attend a General Congregation:

(a) The General or the Vicar General, or both, if the General Congregation is called during the lifetime of the General; the Assistants, the Provincials of the various Provinces; and two Electors, selected by each Province;

(b) The Secretary of the Society, the Procurator General, the General Econome, the Procurators from each of the indepedent Vice-Provinces;

(c) And, finally, those Procurators who may be summoned by the General, or sent by their Provincials with the approval of the General.

2. Only the Vicar General, the Assistants, the Provincials and the two Electors from each Province have the right to vote for the election of a General.

[12] Van Dyke, *Ignatius Loyola*, 155.

encouraged and privileged the Society, and the Society has always been obedient to the Pope, even in 1773 accepting suppression at his hands. In its relations to him, it has, however, not always been as a stick in an old man's hands.

The work which faced the Society at its formation was colossal. When Ignatius Loyola died in 1556, Luther had been dead ten years. Calvin was hard at work in Geneva until 1564; Mary Tudor was Queen of England, but Elizabeth came to the throne in 1558. John Knox was preaching in Geneva, the work of his life being done in Scotland between 1559 and 1572. How the world looked to the members of the Society of Jesus in the days of Loyola, we do not know. Had they sensed its real condition it is hardly likely that they would have centred their first intention so fixedly upon the conversion of the infidels of Syria. Laínez, the second General, is entirely clear about what must be done. Here is the acknowledging speech he wrote six years after Ignatius' death: "The corruption of the little of Christendom left demands penitence and emendation. This must begin with the clergy, and among the clergy with the Supreme Head and his court, whose bad example and bad use of the power he has from God is the principal cause of the disorders among the members of the Church. How great is the need of such a reformation can be judged by the universal scandal and the hatred among some, the contempt among others, of the Holy See because of the abuses in it. In our day we have seen Germany, Scotland, Denmark, Sweden, Norway and Prussia break away and there is very probable danger that the Kingdom of Poland and the States of Flanders and France will follow. Nor is there any security for those which remain, Spain and Italy, because they are scandalized by the abuses of their

Head . . . The abuses which cause this scandal are first to see the Popes not expecting to do anything in the Papacy except to make great their relatives according to the flesh, and for this reason conceding to princes wrong things and putting unfit men into the college of cardinals," etc.[13]

There was much to be reformed if the Church was to be saved from corruption. The religious orders were no longer completely helpful. Parish priests had almost wholly given up preaching. They did not know how. Little care was given to choosing candidates for the priesthood. Their education was grossly neglected. The bishops were some of them incapable and indifferent. In Italy heresy infected a great part of the cities. In Germany Lutheranism held the field; and Calvin's influence was vigorously spreading through northern Europe. Spain was less evil, but only less evil than other countries. The ignorance and evil life of the priests, Ignatius held, "brought the pestilence of heresy upon Germany." The Catholic Church must be revived, and the Jesuits set about its revival. The reform that Rome had talked about for a century at last had come.

The power of the Jesuits was the power of preaching.[14] Wherever they went they employed that. When they went into strange cities they preached in the streets and shortly were asked into the churches. They were educated men who knew what they wanted to do and set about doing it with oratorical force and energy. When Laínez preached in Venice, a large part of the city came out to him. The same was true when he preached at Florence and Siena. Araoz preached to thousands in Valladolid, Valencia, and Madrid. At Azpeitia, Ignatius' birthplace, more than

[13] Van Dyke, *Ignatius Loyola*, 160.
[14] Dudon, *Saint Ignace de Loyola*, 575.

four thousand came from all the countryside to hear him. A similar thronging of people attended Strada's preaching at Barcelona and elsewhere in Spain. Preaching, however, was only the first step in their ministry; after it came the hearing of confessions and the administering of the Sacrament. They attacked characteristic local sins as well as sin in general; they collected money for the poor and defended them against oppression. They were peacemakers, and protectors of orphans. Energy and devoutness characterized their doings and they upheld a standard of life.

The founder Ignatius' original plan was to bring together only a little company of very able men who should pray, preach, study, write, consult, advise, and incessantly care for mankind. The number of that highly selective company in his thought was to have been no more than sixty. Francis Xavier was his mental pattern of the men for such a company. They were to go wherever the Pope might send them, to sit with the cabinets of kings, to advise councils of the Church, to overcome arch heretics and lead universities by their superiority in disputation and their matchless preaching. It was not in Ignatius' thoughts to found an order to conduct academic instruction. But even before the Order was chartered by Pope Paul III in 1540 so many young university scholars sought admission that the question of how to train them had to be faced. They were allowed to take the vows of *scholastics* and were sent at first in small groups to the universities, where they lived together under a superior and followed the daily observances of a religious community. The first of such groups was sent to Paris in 1540. These men were not monks but clerics living in a communal house with communal rules—a Jesuit college whose students by their studies in it earned the degree of the University of Paris.

That was the first stage in the evolution of education in the Society of Jesus. A second development soon followed. Students from outside the Society soon asked to be allowed to study in its college. About 1546 the college originally intended only for *scholastics* of the Society of Jesus admitted secular scholars, externs as well. A third stage of development was reached when colleges with Jesuit teachers but with extern students only began to be opened. The college in which the Society began its work of teaching youth from the world was that of Messina, which was opened in the year 1547.[15]

While these unforeseen developments in the Society were taking place it was actively pursuing its original program. Alfonso Salmerón and Pasquier-Brouet were sent to Ireland to encourage the native clergy and the people to resist the undertakings of Henry VIII. They were discovered and hunted out of the land in about a month. In 1540 Peter Lefèvre was sent to the religious conference at Worms but made no public statement there. Instead he preached here and there to students and to priests and gave them the spiritual exercises. His analysis of the situation in Germany as he reported it was "that the Lutherans have brought about the secession of so many people from the Roman Church through the apparent righteousness of their teaching; the greatest blame for this development lies rather on our own clergy."[16] From Worms Lefèvre went to Regensburg, where he was enthusiastically welcomed. From Regensburg he went to Nürnberg, from which city he was recalled and sent to Spain. Le Jay and Bobadilla succeeded him in Germany. Le Jay addressed the bishops assembled at Salzburg and

[15] See Dr. William J. McGucken, S.J., *The Jesuits and Education,* 7 (Milwaukee: Bruce, 1932).
[16] Fülöp-Miller, *The Power and Secret of the Jesuits,* 346.

preached in the Lutheran churches but was not able to
check the flood of heresy. Bobadilla was sent to repair
conditions at Ingolstadt. Lefèvre returned and renewed
the activity of the Catholic clergy at Spires. From there
he was sent to Cologne but was again detached and
ordered to go to Portugal. Sickness prevented, however,
and he returned to do some effective work at Cologne.
Again he was summoned to Portugal and prevailed upon
the King in 1547 to give the College of Coimbra to the
Society. Other Jesuit colleges were established about the
same time in Valencia, Barcelona, and Valladolid in Spain
through the efforts of Araoz. Le Jay became professor
of theology at Innsbruck. Both Le Jay and Bobadilla
were at the Diet of Augsburg, and at Worms and later
at Vienna. Bobadilla's fiery preaching did effective work
against the Lutherans. Thus was a beginning made of the
recovery of Germany to the Church.

The great ecclesiastical event of those times was the
Council of Trent. The Council, called by the Pope, met
in December, 1545. The Emperor wanted the question
of reform in the Church to come up first; the Pope's party
carried a resolution that reform and dogma should be discussed together. The question was whether the Catholic
Church should in any degree acknowledge the force of
Protestant doctrine. Is what is written in the Gospel
sufficient for salvation? There were some at Trent who
believed it was; but when the question was put an enormous majority held that the unwritten traditions received
from the mouth of Christ Himself and propagated through
the ages by the Holy Spirit are of equal force with the
Gospel. Not the original texts of the Bible but the Vulgate
translation was accepted as authoritative. On the crucial
issue of justification concerning which the Protestants
said, "It is by faith," the Council decided: "The sinner

is justified when through the merit of the most holy passion and through the operation of the Holy Spirit, the love of God is implanted in his heart and abides in it; thus become a friend of God man goes forward from virtue to virtue. Whilst he observes the Commandments of God and the Church, he grows, with the help of faith through good works, in the righteousness attained through Christ's grace, and becomes more and more justified." [17]

Thus the possibility of a common understanding with Protestantism was utterly rejected.

Salmerón and Laínez were the Pope's special theologians at the Council of Trent. Le Jay was the theologian of the Cardinal Archbishop of Augsburg; Cavallino appeared for the Duke of Bavaria; Canisius and Polanco were added later. These, the members of the Society of Jesus, were the ablest men in the Council. Their extreme youth caused astonishment, for theology is a venerable science and they who practice it are expected to be sages, but these master theologians of the new order were mere youths, Laínez, the chief figure in the Council being thirty-four, Salmerón thirty-one, Le Jay thirty-one, and Canisius twenty-six.[18] They were older when the sessions of the Council closed. The Pope's representatives had to attend them all. They began in 1545 and ended in 1563. If Laínez was the greatest force in the Council of Trent, Peter Canisius became the greatest agent of the Catholic cause in Germany. He was the founder of the colleges of the Society of Jesus at Ingolstadt, Prague, Freiburg, and Vienna. Ingolstadt became to the Catholics what Wittenberg was to the Lutherans and Geneva to the Calvinists. Canisius lectured on theology there. Just as Luther had fought the Catholics with the printing press, Canisius now

[17] In Ranke, *History of the Popes*, II, 73 (Philadelphia, 1844).
[18] Campbell, *The Jesuits*, 46.

in turn fought the Lutherans with it. In Germany, he said, a writer is accounted of more worth than ten professors. He was himself an indefatigable writer, compiling catechisms for all ages and every degree of intelligence. He even proposed a Jesuit college for writers. The strength of Protestantism was in the ally it had made of the German language, in its German Bible, its German hymns and German sermons. Canisius made the German language serve the Catholic cause, too.

Ferdinand I wrote to Loyola that the only means to restore the Church in Germany was pious and learned priests. The recatholicizing of Germany was done through Jesuit colleges, which were opened in all the important towns. "Religious instruction in the *Spiritual Exercises,* exhortations to the worldly clergy, mildness and friendliness to the Protestants, instruction in the catechism and the erection of numerous schools—these were the means by which the Jesuits set about the Counter-Reformation in Germany." [19]

It was in 1551 that the Emperor Ferdinand I welcomed thirteen Jesuit fathers, among them Le Jay, in Vienna and set them up a college of the University, making them indeed official University visitors. About 1556 they succeeded in starting a college at Cologne. From Vienna they spread over Austria, and from Cologne over the territory of the Rhine. Ingolstadt, which eighteen Jesuit fathers had occupied without opposition on St. Willebald's Day in 1556, became their centre of theological teaching. The Emperor Ferdinand I gave them a college at Prague in 1556, where the sons of the nobility came for education. An important Jesuit college was established in Tyrnau in Hungary in 1561. At about the same time the Jesuits established a headquarters of influence and operations by

[19] Fülöp-Miller, *op. cit.,* 348.

founding the College of Olmütz in Moravia. From Würzburg they spread through Franconia. Munich, to which
they came indeed in 1539, was theirs. They called it the
Rome of Germany. In 1562 Canisius, who was called the
second Boniface, opened the College of Innsbruck, in 1564
the College of Dillingen, in 1567 Würzburg. To these
Canisius added the College of Halle before requesting
to be relieved of his office as Provincial of Germany, which
office he had held for thirteen eventful years. Von Ranke,
the historian of the Reformation, pauses to note the remarkable progress which the Society was able thus to
make in a very short time: "In the year 1551 they had not
yet any fixed position in Germany; in 1556 they had
extended over Bavaria and the Tyrol, Franconia, and
Swabia, a great part of Rhineland and Austria, and they
had penetrated into Hungary, Bohemia and Moravia. The
effects of their proceedings had already become manifest.
In the year 1561 the papal nuncio asserts that 'they are
winning many souls and doing great service to the holy
see.' This was the first enduring anti-Protestant impression made on Germany. Their labors were above
all devoted to the universities. They were ambitious of
rivaling the fame of those of the Protestants. The whole
learned education of those times was based on the study
of the ancient languages. This they prosecuted with lively
zeal, and ere long it was thought, here and there at least,
that the Jesuit teachers deserved a place beside the re-
storers of classical learning. They likewise cultivated the
sciences . . . But their main concern was, of course,
theological discipline. The Jesuits lectured with the
greatest industry even during the holidays; they revived
the practice of disputation, without which they said all
instruction was a dead letter. Their disputations, which
were held in public, were conducted with dignity and

decorum, were full of matter, and the most brilliant that had ever been witnessed. . . . The Jesuits displayed no less assiduity in the conduct of their Latin schools. It was one of the leading maxims of Laínez, that the lower grammatical classes should be supplied with good teachers, since first impressions exercise the greatest influence over the whole future life of the individual. He sought with just discernment for men who, having once adopted that more limited department of education, were content to devote themselves to it for their whole lives; for time alone could enable the teacher to learn so difficult a business or to acquire the becoming authority. In this the Jesuits succeeded to admiration. It was found that young persons learned more under them in half a year than with others in two years; even Protestants called back their children from distant schools, and put them under the care of the Jesuits. Schools for the poor, modes of instruction adapted for children, and catechizing followed. Canisius composed a catechism that satisfied the wants of the learner by its well-connected questions and apposite answers. The instruction of the Jesuits was conveyed wholly in the spirit of that enthusiastic devotion, which had from the first so peculiarly characterized their order . . . They were learned enough to acquire reputation, to excite confidence, to form and attach scholars; more than this they did not aspire to. Their piety not merely shunned all moral taint, but was positively conspicuous, and so much the less questionable; this was enough for them. Neither their piety nor their learning ventured upon undefined or untrodden paths; but they had one quality that particularly distinguished—strict method. With them everything was subject of calculation, for everything had its special end. Such a combination of competent knowledge and indefatigable zeal, of study and persuasiveness, of pomp and asceticism, of world-wide influence and of unity in the governing principle, was never beheld before or since. They were assiduous and visionary, worldly-wise and filled with enthusiasm; well-comported men, whose society was gladly courted; devoid of personal interests, each laboring for the advancement of the rest, no wonder that they were successful.

"Another consideration," says Professor Ranke, "forces itself upon a German writer. Papal Theology had . . . all but perished in Germany; the Jesuits arose to revive it. Who were those Jesuits who first arrived in that country? They were Spaniards, Italians and Flemings; the name of their order was long unknown; they were called Spanish priests. They occupied the professors' chairs, and found pupils who attached themselves to their doctrines. They received nothing from the Germans; their doctrines and their constitution were complete before they appeared among them. The general progress of their institution in Germany may be regarded as a new instance of the influence of the Latin portion of Europe on the Germanic." [20]

But the Jesuits had need of the help of the ruling princes to bring the Catholic Church back to power. The religious Peace at Augsburg (1555) placed Romanists and Lutherans on an equal footing. The principle of *cujus regio ejus religio* was set up. The creed of the prince and his understanding with his Diet determined which religion should be official in his principality. The Jesuit Bobadilla inveighed openly against the Emperor Charles V for allowing such a concession to the Lutheran heretics. In the end it was found to set the stage for the Catholics. The Catholic Duke of Bavaria needed money and still more money. His Diet demanded Protestant concessions. The

[20] Ranke, *op. cit.*, V, 171.

Jesuits appeared, and soon the Pope offered the duke a tenth of the property of his clergy, making it unnecessary for him to get money from the Diet. Other adjustments with Rome followed, and soon Duke Albert was engaged in making Bavaria wholly Catholic. Everyone must accept the confession of faith which the Council of Trent had decreed. Protestants who would not yield were required to quit the country. In the same way the whole country of Baden once more became Catholic. In the principalities ruled by prince-bishops Canisius was able to bring about concerted action; the resolutions of the Council of Trent were adopted, and the confession of faith was required to be subscribed by all, even in the universities before degrees could be taken in any faculty, including that of medicine. Even the abbot of Fulda called in the Jesuits and exchanged his evangelical councillors for Catholics. Thus did the Counter-Reformation bring back the Catholic Church to southern Germany.

The Society of Jesus was not founded to be a teaching order. The education of youth was not in its original intention. Loyola's first plan was to convert the Holy Land; his second plan was to form a group of Platonic spiritual kings to guide the Church. The problem of reinforcing Catholic Christianity, whichever way he turned, insisted upon showing itself as a problem in education. What was required was Catholic leaders; they had to be made. Hence the Jesuit school system.

The first Jesuit college was opened at Messina in 1547. Before it, however, Loyola had sent a group of scholastics to Paris in 1540. From 1547 to 1550 he was at work drafting the Constitutions of the Society. Ignatius, a grown man of thirty-three, had sat in the classroom with boys at Barcelona to learn the Latin grammar, and after that had spent eleven years of his life with immature youths to gain a university education. How he came by the notion that education was so indispensable to one who would serve God and bring religion to his fellows is by no means clear.[21] But that education must be had at any

[21] "Y siendo esto como es verdad, juzgó N. B. P. con una divina prudencia, que para atajar este fuego, y tener la casa que no se nos caiga encima, es necesario reformar las vidas y emendar las costumbres; y que para esto no hay ningún medio, ni más fácil, ni más eficaz, que criar los niños en el temor santo de Dios, y enseñarlos á ser critisianos desde sustierna edad, para que mamando con la leche la virtud, crezcan con ella, y siendo ya hombres y grandes, ejerciten lo que siendo niños y pequeños aprendieron.

"Esto es lo que todos los que trataron y escribieron leyes para el buen gobierno de las repúblicas, en todas las naciones, y en todos los siglos, enseñaron. Porque para que prenda y heche raíces el árbol que se planta, ha de ser tierno. Y un sabio, aunque gentil, dijo, tanto va en el acostumbrarse á una cosa desde niño. Y otro, que el vaso sabe á la pega, y toma siempre el sabor del primer licor que se echó en él. Y Aristóteles dijo: no va poco, sino mucho en acostumbrarse de una manero ó de otra, desde la mocedad. Pero mucho mejor lo dijo el Espíritu Santo por Salomón en aquellas palabras: Proverbium est, adolescens juxta viam suam ambulans, etiam cum senuerit non recedet ab ea; que es proverbio ya y común dicho de todos, que el mozo acostumbrado á andar por un camino, aunque se haga viejo no le dejará. Y antes de Salomón dijo Job: Ossa ejus implebuntur vitiis adolescentiae ejus. Sus huesos se henchirán de los vicios de su mocedad. Por esto dijo Platón, que él no sabía ninguna cosa en que los hombres hubiesen de poner mayor estudio y cuidado, que en hacer buenos á sus hijos desde niños. Y san Agustín dice, que más cuidado han de poner los padres en criar bien á los hijos que tienen, que no en desearlos ni en tenerlos. El mismo Platón en los libros que escribe de la República, y en los de las leyes, ninguna cosa encarece más, que la crianza y buena institución de los niños, y la toma por basa y fundamento de todo lo que enseña. Porque dice, que della depende el bien de la República, y que más caso se ha de hacer en que haya buenos gobernadores en las ciudades, que no buenas leyes. Y da la razón; porque la ley buena, si no hay buen gobernador que la ejecute, es ley muerta; mas el buen gobernador, aunque no tenga ley scrita, él mismo se es ley viva. Y añade, que no podrá haber buenos gobernadores, si no hay buenos ciudadanos, de los cuales se han de tomar los que han de gobernar; y que para que los ciudadanos sean los que deben ser, también es necesario que lo sean los niños y los mozos, que después de haber crecido han de venir á ser ciudadanos y á gobernar la República; y

sacrifice was in him a fixed idea, and he wanted it for the members of the Society of Jesus. The fourth part of the Constitutions is not under the heading "Education" but "Of the Means of Instructing those who are kept in the Company, in Letters and other means of Helping their Neighbours." "We apprehend that it will be difficult for this Society to grow on the strength of those who are already both good and accomplished. Therefore another way has seemed good to adopt, that of admitting young men who by their good lives and their talents afford us ground to hope that they will grow up into virtuous and learned men." The core of the students must be those under vows, but poor students who did not expect to join the Company were to be admitted if they gave promise that they too would be workers later. The spiritual training of probationers must not be overlooked in zeal for learning; neither must religion set aside study. They must study humane letters in the languages, including rhetoric, logic, metaphysics, natural and moral philosophy, and after them scholastic and positive theology and Holy Writ. All must speak Latin. The probationers should have practice in preaching and public reading of Scripture. "They should be taught to help their neighbors to die well and what should be done in that crisis which may achieve or lose the final end of eternal happiness." Theology is the

---

comunmente serán tales, cuales fueron en su mocedad; y así concluye que si no se echa este cimiento, todo lo que sin él se edificare caerá. Plutarco, filósofo prudentísimo, y maestro de Trajano emperador, dice otro tanto, y escribió un libro entero de la manera con que se han de criar los hijos; en el cual es cosa de ver cuánto encarece este negocio, y dice que es la fuente y la raíz de todos los bienes, y que en él consiste el principio, medio y fin del buen gobierno; y que ninguna de las cosas humanas, como son riquezas, nobleza, honra, hermosura, salud y fuerzas, debrían los hombres estimar en tanto, como la buena crianza de sus hijos."
(Ribadeneyra, *Vida del S. Ignacio de Loyola*, 309-311 [Madrid, 1900]).

study that best prepares one to help his neighbors. "Because the use of Theology in these days demands a good knowledge of humane letters and of Latin, Greek and Hebrew, there should be good teachers of these subjects . . . The natural sciences prepare the mind for the perfect understanding of Theology and they also should be taught together with logic, metaphysics and mathematics." [22]

In the Proemium to this fourth part of the Constitutions which deals with the means of instructing those who are kept in the Company, Loyola wrote: "Since the purpose for which the Society is founded is to help the souls of its members and its neighbors to that end for which they were created; and since with this object in view, besides examples of life, doctrine and the power to express it are also necessary . . . we must now treat of the edifice of letters and the manner of making use of them. For this purpose the Society accepts colleges and sometimes even universities." [23]

Before he finished his revision of the Constitutions, Loyola had decided that the Company was to accomplish a large part of its work through the education not only "of those who are kept in the Company but of secular youth as well." [24] Colleges were rapidly founded as we have seen. At Ignatius' death in 1556 the Company had some thirty-five schools and colleges in Europe and nine in India and America. As yet, the general regulations of the Constitutions directed them; there was no fixed course of study; each college worked out its own tentative course, conforming as nearly as it could to the Roman college which had been opened by Ignatius in 1551. Records

[22] Van Dyke, *op. cit.*, 239–241.
[23] In McGucken, *op. cit.*, 9.
[24] McGucken, *op. cit.*, 20. Dudon, *Saint Ignace de Loyola*, 401.

were kept, however, of all that was done, which show that even before the *Ratio Studiorum* of 1586 there was much uniformity of views and procedures.

In 1584 under the General Claude Acquaviva the Congregation of the Society began to canvass a reform of studies. The General appointed six fathers to remain in Rome and draw up a plan of studies for the entire Society. In nine months they submitted their draft of a plan to the General and to the professors in the Roman college. The General sent it to all the provinces. Each of these gathered its scholars and teachers to discuss and amend it, and each province then sent its report on the plan to Rome. In 1586 the first *Ratio Studiorum* was issued. In 1591 an amended *Ratio* was issued. It did not meet with unanimous approval. The Germans strangely enough objected to its prolixity. In 1599 the General Acquaviva issued the final *Ratio Studiorum*. Fifteen years of coöperative study and discussion had shaped it. It remained the law of the Jesuit schools and colleges until the suppression of the Society by the Pope in 1773.

There is no satisfactory translation in English of the entire *Ratio Studiorum*. In Father McGucken's valuable work, *The Jesuits and Education,* he has included as an Appendix a translation into English of the *Ratio Studiorum* for the lower, that is, the secondary, schools. There is no way to understand what the *Ratio* is like save by reading a part of it, and no way to comprehend the detailed systematization of Jesuit education save by sampling it. We therefore with permission reproduce here the section of Father McGucken's translation of the "Ratio for Lower Schools" entitled "Common Rules for the Professors of the Lower Classes" [25] (the translation is made from Roothaan's *Ratio* of 1832; the footnotes, with one

[25] McGucken, *op. cit.,* 287–296.

or two exceptions, are confined to indicating the particulars in which that text is different from Acquaviva's *Ratio* of 1599):

Common Rules for the Professors of the Lower Classes

1. The master shall so train the youth intrusted for their education to the Society of Jesus that they may acquire not only learning but also a character worthy of a Christian. It should be each master's special aim not only during classes as the occasion may arise, but also outside of class time to prepare the tender minds of these youths for the love and service of God, to inculcate those virtues that are pleasing to Him. In particular, all the masters should observe the following rules.

2. Someone should be appointed to say a brief prayer at the beginning of class. The master and pupils should follow this attentively, kneeling with heads uncovered. Before the beginning of the lesson, the instructor, with uncovered head, should make the sign of the cross, and then begin.

3. The master should see to it that all are present at Mass every day and at the sermon on feast days. Moreover, twice a week during Lent, he should send them to the sermon [in the church] or, if such is the local custom, accompany them thither.*

4. Christian doctrine should be taught in all the classes. In the three grammar classes, and even in the others if necessary, the lesson should be recited from memory on Fridays or Saturdays. Each grade should have ampler explanation and recitations, in proportion to its need.†

5. Likewise on Fridays or Saturdays, each master should

* In American Jesuit high schools, Mass is said daily for the students, but attendance is usually not obligatory, except in the boarding schools. Once a week, however, during class time, all must attend a short service, consisting usually of devotions and a brief talk.

† 1599 *Ratio*: "Christian doctrine should be learned and recited from memory on Fridays or Saturdays, especially in the grammar classes, and also in the other classes, if necessary. In some places and for the new pupils it may be necessary to have these lessons oftener."

give a half hour of pious instruction or explanation of Christian doctrine. He should especially recommend daily prayer to God, in particular, the rosary of the Blessed Virgin, or the daily recitation of the Little Office of the Blessed Virgin, the evening examination of conscience, frequent devout reception of the sacraments of penance and Holy Eucharist, and devotion to the Sacred Heart of Jesus.* He should urge his charges to avoid bad habits, to hate vice, and finally to cultivate the virtues worthy of Christian manhood.

6. In private conversations too, he should strive to instill piety, not, however, in such a way as to seem to influence them to enter our Order. If there be any so inclined, he should send them to their confessor.

7. He should arrange for the recitation of the litanies of the Blessed Virgin every Saturday afternoon in his class; or, if such is the local custom, he should lead his class to the church for the common recitation of the litanies with the other pupils. He should diligently foster devotion to the Blessed Virgin and also to the Guardian Angels.

8. He should strongly recommend the reading of spiritual books, especially the lives of the saints. On the other hand, not only should he be most careful never to read any passage from obscene writers or anything else likely to be dangerous to their virtue, but he should also make every effort to keep his pupils from perusing works of this type, even in their outside reading.

9. The master must see to it that all the students go to confession once a month. They should be told to hand in to their confessors a card bearing their name and class, in order that afterwards the master may know who were absent by inspecting these cards.

10. He should often pray to God for his boys and give them an example of upright character by his own manner of life.

11. In all that pertains to studies and school discipline, the

---

* 1599 *Ratio:* The phrase, "devotion to the Sacred Heart of Jesus" lacking. This Catholic devotion was not so widespread at that time.

master should obey the prefect of lower studies. Without his permission he should admit none to his class, dismiss none, nor take any book for class matter nor give any permission to any-one to absent himself from the common school exercises.

12. Each class must keep to its subject matter. In a separate place rules for the class of rhetoric and humanities will be given. In grammar there should be three classes, each of which has certain definite matter to cover. Hence, all the gram-matical precepts * are to be divided into three parts, and one section assigned to each class in such wise, however, that the matter seen the previous year will always be repeated at the beginning of the next year, as will be indicated below in the rules for the masters of the respective classes.

In teaching the vernacular,† practically the same method is to be observed as in the study of Latin.

13. The Greek grammar should be divided about as follows The first part, assigned to the first class,‡ should begin with the regular nouns, and include the verb "to be," and the regular verbs. The second section for the intermediate grammar class should include the contract nouns, the circumflex verbs, the verbs in *mi,* and the easier constructions. The third class § should take the other parts of speech and all the syntax. The fourth class should study versification and the simpler rules of dialect.**

14. The time schedule for rhetoric class should be at least two hours in the morning, and an equal allotment in the after-noon. For humanities and the other classes, two and a half hours both morning and afternoon should be provided. Even

* 1599 *Ratio:* "the precepts of Emmanuel."

† 1599 *Ratio:* "In teaching the vernacular," etc., lacking.

‡ That is, the second year of lowest grammar, when Greek was com-menced.

§ That is, the highest class of grammar.

** 1599 *Ratio:* "The Greek grammar should be . . . The third class should take the other parts of speech and whatever goes under the terms of rudiments, excepting dialects, and the more difficult exceptions. The fourth class, that of humanities, all of syntax, and the fifth class, that of rhetoric, should study versification."

on the weekly holiday, two hours should be given to class. These should always be at the same hour so that it may be known at any certain hour just what classes are being conducted.

15. The order of classes may be changed with the permission of the provincial to accord with local custom, provided that the same amount of time assigned in the rules of the respective masters be preserved and, provided that once an order of classes is adopted, it be adhered to.

16. If a holiday falls on Saturday, the exercises assigned for that day may be advanced a day or omitted altogether.

17. The same division of time is to have place on a recreation day unless some special exercises are assigned for that day. The ordinary exercises, held on other days, should be curtailed or some of them omitted altogether. Some time should be left for contest in drill work.*

18. Special care must be taken to have the students acquire the habit of Latin conversation. Accordingly, the master should speak Latin, beginning with the highest class of grammar, and he should require the students to speak Latin especially in the explanation of the grammatical precepts, in the correction of their Latin compositions, in the class contests and also in their conversation one with another. In translating into the vernacular, however, he should take special pains to have them use purity of diction in their mother tongue and a correct pronunciation, and he should be intolerant of any mistakes in this matter.†

19. The students should repeat from memory the prelections to the decurions whose duties are explained in Rule 36. If another system seems desirable in the class of rhetoric, it may be used. The decurions themselves recite their lessons to the head decurion or to the master himself. In general, the master

* That is, the concertation.

† 1599 *Ratio:* "The practice of speaking Latin must be particularly promoted, with the exception of those classes in which the students know no Latin. They should never be permitted to use the mother tongue in what pertains to class matter. Demerit marks should be assigned to those who are negligent. For this reason, the master should always speak Latin."

should ask the lesson of the lazier students and from the late-comers so as to check the fidelity of the decurions and to keep all up to the mark. On Saturday, there should be a public repetition from memory of all that has been seen in the past week or even the matter of several weeks. When a book * is finished, some may be chosen occasionally to recite it from beginning to end. For this a prize should be awarded.

20. Written work should be handed in by all the grammar classes every day but Saturday. In the other classes a [Latin] prose composition must be handed in daily except on Saturday and the weekly holiday. Exercises in verse should be handed in twice a week; namely, on Mondays and the day following the weekly holiday. Once a week, at least, there should be a Greek theme, to be handed in on the afternoon of any day the master chooses.

21. Daily the master should correct the written work of all his students, since very great benefit is derived from this. If, however, the number in the class is too great for this, he should correct as many as possible, so that none of the students is ever left long without correction. For this reason, on the days especially when exercises in verse are handed in, he should have some of the class opponents exchange papers [for correction]. To facilitate this, each student should write not merely his own name on his exercise, but also that of his opponent. While the recitation of the memory lesson is being heard [by the decurions] the master himself can correct some of the other papers by individual conference with the pupils in a low voice; the rest of the papers, he should correct in his room, as far as possible.†

22. The method of correcting written work, in general, is to note any grammatical mistake, to inquire how it may be

---

* That is, a book of a Latin author, as a book of Virgil's *Aeneid*.

† 1599 *Ratio:* "Written work is ordinarily to be corrected by individual conference with each pupil in a low voice while the others are given time to practice their [Latin] style. It will be useful, however, daily to select some of the exercises, now from the best, now from the poorest, and to read them publicly at the beginning and end of class and post them in a conspicuous place."

remedied, to require the class opponents publicly to correct any mistake as soon as they notice it, and to quote the grammatical rule that has been broken. Finally, praise should be given for excellent work. While this correction is being done in class, the students should read and correct their own first copy of the exercise which should always be brought to class in addition to the copy handed in to the master. The master * should also try as often as possible to dictate a carefully corrected version to the class.

Moreover, he should see that all the exercises are written neatly and legibly and that the penmanship in general is of good type.†

23. He should demand ‡ different sorts of exercises at different times, suited to the grade of his class. Nothing checks the ardor of youthful spirit more than monotony.

24. Besides the daily written task to be done during class, an exercise in composition should be given to occupy them during an hour of class time, once a week, at least.§

25. The repetition of the previous day's work as well as of the lesson for the day should be done as follows: The entire lesson may be asked of one individual, but it would be better to question several in order that all may have practice. Only the repetition of the most important and useful points should be asked. The better students should be asked first, then the others. They should be made to answer in continued discourse or else in direct answers to the master's questions, the opponent correcting any mistakes in his partner's repetition, or if he hesitates, giving the answer himself.

26. On Saturdays, there should be a repetition of all the matter seen during that week. If any of the students say they are prepared to answer all questions on this matter or even on an entire book, let some of them be chosen whom the others may

* 1599 *Ratio:* "The master . . . of good type" lacking.

† 1599 *Ratio:* The 23rd rule in the 1599 *Ratio* is substantially the same as the 21st rule previously given.

‡ 1599 *Ratio:* "during the time of correction," added.

§ This rule lacking in the 1599 *Ratio*.

ask two or three questions. A reward should be given to those who answer successfully.

27. In the prelections, only the ancient classics, never the modern writers, are to be explained. It will be very advantageous if the master speaks, not on the spur of the moment and at random, but only what he has thoughtfully written out in his room. He should read the whole speech or oration before he begins to teach it. The method of the prelection should generally follow this plan:

First, the master should read aloud the entire passage [for translation], unless it is too long.* Secondly, he should explain briefly the substance of the passage and when necessary the connection with what precedes. Thirdly, as he reads over each sentence, if he gives the explanation in Latin, he should clear up the obscurities, and show the relation of part with part. This should not be done by an inept paraphrase, substituting one Latin word for another, but he should really explain the sentence, by casting it in a clearer version, if it is obscure in the original.† If he is giving an explanation in the vernacular, he should keep, as far as possible, the arrangement of words [in the Latin sentence]. Thus, their ears become accustomed to the [Latin] flow of words. If the vernacular idiom does not permit this, then he should first give a literal translation, and afterward explain the sense in the vernacular.

Fourthly, beginning over again, he should give those necessary observations, that are suited to his class, unless he prefers to give his commentary as he goes along. He should dictate, either during the explanation or later, after the prelection is finished, what he wishes the students to copy out; there should not be much of this. It is usually better for the students of the grammar classes not to write at all unless they are told.

28. The prelection of an historical writer or a poet has this special feature that the former can usually be done more rapidly, while the poet is best rendered by a careful oratorical

* 1599 *Ratio:* "as in the class of rhetoric and humanities."
† 1599 *Ratio:* The phrase "if it is obscure in the original" lacking.

paraphrase. The students must be accustomed to distinguish between the style of a poet and an orator.

Much after the same fashion, the vernacular classics should be read.*

29. In the explanation of rhetorical precepts, the art of versification, Latin, vernacular,† and Greek grammar, and similar subjects, the substance rather than the verbal precepts should be stressed. Brief examples from the best authors should be selected and translated. Particularly in the lower classes of grammar, when some especially difficult precept comes up, they should be drilled on this one point for one or more days. This can be varied by a repetition of some of the easier rules.

30. The assignment for theme should not be dictated *extempore,* but should be thought out beforehand and generally written out. As far as possible, it should be written in imitation of Cicero and built up on the model of some narrative, or argumentative prose, or some expression of congratulation, counsel, or something of that sort. Both the Latin and the vernacular version should be handed in where the master has given a verbal dictation. After the dictation, he should have the assignment immediately repeated, and he should explain the more difficult parts. He should supply the words, the phrases, and other needed helps. With the exception of the class of rhetoric, he should always advise them during the dictation how to write and how to punctuate the theme. An unusual and longer assignment than usual may be given when several feast days come together or when the long or short vacations are announced.

31. During class contests,‡ the master does the questioning and the opponents the correcting of their partners, or else the opponents themselves question one another. These contests are to be highly esteemed and are to be made use of as often as time allows so that praiseworthy rivalry which is a great incentive to diligence may be fostered. For the contest one can

* This sentence lacking in the 1599 version.
† 1599 *Ratio:* "vernacular" lacking.
‡ Or concertations.

be matched against another, or several from each side. It is a good plan to put officer * against officer. Or one student may question several opponents. Generally, private should be matched against private, officer against officer. Occasionally, however, a private may match his skill with an officer, and if he is victorious, he should be awarded the rank of his opponent or given another prize or sign of victory according as the rank of the class and local usage permit.

32. Exercises out of the ordinary and public exhibitions † are very useful. It should be noted that only those should be permitted to take part in a public examination who have been diligently prepared for it. To provide mental training for the student and not merely to exercise his memory, the master should indeed carefully polish what the students are to give before the public, but he should never write the whole of it himself. The same may be said of verse that is to be displayed in public. The students should also be carefully trained in correct enunciation, gesture, and delivery.

33. In the classes of rhetoric and humanities, every other Saturday an explanation of an author may be given or a Greek or Latin speech or poem; one class may play host to the other for this exercise. In the other classes, the explanation of an author not seen previously should not be intrusted to a student; rather he should repeat a prelection he has heard in class. No visitors should be invited to this exercise and they should be held only once a month.

34. Some time during the year, on a day appointed by the prefect of the lower schools, there should be a contest for about an hour between a lower class and the one immediately above it. The subject matter should include only those topics common to both classes. The masters of the respective classes should direct the proceedings. Two, three, or more of the best students of both classes should be matched in contest, either prepared beforehand according to agreement between the two

---

* The class was divided into camps or armies, thus the "Romans" and the "Carthaginians"; and each army had its officers and privates.
† "Public exhibitions" lacking in the 1599 version.

classes on set questions and answers, or asking any questions that their ingenuity suggests, or refuting the objections, especially in rhetoric, that are set forth by one side.

35. The officers [of both sides] in a class should be chosen and rewarded too, if that seems wise, every month, or at least, every other month, unless in some schools this seems unnecessary for the rhetoric class. For this purpose, the students should be given one written test in Latin prose composition and in the higher classes, if it is desired, one written test in Latin verse or in Greek composition. The entire school day should be given for this, unless in the lower classes it seems better to reserve a half hour for the contest in drill. Those who do the best work, should be honored with the highest office. The next highest should also receive honorable titles. To throw an air of erudition about it, the titles should be borrowed from the political or military offices in Rome or Greece. The class should be divided into two equal sides to stimulate rivalry. Each side should have its own officers, opposed by officers of the other side; and each individual pupil should have his opponent assigned. The chief officers of each side should have the seats of honor in the class.

36. Decurions also should be appointed by the instructor to hear the memory lessons, collect the written work for the master, and to mark down in a little book those who fail in the memory work or who fail to hand in their exercises, or fail to bring two copies of their written task to class. They should note down anything else that the master may wish.

37. For the general promotion, the students should be given during the month preceding the examination a thorough repetition of all the main points of the year's work. This holds for all the classes with the possible exception of rhetoric. If anyone has excelled during the course of the year in very marked fashion, the master should refer his case to the prefect so that he may pass at once to a higher class after a private examination.

38. At the beginning of each year, the master should give the prefect an alphabetical list of his students. He should

inspect this list occasionally during the year to revise it, if necessary. Before the general examination, he should do this with special care. In this list, he should classify wherever possible the students according to ability, namely, excellent, good, average, doubtful,* failures. All this can be indicated by numbers, 1, 2, 3, 4, 5, 6.

39. Nothing helps discipline so much as the observance of rules. Hence, the master should take particular care to have the students observe their own rules and those that pertain to studies. This will be more easily attained by the hope of honor and reward, and the fear of disgrace than by punishment.

40. The master should not be hasty in punishing nor petty in his investigation [of wrongdoing]. He should rather pretend not to have seen, when this can be done without disadvantage to anyone. Not only must he never strike a pupil with his own hand—that is the corrector's business—but he should also refrain altogether from sarcastic remarks and discourteous actions. He should never call a student except by his right name. In place of punishment, it will sometimes be useful to add something to the pupil's daily written task. He must leave to the prefect unusual and severe punishments, especially for offenses committed outside of school. To the prefect also should be referred the cases of those students who refuse punishment, especially if they are older boys.

41. The master should demand the greatest diligence of his students. Accordingly, he should not excuse them from class for the purpose of attending public exhibitions or plays. If anyone is absent, the master should send one of his classmates or some other person to his home. Unless proper excuses are forthcoming, the absentee should be punished. If any are absent several days without excuse, they should be sent to the prefect and should not be readmitted without his consent.

42. To avoid any interference with class exercises on account of confessions, the students should be sent to confession at the

* 1599 *Ratio* has *"retinendos, rejeciendos,"* that is, those who must repeat the class, and those who should not be allowed to return to school.

beginning of class [on confession days] in groups of three or
more. When the first return, one or two others should replace
them, unless in some place it should be the custom to have all
go to the church for confession at the same time.

43. The master's first care should be to secure silence and
becoming behavior. He should see that no one wanders about
the classroom, changes his place, or exchanges notes or little
gifts. The students should not leave the classroom, especially
not two or more together.

44. Special care must be taken that none of the pupils be
called out of the room, particularly during the time set for
prelection. To avoid noise and confusion during dismissal time,
the master should stand guard either at his desk or at the door,
and see that those nearest to the doors leave first. Or he can
make any other arrangement, provided the students leave
orderly and quietly.

45. With the rector's approval, the master may organize
academies in accordance with the rules set down later on.
On feast days especially, meetings should be held in order
to ward off idleness and bad habits.

46. If it seems necessary occasionally to confer with parents
about a pupil, the master should consult with the rector about
the advisability of the prefect or some other person summoning them, or if their rank demands it, about paying them a
personal visit.

47. The master should not be more friendly to one student
than to another. Outside of class time, he should speak to
them only briefly and about serious matters. Their conversation should be in an open place, not inside the classroom,
rather at the door of the classroom or in the yard or at the
college gate so that due regard may be had to edification.

48. Without the rector's advice, the master should never
recommend a private tutor to anyone, and he should never
permit these tutors to burden their charges with other lessons
at home, but merely allow the tutors to assist with the lessons
assigned in class.

49. He should never employ a student as a copyist nor for

any other work which does not pertain to the regular school exercises. Nor should he permit the students to spend their money in any way for the school.

50. Finally, the master, with the help of divine grace, should be diligent and persevering in every way, bent only on the advancement of his pupils in their daily lessons and other literary exercises. He should regard no one with contempt but devote the same care to the efforts of poor students as he does to those of the rich. Let him strive for the advancement of each and every one of his charges.

The course of study in a five-year Jesuit school was as follows—the grade being the amount of matter to be covered:

Lower Grammar. The grade of this class is the perfect knowledge of the rudiments, and an incipient knowledge of syntax. In Greek: reading, writing, and a certain portion of the grammar. The authors used for prelection will be some easy selections from Cicero, besides fables of Phaedrus and lives of Nepos.

Middle Grammar. The grade is the knowledge, though not entire, of all grammar; another portion of the Greek grammar; and, for the prelection, only the select epistles, narrations, descriptions, and the like from Cicero, with the Commentaries of Caesar, and some of the easiest poems of Ovid. In Greek: the fables of Aesop, select and expurgated dialogues of Lucian, the Tables of Cebes.

Upper Grammar. The grade is the complete knowledge of grammar, including all the exceptions and idioms in syntax, figures of rhetoric, and the art of versification. In Greek: the eight parts of speech, or all the rudiments. For the lessons: in prose, the most difficult epistles of Cicero, the books De Amicitia, De Senectute, and others of the kind, or even some of the easier orations; in poetry, some select elegies and epistles of Ovid, also selections from Catullus, Tibullus, Propertius, and the eclogues of Virgil, or some of Virgil's easier books. In Greek: St. Chrysostom, Xenophon, and the like.

Humanity. The grade is to prepare, as it were, the ground for eloquence, which is done in three ways, by a knowledge of the language, some erudition, and a sketch of the precepts pertaining to Rhetoric. For a command of the language, which consists chiefly in acquiring propriety of expression and fluency, the one prose author employed in daily prelections is Cicero; as historical writers, Caesar, Sallust, Livy, Curtius, and others of the kind; the poets used are, first of all, Virgil; also select odes of Horace, with the elegies, epigrams, and other productions of illustrious poets, expurgated; in like manner, orators, historians, and poets, in the vernacular. The erudition conveyed should be slight, and only to stimulate and recreate the mind, not to impede progress in learning the tongue. The precepts will be the general rules of expression and style, and the special rules on the minor kinds of composition, epistles, narrations, descriptions, both in verse and prose. In Greek: the art of versification, and some notions of the dialects; also a clear understanding of authors, and some composition in Greek. The Greek prose authors will be Saints Chrysostom and Basil, epistles of Plato and Synesius, some selections from Plutarch; the poets, Homer, Phocylides, Theognis, St. Gregory Nazianzen, Synesius, and others like them.

Rhetoric. The grade of this class cannot easily be defined. For it trains to perfect eloquence, which comprises two great faculties, the oratorical and poetical, the former chiefly being the object of culture; nor does it regard only the practical, but the beautful also. For the precepts, Cicero may be supplemented with Quintilian and Aristotle. The style, which may be assisted by drawing on the most approved historians and poets, is to be formed on Cicero; all of his works are most fitted for this purpose, but only his speeches should be made the subject of prelection, that the precepts of the art may be seen in practice. As to the vernacular, the style should be formed on the best authors. The erudition will be derived from the history and manners of nations, from the authority of writers and all learning; but moderately, as befits the capacity of the students.

In Greek, the fuller knowledge of authors and of dialects is to be acquired. The Greek authors, whether orators, historians, or poets, are to be ancient and classic: Demosthenes, Plato, Thucydides, Homer, Hesiod, Pindar, and others of the kind, including Saints Nazianzen, Basil, and Chrysostom.[26]

Of his own experience of their schools Voltaire, a student at the College of Clermont, wrote in his *Age of Louis XIV:* "What did I observe during the seven years which I spent under the Jesuit roof? A life full of moderation, diligence and order. They devoted every hour of the day to our education or to the fulfilment of their strict vows. As evidence of this, I appeal to the testimony of the thousands who, like myself, were educated by them."

Lamartine writes of his boyhood in the Jesuit college at Balley: "I was a bitter and obstinate boy and I was softened and won over, so that I willingly subjected myself to a yoke which skilful teachers made light and pleasant for me. The whole art was to arouse in us the love of good, and to guide us by their own will and through our own efforts." [27] Bacon writes: "As for the pedagogical part the shortest rule would be to consult the schools of the Jesuits for nothing better has been put in practice." [*De Augmentis Scientiarum, VI, iv.*] For more than two centuries they were the best schoolmasters in Europe. Mingled kindness and firmness was their principle. Their discipline was mild. In marked contrast to the prevailing practice of that day they used little corporal punishment. They devised a method and adhered to it. "We have undertaken to teach, not only members of the Order but youth from the world outside. The

---

[26] Thomas Hughes, S.J., *Loyola and the Educational System of the Jesuits,* 271–273 (by permission of Charles Scribner's Sons).

[27] In Fülöp-Miller, *op. cit.,* 408.

number of this latter class is vast, it includes brilliant talent and represents the nobility. We cannot imagine that we do justice to our functions or come up to the expectations formed of us if we do not feed this multitude of youths in the same way nurses do, with food dressed in the best way, for fear they grow up in our schools without growing much in learning."

The *prelection* was the basis of their method. That, says Père Bainvel, enables us "to summarize their system in a single formula: the study and imitation of a model under the direction of a master." [28] In the higher schools the prelection is a lecture which the professor gives; in the secondary classes it is an explanation or interpretation of a lesson by the teacher. First the teacher states the subject, reads the text, gives the description, goes over the argument, explains the difficult places and the conclusion of the matter. This prereading by the master of course is done in several ways. It is a model for the pupils' imitation, really a study lesson. The master is expected first to go over the whole of the subject under consideration consecutively, that is, without stops of any kind the first time over it. Then he should repeat in the same words indicating by inflection, stops, etc. what is to be taken down by the students in their notes. Then comes the *repetition* in which the students give back to the teacher what he has told them in the prelection in the identical words he used in the prelection. This may of course be done chorus-fashion, but that was not its regular form. The master was to call up the boys, one after another, and each repeated the whole matter from the beginning just as the master had given it. I once asked a student of philosophy in a Jesuit college what the students would do in a class studying the activities of Soc-

[28] In McGucken, *op. cit.*, 41.

rates. He said they would repeat word for word what the professor had given them in the prelection.

The employment of this method of learning indicates that verbal expression of the matters learned was thought capable of something like finished and perfect form, and that the ability to use those perfect or nearly perfect words was held to be the object of instruction. This like every other method consciously used in education was based upon a philosophy, in this case that of the revealed or established perfect truth—the unchanging Aristotelian definitions given by God through His Church.

Provision was made for other studies in the literary course. The Prefect of the lower studies being instructed "to distribute History, Geography, the elements of mathematics, and whatever else is usually treated in these classes in such a manner that each master can satisfactorily and conveniently finish the matter assigned to him." [29] There were additions too to the prelections and repetitions; there were concertations, or debates between rivals who were pitted against one another in the classroom, and rival groups called academies organized within the classes. Competitions and prizes which were conferred with much publicity were made much of.

"Jesuits," Polanco said, "must begin by undertaking preparatory teaching with professors capable of inspiring their young students little by little with a love of Theology." Jesuit education is the result of a great choosing and blending among what Loyola and the early Fathers found going on around them. Their literary course is the result of Renaissance Humanism. It was borrowed tradition, says Father McGucken, from Johann Sturm's school at Strassburg. The assertion is likely—there is much similarity—but the proof that Jesuit education took over

[29] Hughes, *op. cit.*, 270.

Sturm's program is not entirely clear. It may be that both derived from Deventer and the Brothers of the Common Life. At any rate the object of both Sturm's and the Jesuits' endeavor was to give in their schools a general culture. The meaning of that term was no more clear to them than it is to others who use it. The instrument of education, they said, is found in the great literatures of Greece and Rome. These tongues are dead and cannot be picked up by instinct, i.e., by hearing others speak them. To be learned they must be studied, and "when the boy comes to write and speak the language so learned and quickens it with, though dead, the very life of actual speech, we have the supreme test and proof of successful toil." A handsome style was aimed at, and a handsome style was the outcome. Now, that is all specific training; but when the Jesuit educators go on to use such phrases as "In a boy's mind there is need of suppleness of general powers," and the memory, the imagination, and the judgment are to be cultivated, the instrument for this is to be found in literature, they are championing the doctrine of formal or wholesale discipline and are quite beyond the domain of specific and reasonable learning. The training of the mind was their great claim; but the mind was not trained, only habituated to taking orders.

The *Ratio Studiorum* prescribed a three-year course in philosophy and a four-year course in theology, the first year in philosophy being devoted to logic and general metaphysics, eight hours a week, and to mathematics, six hours a week.

The second year: special metaphysics (that is, cosmology, psychology, and natural theology), four hours a week; physics, nine hours a week, and chemistry, three hours weekly. The third year: metaphysics, four hours a week; moral philosophy, four hours a week; physics, two hours a week; mathematics, three hours a week.

When the literary course with its five grades was finished, Jesuit students, both lay and clerical, began their study of philosophy; since the Society of Jesus was bent upon saving Scholasticism, its higher courses followed the Old Learning, while its lower courses followed the New. The course in philosophy meant a three-year study of the physics and metaphysics of Aristotle, since the Society of Jesus has chosen that philosophy as most consonant with the Scholastic theology which is commended to the Society by its Constitutions. The theological course suggested by the *Ratio Studiorium* included Scholastic theology, four years; moral theology, two years; ecclesiastical history, two years; canon law, two years; Sacred Scripture, two years; Hebrew, one year.

The Jesuit scholastic, after finishing his course in philosophy, takes his place in a college as a teacher of the boys in the literary courses. In theory he starts with the class in grammar and goes up with it grade by grade until it finishes its work in eloquence. The Society insists that every scholastic must teach, the rule being that "all Jesuits without exception must spend some time in the instruction of youth."

This universal obligation to teach made the Jesuits the first students of teaching anywhere. An ordinance of the second general assembly, whose date is 1565, resolved that one Seminary should be established in each province for the formation of professors of letters, philosophy and theology. The suggestion was given more definite form in 1586. There was too a considerable output of specially prepared textbooks for use in the schools of the Society.

This outline omits entirely the great missionary labors of the Jesuits, the missions to India, Japan, China, and North and South America. In Fülöp-Miller's *The Power*

and Secret of the Jesuits, Parkman's *Jesuits in America,*
Southey's *History of Brazil* and in many other places that
unequalled story of heroism and devotion unto death
may be read. Life will never be as empty as before to
anyone who reads it.

The means for the spreading of Jesuit education had
to be furnished by the people in the communities which
received it. "Apostolic men," the Jesuits said, "should
not only despise money, they should also have it." The
Society required that a location should be provided by
kings, princes, bishops, churches, or private people or
municipalities, together with buildings and revenues, before the Jesuits would establish a school. This seems to
have been a counsel of perfection, rather than a rigid requirement. Jesuit colleges, nowadays at any rate, seem
to have as much difficulty in raising their necessary money
as other private colleges. The General Acquaviva divided the Jesuit schools into three classes. The lowest
must have provision for professing grammar, humanities,
rhetoric, the languages, and a course in moral theology—
fifty Jesuits to be supported. The medium class consists
of those whose founders desire in addition a three-year
course in philosophy—eighty persons to be supported.
The highest is a *studium generale* in which, besides the
above, there are professed Scholastic theology, Sacred
Scripture, and Hebrew—one hundred and twenty persons
to be provided with necessities. "No obligations or conditions are to be admitted that would impair the integrity
of our principle which is: to give gratuitously what we
have received gratis." But stipends may be accepted if
they are offered as alms and if their destination is left
entirely to the will of the donor.

As to the spread of Jesuit colleges: at the death of the
General Acquaviva in 1615, there were 372; in 1755 there

were 39 provinces, 172 missions, and 728 colleges. In 1912, according to figures which Mr. Sedgwick supplies in his *Ignatius Loyola,* in the United States the Order numbered 2,300 members. It had 6 professional schools with 4,363 students and 26 colleges, besides preparatory and high schools.

INDEX